THE MAKING OF BRONZE AGE EURASIA

This book provides an overview of Bronze Age societies of Western Eurasia through an investigation of the archaeological record. Philip L. Kohl outlines the long-term processes and patterns of interaction that link these groups together in a shared historical trajectory of development. Interactions took the form of the exchange of raw materials and finished goods, the spread and sharing of technologies, and the movements of peoples from one region to another. Kohl reconstructs economic activities from subsistence practices to the production and exchange of metals and other materials. He also examines long-term processes, such as the development of more mobile forms of animal husbandry, which were based on the introduction and large-scale utilization of oxen-driven wheeled wagons and, subsequently, the domestication and riding of horses; the spread of metalworking technologies and exploitation of new centers of metallurgical production; changes in systems of exchange from those dominated by the movement of luxury goods to those in which materials essential for maintaining and securing the reproduction of the societies participating in the exchange network accompanied and/or supplanted the trade in precious materials; and increasing evidence for militarism and political instabilities as reflected in shifts in settlement patterns, including increases in fortified sites and quantitative and qualitative advances in weaponry. Kohl also argues forcefully that the main task of the archaeologist should be to write culture-history on a spatially and temporally grand scale in an effort to detect large, macrohistorical processes of interaction and shared development.

Philip L. Kohl is Professor of Anthropology and Kathryn W. Davis Professor of Slavic Studies at Wellesley College. He is the author of *The Bronze Age Civilization of Central Asia: Recent Soviet Discoveries, Recent Discoveries in Transcaucasia* and coeditor of *Nationalism, Politics and the Practice of Archaeology*.

CAMBRIDGE WORLD ARCHAEOLOGY

SERIES EDITOR
NORMAN YOFFEE, *University of Michigan*

EDITORIAL BOARD
SUSAN ALCOK, *Brown University*
TOM DILLEHAY, *Vanderbilt University*
STEPHEN SHENNAN, *University College London*
CARLA SINOPOLI, *University of Michigan*

The *Cambridge World Archaeology* series is addressed to students and professional archaeologists, and to academics in related disciplines. Each volume presents a survey of the archaeology of a region of the world, providing an up-to-date account of research and integration of recent findings with new concerns of interpretation. While the focus is on a specific region, broader cultural trends are discussed and the implications of regional findings for cross-cultural interpretations considered. The authors also bring anthropological and historical expertise to bear on archaeological problems, and show how both new data and changing intellectual trends in archaeology shade inferences about the past.

CAMBRIDGE WORLD ARCHAEOLOGY

THE MAKING OF BRONZE AGE EURASIA

PHILIP L. KOHL

Wellesley College

CAMBRIDGE UNIVERSITY PRESS
Cambridge, New York, Melbourne, Madrid, Cape Town, Singapore,
São Paulo, Delhi, Dubai, Tokyo, Mexico City

Cambridge University Press
The Edinburgh Building, Cambridge CB2 8RU, UK

Published in the United States of America by Cambridge University Press, New York

www.cambridge.org
Information on this title: www.cambridge.org/9789780521130158

First published 2007
Reprinted 2007, 2008

A catalogue record for this publication is available from the British Library

Library of Congress Cataloguing in Publication Data

Kohl, Philip L., 1946–
The Making of Bronze Age Eurasia / Philip L. Kohl.
p.   cm. – (Cambridge World Archaeology)
Includes bibliographical references and index.
ISBN-13: 978-0-521-84780-3 (hardback)
ISBN-10: 0-521-84780-X (hardback)

1. Bronze Age – Eurasia. 2. Excavations (Archaeology) – Eurasia.
3. Eurasia – Antiquities. I. Title. II. Series.
GN778.28.K64   2007
950'.1 – dc22   2006018838

ISBN 978-0-521-84780-3 Hardback
ISBN 978-0-521-13015-8 Paperback

He cast on the fire bronze which is weariless, and tin with it and valuable gold, and silver, and thereafter set forth upon its standard the great anvil, and gripped in one hand the ponderous hammer, while in the other, he grasped the pincers . . .

He made upon it a soft field, the pride of the tilled land, wide and triple-ploughed, with many ploughmen upon it who wheeled their teams at the turn and drove them in either direction . . .

He made upon it a herd of horn-straight oxen. The cattle were wrought of gold and tin, and thronged in speed and with lowing out of the dung of the farmyard to a pasturing place by a sounding river, and beside the moving field of a reed bed . . .

And the renowned smith of the strong arms made on it a meadow large and in a lovely valley for the glimmering sheepflocks, with dwelling places upon it, and covered shelters, and sheepfolds . . .

Then after he had wrought this shield, which was huge and heavy, he wrought for him a corselet brighter than fire in its shining, and wrought him a helmet, massive and fitting close to his temples, lovely and intricate work, and laid a gold top-ridge along it, and out of pliable tin wrought him leg armour.

(Hephaistos makes Achilleus' shield and armour; Iliad, Book 18, 474–477, 541–543, 573–576, 587–589, 608–612; translated by R. Lattimore 1967: 388–391)

CONTENTS

ILLUSTRATIONS AND MAPS

ABBREVIATIONS

AJA	*American Journal of Archaeology,* Boston
AMI	*Archäologische Mitteilungen aus Iran und Turan,* Berlin
EurAnt	*Eurasia Antiqua,* Berlin
KSIA	*Kratkie Soobshcheniya o dokladakh i polevykh issledovaniyakh Instituta Arkheologii Akademii Nauk SSSR* (Short Bulletins of the Institute of Archeology, Academy of Sciences of the USSR), Moscow (in Russian)
KSIIMK	*Kratkie Soobshcheniya o dokladakh i polevykh issledovaniyakh Instituta istorii material'noi kul'tury AN SSSR,* Moscow (in Russian)
RA	*Rossiiskaya arkheologiya (Russian Archaeology),* Moscow (in Russian)

PREFACE

In a sense, this study has been in the "making" since my first field experiences in southeastern Iran in the late 1960s; ideas first germinated decades ago as a graduate student have taken a long time to mature. The conception and initial writing of this narrative began in fall 1999 when I was completing a Humboldt Fellowship at the Eurasien Abteilung, DAI, in Berlin under the sponsorship of H. Parzinger, then Direktor of this division of the German institute. My stay in Berlin was sandwiched in between participation in two international conferences that were seminal for the formulation of many of the ideas in this account. In late August 1999 I had the good fortune of participating in an international conference at Arkaim in the southern Urals, which was organized by G. B. Zdanovich and which now has been published as *Complex Societies of Central Eurasia from the 3rd to the 1st Millennium BC: Regional Specifics in Light of Global Models* (Jones-Bley and Zdanovich 2002). A few months later, in January 2000, I attended a conference held at Cambridge University entitled *Late Prehistoric Exploitation of the Eurasian Steppe*, which was also the title of a book previously published by the McDonald Institute for Archaeological Research (Levine, Rassamakin, Kislenko, and Tatarintseva 1999). The papers from this conference were published subsequently in two volumes, both of which are extensively cited in this study: *Ancient Interactions: East and West in Eurasia* (Boyle, Renfrew, and Levine 2002); and *Prehistoric Steppe Adaptation and the Horse* (Levine, Renfrew, and Boyle 2003). What began then as a product of these fruitful experiences has taken an additional five years to complete. A semester sabbatical leave from Wellesley College in fall 2004 proved essential to finish what often seemed like an endless (and, at times, hopeless) project.

Numerous scholars have contributed directly or indirectly to the account presented here. I have relied heavily on the ideas and materials of some of these scholars, while I have queried the interpretations of others. Such agreements and disagreements are inevitable when one attempts to write a prehistory on a macro-scale that is compiled from a necessarily incomplete and at least partially unrepresentative database. Likewise, some of the interpretations presented here undoubtedly will be accepted by some and rejected by others. That also is natural, and healthy debate should form part of an ongoing scholarly discourse. Inevitably, I have presented the materials and modified the ideas of countless scholars; whether I have done so correctly or incorrectly, I alone am responsible for the interpretations of the data related in this archaeological narrative.

It is simply impossible to acknowledge my debt to every person who has either influenced this study or sharpened my views on what happened in the remote Bronze Age past and how best to account for it. I thank them all but can list only some of them, including T. Akhundov, D. Anthony, E. E. Antipina, R. S. Badalyan, N. Boroffka, S. N. Bratchenko, C. Chataigner, E. N. Chernykh, M. Frachetti, H-P. Francfort, M. S. Gadjiev, M. G. Gadzhiev, B. Hanks, S. Hansen, Y. Hershkovych, F. T. Hiebert, Z. Kikodze, L. B. Kircho, L. N. Koryakova, V. A. Kruc, K. Kh. Kushnareva, E. E. Kuzmina, S. Kuzminykh, C. C. Lamberg-Karlovsky, E. Yu. Lebedeva, O. LeComte, M. Levine, K. M. Linduff, Kh. Lkhagvasuren, B. Lyonnet, R. G. Magomedov, M. Mantu, M. I. Martinez-Navarrete, V. M. Masson, R. Meadow, G. Mindiashvili, V. I. Mordvintseva, N. L. Morgunova, I. Motzenbäcker, A. Niculescu, A. I. Osmanov, M. Otchir-Goriaeva, V. V. Otroshchenko, H. Parzinger, E. Pernicka, D. T. Potts, L. T. P'yankova, Yu. Rassamakin, S. Reinhold, K. S. Rubinson, S. Salvatori, S. N. Sanzharov, I. V. Sergatskov, A. G. Sherratt, V. A. Shnirelman, A. T. Smith, C. Thornton, H. Todorova, M. Tosi, V. A. Trifonov, J. M. Vicent-García, N. M. Vinogradova, L. Weeks, N. Yoffee, G. B. Zdanovich, and P. Zidarov. Sadly, two very close colleagues with whom I collaborated unexpectedly died during the time in which this book was written: Zaal Kikodze and Magomed Gadzhiev were dear friends and extremely astute and able archaeologists. I learned much from them and miss them terribly.

My initial fieldwork was in southeastern Iran, digging at Tepe Yahya as a participant in the Peabody Museum, Harvard University, Project in Iran that was directed by C. C. Lamberg-Karlovsky. Over the years I have had the good fortune to continue to interact regularly with Karl and the remarkable circle of archaeologists he has mentored at Harvard. Such interactions have always proven stimulating and invaluable for broadening my knowledge and sharpening my interpretations of greater Near Eastern archaeology. I am obviously also greatly indebted to E. N. Chernykh and the "school" of natural scientists that he has assembled in Moscow. Although I sometimes feel like I might be playing Huxley to Evgenij's Darwin, I have tried to maintain a critical perspective and question or "test" as much as possible his macrohistorical interpretations and archaeologically derived concepts, like the metallurgical province. Although many problems remain unresolved and many paradoxes raised by his work are difficult to ponder, it is impossible to overestimate Evgenij's incredible contribution to our overall understanding of Bronze Age Eurasia. In a sense, we all follow in his footsteps.

I also must single out the huge intellectual debt I owe M. I. Martínez-Navarrete for the numerous incisive comments and critical comments on my work that she has provided for several years. Her observations have often exposed the weaknesses of my arguments and forced me to rework them in more parsimonious, scientifically acceptable fashions. Her suggestions have, I believe, helped me maintain a standard of intellectual honesty and academic rigor. When I spent fall 1999 in Berlin, I frequently consulted with Nikolaus Boroffka about aspects of the archaeology of the Balkans and Pontic steppes during Chalcolithic times. He provided me with numerous readings and greatly aided my understanding of early developments in this region in which I had never worked and only briefly visited. Later he also sent me copies of important articles in journals unavailable to me on the social structure of these Chalcolithic societies of "Old Europe." Bertille Lyonnet closely read this manuscript and made numerous constructive criticisms and suggestions. She also provided several important references to still unpublished materials. My close colleague Rabadan Magomedov has also regularly critiqued my work and taught me much about the archaeology not only of Daghestan, but also of the South Russian steppes where he first worked. I particularly want to express my deep thanks to all these friends; their suggestions have immeasurably improved my "archaeological narrative." I also thank the anonymous reviewer for Cambridge University Press who made many useful suggestions that I have tried to incorporate here.

Norm Yoffee, the editor of the Cambridge World Archaeology series, suggested that I add the short biographical sketches of some famous Soviet/Russian archaeologists that appear in Chapters 2–5. I thought Norm's idea was excellent. One of the principal purposes of this book is to introduce Western readers to some of the major Bronze Age discoveries made by Soviet/Russian archaeologists over the course of the last half-century or so. Although I have always tried to evaluate critically the materials presented, I also hope that this book in a real sense celebrates the accomplishments of the Russian tradition of archaeological research. Thus, it is most appropriate to sketch the contributions of some of the leading archaeologists whose works are frequently presented and discussed throughout this study. There are, of course, many other archaeologists whose works could also have been so highlighted, but I knew that my choices had to be restricted. The archaeologists chosen just seemed the most appropriate given the theories and empirical data discussed, and I did not even initially focus on the fact that they all were male and all but one had worked out of the Institute of Archaeology in Moscow! I must emphasize that there has been no attempt to slight the marvelous school of archaeologists working at the St. Petersburg Institute of the History of Material Culture or the accomplishments of the numerous Soviet/Russian female archaeologists whose works also are frequently cited in this study. Very limited choices just had to be made.

Several institutions and foundations have supported this work during the last five years. As already mentioned, the Alexander von Humboldt *Stiftung* allowed me – after a long hiatus – to continue my fellowship in Berlin, and it was during this stay that I began to write this book. An international collaborative research grant from the Wenner-Gren Foundation for Anthropological Research helped support the visits of Dr. M. G. Gadzhiev and R. G. Magomedov to Berlin in January 2000 in which we prepared the initial publication of materials from Velikent that appeared in *Eurasia Antiqua*. The Fulbright Foundation supported research visits to Argentina and Mongolia, the former helping me appreciate the value of grandly conceived culture-history and the latter proving invaluable for understanding how the eastern Eurasian steppes so strikingly differ from the western Eurasian steppes. Dr. Kh. Lkhagvasuren must be acknowledged for providing me with a remarkably comprehensive overview to the archaeological remains of north-central Mongolia. Similarly, Yakiv Hershkovych set up my most informative visits to the gigantic Tripol'ye settlements south of Kiev and to eastern Ukraine in summer 2000; fortunately, I was able to reciprocate by hosting him as a Senior Fulbright Scholar during the academic year 2003–2004. I also want to acknowledge all the colleagues who supported my brief visit to Romania and Bulgaria in summer 2006. Wellesley College supported most of my travels and provided me with two invaluable sabbatical leaves during the academic year 1999–2000 and during the fall semester of 2004–2005. This work would never have been finished without Wellesley College's generous support. Ms. Mattie Fitch, an undergraduate at Wellesley, digitally enhanced most of the illustrations appearing in this book and compiled the general maps showing principal sites discussed in Chapters 1 and 3–5. I hope she will continue her interests in the study of the archaeologically ascertained past.

Though there are many people and institutions to thank, none have been more important and essential for me than my family. They have given me continuous and unquestioning support, putting up with long physical and mental absences when I traveled to remote corners of Eurasia and, even more irritatingly, when I periodically lost present consciousness and immersed myself somewhere in the third millennium BC – with a vacant, eyes glazed expression on my face. I dug with my then quite young daughter Mira at Velikent in Daghestan in 1997 and bounced over the north-central Mongolian steppes with son Owen in 2003. Both have inspired and filled me with pride in ways that I cannot truly articulate. Although, at times, they may have thought that I had lost it, they both helped me – consciously and unconsciously – maintain my sanity. This book is dedicated to Barbara Gard. She first urged me to write it and then made sure that I finished it – despite all the inconveniences and absences that it entailed. She's my best critic. Without her constant support and encouragement, wit, perspicacity, and eminent sense, this study would not even have been begun, much less completed. The ancient poet's verse we cited many years back still applies: Ἔρος δ' ἐτίναξέ μοι φρένας, ὡς ἄνεμος χὰτ ὄρος δρύσιν ἐμπέτων.

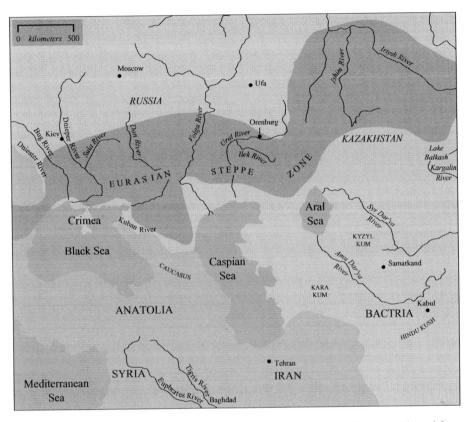

Frontispiece: Eurasian Steppe Zone and the Greater Ancient Near East (adapted from Kohl 2002b: 188, fig. 8, originally from Aruz et al. 2000: XIV–XV)

CHAPTER I

ARCHAEOLOGICAL THEORY AND ARCHAEOLOGICAL EVIDENCE

Cultural change or cultural evolution does not operate on isolated societies but always on interconnected systems in which societies are variously linked within wider 'social fields.'

E. R. Wolf (1982: 76)

Archaeologists gather data about the past and interpret it within distinct research traditions that structure the data they select to find and analyze, and that provide them with the necessary support to carry on their work. The activity of reconstructing the past through the analysis of material cultural remains is necessarily constrained by the social context in which the archaeologist must function. This observation is self-evident, but, during the past twenty years or so, there has been an increasing recognition that these separate traditions of research divide themselves along cultural, linguistic, and, most interestingly, national lines. This too is not surprising, particularly when one considers the very practical nature of conducting archaeological research, that is, obtaining financial support, typically or at least in part, from the state to excavate sites that are now nearly universally considered to form part of some state's – usually the archaeologist's own – national heritage or patrimony. That there exist national traditions of archaeological research also is not surprising when one examines the historical development of the discipline: rooting a people or a nation in the distant past was one of the main stimuli for the development of archaeology, particularly prehistoric archaeology, during the past two hundred years or, not coincidentally, during the period that witnessed the rise of modern nation-states as the world's fundamental unit of political organization.

These observations can be overstated. Clearly, communication across these traditions of research takes place. Archaeological methods and techniques and, even to some extent, theories diffuse throughout the discipline, and such sharing is likely only to increase in the age of electronic mail and the Internet. The process of sharing, however, is neither uniform nor pervasive. Most observers

would consider British and American, or hereafter Anglo-American, archaeology to have features distinctive from those characteristics of separate national
traditions of research in continental Europe (e.g., cf. Coudart 1999; Schlanger
2002), Russia, or China. Although generally laudable, efforts to create a "world
archaeology" (Ucko 1995) have been only partially realized, and the resistances
to such attempts are themselves interesting and deserve further examination.
What some like to see as an admirable universalism, others may resent as a new
form of academic and linguistic imperialism.

There is another division of knowledge that crosscuts these national traditions of archaeological research and affects the current study: the area divisions
of the discipline; specifically, those that divide Classical, Near Eastern or Middle
Eastern/West Asian (*Vorderasiatische*) archaeology from European and Eurasian
prehistory. Political factors here are also at work: the Cold War effectively cut off
the Eurasian steppes from Southwest Asia. With the exception of Urartian sites
in Armenia and the odd cuneiform inscription from Azerbaijan, the former
Soviet Union, as vast as it was, lay beyond the distributional range of ancient
Near Eastern historical sources – at least until the advent of the Achaemenids.
The linguistic barrier, if you will, reinforced this historical accident: most
Western scholars did not read Russian, which, in turn, was reinforced by the
bipolar politics of the Cold War. The result was that scholars' areas of expertise
were arbitrarily circumscribed and unnecessarily and strangely not coincident.
It can be argued, I believe, that this breakdown of knowledge was asymmet-
rical: more Russian/Soviet scholars were aware of research in West Asia than
Western scholars were of their work, say, in the Caucasus, Central Asia, or
on the Eurasian steppes. But this division adversely affected everyone, and
our overall understanding of "what happened in history" suffered. This study
hopes to provide a modest contribution to overcoming this unfortunate legacy.

This book, written in English, is to some extent necessarily addressed to
the practitioners of Anglo-American archaeology. One basic goal is to present
a mass of archaeological materials, largely recovered by archaeologists working within the former Soviet Union, that are not extensively discussed in the
Anglo-American archaeological literature; at this level, its purpose is simply to
make more accessible this incredibly rich database. (Figure 1.1 shows the general area and some of the archaeological sites discussed in this work.) This study,
however, also self-consciously and critically situates itself within an archaeological dialogue that has taken place largely within the Anglo-American tradition
of archaeological research, and the placement of this study within that dialogue
is the principal aim of this introductory chapter.

ANGLO-AMERICAN THEORETICAL ARCHAEOLOGY FROM CA.1960 TO THE PRESENT – A BRIEF OVERVIEW

If the traditions of archaeological research, alluded to earlier, divide themselves
most significantly and typically along national lines, then is it even appropriate

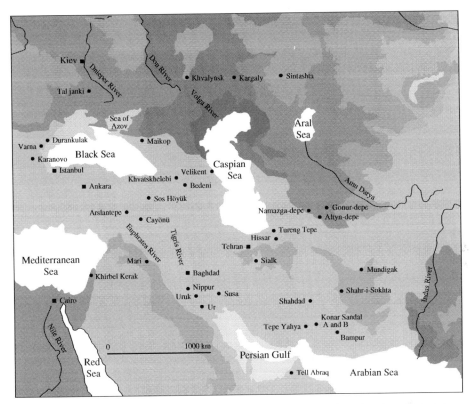

Figure 1.1. Western Eurasia, showing approximate location of selected archaeological sites.

to refer to an Anglo-American archaeology? Despite certain "special relation-ships" that may exist, most English-speaking nations – particularly the United States, the United Kingdom, Canada, and Australia – are politically inde-pendent from one another, and the way archaeological research takes place within each of these countries varies according to its specific national context. Such real differences are not the focus of the current discussion; rather, here the emphasis is on their *similarities*. Since the initial emergence of the then-new or processual archaeology in the early 1960s, an increasing dialogue has taken place largely across the North Atlantic. In the 1960s graduate students in the United States read not only their Lewis Binford and Kent Flannery, but also their David Clarke and Colin Renfrew; the converse was true in the United Kingdom. Today with the advent and establishment of post-processual archaeology as the competing or even possibly dominant paradigm, this pro-cess continues unabated and has even intensified with highly visible, leading practitioners assuming teaching positions on the other side of the Atlantic. The existence of a specific Anglo-American archaeology is recognized not only by archaeologists within it, but also by scholars working outside it (Biehl et al. 2002; Neustupny 2002). What are its common features? Certainly one is an increasing and explicit self-consciousness, a feature that means that much of this ground is very well trodden, obviating a tedious discussion of what has been perhaps overly discussed in the literature. Nevertheless, some cursory review of the recent developments in Anglo-American archaeology is necessary to situate this book appropriately within (or, perhaps, outside) this tradition.

The new processual archaeology, which was proclaimed on both sides of the Atlantic and dominated the practice of Anglo-American archaeology from at least the late 1960s to the early 1980s, was characterized by its emphasis on developing rigorous methods of analyzing archaeological materials, analogous to those that were purported to characterize harder natural and physical sciences, such as biology, physics, and chemistry. The call for an explicitly scientific archaeology meant that archaeologists should adopt the scientific method and test in the field and in the laboratory the hypotheses they had formulated. The aim was both to reconstruct and model past societies and, as far as possible, to explain why the societies had developed or "processed" in the ways the archaeological record indicated that they had. It became much more important to model archaeological evidence than simply to describe and order it temporally and spatially.

For a variety of reasons both internal and external to the discipline, the advent of the explicitly scientific new archaeology coincided with and then subsumed a return to generalizing, comparative evolutionary analysis. All human societies could be ordered and compared as long as one avoided the pitfalls of simplistic late nineteenth-century evolutionary thought and proceeded in a fashion that was deemed sufficiently "multilinear." The favorite scheme adopted – then modified and refined countless times – was to identify archaeological cultures as belonging to the increasingly complex levels of social organization: bands, tribes (now segmentary societies), chiefdoms, and states. This renaissance of neo-evolutionary thought had the virtue of forcing the archaeologist to get behind the artifacts and reconstruct the societies or, more famously, the System that had produced them (Fig. 1.2); it also consciously promoted general comparative analysis. One did not just study one's society or archaeological culture but had to compare it with other societies throughout the world that were ranked at the same evolutionary level. In this sense, the neo-evolutionism of processual archaeology facilitated the development of world archaeology; Childe's concerns with the unique development of European prehistory appeared outmoded and provincial, if not unwittingly imperialist. Since evolutionary ranking now was once more acceptable in social anthropology, one could turn freely to the ethnographic record to flesh out farther the interpretation of one's own archaeological data. If the ethnologies were insufficiently focused on material remains, the archaeologist should go out and study contemporary societies ranked at the appropriate evolutionary level; the subfield of ethno-archaeology rapidly bloomed.

The insistence on a rigorous scientific methodology, the development of new archaeological techniques for recovering material remains, and the rebirth of

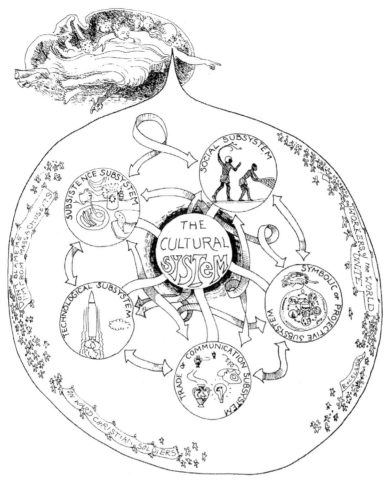

Figure 1.2. Beliefs of an earlier generation of the then-new Anglo-American archae-ologists (adapted from Kohl 1974, vol. II, p. 392, original drawing by R.D. Timms).

evolutionary thought were all applied together and reinforced one another. The new processual archaeology had a strongly materialist focus and became increasingly interested in the reconstruction of past environments and past subsistence economies; ecofacts – ancient floral and faunal remains – were retrieved by new techniques and studied as intensively as, if not more intensively than, traditional archaeological features and artifacts. The neo-evolutionary perspective consciously focused on internal cultural development and gener-ally downplayed external factors of change. Societies adapted to their local conditions and evolved; given enough time and a sufficiently favorable envi-ronment, the emergence of social complexity was virtually assured. One could still model systems of exchange, but concepts, such as diffusion or migration, were vague and unsatisfying, if not scientifically suspect. Evolutionary rigor was

opposed to historical imprecision and particularism. An incorrect and misleading dichotomy between evolution and science, on the one hand, and history,
on the other, was celebrated (cf. Binford 1972) and remained enshrined in the
literature until its critique and rejection by post-processual archaeologists.

A reaction against the particularly hard version of the new processual archaeology was inevitable for the simple reason that much was overstated, simplistic,
and never realized, such as the claims for defining and developing laws of cultural change (cf. the original edition of Watson, Le Blanc, and Redman 1971).
Such shortcomings, of course, were recognized and commented on at the
time (e.g., Flannery 1973; Trigger 1973), but the full critique was articulated
only by the self-named post-processual archaeologists whose writings became
increasingly visible from the early 1980s on.

For many reasons, it is much harder to characterize post-processual archaeology. Diversity has been its trademark from the beginning with one of its only
unifying features being the conscious rejection of what was perceived (and perhaps caricatured?) as the positivist processual program. Its development cannot
be sufficiently explained as a response internal to Anglo-American archaeology
but must also be set against the broader background of postmodern movements in literary criticism, philosophy, and social anthropology, which came
into prominence at the same time and which were avidly read and adopted
by post-processual archaeologists. On the other hand, it is noteworthy that
post-processual archaeology hardly exists or has been very critically received
outside the Anglo-American tradition (Coudart 1999). For our purposes, such
lack of recognition and acceptance only underscores the reality of a distinct
Anglo-American archaeology and its increasing (?) separation or isolation from
continental European and other traditions.

If methods and techniques were the hallmarks and strengths of the new
processual archaeology, then theoretical innovations have dominated post-
processual archaeology. Various historical and social theories have been introduced, modified, and applied to archaeological data by the post-processualists –
the outcome being sometimes more misleading and bewildering than
enlightening (cf. Chippendale 1993). Unquestionably, the post-processual critique made many valid and important points: archaeology was perceived as a
form of history and, as such, had a necessarily contingent and specific character; not everything could be explained in terms of impersonal structural or systemic features, but one also had to consider (and somehow model) the actions
and decisions of individual personal agents actively engaged in making their
own pasts. The opposition between evolutionary and historical approaches was
rejected, and archaeologists were enjoined to interpret their data in all its rich
specificity. Such exhortations should have led logically to detailed reexamina-
tions of archaeological evidence, but the temptation to theorize, proselytize,
and publish proved stronger. There was no single approach to reconstructing

the past; no one had an exclusive claim, a monopoly, on how to proceed – least of all the processual positivists constrained by their inadequate epistemologies.

Rather, diversity was celebrated, resulting sometimes in the articulation of poorly considered and dangerous forms of relativism. The extreme relativism of post-processual archaeology has been sufficiently criticized and has even now been begrudgingly repudiated by most of its practitioners (cf. *Archaeological Dialogues* 1998 and the essays critiquing hyperrelativism in Trigger 2003); there is no need to retread this excessively worn ground. Post-processual archaeology within the Anglo-American tradition has played a positive role in deflating some of the scientistic pretensions and hyperbolic excesses of processual archaeology; that it too committed its share of blunders and overstatements is not surprising. What has not already been corrected or recognized will undoubtedly be addressed by a new generation of archaeologists who will reject features of the post-processual paradigm (if such a single paradigm exists) and develop their own theories as they find employment and gain recognition within the highly competitive Anglo-American academic setting.

Such an ongoing process of development is perfectly healthy and underscores the dynamic, ever-innovative character of Anglo-American archaeology over the past forty years. Whereas post-processual archaeology developed as a reaction to processual archaeology, both approaches share many features that are best understood by locating them within the specific academic context in which they are realized (Kohl 1993). It is also true that a similar contextualization of archaeological research is necessary to understand any national tradition of archaeological research, and the differences between traditions in this respect can be striking.

Two features common both to processual and post-processual Anglo-American archaeology are, however, troubling and must be at least mentioned here: 1) the provincialism of much of this literature; and 2) its sometimes surprising distance from actual archaeological evidence. These features are interrelated. During the last forty years Anglo-American archaeologists have demonstrated that they read – in English, at least – outside their discipline: philosophy, literary and social theory, mathematics, history (to some extent), and so forth; what is less clear is their degree of familiarity with the ever-accumulating archaeological record. Contemporary archaeology is necessarily interdisciplinary, and so this recourse to other fields for *both* methodological and theoretical inspiration is essential and constitutes one of the great strengths of the Anglo-American archaeological tradition. At the same time it is necessary to be aware of what other archaeologists working within other traditions – and not publishing in English – are actually doing. If many other archaeologists – and this picture itself is a caricature – are still engaged primarily in classifying and ordering their materials spatially and temporally, it is essential to be aware of their work and to be basically cognizant of the current state of accumulated

archaeological knowledge. One of the indirect aims of this study is to illustrate
the need and value of overcoming these troubling tendencies.

BACK TO THE FUTURE – OR TOWARDS AN INTERPRETATIVE AND EXPLANATORY CULTURE HISTORY

Historians long have debated the value of "narrative history" (cf. Stone 1979;
Hobsbawm 1980). Those historians who are more inclined to be analytical and
quantitative in their reconstruction of the past tend to resist the notion that they
just tell stories about the past and emphasize that their work is systematic and
grounded in the collection of empirical evidence, and that it is this fundamental
basis that distinguishes their work from, say, that of novelists. Nevertheless,
even such an analytically and theoretically inclined historian as E. Hobsbawm
concedes the value, indeed, the inevitability of the historical narrative if one is
going to do more than gather evidence and just talk to oneself. His own justly
famous accounts of the modern historical era are stories that are very well told
and, of course, extremely well documented.

The concepts of storytelling and of "reading" the past – the archaeological record being a text to be "read" by the archaeologist and then retold as
a story to one's audience – are metaphors, of course, that have been widely
adopted by post-processual archaeologists, and their adoption is consistent with
the notion that multiple pasts (or stories) can be reconstructed from archaeological evidence. The relativism implicit in this perspective must, however, be
constrained, and criteria, such as plausibility and coherence with accumulated
archaeological evidence, exist to distinguish among different readings of the
past. The metaphors of the archaeological record as a text to be read or the
study of the past as a task akin to writing fiction are also misleading, as Trigger
(1989: 380–382) and others have noted, for material cultural remains are rarely
as explicit or as potentially unambiguous as the more complete information
gleaned from written sources, and the creative instincts of the archaeologist
are necessarily constrained to some extent by the nature of the archaeological
evidence considered.

This book accepts these necessary caveats but still consciously tells a story
or constructs a narrative account of the increasing integration of the Eurasian
steppes into the "civilized" literate world of West Asia during the course of
roughly two millennia, or from the Late Chalcolithic period through Middle
to Late Bronze times. This reading of the past is just that: one way of looking
at the archaeological record and attempting to make sense of it. Undoubtedly, other readings are possible and, in some cases, may be more plausible
and consistent with the archaeological evidence than that presented here. The
limitations of my understanding and lack of familiarity with the vast corpus of
archaeological data so cursorily reviewed in this study are all too keenly felt.
Reviewing the literature, however, is also emboldening in that it highlights the

lack of consensus that often exists among the specialists who have assembled this record. Although some reconstructions may be rejected on grounds of plausibility, coherence, or basic lack of awareness of archaeological evidence, other accounts, even contradictory ones, may be equally plausible, coherent, and consistent with the archaeological record. As post-processualists emphasize, archaeological data are often "underdetermined" and multiple acceptable readings of the past are possible given the inherent limitations of the evidence. This book clearly represents only one possible "reading" of the vast, inevitably incomplete, and problematic archaeological record.

Interpretation is not opposed to explanation – the former constituting a subjective search for a personally satisfying account of the past, and the latter aspiring to an understanding based on the use of universally recognized causal principles and procedures. This dichotomy too is false, like that already mentioned between evolution and history or that dichotomy once so numbingly discussed in the processual archaeological literature between deduction and induction. One accounts for the prehistoric past by carefully examining and ordering the archaeological record and seeking to discern recurrent patterns or processes – often necessarily at a coarse-grained or macrohistorical level – that one then invokes to construct the prehistory. Meaning is ascribed, and explanations are offered.

Because this attempt to reconstruct the past is necessarily interpretative, reflecting the perspective and biases of the author, it is incumbent on me to sketch the values that inform the present study. Archaeologists should reconstruct the past on the basis of the evidence they best control. Given the nature of *material* culture remains, this means primary emphasis should be placed on the reconstruction of ancient technologies, environments, subsistence and exchange economies, and, as far as the evidence permits, social organization and structure as indirectly reflected in landscape and settlement patterns, architecture, mortuary evidence, and the like. The symbols, beliefs, and ideologies of the Bronze Age peoples who created the archaeological record cannot be ignored; such beliefs may have been incredibly important for understanding a particular course of development. What people today think and believe informs what they do, and the essential assumption of uniformitarianism, intrinsic to archaeology, dictates that this conscious, ideologically driven, and symbolic production and manipulation of materials must have been true during the Bronze Age as well. Nevertheless, archaeological evidence is more ambiguous in relation to the reconstruction of past belief systems and ideologies; by their very nature symbols are polyvalent, and a given material symbol can be "read" in a variety of different ways, the criteria for preferring one interpretation over another being correspondingly harder to establish. The models archaeologists devise, however elegant and theoretically satisfying, must be constrained ultimately by the very refractory and mute *material* culture remains that constitute the archaeological record.

The limitations of the archaeological record are real but not so deficient, I believe, to prevent reconstructing the broad contours of large-scale historical developments. As Childe recognized, archaeological data usually do not deliberately misinform, and the archaeologists' peculiar ability to reconstruct ancient technologies, environments, and, to some extent, ancient subsistence and exchange economies is sufficient to detect specific large-scale patterns and processes, to write, in essence, an empirically grounded prehistory. This book tells a story, but it does so from the materialist perspective demanded by the archaeological record. Part of its theoretical inspiration is derived from the tenets of processual archaeology sketched earlier, that is, a focus on environmental constraints and economic adaptation to local conditions; where possible, it attempts to reconstruct the less tangible but incredibly important social structural features of the cultures that produced the examined archaeological record. Deviating from the processualist paradigm, it also traces the eminently documentable interconnections among different regions and interprets them as evidence for the diffusion of technologies and ideas, the exchange of materials, and the movements of peoples. Regularity and pattern are sought more in these interconnections than in making cross-cultural comparisons or typing various archaeological phenomena according to elaborately defined evolutionary levels. The prehistoric story that is told exhibits certain recurring features, some of which change imperceptibly with time, and all of which remain at the same time highly specific and contingent.

THE DEVOLUTION OF URBAN SOCIETY – MOVING BEYOND NEO-EVOLUTIONARY ACCOUNTS

The book's title consciously invokes, of course, the historian's emphasis on different peoples actively constructing their own pasts. It also is deliberately meant to place this study outside the neo-evolutionary tradition of processual archaeology, a tradition that with few exceptions has focused more on the internal growth and development of early complex polities than their recurrent collapse (cf. Yoffee 2005: 131–140). The periodic breakdowns of social complexity, as well as the emergence of more advanced social formations, are both traced in the present work. The evolution of specific technologies, such as metallurgy and advances in the means of transportation, which had far-reaching consequences, are described, but many of the societies or archaeological cultures and, indeed, entire regions recounted here exhibit a more complicated pattern of elaboration and development followed by breakdown and collapse. Societies devolve or become less complex, as well as evolve.

One of the aims of the book is to account for these breakdowns in social complexity by considering them first within a larger network of historical interconnections, rather than by accounting for them in terms of the internal structural contradictions and weaknesses of the polities concerned. In part, this focus reflects the sources available to it, namely, an almost exclusive reliance on the archaeological record with only occasional recourse to historic and ethnographic analogy. It is consequently less textured and nuanced than certain justly famous neo-evolutionary studies, such as R. McC. Adams's comparative account *The Evolution of Urban Society* (1966), which combined archaeological, historical, and ethnohistorical data to compare the breakdown of kin-based and the emergence of class-stratified societies and cities in ancient Mesopotamia and pre-Columbian highland Mexico.

With its focus on devolution as much as evolution, this work largely eschews the use of neo-evolutionary labels to characterize specific archaeological cultures. Nothing necessarily is added to our understanding of a given archaeological culture by labeling it a chiefdom (a stage too closely defined by ethnographic evidence from Melanesia and Polynesia), or, because this term is itself too vague and procrustean, by refining our typology and identifying the archaeological materials in question as some subcategory of chiefdom, state, or whatever. Such a neo-evolutionary exercise is just another form of archaeological classification; one might as well just type one's flint tools or pots.

The point is not to deny that cultures evolve, or to argue that there has not been an overall process of cultural evolution; they do and there clearly has been. Cultures manifestly evolve or develop in ways that over the long term exhibit progressive technological change and greater control over the forces of nature, resulting in qualitative changes in social and economic organization. Such processes characterize not only individual cultures, but also human culture as a whole, general as well as specific cultural evolution (Sahlins and Service 1960). To observe similarities in the processes of separate specific cultures' evolution may be a very valuable and enlightening exercise, but many processual Anglo-American archaeologists have overzealously adopted it. Contrasts among separate cultures are frequently more interesting than their similarities (cf. Kohl and Chernykh 2003; Kohl 2005b; and Chernykh 2005), but the quest for evolutionary order tends to overlook these and so reduce the complexity of the ancient past or the ethnographic present to a theoretically preordained scheme, a continuously gradated evolutionary spectrum of social development that is claimed to be diverse and multilinear but that in reality is unilinear in the sense that all societies can be ranked along it (Kohl 2005a).

Neo-evolutionary archaeology is heavily dependent on the ethnographic record, a basic assumption being that one can dip into that record to find the appropriate parallel to the archaeological materials under consideration and then "flesh out" the less tangible features of the archaeological culture to reconstruct its level of social organization. But certain questions must be asked. Does the ethnographic record really contain all relevant examples of past social organization and structure? Were there formations in the prehistoric past that are not readily paralleled in the ethnographic record? Ethnographic evidence, after all, has been basically compiled only during the past 150 years or so. N. Yoffee (2005: 188) recently has highlighted the limitations of this overreliance on the ethnographic record and uncritical quest to find appropriate analogies:

> The danger in the use of 'prior probabilities' in archaeological theory, however, is that the past can be condemned to resemble some form of the historical present, that nothing new about the past can be discovered, and that theory itself cannot be 'ampliative', that is, allow us to find novelty and even singularity in ancient societies and processes of change.

The second chapter describes the gigantic "proto–urban" settlements of the Tripol'ye culture, sites that in their extent are as large as or larger than the cities of southern Mesopotamia and that appear roughly 500 to 1000 years earlier! These gigantic Tripol'ye sites are manifestly not comparable with the later Sumerian cities; they exhibit none of the features of social differentiation so evident in the latter's public architecture, mortuary remains, and, ultimately, texts, as so vividly summarized by Adams. The neo-evolutionary term "proto-urban," which has been applied to these gigantic Tripol'ye settlements, is correspondingly misleading. One must attempt to understand how these sites functioned and, as much as the evidence allows, attempt to reconstruct their social organization and structure. But the question must be raised: do they have a precise parallel in the ethnographic record, or are they, to some significant extent, a unique product of the Late Chalcolithic period?

Similarly, the book tries to trace the early development of a specific form of pastoral nomadism, the mixed herding mounted pastoral nomadism characteristic of the Eurasian steppes and known to us by numerous historical and ethnographic accounts. One of the book's theses is that this form of nomadism emerged essentially only at the end of the Bronze Age and the beginning of the Iron Age, that is, at the end of the second millennium BC – beyond the chronological limits of this study. Clearly it is useful to study much later historical and ethnographic accounts of mounted pastoral Eurasian nomads to understand better the fragmentary archaeological evidence. But were the dominantly cattle-herding societies that were developing a more mobile economy and mode of life along the river valleys and, however tentatively, on the open steppes during the late fourth and third millennia BC directly comparable to those of their later descendants? Many fanciful archaeological reconstructions (for a similar critique cf. Rassamakin 1999: 59; 2002: 66; Fig. 1.3) have appeared that anachronistically imagine these Late Chalcolithic and Early Bronze Age cultures as formed by marauding warriors, wreaking havoc on settled societies as later did Genghis Khan and Timur. Such an image overlooks the fact that, at least at the beginning of our story, horses were not ridden and metals were utilized more as ornaments than as weapons. In other words, the analogy may be more misleading than enlightening and, at the very least, should not be applied indiscriminately.

Figure 1.3. Anachronistically imagined Chalcolithic and Bronze Age marauding mounted hordes from the East (adapted from Rassamakin 2002: 66, fig. 4.12); translated from the German.

Another example of an archaeological phenomenon that may not find a perfectly appropriate ethnographic parallel to allow for evolutionary ranking is provided by the late third/early second millennium BC fortified and symmetrically planned Sintashta-Arkaim sites found in a concentrated area in the southern trans-Ural steppe and forest-steppe region. One of their principal investigators, G.B. Zdanovich (1999), has referred to the landscape over which these sites are regularly distributed as the "Country of Towns" (*Strana gorodov*), an evocative phrase meant to suggest parallels with other areas that witnessed the emergence of urban formations, such as southern Mesopotamia. Once evoked, the image of towns or cities (*goroda*) requires that these settlements then exhibit the cluster of features characteristic of urbanism: social differentiation, craft specialization, intensive agriculture, and so forth. This evidence

will be reviewed in more detail later (Chapter 4), but here just a consideration of scale casts some doubt on the utility of this urban interpretation: the
largest documented Sintashta-Arkaim sites are roughly 3 ha. in extent or hardly
equivalent to the gigantic Tripol'ye settlements or to Sumerian city-states.

Urbanism is, of course to some extent, a relative phenomenon, and the discovery of such sites with substantial planned architecture on the open steppes
forces a major reconsideration of what actually occurred there during the
transition from Middle to Late Bronze times and how it may have affected
other areas of the interconnected world of the Eurasian steppes. There is also
no question that the appearance of horse-driven, spoke-wheeled vehicles, the
elaboration of bronze weapons, including javelin and large arrow heads, and
elaborate funerary rites with costly animal sacrifices, which have all been excavated at Sintashta, represent extremely significant discoveries. But is the concept
of urbanism really appropriate? Is it even misleading? One of the fascinating
aspects of the "Country of Towns" is its disappearance; current evidence does
not support any continuing evolution of "urban" society in this area of the
steppes. How does one account for its absence? If one removes one's neo-
evolutionary blinkers and considers the actual archaeological evidence, one is
struck more with the devolution or, perhaps better, cyclical transformation of
social complexity throughout the steppes than with its continued growth.

This study examines the early development of a more mobile and specialized form of economy that ultimately became the classic form of mounted
pastoral nomadism, characteristic of the broad, physically interconnected area
of the Eurasian steppes. It shows how the early development of this distinctive
way of life began to affect in a detectably patterned fashion more settled, agriculturally based communities to their south. As the process of the emergence
of this new economy occurred during the course of at least two millennia it
can be considered protracted, but its tempo of change was characteristically
punctuated, resulting in the relatively abrupt appearances and disappearances
of certain archaeological cultures and larger formations. As mobility increased,
the movements of peoples occurred more systematically and became one of the
major links connecting the world of the steppes with that of the sown. Mobility
was enhanced with technological developments in the means of transportation,
above all, with the emergence of wheeled vehicles and the domestication, harnessing, and ultimately riding of horses.

Equally significant was the production and exchange of ground stone and
metal tools and weapons; from a macrohistorical perspective, this diffusion of
technologies and exchange of materials can be traced throughout an increasingly more extensive geographical area. Vast, ever-expanding "metallurgical
provinces" (Chernykh 1992) subsumed within them countless archaeological
cultures and even larger related archaeological communities (*obshchnosti*). Here
too, the process of expansion was not regular and uniform but sharply punctuated, with earlier areas suddenly collapsing and others emerging in a rapidly

successive fashion (e.g., the relatively sudden dissolution of the Carpatho-Balkan Metallurgical Province and consequent rise of the Circumpontic Metallurgical Province during the second quarter of the fourth millennium BC). Most significant was the growing need to obtain materials, above all metal resources, which were not evenly distributed across the interconnected area stretching from the Balkans to western Siberia and the Kazakh steppes. The interregional exchange of these materials then became as significant as their actual production.

All these factors were interrelated, synergistically affecting each other: adaptation to the open steppe required the increasing elaboration of a mobile economy initially based on foraging and the intensive hunting, then herding of animals both introduced and indigenous to the steppes. This mobility subsequently was ultimately transformed first by the introduction of wheeled vehicles and then by the innovation of the harnessing and riding of horses. Over time, this enhanced mobility facilitated the specialized production and exchange of goods. Initially, the exchange of ornaments and prestige goods functioned in part to differentiate members within a given social group or community; later the production and exchange of weapons served to establish and maintain relations between communities. The increasing militarism evident on the steppes from Early to Late Bronze Age times finds its reflection farther south in dramatic shifts in settlement patterns and, ultimately, in an increase in the number of fortified sites, such as the countless Late Bronze/Early Iron Age cyclopean fortresses (cf. Smith 2003: 165–172) found throughout the southern Caucasus. The Eurasian steppes interact increasingly with the Ancient Near East through both the exchange of materials, particularly metals, and through the continuous, protracted movements of peoples. Occasionally, agriculturalists moved north and participated in the development of the more mobile economy with its greater reliance on animal husbandry; more typically, pastoralists moved south to escape the rigors of life on the steppes and settled down and changed their way of life. Ultimately they learned to disrupt the agricultural settlements and preyed on their more sedentary and vulnerable neighbors. Later after our story ends, a pattern of interregional interaction between the steppes and the sown will be established that will continue significantly to affect world history until the advent of modern times.

STEPPE ARCHAEOLOGY AND THE IDENTIFICATION (AND PROLIFERATION) OF ARCHAEOLOGICAL CULTURES

The perspective adopted here can be compared and contrasted with that recently articulated by A.N. Gei (1999) in a thoughtful article assessing current difficulties in interpreting the incredible amount of archaeological materials that were recovered from the excavations of literally thousands of Bronze Age barrows or kurgans on salvage projects during the 1970s and 1980s, the so-called golden age of kurgan archaeology. Gei trenchantly criticizes the current state of affairs, lamenting the bewildering confusion of names and inadequate conceptualizations of closely related archaeological remains; as an example, he lists twenty-four terms (1999: 37) used to describe Chalcolithic to Middle Bronze remains just within the Rostov province in the lower Don region! According to Gei, the tendency to split or subdivide these remains into countless archaeological cultures is due not only to the recent tremendous accumulation of materials, but also to the interregional breakdown in communication and standardization associated with the dissolution of the Soviet Union. One can add also that the structure of research in the Russian archaeological tradition promotes this same tendency: senior scholars stake out their distinctive research territories, which they then naturally highlight in a variety of ways, including incessantly defining and naming new archaeological cultures.

Gei eloquently argues against these trends and for greater systematic treatment of these materials, insisting on the necessity of creating computer data banks to process and prepare the materials, work that he and his colleagues have already begun at the Institute of Archaeology in Moscow. I concur with Gei's assessment, applaud his recommendations, and even confess to feeling a bit relieved to learn that it is not only I who am confused by the formidable roster of archaeological cultures characteristic of "kurgan archaeology." It is reassuring to realize that even a scholar as intimately familiar with these remains as A.N. Gei is similarly bewildered. Consequently, I feel more emboldened to offer my own, admittedly less informed interpretation of these materials. This reaction, of course, is not an excuse for shabby scholarship but again represents a recognition of the fact that no one can claim perfect understanding, that there is no final word to utter.

It is on this recognition, however, that Gei and I differ. Implicit in his article and recommendations is the belief that it is just a question of doing more systematic work to get to that stage of understanding where one has defined and named all the real archaeological cultures that once roamed the steppes. Create a sufficiently comprehensive data bank and the ambiguities and uncertainties will be resolved; once this work is done, the cultural terminology will reflect past reality. His article, reflective of a distinctively different national archaeological tradition, ironically is perfectly consistent with the positivist approach of the "explicitly scientific" archaeology of the Anglo-American tradition in the late 1960s and 1970s.

"Kurgan archaeology" consists almost exclusively of the analysis of mortuary evidence and, as such, is inherently limited. In many cases, more understanding may be achieved through the systematic discovery and excavation of settlements than through the standardized processing of the inventories from thousands of excavated kurgans. Rigorous ethnohistoric and ethno-archaeological studies documenting adaptations to the open steppe and recording the distinct environmental conditions characteristic of specific regions would also illuminate this archaeological record and aid tremendously in reducing the "noise" of all those listed archaeological cultures. Many suggestions can be made – more radiocarbon dates, more analyses of the provenience of materials, and so forth; such recommendations are easy to make, but they miss the point. More and better information will always need to be collected and analyzed, but that does not mean that at a certain point the data will speak for themselves, that past reality will be clear. The historian must always interpret his/her materials, and so must the archaeologist. In fact, it is important to do so even when the database is far from satisfactory.

In reality, we all know that the archaeological culture is a problematic concept, sometimes nothing more than a convenient device for grouping together similar looking assemblages of artifacts and often employed unreflectively – assuming the fit between the defined culture and a past people. The fit between the archaeological culture and the culture of the ethnographer or ethnic culture is typically imprecise; we can never be certain that similar material remains relatively restricted in space and time signify a single or multiple groups. Similarly with different material remains. Are we dealing with two or more groups or the same group performing different activities? Even more problematic is the attempt to identify such archaeological cultures as ancestral to much later, historically mentioned ethnic groups, and this latter tendency unfortunately remains very much alive in the Russian archaeological tradition of research.

It is essential to question such identifications and the implicit concept of the *ethnic* culture with which the archaeologist hopes his materials corresponds. At times – the best of times – there may be a direct correlation between the archaeologically defined culture and some collective people who recognized itself and existed in the prehistoric past. Even then when this elusive correspondence is real, however, we should reflect more seriously on what contemporary social anthropologists mean by a culture or an ethnic group. As Eric Wolf (1984: 399) reminded archaeologists some years ago, the determination of the archaeological culture represents only the beginning, not the end point of the analysis.

> Cultural construction, reconstruction, and destruction are ongoing processes, but they always take place within larger historical fields or arenas. These arenas are shaped, in their turn, by the operation of modes of mobilizing social labor and by the conflicts these generate internally and externally, within and between social constellations. . . . We must come to understand [cultural forms and sets of forms] as human constructions built up to embody the forces generated by the underlying mode of mobilizing social labor. They are not static and given for all times . . . they are subject to a continuous process of social ordering and dismemberment.

We must realize that cultures are dynamic entities that can change dramatically over very short periods of time, particularly as they get caught up in larger historical processes that can overwhelm and transform them. Such large-scale processes, involving the development of new technologies and economies and the large-scale movements of materials through various forms of exchange and of peoples through their migrations, were at work on the Eurasian steppes, the southern Caucasus, and the Central Asian plains of Bactria and Margiana during the Bronze Age. These processes profoundly affected the countless archaeological cultures with which they came into contact.

In other words, the cultures that ethnographers study are not pure, pristine entities developing in a vacuum. Rather, they are almost always hybrids, fissioning or coalescing, assimilating or modifying the customs of the neighboring peoples with whom they constantly interact. Cultures are not primordial entities or essences once crystallized in time and then remaining forever the same; they are never made, but always in the making (again justifying the title of this study). Finally, both ethnographic and historical sources make it patently clear that the same people can change its way of life, including its basic subsistence economy – more agricultural, more pastoral nomadic, or whatever – within a single generation. As that is true, it means the material culture of a group or people can quite quickly and profoundly change as well. The point is not that cultures *have* to change so quickly but rather that they are capable of doing so.

The Kura-Araxes Early Bronze "culture" of Transcaucasia has no single point of origin. As bearers of this cultural formation moved farther south, they changed and adopted some of the features of the peoples with whom they came into contact. Similarly, the peoples from the steppes who moved into the southern Caucasus with their oxen-driven wagons and buried their dead in impressively large kurgans also assimilated features of the Kura-Araxes folks who stayed behind. The roots of the so-called Bactria Margiana Archaeological Complex (BMAC) are not to be sought in southern Turkmenistan, eastern Iran, Baluchistan, the Indian subcontinent, or, later, the Eurasian steppes but in all these areas combined. Like other cultural entities, this complex phenomenon or regional secondary state was a hybrid, the product of a unique convergence of different cultural traditions.

Ethnographers dealing with ethnic or living cultures tell us also that that group is a distinct cultural community that considers itself such and, to a great extent, is also considered such by its neighbors. An ethnographer's culture that is ultimately based on the self-recognition of the group and/or the recognition of neighboring groups is not directly recoverable archaeologically. That does not mean that the concept of the archaeological culture should be abandoned but just that it should be distinguished from the culture of the ethnographer. It should also lead to caution in making ethnic and linguistic identifications on the basis solely of material remains. That is, there is no necessary material correlate to such reflection and consciousness. Such self-recognition is archaeologically invisible, and, correspondingly, ethnicity and language cannot be determined in the absence of intelligible inscriptional evidence. Until such inscriptions are discovered, we will never be able to ascertain whether the Kura-Araxes folks were Hurrians or the BMAC peoples were "Aryans" or someone else. Quests to make such identifications have a sorry and, at times, even dangerous history. From the perspective adopted in this study, the archaeology of ethnicity is a mistaken enterprise; indeed the term itself is an oxymoron.

CHRONOLOGICAL CONUNDRUMS – THE APPLICATION OF CALIBRATED C14 DETERMINATIONS FOR THE ARCHAEOLOGY OF THE EURASIAN STEPPES

If the archaeology of the steppes is characterized by an excessive proliferation of archaeological cultures, the lack of chronological consensus is also striking, particularly as regards an absolute chronology. Wherever available, I have made use of calibrated radiocarbon dates to help anchor the relative chronological relations. Fortunately, chronological correspondences today can be based on substantial sequences of calibrated dates that have recently been published, and these will be utilized throughout this work (cf. Rassamakin 1999; Chernykh, Avilova, and Orlovskaya 2000; Telegin et al. 2001; Trifonov 2001; Chernykh and Orlovskaya 2004a and 2004b; and the periodization of Trifonov based on calibrated dates that is presented in the Appendix).

Some scholars (e.g., Sarianidi 1998: 78; Lichardus 1988: 88–89) still prefer to work with uncalibrated dates because they better fit their preconceived theories and typologically derived chronologies that in turn are ultimately connected to Troy, Mycenae, or some presumably securely dated culture with which their materials exhibit parallels. The refusal to adopt calibrated dates also conveniently fits their preconceived notions about the relations and the directions of movements of materials and peoples between regions. Unfortunately, however, there is no choice. Radiocarbon dating has become more accurate and "scientific" and has done so on the basis of making these calibrations. In fact, one of the great virtues of calibrated radiocarbon dates is that they are independently derived and not based on the preconceptions of archaeologists. One is compelled to rethink one's materials and, if need be, abandon one's pet theories. Thus, calibrated dates have to be adopted, and there is real hope for the eventual establishment of a secure, mutually accepted absolute chronology – though we have not yet arrived at this desired state.

Adding to the confusion is the lack of standardization of basic periodization sequences despite various recent attempts (cited above) to anchor the chronology of the steppes through the compilation and calibration of hundreds of radiocarbon dates. These efforts have solved some vexing chronological issues, such as the seemingly now well-established second quarter to mid-fourth millennium date for the beginnings of the Maikop culture, but have not yet led to a generally accepted or uniform sequence. There are lumpers and splitters; Telegin et al. (2001) define three periods – early, middle, and late – from 5700–2700 BC, whereas Trifonov (2001) distinguishes six periods of development during essentially the same absolute time frame (see his periodization presented in the Appendix). Relying on their compilation of dates, Chernykh and his colleagues emphasize the so-called Chalcolithic hiatus, associated with the collapse of the Balkan Chalcolithic cultures and the breakup of the Carpatho-Balkan Metallurgical Province, and see this as lasting for roughly half a millennium from ca. 3800–3300 BC, whereas Rassamakin (1999: 128) sees such a hiatus as insignificant, lasting 200–300 years and dating it slightly earlier to the very beginning of the fourth millennium. Trifonov (personal communication) doubts the very existence of this postulated hiatus, seeing it as a temporary product of a still-incomplete record of steppe radiocarbon dates.

If one compares the lists of dates of Rassamakin (1999) and Telegin et al. (2001), on the one hand, with Chernykh et al. (2000), on the other, it is clear that series of dates occur in the former that do not appear in the latter and vice versa, including several bridging the gap of the postulated hiatus. Many dates are contradictory and/or have large +/− ranges, limiting their overall utility; the compiled dates come from different laboratories, made on different materials and at different times, including during the early years of radiocarbon analysis (i.e., when and in places where the dates obtained were less reliable). It is very useful to have such compilations of calibrated dates, though they do not as yet − and maybe never will − provide the perfect panacea for resolving the relative and absolute chronology of the later prehistory of the steppes given both the inherent limitations of calibrated C14 dating and the theoretically rapid movement of materials, technologies, and peoples across this vast, open, and interconnected area.

To conclude this long discussion of chronological uncertainties, three caveats must be emphasized. First, we are still a long way from achieving an absolutely anchored and consensually accepted chronology; not only are there many regions that lack a sufficient number of radiocarbon determinations, but many of the dates obtained, particularly those processed some time ago, have too wide a +/− range of probability to be useful. Many more samples have still to be systematically collected throughout this vast region and submitted to the appropriate well-regarded and equipped laboratories. This will take considerable time and money.

Second, though extremely useful, calibrated C14 dates do not provide a panacea for all problems of dating archaeological materials. The term "absolute" may be misleading. There is always that range of probability within which they fall, and that range can be sufficiently large to substantially diminish their utility. This problem is particularly acute in the interconnected world of the steppes. Materials and peoples demonstrably moved across and between regions in Chalcolithic times, and these movements intensified during the Bronze Age; such processes may have unfolded simply too quickly for calibrated radiocarbon dates to determine their origins and basic directions or to solve critical historical questions as to which cultures influenced which. Only the development of an absolute dendrochronological system for the steppes could potentially resolve these problems, but the establishment of such a chronology lies – if it is at all possible – only in the distant future.

The final caveat is more epistemological: absolute chronologies help resolve many difficulties, and effort always should be made to improve them, but chronologies are not history. Just knowing when something happened does not mean that one has understood why it happened. Contemporary historians are free from the chronological difficulties that beset prehistorians; nevertheless, they account for the same events in remarkably diverse ways.

INHERENT LIMITATIONS OF THE PRESENT STUDY

There is at least one advantage in adopting a post-processual perspective and writing an interpretative prehistory: there is no claim to the final word or truth. Although this study would prefer to eschew the post-processual label, it does acknowledge the practical limits of what it can hope to accomplish. My own inadequate familiarity with some of the sources reviewed in this study is part of the problem. Regardless of what is personally or currently known, no one reconstructs the past so definitively as to obviate the need for future studies and alternative explanations. Whether one is dealing with more complete and satisfactory historical sources or piecing together as best one can the fragmentary prehistoric record, the historian or archaeologist engages always in a process of selection based on criteria of values and judgments that may or may not be made explicit (cf. Carr 1961). The result of such a process is neither a fanciful story, unconstrained by evidence, nor a definitive account that lays to rest forever the need for someone else to reexamine the materials and produce a separate, perhaps even more convincing and plausible account in the future. One's aspirations must be limited from a sense not of false modesty but of acquiescence to reality.

Although all reconstructions are partial, the limitations of the present study must be more explicitly specified. I am much more familiar with the archaeology of the Caucasus, Central Asia, and the greater Near East broadly speaking than I am with that of the Balkans and the western Eurasian steppes stretching from the Dnieper across the Urals. Even in those areas where I can claim some expertise, I certainly must defer to specialists who have concentrated on reconstructing the prehistories of their regions throughout their careers. My own research has followed a more peripatetic or, if you will, "nomadic" course, beginning in Iran and Afghanistan, then migrating to southern Central Asia and the Caucasus. For a variety of reasons, I continued to move around and work in different regions within those broad areas (e.g., in southern Georgia, northwestern Armenia, southeastern Daghestan, and northeastern Azerbaijan within the Caucasus). I have tried also to familiarize myself at least second hand with the materials and literature from the areas covered in this study, participating in several international conferences on the steppes and making an initial short study trip to Kiev and the Lugansk region of eastern Ukraine and the Middle Volga region of southern Russia in summer 2000 and even to north-central Mongolia in summer 2003 to round out my overview. Such field experiences do not allow me to write the definitive account of the integration of the Eurasian steppes into the "civilized" Bronze Age world, ca. 3500–1500 BC, but they are essential for informing the interpretative narrative account that follows.

CHAPTER 2

THE CHALCOLITHIC PRELUDE: FROM SOCIAL HIERARCHIES AND GIANT SETTLEMENTS TO THE EMERGENCE OF MOBILE ECONOMIES, CA. 4500–3500 BC

> Unter Kupferzeit verstehe ich jenen Zeitabschnitt in der Geschichte der Menschheit, der durch das Auftreten des frühesten Kupfers in Form von Schwergeräten, bzw. durch die Anfänge der zweiten gesellschaftlichen Arbeitsteilung gekennzeichnet ist.
>
> By the Copper Age I understand that period in the history of humanity in which one encounters the earliest copper in the form of heavy functional tools, or in which the beginnings of the second division of labor in society can be recognized.
>
> (H. Todorova 1991: 89)

The Copper Age settlements and cemeteries of southeastern Europe, extending from the northern Balkan Peninsula to the northeast across Romania and western Ukraine to the Dnieper, have long been recognized as exceptionally rich and significant. The history of the research on Chalcolithic sites found throughout this interconnected area extends back into the late nineteenth century when scholars first began to excavate the upper levels of what were recognized as settlement mounds with thick cultural deposits (for summary accounts of the histories of research cf. Todorova 1978: 3–6; 1995: 79–82; Fol and Lichardus 1988: 19–26; Monah and Monah 1997: 21–34; *Arkheologiya Ukrainskoi SSR* 1985: 189–193).

State-funded archaeological research led to an enormous compilation of archaeological materials, a record which for sixth- and fifth-millennia times is arguably as, or more, complete than any other area of the world. Numerous artificially raised settlement hills, *tepes* and *tells* of the Near Eastern type, are distributed throughout Bulgaria and southern Romania (Figs. 2.1–2.3). Many are multiperiod sites with thick cultural deposits (e.g., 12.4 m. at the famous type site of Karanovo in southeastern Bulgaria). Unlike the Chalcolithic deposits on mounds in the Near East that are frequently found stratified beneath later Bronze, Iron, or even later levels, such as is the case for many Ubaid-related sites (cf. E. Henrickson and Thuesen 1989) – some of which have even been found

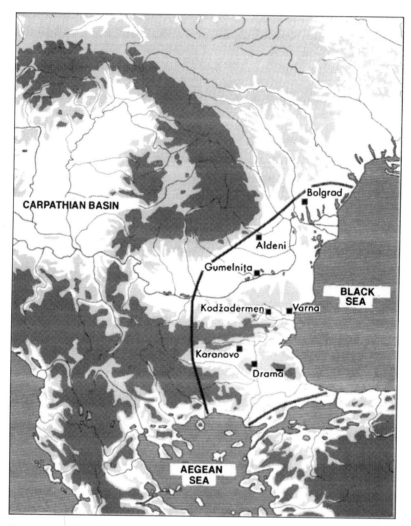

Figure 2.1. Distribution of the related Balkan Chalcolithic cultures or community of cultures – Kodzadermen, Gumelnitsa, and Karanovo VI (adapted from Lichardus 1988: 85. abb 43).

buried beneath the Mesopotamian alluvium, the southeastern European Copper Age remains typically cap their long-lived settlement mounds or occur as the topmost levels on natural raised promontories or hills, making them much more accessible to the archaeologist's spade (Fig. 2.3). The striking ceramics, anthropomorphic figurines, and exotic prestige goods (Fig. 2.4) recovered from these settlements have also stimulated archaeologists to excavate them, as well as to uncover hundreds of graves found in cemeteries (e.g., from 1975 to 1991 more than 1200 graves have been uncovered alone at Durankulak on the Black Sea coast northeast of the famous Varna cemetery; Todorova [ed.]2002: fig. 2.4).

1. Ariuşd
2. Bereşti
3. Bod
4. Bodeşti
5. Bondarka
6. Bonţeşti
7. Brad
8. Brânzeni
9. Ceapaevka
10. Cicerkozovka
11. Corlăteni
12. Costeşti
13. Costişa
14. Cuconeştii Vechi
15. Cucuteni
16. Doboşeni
17. Drăguşeni – Botoşani
18. Druţa
19. Dumeşti
20. Evminka
21. Fedeleşeni
22. Ghelăieşti
23. Glăvăneştii Vechi
24. Hăbăşeşti
25. Harbuzin
26. Iablona
27. Izvoare – Neamţ
28. Jura
29. Kasenovka
30. Klişcev
31. Krasnotavka
32. Lacul Soroca
33. Luka Vrubleveckaya
34. Lunca
35. Malnaş Băi
36. Mărgineni – Cetăţuia
37. Mihoveni
38. Mitropolye
39. Pesceanaya
40. Piatra Şoimului
41. Podgorcy
42. Poduri
43. Poieneşti
44. Polivanov – Jar
45. Preuteşti
46. Putineşti
47. Racovăţ
48. Răuceşti
49. Rogojeni
50. Ruseştii Noi
51. Sărata Monteoru
52. Scânteia
53. Solonceni
54. Staraia Buda
55. Skarovka
56. Şipeniţ
57. Ştefăneşti
58. Tal'ianki
59. Târgu Frumos – Buznea
60. Târgu Ocna – Podei
61. Târpeşti
62. Toflea
63. Traian
64. Tripolye
65. Truşeşti
66. Ţipleşti
67. Valea Lupului
68. Văleni
69. Varvareuca
70. Vermeşti
71. Veselyi Kut
72. Vignanka
73. Vladimirovka
74. Zurubincy

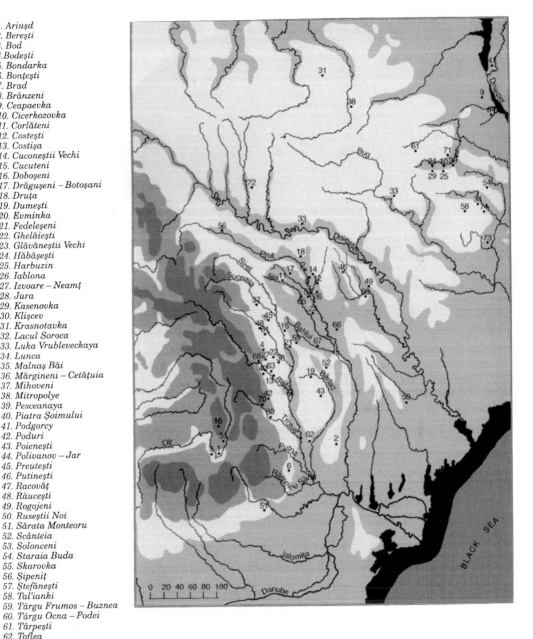

Figure 2.2. Location of some major Cucuteni-Tripol'ye sites (adapted from D. Monah and F. Monah 1997: 36-37); list of numbered sites at left (no. 58 is the giant settlement of Tal'yanki).

Figure 2.3. Brad Cucuteni settlement, Romania (adapted from D. Monah and F. Monah 1997: 81).

Indeed, the very accessibility of the Chalcolithic remains of southeastern Europe and the fact that they have been investigated for so long and on such a large scale may distort our understanding of their significance; that is, the tendency is to overevaluate this "last great Chalcolithic civilization of Europe" relative to areas with less accessible and less well-investigated Chalcolithic remains, such as those from Anatolia, Iran, or northern Mesopotamia to the south. There is no satisfactory solution to this problem of relative overrepresentation or incommensurate information. This problem is hardly uncommon in archaeology, and the only partial "solution" or correction to it is cognizance of it, particularly when there is good reason to believe that future research may radically change current understanding.

From this perspective, the use of the term "civilization" to describe the Chalcolithic materials from southeastern Europe may be misleading or perhaps is to be understood only in the same sense as Possehl (2002: 5–6) refers to the Indus *Civilization* as an example of "archaic sociocultural complexity, but without the state," that is, without well-defined archaeological markers for political rulers, sharply differentiated social classes, and monumental art and architecture suggestive of a political organization with a monopoly of force

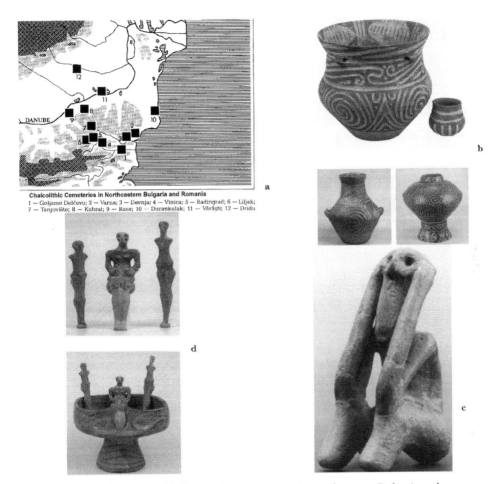

Figure 2.4. "Old Europe." (a) Copper Age cemeteries in northeastern Bulgaria and Romania (adapted from Lichardus 1988: 93, abb. 50); (b–d) selection of Cucuteni-Tripol'ye ceramic vessels and figurines (Mantu et al. 1997: 144, 111, 157)

for maintaining social control. The differential accumulation of wealth that is clearly evident in the burials from cemeteries, such as Varna and Durankulak, is most plausibly interpreted as documenting significant social ranking within these societies at least into an elite, a more numerous middle, and lowermost social strata (Todorova 2002b: 275–277). Nevertheless, the term *civilization* here does not imply that these striking fifth-millennium Chalcolithic cultures of southeastern Europe had achieved literacy or had attained the commonly understood, anthropologically defined neo-evolutionary level of an ancient state. Some of these societies, like Varna, may have approached the "threshold" to state organization, but they never crossed it; the Chalcolithic societies of southeastern Europe were not class-stratified as were the later Bronze Age "civilizations" to the south in western Asia, such as those which arose in Mesopotamia, Egypt, and slightly later in Iran, southern Central Asia, and lands farther east. Such hyperbole is unnecessary, particularly since these Chalcolithic remains north of the Black Sea are spectacular enough in their own right and intrinsically interesting as a "failed state" or as an interrupted trajectory of social development that became less complex or "devolved" during the subsequent Early Bronze period.

The situation is strikingly different as one extends one's horizon east across the Dnieper and into the Eurasian steppe and forest-steppe zones stretching to western Siberia and northern Kazakhstan. Here most of the archaeological evidence has been obtained from excavating burials; the few settlement mounds, such as Dereivka and Mikhailovka in Ukraine or now the Botai culture settlements in northern Kazakhstan, which have been located and partially excavated, assume correspondingly tremendous – perhaps disproportionate – significance just because of their exceptionality. Thus, in comparing and contrasting Chalcolithic remains from these two areas – the Balkans and the steppes east of the Dnieper – one must always be aware of the qualitative and quantitative differences in the recovered archaeological materials.

This chapter attempts to sketch fifth- and early fourth-millennium interconnections from the northern Balkans in the west to the steppes beyond the Ural Mountains in the east as the necessary introduction to later Bronze Age developments across these steppes and south into Caucasia, Central Asia, and the Anatolian and Iranian plateaus. The coverage of this "Chalcolithic prelude" is selective, focusing on evidence linking these areas, particularly the exchange of prestige goods and, above all, copper; on the emergence and collapse of the gigantic Tripol'ye settlements, several encompassing hundreds of hectares; and reconstruction of the economies and social structures of specific cultures throughout this vast region. Numerous syntheses of these materials, some of which exhaustively document cultural and chronological correspondences, have recently appeared, and these can be consulted for farther information (cf. for example the articles in the edited volumes of Lichardus 1991; Bailey and Panayatov 1995; Hänsel and Machnik 1998; and Levine, Rassamakin, Kislenko, and Tatarintseva 1999; very useful contemporary overviews are provided also by Parzinger 1998a and 1998b).

THE PRODUCTION AND EXCHANGE OF COPPER FROM THE BALKANS TO THE VOLGA IN THE FIFTH AND FOURTH MILLENNIA BC – THE CARPATHO-BALKAN METALLURGICAL PROVINCE (CBMP)

It is no accident that European prehistorians adopted the Three Age System in the nineteenth century to order their materials. Arguably, large-scale developments and processes in later Eurasian prehistory are most clearly discerned by documenting changes in metallurgical production and exchange. There are several reasons for this. As Childe perhaps overly emphasized, the birth of true metallurgy – the smelting of metal ores and the melting, casting, and alloying of metal objects – implied the emergence of full-time craft specialization; to pursue their craft, smiths had to be fed by societies capable of regularly producing food surpluses. With the emergence of metallurgy and the production of substantial metal artifacts, another great division of labor in human society was achieved.

Conveniently for archaeologists, metallurgical developments are technologically cumulative: a traceable progression from treating metals as colored rocks to fashioning alloys, creating artificial materials from what nature itself provided. Each step in the sequence from native copper to arsenical copper/bronze, tin bronze, and iron required technological advances, particularly those associated with the control and manipulation of fire (or pyrotechnology), and these can be documented archaeologically. Though in the long term this process is technologically "progressive," it does not typically proceed in a gradual, cumulative fashion, but rather is characterized by punctuated changes, such as the sudden appearance of new metal types and resources that distinguish Early Bronze from Late Chalcolithic remains. Individual sequences do not necessarily exhibit a smoothly progressing developmental curve. Some of the most intriguing problems requiring explanation are those sequences that fail to develop or experience reversals, that is, devolve – a quintessential example being the collapse of the spectacularly precocious Copper Age cultures of southeastern Europe.

Metal resources, the components of bronze more so than iron, are unevenly distributed spatially, and this reality distinguishes the value of metals for reconstructing prehistory on a broad scale from, say, ceramics, the technological progression of which is also related to pyrotechnological advances and can be traced archaeologically. The potter's clay is not ubiquitous but much more widely distributed than the miner's metalliferous ores; ceramics were traded in later prehistory but never on the scale of metals. That is, *for transforming late prehistoric societies, the exchange of metals was as important as their production, if not more so.* The earliest metals were more ornamental than functional, but as such, they were not unimportant, particularly as they became caught up in prestige-goods networks of exchange that could have significant transformative effects on local societies. The importance of the production and exchange of metals, however, increased over time as they became more functional, as metal tools and weapons replaced earlier chipped stone artifacts and became essential to the survival of the societies acquiring them.

The earliest occurring copper ornaments and even tools have been found in Early Holocene Neolithic contexts in West Asia at sites such as Zawi Chemi Shanidar in northwestern Iraq and particularly Çayönü Tepesi in southeastern Anatolia (A. Özdogan 1999: 54). The regular occurrence of copper and lead ornaments at later seventh- and sixth-millennium sites in northern Mesopotamia and Anatolia, such as Tell Sotto and Yarim Tepe I (Merpert and Munchaev 1993) and Çatalhöyük, is significant for it shows that the earliest regular use of metal was associated with the early food-producing cultures of West Asia, and the general spread of the Neolithic food-producing economy from

Figure 2.5. Copper tools, weapons, and ornaments from Bulgaria (from Pernicka et al. 1997: 81, fig. 12).

Anatolia into southeastern Europe is accepted by all scholars, even those with a penchant for emphasizing autonomous evolutionary processes (e.g., Renfrew 1969; 1987: 145–159). Some scholars refer even to a common Balkan–Anatolian cultural area (or "Balkano-Anatolische Kulturbereich", cf. Todorova 1998: 31) to emphasize the close, historically connected relationship between developments in the two areas until the beginning of the Bronze Age.

Thus, the ultimate origins of metalworking in southeastern Europe can be traced back to its sporadic use within the early food-producing economies of the ancient Near East, but the metallurgical production, which involved the casting and forging of large and eminently functional tools and weapons

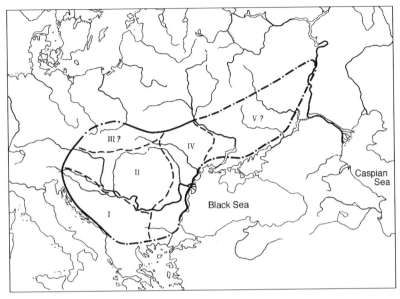

Figure 2.6. The Carpatho–Balkan Metallurgical Province (CBMP) (from Chernykh 1992: 49, fig. 15); main foci of the CBMP: I – northern Balkans; II – Transylvanian/Middle Danubian; III – northern Carpathian (postulated); IV – western Black Sea region; V – steppe (postulated).

(Fig. 2.5) that developed in the Carpathian–Balkan area during the fifth millennium BC, represented a qualitative transformation of these earlier metalworking practices. If one anachronistically wishes to accord "Europe" due credit for these innovations, then one can consider the development of copper-based metallurgy in southeastern Europe as an indigenous process – though with its roots firmly planted in the early agricultural soil of Anatolia.

E. N. Chernykh's concept (1992: 48–53) of a "Carpatho–Balkan Metallurgical Province" (or CBMP, Fig. 2.6) usefully elucidates the qualitatively distinctive production and exchange of metals that originated in southeastern Europe during the fifth millennium BC. According to Chernykh, it is possible to distinguish at least three separate metalworking areas during Chalcolithic times just within the confines of the former Soviet Union: southeastern Europe; the southern Caucasus; and what was Soviet Central Asia, particularly southern Turkmenistan. Metalworking in each of these areas can be traced back ultimately to the same Near Eastern Neolithic roots, but each then developed its own distinctive metalworking practices to a great extent independently of one another. Undoubtedly, other contemporaneous metallurgical "foci" existed farther south in Anatolia, on the Iranian plateau, and elsewhere, but it is only in southeastern Europe that one can trace the spread of related metalworking practices, metals, and probably finished objects over a vast, naturally and culturally heterogeneous area that stretched east to the Volga, encompassing what Chernykh has defined as a unified metallurgical province – the Carpatho–Balkan Metallurgical Province (CBMP).

The concept of a metallurgical province (ibid., 8–9) is a lumping category meant to order the archaeological record as based principally on the general typological uniformity of the metal tools and weapons and the fundamental similarity in the technological production of the metal tools and weapons found within it. Utilization of the concept of a metallurgical province, like any classificatory concept or model in archaeology, has certain inherent limitations. Did such provinces really exist or have they merely been constructed for the convenience of the archaeologist, and are they, in that sense, artificial? As a macroarchaeological concept, there is always the danger of the metallurgical province's reification, ascribing to it a reality that it did not possess and then invoking it indiscriminately as an explanatory device, a convenient *deus ex machina* to be employed when trying to account for changes in the archaeological record.

Nevertheless, archaeologists cannot proceed without ordering their data and must utilize concepts that aggregate their data for purposes of analysis; for example, archaeological cultures, cultural unified communities (*kul'turnie obshchnosti, Kulturbereich, Kulturverband, etc.*), peer-polity interaction spheres, world systems, and the like. The "metallurgical province" has the great virtue of having been constructed directly on the empirical basis of the analyses of tens of thousands of metal artifacts; oftentimes concepts borrowed from social theorists lack this direct connection and their appropriateness for a given reconstruction may be much more seriously questioned. The "metallurgical province" is a particularly useful concept for tracing the interregional relations basic to the theme of this study – the increasing integration of the Eurasian steppes into the "civilized" agriculturally rooted world of West Asia – and will be regularly utilized throughout this work.

According to Chernykh, such "metallurgical provinces" were few in number; he was able to define only seven of them within the former Soviet Union during the "Early Metal Age." They also become more extensive over time, ultimately incorporating most of Eurasia. The first such qualitatively distinct "metallurgical province" was the CBMP (Fig. 2.6). It stretched from the northern Balkans to the Middle Volga and encompassed five distinct "foci": the northern Balkans; Transylvania and the Middle Danube area; the northern Carpathians; the western Black Sea region; and the west Eurasian steppes between the Dnieper and Volga rivers. We are concerned principally with the integrated developments that occurred within these last two "foci," but it is important to understand the broader context in which relations developed between the western Black Sea region both south and north of the Lower Danube and northeast to the Middle Dnieper, on the one hand, and the steppes and forest-steppes to the south and east, on the other, particularly in terms of the procurement of metals.

Several early copper mines in the northern Balkans have been investigated, such as Rudna Glava in Serbia (Jovanovic 1971, 1982) and Ai Bunar in southern

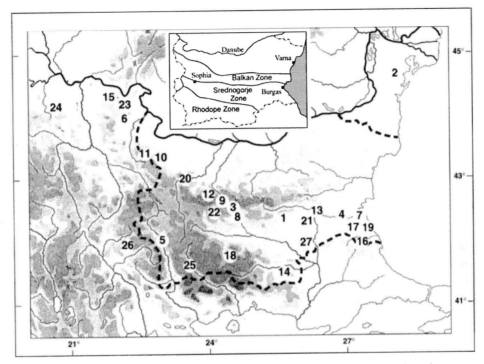

Figure 2.7. Bulgaria: its mineralized regions and analyzed copper ore sources (adapted from Pernicka et al. 1997: 83, fig. 14). Numbers relate to the following sites. 1 Ai Bunar; 2 Altin Tepe (Ro); 3 Assarel; 4 Bakadzic; 5 Bobosevo; 6 Bor; 7 Burgas; 8 Car Assen; 9 Celopec; 10 Ciprovci; 11 Cuprene; 12 Elacite; 13 Gorno Alexandrovo; 14 Madzarovo, Posko; 15 Majdanpek; 16 Malko Tamovo, Strandza, Ikiztepe; 17 Medni Rid, Rosen, Zidarovo; 18 Mihalkovo; 19 Kiten; 20 Plakalnica; 21 Prochorovo; 22 Radka; 23 Rudna Glava; 24 Rudnik; 25 Skrebatno; 26 Sletovo; 27 Ustrem.

Bulgaria (Chernykh 1978; 1988). More than 20,000 tons of metal-bearing ores are estimated to have been mined at the latter site, which may have yielded as much as 1000 tons of smelted copper (Chernykh 1988: 149), and the principal initial exploitation of Ai Bunar has been positively dated to the Karanovo VI period (or the Kodzadermen-Gumelnitsa-Karanovo VI *Verband* [cf. Lichardus 1988: 84–89], fig. 2.1) or, in other words, contemporaneous with the metal-rich cemetery of Varna. Recent analytical work (Pernicka et al. 1997: 134) has demonstrated that "the ores utilized during the Bulgarian Late Chalcolithic 'metal boom' must have come from a variety of sources" that were exploited at the end of the fifth millennium BC, and the same work has shown that much of the copper found in the Cucuteni-Tripol'ye culture to the northeast is probably better associated with the ores found in the Medni Rid area near the Black Sea coast than principally with the Ai Bunar mine (ibid., 141), as had been previously suggested.

The picture that emerges with a more detailed testing of different mineralized regions and ore sources in Bulgaria (Fig. 2.7), thus, is one in which several production centers with overlapping distribution zones operated simultaneously rather than a single source, such as Ai Bunar, that supplied areas throughout Bulgaria and far to the northeast (ibid., 146). Such a conclusion, however, is still consistent with a presumed maritime trade in copper to the northeast that entered the same exchange network of other prestige goods, such as *Spondylus* shells, and with the movement of Bulgarian copper across the steppes north of the Black Sea or the region encompassing the CBMP.

Calculations as to the amount of copper mined in Bulgaria and Romania during this Chalcolithic boom relative to the amount of copper artifacts actually recovered yield a striking discrepancy: only .1% to .01% of the copper presumably produced – estimated at 5000 metric tons – has been recovered (cf. Taylor 1999: 25–26). Such a recovery rate is, perhaps, not surprising given the fact that the archaeological record is always incomplete (and "underdetermined"), but it may also suggest that many copper artifacts had been continuously recycled and graves plundered for their metals, reducing correspondingly the amount recovered and making much more difficult the archaeological interpretation of the scale and significance of this early exchange and use of metals.

Complications also arise as to whether eastern Ukrainian copper sources might not also have been exploited by the peoples occupying the numerous Cucuteni-Tripol'ye culture settlements stretching northeast across Romania, Moldova, and western Ukraine (ibid., 27), although such exploitation has not yet been analytically demonstrated, and there is no question that Bulgarian copper was reaching these settlements as well as areas farther east during the late fifth and early fourth millennia BC. Exploitation of these latter sources has been empirically documented only for the Late Bronze Age, not earlier periods (Sanzharov and Bratchenko, personal communication; Brovender and Otroshchenko 2002: 55–56; and cf. also L. Cernych 2003).

The exchange of metals within the CBMP to the northeast, possibly as far as sites on the middle Volga, has been demonstrated, though the nature of this exchange and its differential social effects on all the cultures participating in this exchange network are more difficult to assess. Chernykh (1992: 50–54) notes several unusual features of this earliest "metallurgical province": 1) the sudden appearance of sophisticated metalworking in the core production area of the northern Balkans, which involved the casting and forging of large artifacts, such as shaft-hole axe-hammers, cruciform axe-adzes, and large adze-chisels; 2) the distinctive and relatively primitive or archaic metalworking characteristic of the Cucuteni-Tripol'ye settlements, as well as the distinctive metal assemblages found farther east in cemeteries and settlements of the so-called Khvalynsk and Sredny Stog communities; and 3) the equally spectacular collapse of metallurgical production within this province during the early centuries of the fourth millennium, a phenomenon associated with the progressive deterioration and abandonment of many settlements from the northern Balkans to the Middle Dnieper. This last phenomenon of the so-called Chalcolithic hiatus or advent of a "Dark Age"/ Transitional Period, encompassing the Final

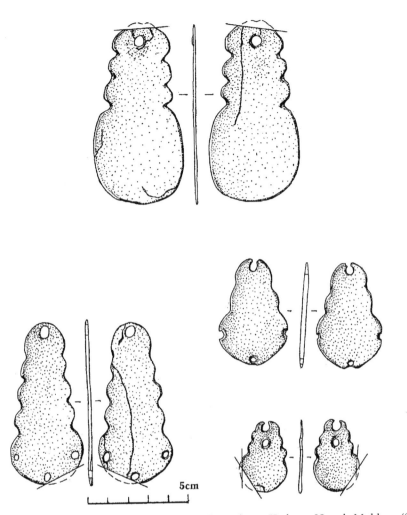

Figure 2.8. Copper "anthropomorphic" pendants, Karbuna Hoard, Moldova (from Dergachev 1998: 78, fig. 6).

Chalcolithic and Proto-Bronze periods of the second and third quarters of the fourth millennium (Pernicka et al. 1997; Todorova 1995, 1998, 2002: 22), will be considered at the end of this chapter.

As stated before, the beginnings of metallurgical production in the Balkans are clearly associated with the spread of agriculture and livestock raising from Anatolia and the consequent spread of sedentary settlements and demographic growth. Although there is a sharp punctuated increase in the scale and nature of metallurgical production from the Early to the Middle Chalcolithic periods or during the first half of the fifth millennium BC, these developments are best conceived as an internal evolutionary process associated with advances in pyrotechnology (as seen, for example, in the production of the positive, then negative graphite-ornamented ceramics of the Early and Middle Chalcolithic

Copper hammer-axe

Figure 2.9. Cucuteni–Tripol'ye copper hammer and crossed arms axes (adapted from Mantu et al. 1997: 159).

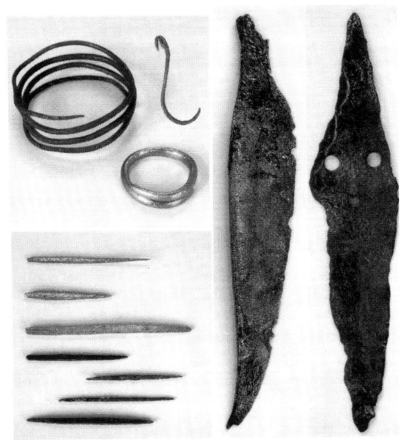

Figure 2.10. Cucuteni-Tripol'ye copper tools and ornaments (adapted from Mantu et al. 1997: 160).

periods), and the exploitation first of native copper and gold and, subsequently, of attractive and relatively accessible oxide ore sources. It is not surprising that the most sophisticated metalworking occurs within the core northern Balkan region where the copper and gold were obtained.

The relatively primitive character of metalworking farther to the northeast reflects the less central role that metals assumed in these societies. Thus, for example, ornaments dominate the metal assemblages of the Cucuteni-Tripol'ye culture sites (e.g., the characteristic "anthropomorphic" [?] pendants from the Karbuna Hoard in Moldova) (Fig. 2.8); relatively few functional tools and weapons, such as awls, fishhooks, and hammer axes (Figs. 2.9 and 2.10), have been found, though their infrequent occurrence suggests that the Cucuteni-Tripol'ye cultivators at least occasionally used copper implements to conduct essential, practical tasks. Farther east in sites of the Khvalynsk and Sredni Stog communities, bracelets, earrings, and very distinctive shell-shaped copper pendants are typical, with only occasional finds of shaft-hole axes and axe hammers. Similarly, the technology of the manufacture of copper ornaments and tools on Cucuteni-Tripol'ye sites is less developed than that found on sites farther to the southwest. Tools from the Karbuna Hoard in Moldova, for example, were hot-forged, and although subsequently during Tripol'ye B times cast axes have been recovered that exhibit parallels with materials found much farther west in Transylvania, smithing continued to dominate over casting in the Cucuteni-Tripol'ye settlements (Chernykh 1992: 41).

The picture then is one of sophisticated casting metallurgical production in the core resource-rich north Balkan area and less developed metalworking on the northeastern periphery of the CBMP, and this distinction implies that most of the copper that was being exchanged to the northeast must have arrived as a raw material or in semifinished form where it was subsequently worked by local smiths (ibid., 40). Unfortunately, ingots have not yet been found in the northeastern extension of the CBMP that would support this conclusion. Most of the metal artifacts from Cucuteni-Tripol'ye sites have been found in hoards (D. Monah and F. Monah 1997: 82–83), such as the already mentioned Karbuna Hoard. What this distributional evidence signifies in terms of the culturally defined envaluation of the metals and patterns of recycling and reuse is unclear, though it certainly also reflects the fact that Cucuteni-Tripol'ye settlements, rather than cemeteries, have been excavated, the latter nearly always yielding more prestigious metal artifacts than the former. Occasional discoveries of slag and crucibles on Cucuteni-Tripol'ye settlements, such as were found at the site of Branzeni VIII in Moldova, show that metal was worked by local, possibly itinerant smiths, and the complicated repairs that sometimes can be observed on the metals demonstrate the high value accorded this imported material (ibid.), as well possibly as lack of regular access to it.

East of the Cucuteni-Tripol'ye settlements, most metals have been found in cemeteries, some burials of which have been interpreted as representing a newly emergent social elite whose status is derived from participation in the luxury exchange network not only of copper tools and ceremonial weapons, but also of long flint and obsidian knives and arrowheads, ceremonial stone axe-hammers and animal-headed scepters, and marble and jet beads (Rassamakin 1999: 75–102; cf. Chapter 4). For example, recently excavated burials from the Krivoi Rog cemetery, which is located west of the Dnieper in the intermediate area between the Cucuteni-Tripol'ye settlements and the steppe cultures to the east, contained hundreds of copper beads, and bracelets, rings, an awl, copper scrap, and even a Varna-like gold baton; such materials are attributed to the newly defined Skelya culture, which is centered principally in the Dnieper-Don interfluve, and this culture is interpreted as playing "an essential role in the inception of the prestige exchange system" and serving "as a link between the developed agricultural world, the Volga region, and the pre-Caucasus" (ibid., 100; cf. Chap. 4, Figs. 4.5 and 4.6).

The evidence is more supportive of such an exchange network than any concerted movement of peoples east to west during the late fifth and early fourth millennium. The stone scepters, for example, particularly those that more realistically depict animal heads (the so-called type B), which have been interpreted as documenting the infiltration of Sredny Stog pastoralists into the agricultural world of the northern Balkans and lower Danube (Lichardus 1988), are much more reasonably seen as having been exchanged west to east, probably in association with the exchange of copper, than with any elusive mounted nomadic migration (Häusler 1995: 44–48; for a complete catalogue of these scepters, cf. Govedarica and Kaiser 1996; cf. Chap. 4, Figs. 4.2, 4.3, and 4.4). A few such scepters somehow ended up in burials far to the east in the Middle and Lower Volga region, but their overall distribution not only reveals how isolated these eastern examples actually are, but also suggests that such "prestige items" may have moved principally by sea. Such a maritime route along the Black Sea has been postulated also for the movement of copper, a trade that may partially explain the incredible accumulation of wealth in the Varna cemetery (Frey 1991).

The main point is that there is little, if any, evidence for the circulation of metals from the Caucasus or the southern Urals during this period and that substantial amounts of copper had to move from the northern Balkans east as far as the Volga (Chernykh 1992: 46); some of this movement most likely was by sea, but some of it also had to go overland, at least to get to the Lower Volga. Not surprisingly, a general falloff in the accumulation of copper, gold, and silver artifacts from west to east can be traced from the core northern Balkan area of production to the distant cultures on the steppes east of the Dnieper.

THE FORM AND ECONOMY OF THE GIGANTIC TRIPOL'YE SETTLEMENTS – NUCLEATION OF POPULATION AND THE DEVELOPMENT OF EXTENSIVE AGRICULTURE AND ANIMAL HUSBANDRY, PARTICULARLY THE HERDING OF CATTLE

Settlements of the Cucuteni-Tripol'ye culture were explored initially at the end of the last century by scholars such as D. Beldiceanu and Gr. Butureanu in Romania and V. V. Khvoiko in Ukraine, and their later correlation and periodization was established by archaeologists such as Vl. Dumitrescu and T. S. Passek. More recently, calibrated radiocarbon dates have provided a firmer basis for relating developments of the culture or cultural community in terms of an absolute chronology (cf. lists in Rassamakin 1999; and Mantu 1998a and 1998b). This section is concerned principally with describing the main features of the gigantic Tripol'ye settlements, as conveniently summarized by M. Videjko (1996); reference is made to the gigantic Tripol'ye settlements because such large sites have been intensively excavated in Ukraine only since the late 1960s. It must be mentioned, however, that related large

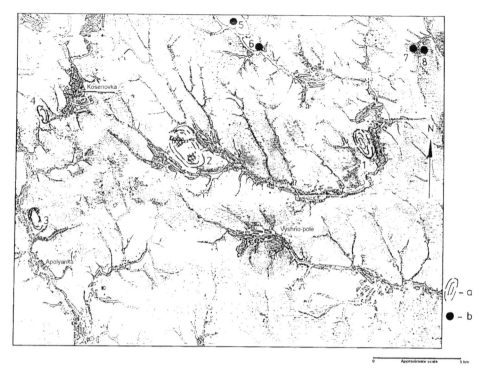

Figure 2.11. Concentration of gigantic Tripol'ye settlements (adapted from Kohl 2002b: 181, fig. 1, originally from Videjko 1995, 67, fig. 13). 1. Majdanetskoe; 2. Tal'janki; 3. Dobrovody; 4. Kosenovka; 5. Mosurov 2; 6. Mosurov 3; 7. Tal'noe 2; 8. Tal'noe 3; a. giant settlements; b. smaller settlements. (Originally from Videjko 1996: 67, Fig. 13.)

settlements (30–100 ha.) have been found also in northern Moldova and farther west.

The Cucuteni-Tripol'ye culture emerged in the second quarter of the fifth millennium BC with clearly established Neolithic roots extending back into the sixth millennium (Starcevo Cris, Bug-Dniester, etc.). Over time there is a clear expansion of Cucuteni-Tripol'ye settlements to the northeast from an original concentration along the numerous left-bank tributaries of the Danube and the Middle Dniester (Fig. 2.2) towards the Bug and Middle Dnieper area near Kiev; some later Tripol'ye settlements are even located east of the Dnieper (cf. *Arkheologiya* 1985: maps 5, 192; 6, 204; and 7, 224). Before the discovery of the gigantic settlements the largest known and excavated settlement was Vladimorovka, which contained about 200 houses spread over an area of about 34 ha. The picture radically changed in the late 1960s when K. Siskin utilized aerial photos and discovered a series of extremely large settlements, located mostly in the forest-steppe region between the Bug and Middle Dnieper rivers (Fig. 2.11); these included the settlements of Majdanetskoe (270 ha.),

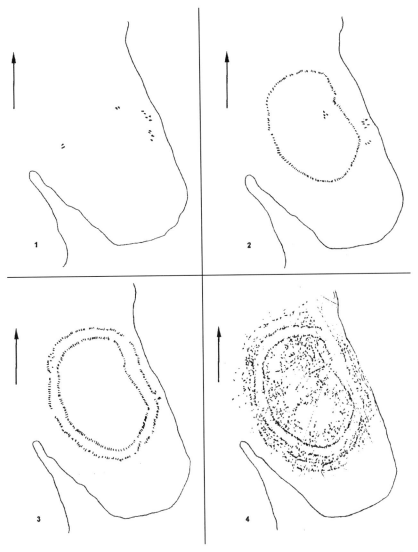

Figure 2.12. Majdanetskoe – building phases (adapted from Kohl 2002b, 182, fig. 2, originally from Videjko 1996, 55, Fig. 6); 1 – first buildings; 2 – inner "fortification" oval; 3 – second "fortification" encircling houses of the standing inner "fortification" ring; 4 – final phase.

Dobrovody (250 ha.), Tal'janki (400 ha.), Veselyj Kut (150 ha.), Miropol'e (200 ha.), Kosenkova (70 ha.), Cicerkozovka (60 ha.), Onoprievka (60 ha.), and P'janezkovo (60 ha.). Extensive field investigations began in the early 1970s and included geomagnetic surveys to locate houses and plot more precisely the overall plan of these gigantic settlements.

Settlements increase in size from Tripol'ye A (20–60 ha.) to Tripol'ye B I (150 ha.), or from the middle to the last quarter of the fifth millennium, but

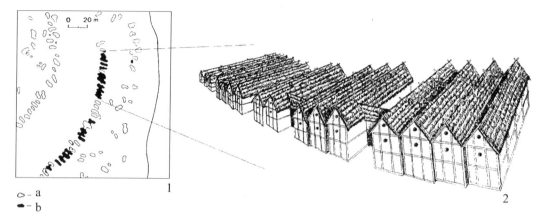

Figure 2.13. Majdanetskoe settlement (adapted from Kohl 2002b: 183, fig. 3; originally from Videjko 1996: 62–63, figs. 9 and 10). 1. Part of ring of houses; 1a. House contours according to geomagnetic measurement; 1b. Discovered houses; 2. Interconnected houses reconstruction.

the largest settlements, such as Majdanetskoe and Tal'janki, date from the last quarter of the fifth towards the middle of the fourth millennium BC; in general, one can refer to an approximately 500 to 700 year period of existence for these extremely large settlements, or ca. 4200–3500 BC (Videjko 1996: 53).
Comparatively, in terms only of the *overall size* of the settlements, these gigantic Tripol'ye settlements are as large, or larger, than the earliest city-states of Sumer and precede them chronologically by more than half a millennium; the evidence for specialization and internal social differentiation, on the other hand, is much less, and for this reason we consciously have eschewed the term "cities" and have referred to these incredibly large nucleated settlements as "giant sites" or "gigantic settlements."

Excavations of the houses and study of their materials, particularly the ceramics, led the archaeologists to conclude that most of the gigantic settlements experienced two phases of growth: a cluster of unplanned houses expanded outwards forming two to three concentric oval rings of interconnected houses (Fig. 2.12). The ceramics show little differentiation within the settlements, suggesting that each settlement in its final phase of maximum extent was occupied simultaneously for a relatively short period of time, possibly less than a century, before its abandonment, typically after having been deliberately burned down.

Scores of houses have been excavated, particularly from the settlements of Majdanetskoe, Tal'janki, and Veselyj Kut. The houses are made of loam and are rectangular in shape (20–30 m. long and 6–10 m. wide), possibly reinforced with wooden posts; most are thought to have been two-storey structures, with the living areas with hearths and benches/beds in the upper storey, and kitchens, work rooms, and animal stalls (?) downstairs. The houses arranged in the oval rings are thought to have been connected with one another, forming their own separate system of enclosures, possibly for controlling their large herds of

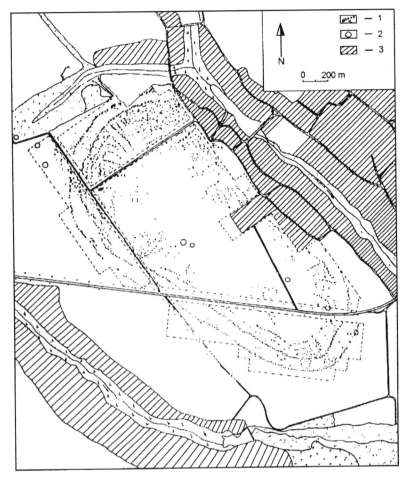

Figure 2.14. Plan of the settlement of Tal'janki (adapted from Kohl 2002b: 184, fig. 4; originally from Kruc 1994: 12, fig. 2). 1. Homesteads of the Tripol'ye culture according to the geomagnetic image; 2. Kurgans; 3. Contemporary buildings and gardens of Tal'janki village. (Adapted from Kruc 1994: 12. Fig. 2).

cattle and other animals (ibid., abbs. 7–10; Fig. 2.13). It is clear at least at the largest site, Tal'janki, that the central area formed by these concentric circles lacked architectural structures and formed a large open space (Fig. 2.14). The interconnections linking the houses together did not constitute any system of fortifications; references to such fortifications are illusory and driven by the myth of the invasion of kurgan-building pastoral nomads from the east. The later kurgans located within the area of the Tal'janki settlement are just that: later and unrelated to the occupation or final abandonment of this gigantic Tripol'ye site (Kruc and Korvin-Piotrovsky, personal communication).

Some of the plastered walls of the houses were painted. There are some special or "public" structures, such as the "M" complex at Majdanetskoe, which are larger in size (336 sq. m.) and more richly decorated, but the vast majority of the houses (over 80%) are very similar to one another with little difference in shape or size (60–120 sq. m.). Videjko believes that the distribution is basically bimodal with roughly 10% of the houses being substantially larger (270–400 sq. m.). It also must be mentioned that the sites are so large that many open areas, including the centers of the settlements, have not yet been thoroughly investigated, and, consequently, the final interpretation of the settlement structure may require revision. Nevertheless, the overall picture is one of extremely large, "planned" unfortified settlements with very little indication of internal social differentiation.

The aerial photos and geomagnetic surveys have shown that there were large areas within the settlements that were unoccupied, possibly again for securing their herds of cattle. The two ellipses at Tal'janki, for example, were separated from each other by an unbuilt area 70–100 m. wide; within the inner ellipse radial rows of houses extend towards the center in the northern part of the settlement, but as currently understood, the center of the site, encompassing roughly 60 ha., also comprised an open, unbuilt area. Excavations at Majdanetskoe have also revealed that only about two-thirds of the investigated buildings were dwellings, a finding that necessitated, correspondingly, a one-third reduction in the estimated population of the settlement (cf. below). In terms of their forms and dimensions, the houses of the contemporaneous smaller settlements are essentially identical to those found in the giant sites.

There is a three-tiered settlement pattern: the gigantic settlements (100–400 ha.); middle-sized (20–60 ha.); and small (2–10 ha.). The settlements are clustered in groups. Typically there are one to two middle-sized and/or two to three smaller settlements found within 3–10 km. from one of the gigantic settlements (ibid., 66). Demographic reconstructions are based on the assumption of five-to-seven persons/house, and the houses within the settlements form groups (of related families?) of up to 20 houses or 100–140 people. The large settlement of Tal'janki with 2700 houses was inhabited possibly by more than 15,000 people, and, adding then the numbers for the satellite settlements within its cluster, the total population may have exceeded 30,000 (ibid., 72). These calculations are, of course, rough and preliminary, but, taken all together, they show that tens of thousands of people occupied a relatively restricted area of the forest-steppe between the Bug and Middle Dnieper rivers at the end of the fifth and beginning of the fourth millennium.

It is essential to reconstruct the basic subsistence economy of the gigantic sites and their satellite communities. Cucuteni-Tripol'ye settlements inherited the basic constellation of plant and animal domesticates that had diffused into the Balkan peninsula from the Ancient Near East: emmer, einkorn, and bread wheat (*Triticum aestivum*), naked and hulled barley, peas, vetch, lentils; and sheep, goat, cattle, and pigs. They also grew buckwheat (*Fagopyrum esculentum*) and millet (*Panicum miliaceum*), the latter particularly in the eastern area where the giant sites are located; cultivated both wild and domesticated grapes (*Vitis vinifera*), though the latter may have been introduced later in middle Tripol'ye times (Masson and Merpert 1982: 235); and gathered wild and, apparently, domesticated fruits, such as plums. Hunting and fishing were always important subsidiary activities, as indicated both by the osteological finds of species such as aurochs, deer, elk, and horses, and artifactual remains, such as copper and bone fish hooks and flint arrowheads; there is some indication that hunting and fishing may have even increased in importance as the Cucuteni-Tripol'ye culture began to break up and expanded into the dry steppe zone to the south (ibid., 237).

An extensive form of sowing summer wheat and barley interspersed with the growing of vegetables, such as peas and lentils, most likely occurred on the extensive meadows that surrounded the gigantic settlements. A strong indirect case for the use of a primitive plow or ard to create furrows in soils possibly already loosened by hoes can be made by the discovery of large elk antlers with clearly worked ends, such as that found on the settlement at Novyie Ruseshty I (ibid., 233, fig. 18; 234); two types of ards, fashioned from deer and elk antlers, have been recovered: one with a vertically set blade for working recently cleared land; and the other with a horizontal blade for working intensively cultivated fields (D. Monah and F. Monah 1997: 80). A clay model of two yoked bulls (oxen?) drawing a sledge was recovered from Majdanetskoe, and traces of yoking and harnessing have been found on steer bones from Tal'janki and other giant sites (Videjko 1996: 70, fn. 68). It is difficult to imagine how these large sites with their thousands of inhabitants could have maintained themselves without harnessing oxen to draw these plows, a development that would have increased several times the arable area (ibid., 70 with references).

Similarly, it is reasonably conjectured that the short duration of these settlements suggests an extensive form of possibly shifting cultivation, involving the burning of vegetation and trees and the periodic movement of fields for renourishing the soil. It is hypothesized with supporting palynological evidence that such ecologically destructive practices led to deforestation and an anthropogenic-induced environmental crisis that was one of the factors responsible for the breakup of the giant sites and the fissioning of the culture into separate regional components by the middle of the fourth millennium, if not somewhat earlier.

Animal husbandry also played an extremely important role in the subsistence economy of these gigantic settlements. Although some regional variation can be observed, cattle were clearly the most important domesticated species and kept for meat and milk production, as well as some most likely for draft purposes. Large numbers of pigs were also raised, whereas sheep and goats, in general, assumed a much more subsidiary role (Masson and Merpert 1982: 234), though their numbers and significance seem to increase after the breakup of the settlements and occupation of the open steppe on Usatovo-related sites, when livestock herding formed a more central role in the economy and when influences from the steppes to the east and the Caucasus to the southeast are more discernible. Rustling of cattle among the different Tripol'ye communities must have been a constant problem, and, as already suggested, the large open spaces within the gigantic settlements may have functioned, in part, to secure their herds at night.

The relative insignificance of sheep and goats in the overall economy of the Cucuteni-Tripol'ye culture may suggest an extremely limited production of woolen textiles, despite the evidence for weaving as suggested by the very occasionally encountered spindle whorls and more numerous finds of what are interpreted as loom weights, but which may also have been used to help secure and weigh down the roofs of houses. There is some evidence for the use of wool (e.g., spun balls of wool recovered from the Cucuteni A–B settlement of Iablona I [D. Monah and F. Monah 1997: 71]), but it is extremely limited and some zoo-archaeologists even questioned whether the sheep that they kept were covered with wool (ibid.). Linen indisputably was woven, as well as other plant fibers, such as hemp, and the numerous bone scraping tools for working skins and animal pelts suggest that the Cucuteni-Tripol'ye peoples also typically clothed themselves in leather garments. The use of wool may have been much more restricted, suggesting that their extremely extensive agricultural and herding economy had not fully experienced the benefits of the "Secondary Products Revolution" (Sherratt 1981, 1983) that may have already been getting underway farther south and soon would take off; in other words, the Cucuteni-Tripol'ye cultures of "Old Europe" – to use M. Gimbutas' evocative phrase – may have functioned largely in the absence of woolen textiles.

AN OVERVIEW OF THE SOCIAL ARCHAEOLOGY OF THE CHALCOLITHIC FROM THE NORTHERN BALKANS TO THE VOLGA AND BEYOND FROM THE FIFTH TO THE SECOND HALF OF THE FOURTH MILLENNIUM BC

This section will review briefly and sequentially the social organization of Chalcolithic societies stretching west to east from the Balkans to the Lower Volga. Its coverage will be selective and focus on the contrasts that distinguish the cultures that were distributed across the different environmental zones incorporated within the Carpatho-Balkan Metallurgical Province (CBMP).

The greatest accumulation of wealth, particularly in the form of copper and gold artifacts, and evidence for internal social differentiation is found in the northern Balkans near the area where the copper was mined. The Varna cemetery is most striking in this respect, though now the excavations of the cemetery *and* part of the contemporary settlement at Durankulak located on an island near the coast roughly 100 km. northeast of Varna must also be considered (Todorova 2002). Lichardus (1988: 94 ff.; 1991) has provided a useful social analysis of the Varna cemetery, dividing the then-excavated 281 graves from the cemetery into five types: A) rich – with copper, gold, and shell ornaments, some of which were sewn on their garments, and ceremonial symbolic artifacts, symbolizing power and status, such as long flint blades, axe-hammers, and gold

Figure 2.15. Grave 43, Varna cemetery – the so-called "king's" grave during excavation (adapted from Ivanov 1988: 55, abb. 25).

batons and scepters; nearly all of these rich graves also contained metal tools and ceramics; B) graves with rich gold, copper, and shell ornaments but lacking symbols of power and status; C) graves with a few copper tools (flat axes, wedges), polished stone axes, simple copper and gold ornaments, and ceramics; D) graves with simple stone or bone tools, some ornaments, and pottery; and E) graves with one to three ceramic vessels. The richest graves include several cenotaphs or symbolic graves interpreted to represent the burials of men (graves 1, 4, and 36) and women (graves 2, 3, and 15), as well as the famous "kingly" or "royal" burial no. 43 (Ivanov 1991: 143–144; Todorova 1998: 43) of a 40- to 50-year-old man with numerous gold, copper, shell, and stone symbols of power and status, including what has been interpreted as a golden penis sheath (Fig. 2.15).

According to Lichardus's analysis, the richest graves are concentrated in one small section (15×15 m.) of the cemetery that he defines as its core, though it should be noted that this same core area also contains examples of the remaining four poorer types of burials. Other smaller excavated contemporary cemeteries near Varna, such as Vinica and Devnja, contain only types C, D, and E, but the richer of these, or type C, are similarly concentrated in one small area of the cemetery (cf. Fig. 2.4a above). Excavations farther north along the Black Sea coast at the Durnakulak cemetery have uncovered more than thirty "princely" graves (listed in Todorova 2002b: 272–275), not quite comparable to the richest (type A) at Varna, but richer than those of the smaller inland cemeteries; possibly the richest Varna-period burials at the Durankulak cemetery may lie under the level of the sea and have not been excavated. The rich graves at Durankulak are plausibly interpreted as belonging to an elite or princely stratum (*Häuptlingsfamilie*) indicative of the differentiation in this society that separated this elite stratum from the rest of the society. These graves probably are best compared to Lichardus's type B from Varna. It may not be fortuitous that there appears to be a difference between the cemeteries located on the Black Sea coast and those located farther inland: the richest Copper Age burials have been found near or on the Black Sea, suggesting that the impressive accumulation of wealth evident in these elite burials may have been associated at least in part with the maritime exchange of exotic prestige goods (ibid., 277).

There is a clear differentiation between male (typically extended) and female (contracted or crouched) burials not only in their form, but also in the accompanying grave goods (males typically with more metal objects and ceremonial weapons and symbols of power; females with greater numbers of ornaments, such as necklaces and hair pins). In the Durankulak cemetery, male burials contained nearly eight times as much copper (by weight) than female burials, which, in turn, contained only slightly more copper than that found in children's burials (Todorova 1999: 245, table 2). It has been claimed, however, that roughly 10% of the burials may have been sexed incorrectly on the basis of their accompanying grave goods (Bailey and Hofmann 2005: 221). Nevertheless, the archaeological, particularly mortuary, evidence completely contradicts the fanciful notion that these Balkan Copper Age societies were matriarchal and peace loving (e.g., Gimbutas 1989; cf. Anthony's devastating critique 1995).

Additional evidence for social differentiation and craft specialization comes from the excavation of settlements. A vase, for example, from the Hirsova settlement contained broken pieces of *Spondylus* arm rings or bracelets, which were presumably hoarded to be made into beads, and it is noteworthy that one of the *Spondylus* bracelets from the "royal" grave 43 at Varna had been repaired and held together with a gold band, emphasizing the high value accorded to objects fashioned from *Spondylus* (Lichardus 1988: 91, 106, and 203 cat. 14 [31]). A fireplace or smelting pit (*Kupferschmelzgrube*) in a house of the VIth building level of the Durankulak settlement was apparently used to produce copper (Todorova 1999: 242–244), and the architecture of the fortified Chalcolithic settlement (layers III–VIII) at Durankulak, which is located on the "Great Island" (ca. 18 ha.) in a lagoon just opposite its cemetery, includes substantial megaron-like houses and two-storey buildings, including a "palace" and two "sanctuaries" (Pernicka et al. 1997: 59; Todorova 2002c: 15). Whether such identifications are correct or speculative/premature, references still are to G. Twenty excavated large structures comparable in some features and dimensions to much later houses and palaces in the Aegean, though nowhere near to the scale, say, of the public buildings, particularly the temples within sacred precincts, found in Mesopotamian city-states from the second half of the fourth millennium on. Indeed, what seems distinctive about the stone buildings uncovered on the "Great Island" is that they all appear to be well-made, substantial structures; that is, they are roughly comparable in size and do not as clearly reflect the social differentiation so evident in the burials (cf. Todorova 2002c: 15, abb. 8b).

Nevertheless, the overall picture of the late fifth millennium Chalcolithic society that developed in the northern Balkans is most impressive. In terms of the mortuary remains, there is far greater evidence for social differentiation in the Varna cemetery than that which can be detected, say, in the much later cemeteries of the Indus Valley civilization or from the late third/early second-millennium cemetery of Shahdad in eastern Iran, which is associated with extensive metalworking activities and with a settlement, possibly several hundred hectares in extent (Hakemi 1997). There are no known large urban settlements of the Kodzadermen-Gumelnitsa-Karanovo VI *Verband* (Fig. 2.1). As we have seen, the gigantic Tripol'ye settlements show little internal social differentiation and, for that reason, have not been referred to as urban formations or cities. Simple evolutionary categories are difficult to apply. Varna may represent an individualizing chiefdom on the threshold of becoming a state-structured society, but it never quite made it. How then does one categorize the Cucuteni-Tripol'ye or the contemporaneous steppe societies, such as Sredny Stog, Novodanilovka, Khvalynsk, Botai, or the recently identified and highlighted Skelya cultures?

Craft specialization is certainly suggested for the Tripol'ye settlements, particularly in the fields of pottery making, flint knapping (the production, for example, of bifacial blades sometimes exceeding 20 cm. in length), smithing, and, possibly, weaving (Videjko 1996: 71–72). The ceramics exhibit a tendency for a greater standardization of form and a decrease in painted ornamentation, suggesting an overall speeding-up of production, reflective possibly of greater specialization. As already noted, the Tripol'ye metalworking tradition is local but strikingly primitive relative to that of the Varna-related sites farther west, and metalworking is even more limited and primitive farther east on Khvalynsk culture sites in the Volga-Don interfluve, where only 330 metal artifacts, mostly ornaments, have been recovered (Rassamakin 1999: 104). Shell working and ground-stone working to produce bracelets, perforated axe-hammers, and the occasional abstract and animal-headed scepters also most likely constituted separate specialized activities on these eastern sites.

Tripol'ye social structure has to be reconstructed principally from the settlement architecture, whereas those of the steppe and forest-steppe cultures farther east are reconstructed principally on the basis of differential grave good assemblages. None of the available evidence allows for the reconstruction of an elaborate multitiered social hierarchy, such as that postulated for Varna, but the bimodal distribution of house sizes in the gigantic Tripol'ye settlements (see above) – as well as the presence of wealthy graves on Skelya culture sites (Rassamakin 1999), in the Mariupil cemetery on the Sea of Azov (Makarenko 1933), and in the Khvalynsk cemetery near the Volga – suggest some division at least between "elite" and commoner strata. For example, one burial in the Khvalynsk cemetery contained over 2000 beads, which had originally been sewn onto clothing, and around 50 round-bottomed pots (Chernykh 1992: 44); the "elite" burials of the Skelya culture to the west are even more striking.

Moving farther east beyond the Urals and into northern Kazakhstan and western Siberia, one enters essentially a strikingly different "Chalcolithic" world, one largely without metals or beyond the stretch of the Carpatho-Balkan Metallurgical Province. The cultures, particularly now the Botai culture (Kislenko and Tatarintseva 1999) of northern Kazakhstan, develop both out of an earlier local Mesolithic and a "Neolithic" (presence of pottery) base, with influences emanating also from the Mesolithic and Neolithic cultures which have been documented near the Aral Sea and in the Kyzyl Kum desert (e.g., Kelteminar-related sites). Hunting, gathering, and fishing constitute the principal productive activities, including, as at Botai, the specialized hunting of wild horses. Some of these hunting sites were impressively large (up to 15 ha.) and contained scores of rectangular, circular, and polygonal semisubterranean houses (158 dwellings in the last level at Botai), attesting to the success of this specialized adaptation to the open steppe. It is important to note that the available calibrated radiocarbon dates from Botai and the related site of Krasni Yar are consistent and date them to the middle of the fourth millennium BC or, roughly, to the end of the period discussed in this chapter (ibid., 215, Appendix 4.1); in other words, at the end of the Chalcolithic period, the steppes east of the Urals were occupied by successful hunters, intimately familiar with wild horses.

THE COLLAPSE OF THE SOUTHEASTERN EUROPEAN COPPER AGE – SINGLE- AND MULTICAUSAL EXPLANATIONS FROM INVADING NOMADS AND ENVIRONMENTAL CRISES TO SHIFTS IN INTERREGIONAL RELATIONS

Much scholarly ink has been spilled on explaining the end of the Chalcolithic Kodzadermen-Gumelnitsa-Karanova VI *Verband* at the end of the fifth millennium and, subsequently, of the breakdown of the Cucuteni-Tripol'ye Culture into numerous regional post-Tripol'ye variants or groups (cf. Parzinger 1998a: 465; and 1998b). The final section of this chapter will briefly consider the various factors that have been proposed to explain this process of "devolution," as well as consider the fundamental shift in the procurement of metals that occurred from the Carpatho-Balkans to the Caucasus, principally, as well as to the southern Urals, heralding the advent of Chernykh's Circumpontic Metallurgical Province in the second half of the fourth millennium BC. The two main competing theories have been to emphasize the destructive effects of a concerted movement of mounted pastoral nomads from the steppes to the east (e.g., Lichardus 1988, 1991), on the one hand, or to document major climatic changes, involving an increasing aridization that proceeded south/southwest to north/northeast, first affecting cultures in Anatolia and the Aegean, then in the northern Balkans, and finally in Romania and western Ukraine, on the other (notably in numerous articles by Todorova, e.g., 1991, 1993, 1995, 1998a,

1998b, and 2002d). Some have also mentioned the exhaustion of the exploited, easily accessible copper ores in the Balkans, leading to a search for alternative sources, including those farther north and northwest into central Europe.

The theory of a movement of mounted nomads from the east relies heavily on the evidence for Copper Age horse domestication from the Sredny Stog site of Dereivka (Telegin 1986), particularly the demonstration of bit wear on the famous "ritual" stallion skull found at the site (Anthony and Brown 1991; Anthony 1996). The calibrated C14 date taken from this skull has shown it to date at least 1000 years later in the Bronze Age (Levine 1999: 14, table 2.1), and there is indisputable evidence now for the mixing of materials from later levels at the site, leading Levine (1999: 15–19) to refer to the entire evidence for Copper Age horse domestication at Dereeivka as a myth; other skeptics (e.g., Häusler 1994; 1995) had come to this conclusion even prior to these new radiocarbon determinations, dismissing the evidence for a Chalcolithic horse cult at Dereeivka or at Khvalynsk (cf. the discussion in Chapter 4 on the highly contentious, still unresolved debate over the origins and process of horse domestication). As mentioned above, the archaeological evidence cited to support an east-west movement of peoples, such as the distribution of the abstract and animal-headed stone scepters, is much more reasonably interpreted as indicating the existence of a prestige-goods exchange network than such a migration. If one is going to attribute the collapse of the Varna-related cultures to an invasion from the east, one also has the problem of circumventing the giant Tripol'ye-culture sites, which are beginning to develop at the time of the first postulated migration (Videjko 1996: 73). The environmental-crisis model has the virtue of proceeding in the right direction: the observed sequential archaeological collapse from the southwest to the northeast corresponds to different latitudinal zones being affected at different times owing to this progressive onset of more arid conditions and changes in sea level.

Some of the settlements described in this chapter were fortified, and many, including all the giant Tripol'ye settlements, show considerable evidence for burning and for having been destroyed by fire. Such destruction may be due to natural, as well as human-related, causes, though it is clear that the Copper Age peoples of southeastern European were not averse to fighting among themselves. Videjko (1996: 74) attributes the emergence of the gigantic settlements with their enclosures to internal competition and fights (*Konkurrenzkamp*) among different Tripol'ye groups, an interpretation that also is consistent with the environmental crisis model; times get tough – for whatever reason – and people get nasty. The direct archaeological evidence for such conflicts, however, is rather limited; the burning of the settlements may have been directly associated with their sequential abandonment and may have been conducted for ritualistic purposes, possibly associated with efforts to rejuvenate the soil. Many parallels to such ritualistic burning of houses are attested in the archaeological record from related regions – both in earlier periods, as perhaps occurred at Çatalhöyük (VII–VIA), and later times, such as possibly on many seemingly abandoned Kura-Araxes settlements in Transcaucasia.

A strong circumstantial case can be made also for a complementary human-induced environmental crisis; the construction alone of the giant settlements would have seriously reduced the forests within the forest-steppe zone in which they were situated. Similarly, their agricultural economy was extensive, probably involving forest clearance and the periodic shifting of fields or a form of swidden cultivation. They kept large herds of cattle and substantial numbers of pigs, the utilization of which too would have had serious environmental consequences. Although it would be nice to have more direct confirmatory evidence, the available pollen analyses from the gigantic settlements are consistent with a pattern of deforestation and an overall reduction in biodiversity (Videjko 1996: 57, 70–71). As will be described later, the ecology of the Eurasian steppes is very fragile, and even minor climatic changes affect differentially the open steppes proper from the forest-steppe and forest zones to the north (cf. also Parzinger 1998a: 459).

Thus, the environmental-crisis model championed by Todorova seems consistent with the archaeological record. She (1995: 89) summarizes this model as follows:

> The brilliant development of the late Eneolithic cultural block was terminated at the end of the fifth millennium and the beginning of the fourth millennium B.C. by a colossal, global and multi-causal environmental catastrophe: the final stage of the climatic optimum, when the mean annual temperatures reached their post-glacial maximum. . . . This was a catastrophic event. The rising sea levels caused the water table to rise resulting in the swamping of the plains (i.e., in Thrace and south Muntenia). . . . The final blow to the Eneolithic economy was delivered by prolonged droughts which deprived the people of their means of existence and forest fires and erosion put paid to any chance of survival. . . . Sea waters continued to rise during the first half of the fourth millennium B.C., bringing them above their present level and flooding the land. This phase of sea ingression . . . reached its culmination around 3,500 B.C. . . . These movements can be seen very clearly along the Bulgarian Black Sea coast. The steppes dried up, becoming deserts or semi-deserts in the south and spread beyond their Neolithic boundaries.

One should not apply this model too mechanically. Different regions and different cultures respond in diverse ways to environmental crises, and there were other factors at work, such as the opening up of new sources to procure metals, that must also have played a fundamental role in reconstructing the world of the Eurasian steppes in the second half of the fourth millennium BC.

What is indisputable is that two major shifts in settlement occurred: first, the abandonment of the Karanova VI Varna-related sites of the northern Balkans at the end of the fifth millennium and the consequent spread to the northeast and growth in size of the Cucuteni-Tripol'ye sites, culminating in the emergence of the gigantic settlements; and second, the subsequent collapse of these gigantic, agriculturally based Tripol'ye settlements around the end of the second quarter of the fourth millennium. If the demographic calculations for the giant sites that were presented above are at all accurate, tens of thousands of people were engaged in adopting an even more extensive, more mobile economy, relying principally on animal husbandry, both cattle-raising and increasingly the herding of sheep and goats (Masson and Merpert 1982: 237), an economy which has been characterized as seminomadic.

As Parzinger (1998a: 464–465) notes, the changes in settlement patterns, burial rites, and basic economy were fundamental, justifying the term *post-Tripol'ye* to refer to the new regional groups that emerge at this time. New areas of the steppe are occupied, such as the Lower Dniester region by the Usatovo post-Tripol'ye group (cf. *Arkheologiya* 1985: 224–225), and the house remains of their settlements, such as at Usatovo-Bolshoi Kuyalnik and at Mayaki, are so insubstantial to nonexistent that it is reasonable to identify them as seasonal, possibly summer encampments, despite their size (possibly up to 5 ha. at the former site) and surrounding ditches (Parzinger 1998a: 466; Chernykh 1992: 93). Such ditches, of course, could have served different purposes: not only or even primarily for defense, but also for enclosing and securing their herds. In any case, the change from the time of the giant agricultural settlements is striking, and clearly what is being recorded is a shift from a more sedentary to a more mobile way of life, or, if you will, groups that are predominantly cultivators are transforming themselves to become groups that are principally herders.

If agriculture provides the basis for a more advanced form of society, whereas livestock herding signifies less advanced society, then the term "devolution" seems appropriate to describe the process of change on the western Eurasian steppes from Chalcolithic to Bronze Age times. But this assumption itself is problematic, based on preconceived criteria for ranking societies. The term "devolution" must be employed circumspectly and is thus here placed in quotes. Our categories of analyses – whether they are strictly archaeological, like an archaeological culture, or partly ethnographically derived, such as pastoral nomadism – should not be conceived as fixed and immutable. The same people or culture can adopt a new economy and change dramatically its way of life in a short period of time, even within the lifetime of individuals within it, as numerous ethnographic studies have shown (e.g., Barth 1964; Beck 1986). Agriculturalists may become pastoralists, and, as we will see later when we consider the Late Bronze Age evidence from Central Asia, livestock herders may become agriculturalists, adopting certain features of the material culture of their agricultural neighbors. Both agriculturalists and herders may practice metallurgy or an entire range of different crafts. The categories we employ must reflect this basic fluidity or interchangeability.

A major shift in intercultural relations also begins around the middle of the fourth millennium BC or slightly earlier and greatly affects these changes in the

North Pontic and East Eurasian steppes. The advent of the well-known Early Bronze cultures of the Caucasus – the Maikop and later Novosvobodnaya cultures of the northern Caucasus and the Kura-Araxes (or Early Transcaucasian) "cultural community" of the southern Caucasus, eastern Anatolia, and northwestern Iran – marks a radical change in the production and exchange of metals throughout the entire interconnected area. Arsenical copper/bronzes, most of which originate in the Caucasus, replace the copper artifacts, which had been procured originally from the Balkans. Chernykh's Circumpontic Metallurgical Province emerges to replace the no-longer functioning Carpatho-Balkan Metallurgical Province (cf. the discussion on the use of the term arsenical copper/bronzes in Chapter 4). Its emergence and the advent of these Early Bronze Caucasian cultures must somehow be related also to roughly simultaneous developments occurring farther south that involve the greater integration of northern Mesopotamia, including the Upper Euphrates drainage on the Anatolian plateau, into a larger Mesopotamian world, involving ultimately the movement of colonists and traders from southern Mesopotamia, or what now is referred to in the literature as the Uruk expansion (e.g., Algaze 1993; Stein et al. 1996; *Paléorient* 1999; and Avilova, Antipina, and Teneishvili 1999). Our interpretative narrative history continues by tracing Early and Middle Bronze developments in the Caucasus and the role they played in the establishment of intercultural patterns of exchange throughout the even more extensive Circumpontic Metallurgical Province (CMP).

BIOGRAPHICAL SKETCH

E. N. CHERNYKH

Photo 2.1. E. N. Chernykh leans against his field vehicle and relaxes briefly after a trip across the steppes.

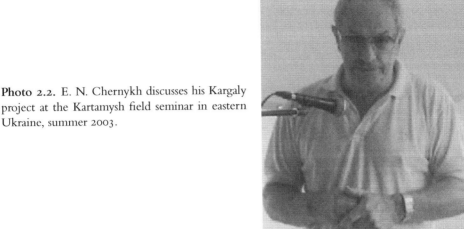

Photo 2.2. E. N. Chernykh discusses his Kargaly project at the Kartamysh field seminar in eastern Ukraine, summer 2003.

The seventieth birthday of E. N. Chernykh, Deputy Head Editor of *Rossiskaya Arkheologiya* and Director of the Laboratory of Natural Scientific Methods of the Institute of Archaeology, Russian Academy of Sciences, was celebrated in Moscow on December 11, 2005 (Kuz'minykh 2005). Chernykh has worked at the Institute of Archaeology since completing his degree in the Faculty of History at Moscow State University in 1958. As an undergraduate, he principally studied Palaeolithic archaeology under the direction of O. N. Bader and was one of the first to conduct reconnaissance investigations of the well-known Palaeolithic site of Sungir'. His initial investigations were extensive, covering different periods and areas, and included fieldwork along the Kama River in central Russia, in the Baikal region of eastern Siberia, and in the Kuban region of the northwestern Caucasus.

His studies fundamentally changed in 1960 when he had the opportunity to work under B. A. Kolchin to establish the first natural scientific archaeological laboratory in Moscow. Lacking the necessary training and experience to establish such a laboratory, Chernykh completed his second university degree at the Moscow Institute of Steel and Alloys in 1962 and worked at a series of academic laboratories and technical institutes in Moscow, familiarizing himself with the earlier studies of the Spectral Chemical Laboratory of the Leningrad Branch of the Institute of Archaeology and with the works of various groups of foreign scientists. From its very inception, Chernykh established this laboratory to specialize in historical metallurgical investigations. For the next three years he chemically analyzed the compositions of copper and bronze samples that he had collected from Chalcolithic and Bronze Ages sites throughout eastern Europe. This work resulted in the completion of his candidate's (first PhD) degree in 1963, which was subsequently published as *Istoriya Metallurgii Vostochnoi Evropy* (1966). He then collected Late Bronze Age samples from eastern Ukraine, the Caucasus, and the Urals, the analyses of which formed the basis of his doctoral (second PhD) dissertation, which he completed at the age of 37 in 1972: *Drevneishaya Metallurgiya Ural i Povolzh'ya*. In 1969 Chernykh joined the collaborative Soviet-Bulgarian expedition at Ezero, began to collect metal samples from that site and other Chalcolithic sites in Bulgaria, and initiated the investigations at the copper mining site of Ai Bunar, first demonstrating that copper from the Balkans was distributed as far east as the Volga basin during Chalcolithic times.

Since then Chernykh has published more than 250 scientific articles and monographs of significant empirical and theoretical interest, including in English *Ancient Metallurgy in the USSR: The Early Metal Age* (1992), a synthetic work that is extensively cited throughout our study. His fieldwork has continued unabated, including investigations in the Caucasus, Central Asia, Mongolia, and, most significantly since 1989, at the huge copper mining complex of Kargaly near Orenburg, an ongoing project that has already resulted in numerous articles and monographs, many of which are referred to here and listed in the bibliography. This work is forcing us to reevaluate the scale and nature of metallurgical production in Eurasia, particularly during Late Bronze times.

His colleague S. V. Kuz'minykh (2005) succinctly summarized his immense contribution to the field:

> It would be difficult to imagine the history of Russian archaeology in the second half of the 20th century up to the present without [the works of] E. N. Chernykh.... He reacts to his accomplishments with self-effacing humor, one of his most attractive traits. Although he values his ideas and works, he lives for the present and future, striving to attain the limits of the unknown, yet knowing full well that in such attempts, there is no beginning, nor end.

CHAPTER 3

THE CAUCASUS – DONOR AND RECIPIENT OF MATERIALS, TECHNOLOGIES, AND PEOPLES TO AND FROM THE ANCIENT NEAR EAST

Issledovateli arkhaichnogo obmena na dalekie rasstoyaniya neodnokratno obrashchali vnimanie na to, shto ego ob'ektami vystupali ne predmety pervoi neobkhodimosti, a roskoshnye i prestizhnye veshchi. Stremlenie obladat' imi sluzhilo intensifikatsii proizvodstva, polucheniyu vse bol'shikh izlishkov. . . . Hesomnenno, obmen okazyval bol'shoe vliyanie na obshch-estvo gortsev, stimuliruya dobychu i pervichnuyu obrabotku metallov, shto trebovalo organizatsii proizvostva i neminuemo velo k uslozhneniyu sot-sial'noi strukturi

[Investigators of long-distance exchange frequently have observed that the objects exchanged were not in the first instance necessities, but luxuries and prestige items. The desire to obtain them led to the intensification of pro-duction and the acquisition of large surpluses. . . . Undoubtedly, exchange exerted great influence on the society of the mountain peoples, and stim-ulated the extraction and initial working of metals, tasks that demanded an organization of production and inevitably led to a more complex social structure].

(Avilova, Antonova, and Teneishvili 1999: 61, 64)

The Copper Age of the Caucasus – or, more precisely, the immediately pre-Maikop and pre-Kura-Araxes horizons of the northern and southern Cauca-sus, respectively – appears remarkably impoverished relative to the spectacular Chalcolithic developments considered in the previous chapter. Nothing com-parable to the Cucuteni-Tripol'ye complexes exists in the Caucasus during the sixth through the first half of the fourth millennium BC; even more striking is the underdevelopment of the northern Caucasus before the emergence of the famous Maikop culture, which most specialists (Munchaev 1994: 169–170) now date as beginning at least towards the second half of the fourth millen-nium, if not somewhat earlier (Trifonov 1996, 2001; Lyonnet 2000, n.d.c.; Chernykh and Orlovskaya 2004a; cf. later discussion).

Such underdevelopment in Chalcolithic times, of course, contrasts sharply with what occurs during the Early Bronze Age when the Caucasus becomes one of the main suppliers of arsenical copper/bronzes to the peoples of the steppes, particularly to the Pit and Catacomb Grave cultural communities. As Chernykh (1992: 159–162) has argued, the northern Caucasus from Maikop times through the Middle Bronze period may have functioned as *the* critical intermediary for receiving metals that originated in Transcaucasia and for producing and shipping bronze artifacts to the steppes. Clearly a major shift in interregional relations occurred initially sometime during probably the second quarter to middle of the fourth millennium BC, a shift that brought the Caucasus onto the main stage of developments encompassing both the steppes to the north and the mixed agricultural/herding and settled agricultural regions of the Ancient Near East to the south.

Specialists differ in their assessments of which regions contributed to the formation of the Maikop culture, some emphasizing its steppe (Nechitailo 1991) or Central European (Rezepkin 1991; 2000: 31) components, the latter via links with the tradition of megalithic constructions, and others (Andreeva 1977; Trifonov 1987) its links with northern Mesopotamia. In a recent reappraisal and comparison of the so-called royal tomb at Arslantepe with the Novosvobodnaya-phase Maikop burials, Trifonov (2004) even argues for an eastern Anatolian Chalcolithic origin for the Novosvobodnaya megalithic tombs, such as documented at Korucutepe. Thus, if Trifonov is correct and if the calibrated radiocarbon dates securely place Maikop chronologically prior to the emergence of the Pit-Grave (*Yamnaya*) horizon, then, somewhat counterintuitively, the origins of raising large barrows or kurgans above the broad, flat expanse of the steppes may not have been indigenous to the steppes, but may have derived from eastern Anatolia or the northern periphery of the greater Ancient Near East. It is also well established that Mesopotamian elements, such as Halafian pottery, have occasionally been found on Chalcolithic sites, such as at Kyul-tepe I in Nakhicevan (Fig. 3.7), in the southern Caucasus, finds that push back some form of contact between the Caucasus and northern Mesopotamia at least into the fifth millennium BC.

The redating of the well-established Caucasian Early Bronze horizons, both the Maikop and Kura-Araxes formations, which are based now not only on typological considerations, but also on calibrated radiocarbon determinations (for Maikop see Rassamakin 1999: 163–164; Chernykh et al. 2000: 74–75; and Trifonov 2001: 76–77; for Transcaucasia cf. Kavtaradze 1983, 1999 and the partial *uncalibrated* list of Kushnareva 1997: 52; also Chernykh and Orlovskaya 2004a), suggest that Maikop began to emerge towards possibly the second quarter of the fourth millennium and the Kura-Araxes cultural formation slightly later, towards the middle to third quarter of the fourth millennium, or, perhaps not coincidentally, at roughly the same time that the so-called Uruk colonies have been documented in Anatolia on the middle to upper reaches of the Euphrates (cf. Rothman 2001).

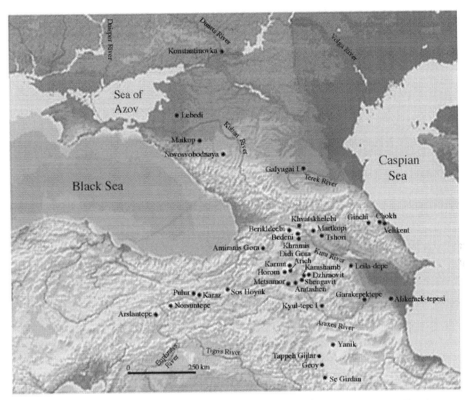

Figure 3.1. Caucasus and adjacent regions, showing approximate locations of selected archaeological sites.

The calibrated high dating for the beginnings of the Maikop culture also demonstrates that this culture/cultural community predates the formation of the *Yamnaya* (or Pit Grave) cultural community and possibly suggests that it was somehow formative in the development of Early Bronze kurgan-building cultures on the steppes (Chernykh and Orlovskaya 2004a: 97; cf. also the internal stratigraphy and C14 dates of Maikop, Pit Grave and Catacomb Grave burials in the recently excavated Ipatovo kurgan, about 120 km. northeast of Stavropol; Belinskij et al. 2000). Although relatively uncommon, earlier Chalcolithic kurgans on the steppes and in the southern Caucasus (cf. below) have occasionally been excavated, and some of these, particularly north in the Lower Don and, to a lesser extent, northeast in the Lower Volga regions, show clear evidence for contact with the Maikop-Novosvobodnaya cultural community (Rassamakin 2002: 56–60; Figs. 3.2 and 3.3). If the Novosvobodnaya component or phase of the Maikop cultural community is historically/genetically antecedent at all to the later megalithic dolmen constructions found near the Black Sea coast south of Novorossiisk, then it would suggest a chronological extension in some transformed variant of the Maikop/Novosvobodnaya community at least into

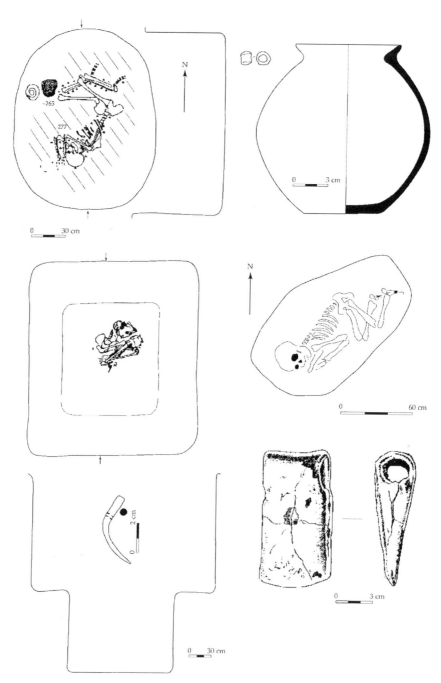

Figure 3.2. "Steppe Maikop-type" burials (adapted from Rassamakin 2002: 58, fig. 4.5).

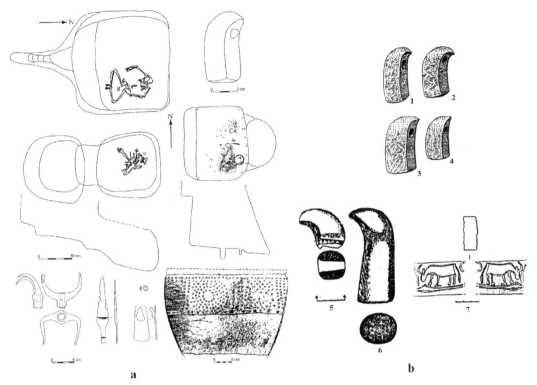

Figure 3.3. (a) Konstantinovka burials and artifacts with Maikop/Novosvobodnaya cultural community parallels (adapted from Rassamakin 2002: 59, fig. 4.6); (b) perforated stone "beaks" (1–4) from Chegem I and II, northern Caucasus; 5–6 perforated stone "beaks" and 7 cylinder seal from Sarazm, Tadjikistan (adapted from Lyonnet 2000: 320, fig. 8).

the early third millennium BC. The Black Sea coast dolmens continue to be built much later, at least into the second half of the second millennium BC (Markovin and Munchaev 2003: 101–102).

This chapter begins by briefly considering the physical and environmental characteristics of the Caucasus and reviewing earlier Chalcolithic developments in the southern and northern Caucasus. It then presents in greater detail features of the Maikop and related Novosvobodnaya cultures of the northern Caucasus and the intriguing Kura-Araxes or Early Transcaucasian cultural community of the southern Caucasus and focuses on the metal-rich, syncretic Early Bronze Age site of Velikent, which is located on the Caspian littoral plain, the only natural corridor linking the Eurasian steppes to areas south of the Great Caucasus range.

It presents evidence for movements of peoples into and out of the Caucasus, discussing the well-known spread of Kura-Araxes related settlements to the southwest ultimately to Syria-Palestine and south into west-central Iran, and the likely movement of peoples with oxen-driven carts from the steppes into the southern Caucasus beginning on a substantial scale possibly towards the middle of the third millennium BC. The material remains found in the monumental kurgans in Transcaucasia during the late Early and Middle Bronze periods are briefly described, and the settlement pattern of this time is contrasted with what has been documented for the immediately preceding and succeeding periods. The exchange, particularly of metals, and contacts with the Early and Middle Bronze Age cultures of the Eurasian steppes are discussed, and the refractory epistemological problem of detecting the movements of peoples on the basis of archaeological evidence is considered.

The chapter concludes with a summary characterization of the reemergence of settlements in Transcaucasia in the second half of the second millennium BC and the massive production of dominantly tin-bronzes for internal consumption that characterizes Caucasian metallurgy at least into the first millennium BC. Our analysis of the Caucasus materials extends somewhat beyond the lower chronological boundary of our study and violates, in a sense, its basic principle of presenting the materials historically or in correct temporal order. Such an extension is necessary to complete our review of the extremely rich and highly specific late prehistoric record of the Caucasus.

THE CAUCASUS – PHYSICAL AND ENVIRONMENTAL FEATURES AND A CONSIDERATION OF EARLIER CHALCOLITHIC DEVELOPMENTS

The Caucasus Mountains form a sharp geographic boundary between the Eurasian steppes to the north and the highland plateaus of Anatolia and Iran to the south (Fig. 3.4). The *physical* border created by the Caucasus is much sharper than that which divides the steppes and deserts of Central Asia from northern Afghanistan and northeastern Iran on the eastern side of the Caspian Sea. There the Kopet Dagh and Hindu Kush ranges also separate highland areas to the south from the flat Kyzyl Kum and Kara Kum deserts with their systems of internal drainage to the north, but the borders formed by these mountains are more easily traversed by following upstream rivers, such as the Tedjen then Kashaf Rud or the Murghab into, respectively, northeastern Iran or northwestern Afghanistan. Alternatively, one can move west-southwest onto the extensive Misrian plain, which extends along the southeastern shore of the Caspian (or today's southwestern Turkmenistan), or cross the Kopet Dagh via the Darreh Gaz plain and continue south into the upper Atrek valley, the river of which flows west towards the northern Gorgan plain of northeastern Iran. All these areas were densely occupied during late prehistoric times (cf. Chap. 5, pp. XX – and Figs. 5.0, 5.1, and 5.2).

The Central Asian deserts, in other words, effectively extend the *range of transition* between the steppes and the highlands and find no real parallel on

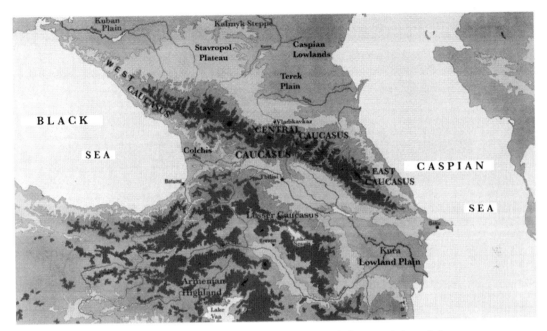

Figure 3.4. The Caucasus and adjacent regions: physical features (adapted from Kohlmeyer and Saherwala 1984: 9, abb. 2).

the western side of the Caspian, though in this latter area the dry Nogai and Kalmyk steppes also merge with each other and extend north around the Caspian. Paradoxically, the Central Asian deserts functioned as a more effective *cultural* barrier until later in the second half of the third millennium, when the pastoralists and agriculturalists of Central Asia were able to traverse the extensive arid expanses by developing more mobile economies, presumably with the help of horses and Bactrian camels (cf. Frontispiece and discussion at the beginning of Chapter 5).

Therefore, from a strictly geographical perspective, it is not surprising that contacts between the western Eurasian steppes and the ancient Near East developed earlier on the western side of the Caspian because the steppes and the Caucasus mountains, particularly in the northwest along the Kuban basin, were directly contiguous with one another, not separated by waterless deserts. Here the only problem more mobile pastoralists confronted was how to get around or over the mountains. One can visualize this important physical distinction between steppe and sown on either side of the Caspian as like a wedge opening west to east in which the northwest Caucasus mountains practically touch the Crimean and east Ukrainian steppes, whereas the oasis irrigation agricultural settlements of southern Central Asia are physically removed from the vast steppes of southern Russia and northern Kazakhstan by the formidable Kyzyl Kum and Kara Kum deserts.

In other words, the transitional zone separating the steppes from the piedmont and into the high Caucasus with their unbroken wall of perennially snow-capped peaks is much narrower. As soon as one travels north of Makhachkala, the capital of Daghestan, the steppes simply open up to the north and west. The small mountains that surround Pyatigorsk form a restricted enclave famous for their salubrious mineral waters, but the massive peaks of the Caucasus looming immediately to their south dwarf them. The flat plains north of the Caucasus, such as those forming Krasnodar and Stavropol' provinces, are today intensively cultivated and constitute some of Russia's richest and most productive agricultural land. Their use during Bronze Age times was totally different, when more extensive and more mobile economies exploited them. Farther west the heavily wooded slopes of the northwestern Caucasus descend almost directly into the Black Sea, creating strikingly beautiful landscapes and today a potentially lucrative tourist area extending from Novorossiisk in the north through Abkhazia into western Georgia in the south.

The Caucasus contain extremely diverse environments, particularly marked by altitudinal differences, ranging from the perennial glaciers to countless steep and well-protected mountain valleys, to open volcanic highland plateaus, to broader plains, and even to subtropical depressions such as the Colchidean plain of western Georgia. Such environmental diversity explains, to a certain extent, the incredible ethnic and linguistic diversity for which the Caucasus is renowned; this human cultural diversity, however, is foremost the product of a long history of movements into the Caucasus of peoples who then zealously defended the separate valleys and environmental zones that they had entered and occupied.

The Caucasus region, in general, consists of the isthmus between the Black and Caspian Seas that is cut by the Great Caucasus range. The mountains extend roughly 1200 km. northwest to southeast, encompassing a total area of about 440,000 sq. km. The region can be subdivided into five basic zones (for more detail, cf. Motzenbäcker 1996: 13–20):

1. the pre- or Cis-Caucasian northern plain bounded by the Kuma and Manych Rivers;

2. the Great Caucasus Mountains themselves, the highest peaks of which extend in the central part of the range between the Elbrus (5633 m. above sea level) and the Kazbek (5047 m.) mountains and include an additional four peaks over 5000 m. and none under 4000 m.;

3. the southern or Transcaucasian river basins consisting principally of the Rioni River and its tributaries that flow through the Colchidean depression into the Black Sea, and the basin of the Kura River that originates in northeastern Anatolia and flows through central Georgia (Shida Kartli), being joined in its lowermost course before debouching into the Caspian

by the Araxes River, which originates even farther west in Anatolia near the headwaters of the Upper Euphrates; in its middle course the Araxes has demarcated the political border with Iran and Turkey since the early nineteenth century;

4. the so-called Smaller Caucasus ranges, which also contain peaks exceeding 4000 m. in height, such as Mt. Aragats in western Armenia; the Smaller Caucasus consist of several ranges, some of which run perpendicular to each other (e.g., the Trialeti and Djavakheti ranges in southern Georgia);

5. the volcanic, obsidian-rich Armenian highland or plateau that extends imperceptibly into eastern Anatolia or today's eastern Turkey to the south.

Relatively broad valleys and plains are found in central and eastern Georgia (Kakheti), and the broad Ararat plain (ranging between about 800 and 1200 m. above sea level) of southern Armenia and the Nakhichevan province of Azerbaijan extends along the middle course of the Araxes River and represents a particularly productive subregion that today is as intensively cultivated as it was in the prehistoric past.

Forests, consisting of an oak and juniper canopy, may have largely covered southern Georgia, including the Tsalka plateau, from Neolithic through Middle Bronze times, ca. 1500 BC (Connor et al. 2004). This thick forest cover may affect our interpretation of later prehistoric sites. Thus, the Tsalka plateau today consists of open grassy terrain, and the large kurgans dotting it, which are occasionally connected with one another via impressive stone causeways (cf. Fig. 3.27), are strikingly visible. Such might not have been the case when they were built. Similarly, geomorphological factors, which are still imperfectly understood, must also be considered in evaluating the distribution of later prehistoric sites. Much of the Central Caucasus has experienced considerable alluviation that has buried sites, particularly small one-period sites, sometimes beneath more than two meters of alluvial sediments and small river pebbles. This phenomenon obviously also affects our understanding of Bronze Age settlement patterns.

The only unimpeded route from the steppes to the south is to circumvent the Great Caucasus on their eastern side by following the Caspian littoral plain from the Nogai steppes, and Herodotus says that it was by this route that the Cimmerians and Scythians moved into the Ancient Near East beginning in the first half of the first millennium BC, thereby setting a pattern for numerous mounted nomadic incursions that continued into the first half of the second millennium AD. In other words, this so-called Caspian corridor forms the only natural unbroken route linking the south Russian steppes to the north with Transcaucasia and the eastern Anatolian and northwest Iranian plateaus to the south (Fig. 3.5).

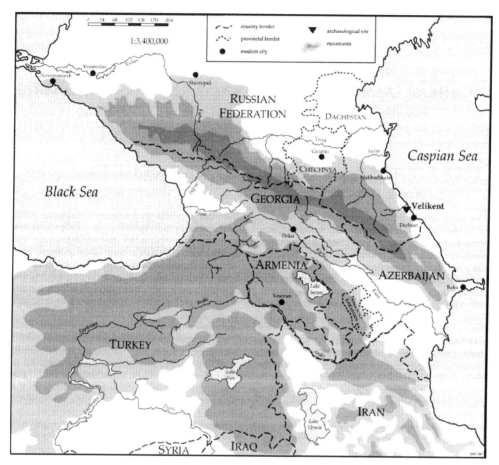

Figure 3.5. General Map of the Caucasus, showing the Caspian corridor and the Bronze Age site of Velikent (adapted from Kohl, Gadzhiev, and Magomedov 2002: 114, fig. 7.1).

The corridor consists actually of a series of plains or bays successively interrupted by rivers and streams flowing down from the mountains and by the mountains themselves extending eastwards to "pinch" the plain at several critical points, the narrowest being at the town of Derbent (or literally "closed door"), where the Sasanian ruler Khosrow I in the early sixth century AD erected a fortress and a long fortification wall, which stretches about 45 km. along the ridge of mountains directly west of the town, attempting unsuccessfully to stop the periodic nomadic invasions off the steppes to the north (Fig. 3.6). This wall was only one of a series of long parallel walls constructed by the Sasanians to defend their realm against nomadic incursions from the north; remnant lines of the southernmost walls are found north of Baku in eastern Azerbaijan at Beshmarak and then along the Ghilghilchay River, extending into the high mountains (Aliev et al. n.d.).

There are also several passes through the Great Caucasus, the most famous being the Darial ("door of the Alans") or Cross Pass (2388 m. high and, significantly, open year-round) that connects the Upper Aragvi valley with the Upper Terek River that originates to the north off Mt. Kazbek along what is known today as the Georgian Military Highway running between Vladikavkaz (formerly Ordjonikidze) and Tbilisi. Most of these passes are only seasonally accessible from late spring to early fall, and all are narrow and easily defended by mountain tribes, such as historically the Khevsurs and Svans of mountainous Georgia.

Finally, it must be mentioned that both the Great and Small Caucasus ranges contain numerous mineral deposits. Chernykh (1992: 60) refers to more than 400 deposits and ore bodies of copper, arsenic, antimony, and gold, though characteristically most of the copper deposits are composed of sulphidic minerals with weakly developed oxidized zones; many of these presumably would have been exploited only from the Late Bronze period onwards when people were able to extract and smelt them. Their modern exploitation has destroyed many of the traces of ancient mining activities, though

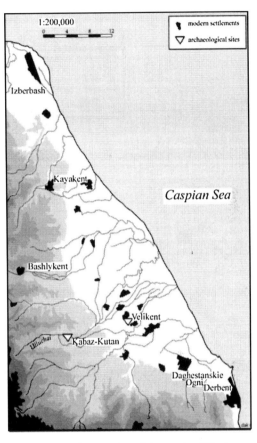

Figure 3.6. The Caspian plain north of Derbent (adapted from Kohl, Gadzhiev, and Magomedov 2002: 115, fig. 7.2)

ancient slag heaps and mines have been discovered, particularly in the Zangezur region of southeastern Armenia (Gevorkyan 1980) and in the western and central Great Caucasus (Tschartolani 2001; Maisuradze and Gobedschischwili 2001). Much archaeometallurgical research still needs to be done, particularly in the metal-rich eastern Caucasus Mountains of northern Azerbaijan, Daghestan, and Chechnya.

The best documented food-producing Late Neolithic to Early Chalcolithic horizon in the Caucasus is known as the Shulaveri–Shomu complex and dates principally to the sixth millennium BC (Kiguradze 1986: 112; Kavtaradze 1999: 70–71; Narimanov 1987), exhibiting clear relations with the Umm Dabaghiyeh–Tell Sotto and Hassuna cultures of northern Mesopotamia. The internal development of the Shulaveri–Shomu complex has been traced over

several centuries for the sites found along the Khramis tributary of the Kura
River in Kvemo Kartli south of Tbilisi by Kiguradze (1986) and in the neighboring region of western Azerbaijan by Narimanov (1987; cf. also Chataigner
1995). This cultural horizon clearly predates considerably our period of interest
and will not be reviewed in detail here.

Some features, however, are interesting for they shed light on later Chalcolithic and Early Bronze developments in Transcaucasia. The sites group together
in clusters of *tells* or *tepes* of the Ancient Near Eastern type composed of
successive building levels formed by the decomposition of their distinctive
interconnected circular mud-brick architecture forming cultural deposits that
sometimes exceed 10 m. in depth (Kushnareva 1997: 21). They are located in
a well-watered district of south-central Transcaucasia but are totally isolated or
set off from any other known contemporary food-producing cultures, except
possibly for some Late Neolithic/Early Chalcolithic settlements on the Ararat
plain of southern Armenia (ibid., 33; cf. also now the ongoing Armenian-
French excavations at Aratashen [Lombard 2003; Badalyan et al. 2004]). For
example, the earliest food-producing remains found on the contiguous high
Djavakheti plateau to the west or on the Shirak plain of Armenia to the southwest relate to the much later Kura-Araxes cultural community that begins
roughly in the middle of the fourth millennium BC.

There is a clear disjunction between the Shulaveri-Shomu remains and those
of the Kura-Araxes culture; the later dwellings of the latter *in these mountainous
areas* are typically made of stone, not mud-brick, and, correspondingly, do
not form classic Near Eastern-like *tells*. It can be argued, in other words, that
the Shulaveri-Shomu horizon represents something intrusive in Transcaucasia,
presumably from southeastern Anatolia and northern Mesopotamia, consisting
of small colonies of early food-producers who lived in this area for several
centuries before returning (?) to their southern homelands and/or possibly
assimilating with the local highlanders and disappearing from the archaeological
record.

Later Chalcolithic horizons in Transcaucasia, which now occupy different
areas, such as the Ararat plain (Tekhut, Aratashen), central Georgia (Sioni),
Nakhicevan (Kyul Tepe I), the Mughan steppe (Alikemek tepesi) and the
Karabakh steppe (Chalagan-depe, Leila-depe), also exhibit parallels with cultures documented farther south; a few Halafian ceramics were recovered from
Kyul Tepe I (Abibullaev 1982: 292, table XII; Fig. 3.7), and ceramic parallels with northern Mesopotamia have been observed for the remains from
Tekhut and from Leila-depe, where the excavator I.G. Narimanov (1985:
271–272), who had also dug at the site of Yarim Tepe III in northern Iraq,
believed that Leila-depe, located on the Karabakh steppe, had been founded
by Ubaid "tribes" that had moved into the area from the south. His interpretation was based on very specific ceramic parallels with late Ubaid ceramics
from Yarim Tepe III (Aliev and Narimanov 2001: 48–53). Later examination

Figure 3.7. Painted Halaf vessel from Kyul Tepe I, Nakhicevan (photo by G. Guseinzade, Baku).

of these materials by B. Lyonnet (n.d.c.; personal communication) suggests that the parallels are better made with Early and Middle Uruk ceramics, making these sites contemporary with the earliest materials from Berikldeebi in Shida Kartli (Central Georgia) and early Maikop remains from the northwestern Caucasus.

Leila-depe also revealed evidence in the form of slag fragments, metal drops, a possible ingot, and a relatively high concentration of copper artifacts for local metalworking (Aliev and Narimanov 2001: 70–73, table XXXVIII; Kiguradze 2001: 50–51). With the exception of Leila-depe, however, metal artifacts are remarkably scarce during the so-called Chalcolithic period of Transcaucasia, a relative paucity that leads Akhundov (2004: 425, 432) to question the standard terminology and even the validity of the concept of a Copper Age for the southern Caucasus. This picture changes radically during the subsequent Kura-Araxes Early Bronze period.

The painted pottery from Alikemek tepesi shows clear parallels with Dalma-related wares from northwestern Iran (Masson and Merpert 1982: 120–121), and this site in southeastern Azerbaijan is also interesting for its rich collection of bone tools, including horse bones, which constituted 7.5% of the identified faunal assemblage. The claim (ibid., 135) that the horse bones, coming apparently from both small and large types of horses, demonstrates that horses were domesticated here is questionable, though their recovery must indicate minimally that the distribution of wild horses extended at least as far south as the border with northwestern Iran and probably into northern Iran as well (cf. Mashkour 2003: 133). There is no artifactual evidence at all that the horses were ridden.

Most of these Chalcolithic Transcaucasian sites also reveal a basic disjunction with the Kura-Araxes remains. Typically, there is a recognizable break in the stratigraphic sequence, as at Kyul Tepe I, between the Chalcolithic and Kura-Araxes levels, or there is a shift/abandonment of settlements from one period to the other, as on the sites near Agdam on the Karabakh steppe. Kushnareva's recent review of the Kura-Araxes culture emphasizes the continuities between these Late Chalcolithic Transcaucasian cultures and the early stages of the Kura-Araxes culture. She believes the latter dispersed initially from the "flatlands of the southern Caucasus" but admits that the problem of locating the "homeland" of the Kura-Araxes cultural community remains unresolved (1997: 49).

Currently available (i.e., published) evidence does not allow one to determine the origin/homeland (assuming there was only one) of the Kura-Araxes culture. Ceramics from the site of Ovchular-tepesi in Nakhicevan exhibit features that may be considered "transitional" typologically between the Late Chalcolithic and Kura-Araxes forms, but their stratigraphic relationship is unclear, and the site needs to be reexamined and published. Farther north in Shida Kartli, the site of Berkikldeebi has been meticulously excavated by L. I. Glonti and A. I. Dzhavakhishvili (1987) and does contain a sequence that extends from pre- to post-Kura Araxes, or what are termed Bedeni and even later Bronze Age remains; its deposit, however, is shallow and badly pitted. It alone cannot solve the problem of the seemingly sudden and quite massive emergence of Kura-Araxes settlements throughout Transcaucasia, the northeastern Caucasus, and parts of eastern Anatolia beginning towards the middle of the fourth millennium BC (cf. discussion that follows).

The claim for a broadly uniform Sioni horizon immediately preceding the beginnings of the Kura-Araxes culture and directly ancestral to the culture as a whole (cf. Kiguradze 2000) covers only part of the broad area over which the subsequent Kura-Araxes settlements are distributed. Lyonnet (n.d.c.) emends this interpretation somewhat and, based principally on a detailed analysis of ceramic parallels, relates the emergence of this Late Chalcolithic Sioni horizon from Transcaucasia and the initially pre-Maikop fortified Meshoko settlements found in the northern Caucasus with an intrusion of northern Mesopotamian cultural elements or peoples (?), predating the subsequent well-known southern Mesopotamian Uruk expansion. In other words,

> Le phénomène que l'on observe dans les régions du Caucase...est très proche de celui qui se manifeste sur d'autres sites d'Anatolie orientale, comme Haçinebi au cours des phases A et B1. Il est clair qu'il précède l'intrusion urukéene sud-mésopotamienne de plusieurs centaines d'années....Il est néanmoins clair que le phénomène entrevu ici ne représente qu'un maillon supplémentaire de celui déjà connu en Anatolie orientale.

She believes that this pre-Uruk northern Mesopotamian intrusion into the Caucasus may have been related ultimately to advances in metallurgy

> qui se serait développée dès las fin du 5eme millénaire dans le Caucase, très probablement sous l'influence principale du foyer des Balkans-Carpathes.

This latter opinion may be correct, but it is hard to confirm given the minimal occurrence of copper artifacts in both the northern and southern Caucasus prior to the emergence of the Maikop "cultural-historical community" and the minimal evidence in general for the participation of Caucasian Chalcolithic cultures in the Carpatho–Balkan Metallurgical Province (CBMP) to the north. The more important original stimulus for metallurgy in the Caucasus may have come ultimately from earlier Chalcolithic developments in Iran that also influenced the metallurgical practices of Ubaid peoples in both northern and southern Mesopotamia (Pigott 1999; Avilova 2005: 27–28).

Other evidence for the initial emergence of food-producing economies and subsequent developments during Chalcolithic times can be traced independently for western Georgia and for the mountains of Daghestan in the northeastern Caucasus (Kushnareva 1997: 10–21). The latter are particularly interesting for here reexcavations at the site of Chokh (Amirkhanov 1987) defined a sequence extending from the Mesolithic to the Neolithic, which probably represents an essentially independent evolutionary trajectory culminating in food-production. Excavations of later Chalcolithic sites, such as the settlement of Ginchi (Gadzhiev 1991: 61–78), continued this process of development and adaptation (including the beginnings of terraced agriculture?) to mountainous terrain. Ginchi's bone- and stone-working and ceramic traditions clearly constituted one of the formative components to the distinctive hybrid Early Bronze Kura-Araxes-related culture at Velikent that was established on the Caspian plain by the middle of the fourth millennium BC, though it is also possible that the Chalcolithic Ginchi settlement essentially overlapped chronologically with the initial settlement at Velikent on the Caspian plain which began around the middle of the fourth millennium.

Chalcolithic remains in the Northwest and North-Central Caucasus are not well documented despite some recent investigations, particularly at the site of Svobodnoe (Nekhaev 1990). The excavator of the Svobodnoe settlement, A. A. Nekhaev (1992: 83), emphasizes its connection with the steppes to the northwest, even suggesting that it may have formed as a result of a movement of peoples from the steppes into the northwestern Caucasus. Rassamakin (1999: 108), however, explains the similarities differently, observing that materials from this site, such as its characteristic serpentine bracelets, can be paralleled with materials found on the steppes to the northwest and argues that the northwestern Caucasus in the late fifth millennium was involved also in the prestige exchange network linked with the newly defined Skelya culture.

Possibly, but, if so, the connection was rather tenuous, and they were only marginally, if at all, caught up in the Carpatho–Balkan Metallurgical Province, which, as we have seen, stretched from the Balkans to the Volga. A single copper artifact, presumably of Balkans origin (Rassamakin 1999:108), is reported from Svobodnoe, and only one small copper fragment was found in the Nal'chik cemetery, despite the excavation of more than 100 burials (Masson and Merpert 1982: 130). Most of the graves lack funerary goods altogether, and those (e.g., graves 86 and 41) with a more substantial burial inventory, including the stone bracelets, contain principally objects most reasonably interpreted as local in origin, such as perforated pendants made from the teeth of wild animals. The social differentiation evident in this Chalcolithic cemetery is certainly far less than that described for the Balkan cultures of "Old Europe" reviewed in the previous chapter.

What is most striking and contrastive with what immediately follows in Maikop times is the extreme paucity, indeed almost complete absence of metal artifacts in Caucasian Chalcolithic contexts. Such absence could partly be a product of the lack of sufficient research on this period in the northern Caucasus, but the negative evidence from the Nal'chik cemetery and from other sites, such as the Agubekov settlement (ibid., 129) suggests that metalworking and the exchange of metal goods did not develop gradually in the northern Caucasus, although it may have been stimulated ultimately by contacts with the steppes and distant familiarity with the metals of Balkan-Carpathian origin, as Nekhaev, Rassamakin, and Lyonnet suggest. This picture is radically transformed when local metallurgical activities suddenly and spectacularly burst on the scene with the advent of the Maikop culture in the second quarter to the middle of the fourth millennium BC.

THE MAIKOP CULTURE OF THE NORTHERN CAUCASUS – A REVIEW OF ITS KURGANS, SETTLEMENTS, AND METALS; ACCOUNTING FOR ITS ORIGINS AND WEALTH AND A CONSIDERATION OF ITS SUBSISTENCE ECONOMY

In 1897, N. I. Veselovskii excavated the very large, nearly 11 m. high Oshad kurgan or barrow in the town of Maikop in the Kuban region near the foothills of the northwestern Caucasus (today's capital of the Adygei Republic). The kurgan contained a spectacularly rich burial assemblage, including bronze weapons and cauldrons; scores of figured gold appliques, which had been sewn on the clothes of the principal male burial; six silver rods (some over 1 m. long) with gold and silver terminals depicting bulls (Fig. 3.8); silver, gold, stone, and ceramic vessels; and numerous gold, turquoise, and carnelian beads. This discovery stimulated the excavation of other large kurgans located in the same general region, some of which seemed "royal-like" in their dimensions and, when not robbed in antiquity, in their materials; this research has continued to the present day, and spectacular discoveries are still being unearthed, such as hoards from the Klady kurgan necropolis near the village of Novosvobodnaya that have been excavated from 1979 on (Rezepkin 2000), containing distinct but clearly Maikop-related bronze, gold, silver, polished stone, ceramic, turquoise, and carnelian artifacts.

The Maikop materials were brought to the attention of Western scholars initially through the writings of A. M. Tallgren, M. I. Rostovtseff, and, later,

Figure 3.8. Maikop kurgan: gold and silver bulls (adapted from Markovin and Munchaev 2003: 54, fig. 10).

V. G. Childe. The "absolute" dating of the "first early" or "large Kuban kurgans" was debated for years, with some scholars (Degen-Kovalevskii 1939) relating them to the Scythians or immediately pre-Scythians and dating them as late as the early first millennium BC, whereas most (Iessen 1950) dated them back to the middle or second half of the third millennium BC. The demonstration of convincing parallels to still earlier northern Mesopotamian/Syrian remains (Andreeva 1977), the new excavation of related Maikop settlements (e.g., Korenevskii 1993, 2001), and the application of a consistent sequence of more than forty calibrated radiocarbon determinations (Trifonov 1996, 2001; Chernykh et al. 2000; Chernykh and Orlovskaya 2004a) have all combined to place them on a much firmer chronological footing and date their earliest appearance much farther back towards the second quarter to the middle of the fourth millennium BC, practically to the transitional period between late Ubaid and early Uruk times (cf. also Lyonnet 2000). The spectacular early discoveries, particularly of Veselovskii, have never been published completely, but the Maikop culture itself has been defined and described in two long treatments in Russian by R. M. Munchaev (1975; 1994; for a recent summary treatment cf. Markovin and Munchaev 2003). A convenient short English description with a focus on the Maikop metals is provided by E. N. Chernykh (1992: 67–83) (unfortunately, I was unable to consult the recently published catalogue of some of the Maikop materials in the Hermitage Museum: *Shliman, Peterburg, Troya* by Yu. Piotrovskii [1998]).

Munchaev (1994: 178, 174) estimates that roughly 150 Maikop burial complexes (or 250, according to Korenevskii 2004: 15) have been excavated, whereas there are only about 30 known Maikop settlements (or even fewer, cf. Korenevskii 2001; 2004: 12; Lyonnet, personal communication), only a handful of which have been substantially excavated. The mortuary assemblage to settlement ratio for Maikop remains is heavily weighted towards the former, and this situation is almost the opposite of what is known for the slightly later but overlapping Early Bronze Kura-Araxes "cultural community" of Transcaucasia to the south. Hundreds of Kura-Araxes settlements have been found, scores of which have been excavated, whereas very few Kura-Araxes cemeteries have been located and investigated. As Chernykh (1992: 73) is at pains to observe, it is primarily this difference in the nature of the archaeological evidence that explains the apparent greater wealth of the Maikop metals relative to that of the Kura-Araxes culture.

Both areas were working – and probably producing – metals on a large-scale, though we have more evidence from the Maikop culture just because more "royal" kurgans and hoards have been uncovered. Indeed, the recent discovery of the grave of the "Signore di Arslantepe" (Frangipane 1998, 2000; Frangipane et al. 2001), with its wealth of bronze weapons, bronze, silver, and gold ornaments and local Mesopotamian-related and "Transcaucasian" (Kura-Araxes) vessels, underscores the degree to which our knowledge of Kura-Araxes metallurgy and social differentiation is partial and distorted. This important discovery also suggests that significant interaction, possibly involving migration and armed confrontation, occurred between Transcaucasia and eastern Anatolia already at the end of the fourth millennium (Arslantepe VII), becoming more significant at the beginning of the third millennium BC (Arslantepe VIB1), a pattern that may have continued for several centuries with the subsequent spread of the Kura-Araxes peoples far to the south.

Munchaev (1994) divides the Maikop culture into three successive phases – labelled Maikop, transitional, and Novosvobodnaya – on the basis of changes in the features of the construction of the kurgans and their accompanying ceramic and metal artifacts. He accepts completely the ceramic parallels first noted by Andreeva between the early Maikop ceramic vessels and those found farther south in Syria and northern Mesopotamia (Amuq F and Gawra XII–IX); a detailed comparison of their specific attributes reveals a "similarity that is simply striking" (ibid., 169), and it has now been claimed that some of the spherical Maikop vessels may have been turned on a slow wheel, a technological development that may also reflect direct borrowing from the south, though this also could be either a local innovation or even reflect diffusion from the north, for the slow potter's wheel may also have been used in late Tripol'ye CI specialized ceramic workshops, such as at Varvarovka VIII (Ellis 1984: 162; Anthony 1996).

The depiction of a deer and a "tree of life" on a cylinder seal from an early Maikop burial at Krasnogvardeisckoe (Nekhaev 1986) can be paralleled to depictions on earlier stamp seals and on late fourth-/early third-millennium seals from northern Mesopotamia (Tepe Gawra) and eastern Anatolia (Degirmentepe), whereas a toggle-pin with a triangular-shaped head from the Late Uruk-related Arslantepe is identical to a pin found in an early Maikop burial at the Ust'dzhegutin cemetery (for references, cf. Munchaev 1994: 169). Surprisingly, microlithic chipped stone tools were found in the great Maikop kurgan, and Munchaev (ibid., 189) relates their late presence there to the long-rooted Mesopotamian tradition of depositing such archaic artifacts beneath the floors of public buildings or temples (e.g., in the earlier Yarim Tepe 2 and at Uruk itself); in other words, the fact that such a symbolic Mesopotamian practice is attested in the richest known "royal" or chiefly Maikop burial must have significance not only for the earlier dating of the Maikop culture, but also for determining its cultural affiliation and formation (Fig. 3.9).

Other scholars have focused on the northern steppe component of the Maikop culture. Most fundamentally, kurgan or raised earth burials are not characteristic of northern Mesopotamia, but at least eight Chalcolithic and presumably pre-Maikop kurgans have been excavated in central Ciscaucasia (work of S. N. Korenevskii, cited in Munchaev 1994: 178–179) and in the Kuban area (Nekhaev 1990). Early kurgans with Maikop or Maikop-related materials also appear on the Middle and Lower Don on sites of the so-called Konstantinovka culture, some materials of which show clear parallels with Maikop remains, such as characteristic asymmetric flint arrowheads (Rassamakin 1999: 117–122; compare Fig. 3.3 and Fig. 3.9 above). Although not common, pre–Kura-Araxes Chalcolithic kurgans or raised burial mounds have also now been documented in northwestern Azerbaijan and central Georgia (Akhundov n.d., Makharadze n.d.).

The Maikop settlements, with their relatively thin cultural deposits, light-framed, clay-plastered wattle-and-daub houses, some of which were supported with wooden posts, and many of which contain numerous pits, hardly recall characteristic Mesopotamian building traditions and techniques. Similarly, the subsistence economy of the Maikop culture, as understood from the excavations of a few of the settlements, seems to have focused more on animal husbandry, cattle and possibly pig raising (cf. next), than agriculture. Such subsistence practices too bespeak more of a northern steppe connection (ultimately, to the breakup of the Tripol'ye settlements?) than a southern-related Near Eastern heritage. The Maikop culture clearly has multiple origins or is syncretic in character, with local roots that extend naturally north onto the steppes and with surprisingly close and novel connections with northern Mesopotamia.

Some pre-Maikop or "Maikop-related" settlements, such as Meshoko and Yasenova Polyana (Munchaev 1994: 174), were perched on the top of steep ravines and fortified with stone walls, whereas others, such as the Galyugai series of settlements along the Middle Terek or those now being investigated by B. Lyonnet and A. Rezepkin along the eroded southern shore of the large Krasnodar reservoir, were open and easily accessible. Rock shelters, containing Maikop materials, also have been excavated. The apparently earlier fortified settlements (cf. Korenevskii 2001: 24–25) may have been occupied permanently and over a longer period of time than the other types of settlements, which possibly were occupied seasonally (Korenevskii 1995: 80–81). Korenevskii's work has shown that Maikop settlements appear to have extended at least as far east as along the Middle Terek in the Kursk region of Stavropol' province. The cultural deposits of the Meshoko "Maikop-related" fortified settlements in the piedmont rarely attain 1.5 m. and never exceed 2 m. in depth, and the open settlements along river valleys in the north Caucasian plain have much thinner deposits (roughly up to 40 cm.) and, in some cases, are totally buried, a fact that long impeded their recognition and excavation. According to Korenevskii (2004: 13), the Galyugai 1 settlement extended over an area of about 2 ha.

In this respect, the Maikop settlements sharply contrast with those of the Kura-Araxes culture sites south of the Great Caucasus range, particularly those with mud-brick architecture, the deposits of which can exceed seven meters in depth (e.g., at Dzhraovit on the Ararat plain or at Garakepektepe in southeastern Azerbaijan). Maikop houses are typically light-framed surface structures, plastered with clay and reinforced with reeds (wattle-and-daub); the small villages or encampments now being revealed in the Krasnodar area contain up to twenty or so circular wattle-and-daub structures, some of which exceed 6 m. in diameter, and strangely reveal evidence of being partially burned or deliberately set on fire (Lyonnet, personal communication).

Direct evidence for agriculture in the form of palaeobotanical remains retrieved through flotation or seed impressions on vessels currently are generally not yet available or, when attempted, yield minimal results, though grinding stones, occasional flint sickle blades (Korenevskii 1995: 62), and what may be bronze hoes (ibid., 170) seem to attest indirectly to the practice of some form of extensive field preparation and cultivation and collection of plant remains, though it is also possible that such "hoes" really functioned as adzes to work wood. Consistent with the lack of direct evidence for agriculture elsewhere on the Bronze Age Eurasian steppes, the Maikop settlements have yielded very little macrobotanical remains, only about 10 grains of wheat, for example, being recovered via flotation from the recent excavations near the Krasnodar (B. Lyonnet, personal communication). Relative again to the Kura-Araxes settlements in Transcaucasia, agriculture apparently played a far less significant role in the subsistence economy of the Maikop culture, and in this respect

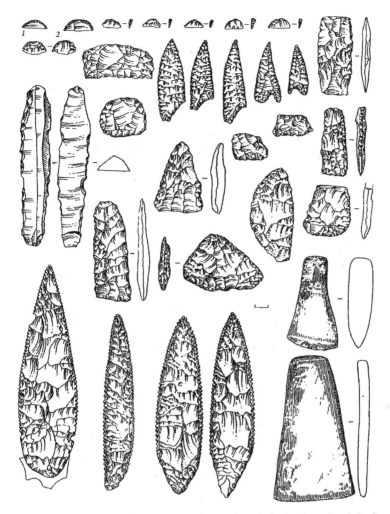

Figure 3.9. Maikop culture: stone points and tools, including microliths from Maikop kurgan (1–2) and asymmetric points (adapted from Markovin and Munchaev 2003: 70, fig. 21).

the "Maikop phenomenon" prefigured later developments on the Bronze Age Eurasian steppes.

Animal husbandry, probably involving at least some form of transhumance, was the more dominant activity. Interestingly, the most thoroughly investigated earlier "Maikop-related" settlements in the foothills, which are located along tributaries of the Kuban River, such as Meshoko and Yasenova Polyana, reveal a surprisingly high concentration of pig remains (40% at the former site; 22.2% at the latter [Cernych, Antipina, and Lebedeva 1998: 245, table 2]). Maikop settlements farther east along the Middle Terek, such as Galyugai I, contain far fewer pig bones (3.3% at Galyugai I) and have a much greater concentration of sheep and goats (44.6% at Galyugai I compared to 15.2 and 12.3%, respectively, at Meshoko and Yasenova Polyana) (ibid.). Cattle (steers and cows) were always the principal animals raised by the Maikop herders, constituting 44.5, 65.5, and 49.6% of the assemblages from these three sites (Meshoko, Yasenova Polyana, and Galyugai I). Cattle were the principal animals raised by the late Tripol'ye peoples, who also kept a considerable number of pigs. The adoption of such practices by the Maikop herders may not be totally coincidental. The importance of cattle in the Maikop subsistence economy is reflected also in their art, such as the silver and gold long-horned bulls that capped the "royal" staffs in the original great Maikop kurgan (Fig. 3.8).

It is commonly accepted that keeping pigs implies sedentism, but this assumption may rely too much on the characteristics of contemporary pigs that have been bred for centuries to produce maximum meat/animal, making them less mobile. Hittite texts refer to the neighboring Kashka peoples to their northeast as "pig-raising nomads" (Matthews, personal communication). Mobile, quite wild-appearing, and apparently very tasty "Kakheti" pigs were moved seasonally between high and lowland areas in central and eastern Georgia in the recent past; during Soviet times, pig herders, who also farmed, drove these animals into the high wooded Georgian forests (in the Aragvi valley, Svaneti, and eastern Georgian mountain valleys) during the summer and let the animals forage freely in the forests, driving them to more protected lowland areas during the late fall (Kikodze, personal communication).

The extremely low percentage of horse bones found on Maikop settlements suggests minimally that horses were not a basic component of their diet, and the only "evidence" for horse-riding consists of the problematic interpretation of distinctive handled circular bronze objects as cheekpieces (or *psalia* in Russian), an interpretation very much open to question (Trifonov 1987; cf. below); such "cheekpieces" have never been found directly associated with horse remains (Fig. 3.10). In any event, the Maikop culture is very distinctive, not only in terms of its metals, to which we turn next, but also in terms of what current evidence reveals about its basic subsistence economy, where a range of gathering and herding practices are suggested, indicating some distinctive form of transhumance, not directly comparable with later, ethnographically documented practices of steppe nomads.

The wealth of the metals – arsenical copper/bronzes and silver and gold artifacts – found in the Maikop "royal" kurgans is truly extraordinary, leading Chernykh (1992: 142–144) to reflect on the "problem of gold" at this time. Indeed, if we trace the occurrence of gold in the area of our concern, we see a conspicuous shift from north to south that continues through Middle Bronze times: the early Chalcolithic florescence of gold consumption in the Balkans, particularly in the Varna cemetery; the abundance of gold (and silver) objects in the Maikop kurgans of the northwestern Caucasus during the Early Bronze period; and the spectacular discoveries of precious gold and, to a lesser

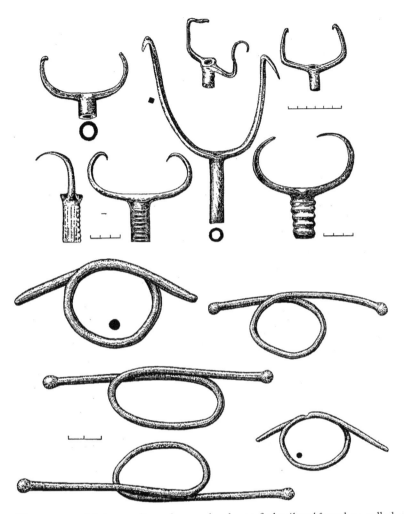

Figure 3.10. Maikop culture: bronze hooks or forks (*kryuki*) and so-called cheek-pieces (*psalia*) or, possibly, Mesopotamian cult symbols (adapted from Markovin and Munchaev 2003: 68, fig. 20).

extent, silver objects in the monumental early kurgans of Transcaucasia and the famous hoards of Anatolia during the Late Early and Middle Bronze periods. Although accidents of discovery undoubtedly play a part here, the trend is unmistakable and must reflect underlying historical processes. For example, Avilova, Antonova, and Teneishvili (1999: 57–58) calculate that approximately 7400 gold and 1000 silver artifacts have been found in Maikop-related kurgans in the northwestern Caucasus. These practically disappear in this area towards the middle of the third millennium, while at the same time the number of gold and silver artifacts in Anatolia and Transcaucasia (and, not incidentally, in Mesopotamia, such as at the Royal Cemetery at Ur) sharply rises (calculated at around 32,000 objects, ibid.). This shift reflects not only changes in the

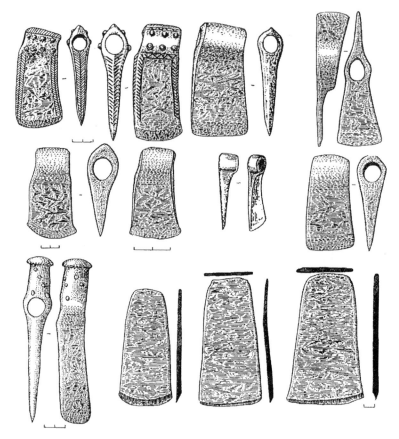

Figure 3.11. Maikop culture: bronze shaft-hole axes and adzes (adapted from Markovin and Munchaev 2003: 76, fig. 25).

production and supply of precious metals, but also the movements of peoples with their leaders or chiefs south – across or around the Great Caucasus range.

The Maikop arsenical copper/bronzes include not only ceremonial prestige weapons, which were potentially also useable, such as ribbed tanged daggers and shaft-hole axes, and ornaments, but also functional tools, such as the already mentioned "hoes", chisels, and awls (Figs. 3.11 and 3.12), and bowls and large distinctive cauldrons (Fig. 3.13); characteristic objects of uncertain significance include the so-called twisted circular cheekpieces (or *psalia*, Fig. 3.10) (Munchaev 1994: 211, for a different interpretation cf. Trifonov 1987) and the large, pitch-fork-like shafted hooks (or *kryuki*, Fig. 3.10).

Chernykh's work has shown that the Maikop bronzes could be divided into two groups – copper-arsenic alloys and copper-arsenic-nickel alloys – and he has postulated that the sources for the former were appropriate ore deposits in Transcaucasia, and for the latter deposits located farther south, possibly in Anatolia and/or Iran, which were also utilized by Mesopotamians. Chernykh

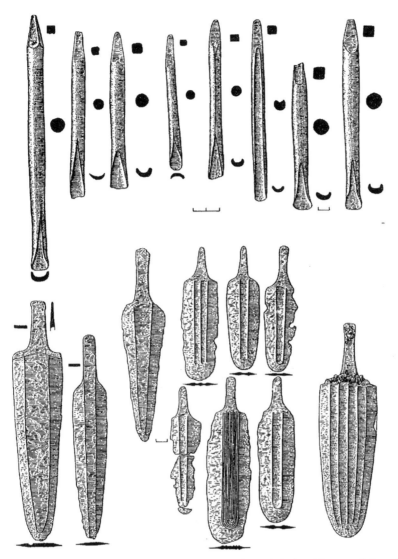

Figure 3.12. Maikop culture: bronze chisels and knives/daggers (adapted from Markovin and Munchaev 2003: 74, fig. 24).

(1992: 159–160) refers to the "North Caucasian Bridge," which brought metals, presumably as ingots or in semiworked form, across the Caucasus, and explains the wealth of the Maikop chiefs as associated with their unique role as intermediaries in this south–north metals trade, supplying vast areas of the steppes to the north and east with Caucasian-derived bronzes.

More recent work by B. A. Galibin (cited in Munchaev 1994: 199) has proposed that an appropriate nickel-bearing copper source exists locally in the northern Caucasus at Belorechensk and could have been utilized by the Maikop miners. This question must, however, still remain open, reflecting the lack of systematic archaeometallurgical research in the northern Caucasus, a situation that also adversely affects our understanding of Early and Middle Bronze metal production in Daghestan to the east. In short, Chernykh's interpretation of the Maikop culture's principal role as intermediaries participating in an extensive metals trade linking the Kura-Araxes culture of Transcaucasia with the steppe cultures farther north remains somewhat speculative, or at least in need of further documentation through future systematic archaeometallurgical research throughout the northern Caucasus.

What happened to the "Maikop phenomenon"? Why did it disappear, or why was it seemingly supplanted by cultures, such as *Novotitorovskaya* and later regional variants of the *Katakombnaya* "cultural-historical community," that are also known to us largely from their mortuary remains? Here the focus is on the virtual post-Maikop disappearance of archaeological evidence for the differential accumulation of substantial wealth – particularly in the form of precious metals, that is, gold and silver artifacts – on the western Eurasian steppes throughout the rest of the Bronze Age. That is, the Bronze Age cultures that subsequently develop on the western Eurasian steppes contain little evidence for social differentiation and appear much more egalitarian, if not actually impoverished, relative to Maikop.

The "Maikop phenomenon" stands out for its uniqueness or singularity, particularly in terms of the precious metals buried with its presumed leaders or chiefs. From this perspective, it is not surprising that initially some scholars attempted to date the Maikop materials to immediately pre-Scythian times. In terms of the concentration of wealth, the Maikop "royal" kurgans resemble the much later "royal" kurgans that appear on the steppes only with the advent of real nomadic societies interacting regularly with sedentary states to their south at the beginning of the Iron Age. How does one account for Maikop's singularity? If true Eurasian nomadism finally emerged only when relations with settled state societies were firmly established – as has been convincingly argued by A. M. Khazanov (1994: 94–95) and, more recently, by L. N. Koryakova and A. V. Epimakhov (n.d.: 160) – then does Maikop's singularity or precocity in terms of its accumulation of wealth suggest, albeit indirectly, that it had established relations by the middle of the fourth millennium BC with a settled state(s) to south? These much later Iron Age nomadic societies and ultimately the first steppe empires (and first appearance of truly "royal" kurgans) came into being in part because they were caught up in larger systems of interregional interaction and exchange, including regular relations with sedentary states to their south (from China to Rome, including the states of southern Central Asia, such as the Parthian and Kushan states).

If this thesis/relationship is essentially correct, then with what settled complex state society was the Maikop culture regularly interacting? Although convincing archaeological documentation for such relations is still largely lacking, the calibrated radiocarbon dates show that Maikop's demise roughly

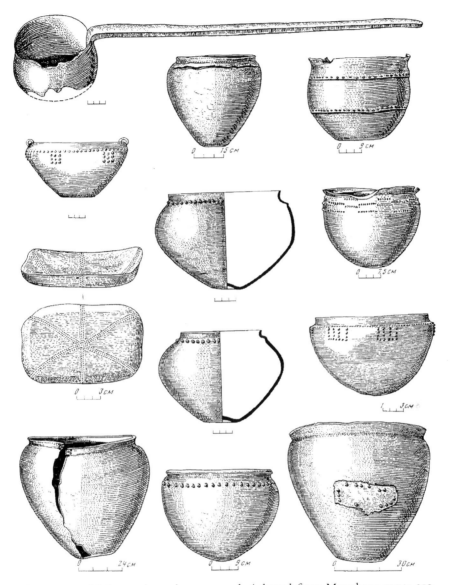

Figure 3.13. Maikop culture: bronze vessels (adapted from Munchaev 1994: 210, table 56).

coincides with the collapse of the "Uruk expansion," the complex, multi-faceted, and relatively long-lived phenomenon that represented some form of southern Mesopotamian presence and/or interest in the Anatolian highlands, particularly along the Upper Euphrates drainage. The end of this southern presence, the "Uruk contraction," if you will, corresponds roughly with the initial dispersal of Kura-Araxes or Early Transcaucasian peoples to the south and southwest, a similarly complex and protracted development that will be discussed in the following section.

As far as is known, state societies do not reappear in the eastern Anatolian highlands or in Transcaucasia until the advent of the Iron Age kingdom of Urartu at the end of the ninth century BC. Southern Mesopotamia (including Southwest Iran) subsequently directed their primary political and economic interests first to the east, culminating in the rise of secondary states in eastern Iran, Central Asia, and western South Asia in the second half of the third and first centuries of the second millennia BC, and then to the west, particularly to the eastern Mediterranean basin during the second millennium BC (cf. Chapter 5). The western Eurasian steppes developed largely on their own during the remainder of the Bronze Age, moving and exchanging materials and ideas over vast distances and constantly developing their mobile herding economies, activities that gradually led to the development of mounted nomadism, social differentiation, and states on the steppes during the first millennium BC. From this macrohistorical perspective, the "Maikop phenomenon" seems remarkably precocious and singular.

The differences between the overlapping Maikop and Kura–Araxes cultures in nearly all their material remains (from settlement patterns and domestic architecture to their subsistence economies and metal assemblages) are also striking. There is very little evidence for direct contact between these two "cultural communities," though some contact is now suggested possibly in the Krasnodar settlements currently being investigated (Lyonnet, personal communication) and possibly also at the Lugovoe settlement in Ingusheti (cf. Krupnov 1954). These two Early Bronze "cultural-historical communities" are totally distinct phenomena, though part of the same overarching, interconnected system that Chernykh has defined as central to his Circumpontic Metallurgical Province (or CMP).

It is only during this Early Bronze period when such a pronounced cultural divide so sharply separates the material remains of the northern and southern Caucasus. Later, the Great Caucasus Range appears to have been more porous, with greater evidence for connections on either side of the mountains (e.g., the close similarity between the Colchidean Late Bronze culture of western Georgia and the Koban culture first documented in northern Ossetia and then south of the Caucasus in the Tli cemetery, cf. Tekhov 1980, 1988; Lordkipanidse 1991). This later pattern of close interaction and cultural assimilation across the Great Caucasus seemingly had not yet been established during the Early Bronze period, and one can only speculate as to the nature of the relations – possibly hostile and/or competitive? – between the bearers of the distinct Maikop and Kura–Araxes "cultural-historical communities."

Clay models of disk wheels have been found at the Late (or Post-) Tripol'ye site of Velyka Slobidka on the Dniester, and two early pre–Pit-Grave kurgan burials with the actual remains of wooden wheels have been found respectively in the Lower Don (Koldyri, burial 7, kurgan 14) and Kuban (Starokorsun, burial 18, kurgan 2) areas. Rassamakin (2002: 53) believes that their appearance in these latter areas was due to "the migration or re-settlement of groups from the agricultural population" farther west. The latter discovery, which consisted of the remains of a wagon with wooden wheels (approximately 60 cm. in diameter), has been attributed to the "early Novosvobodnaya" phase of the Maikop culture (Munchaev 1994: 180, table 44, no. 3), and the partial remains of a similar wheeled cart were found in a kurgan at Tsagan-nur in Kalymykia to the northeast that also apparently contained Maikop-related materials (ibid., 187).

Such vehicles are among the earliest known examples of wheeled transport found on the Eurasian steppes. They may be roughly contemporaneous with or perhaps a few hundred years later than the now earliest well-documented carts from moors in northwestern Germany and Denmark (Hayen 1989; 1991: ptc. 7; and Häusler 1981; 1994). On current evidence, the diffusion of the technology of wheeled transport may have just as plausibly spread north to south from northwestern Europe with its forests of useable hard woods to the more open steppes to the southeast and then farther south into Mesopotamia as the reverse (cf. Bakker et al. 1999). The important point is not where this revolutionary technology first originated but rather how quickly it diffused across western Asia, Eurasia, and Europe during the Early Bronze period, underscoring the interconnections among disparate cultures throughout this vast area. Later during Late Early and Middle Bronze times or beginning in the first half of the third millennium BC such wheeled vehicles are well documented in eastern Ukraine (Pustovalov 1994: 99–101; 1998), the northern Caucasus (Gei 1991, 2000), and in Transcaucasia (cf. Miron and Orthmann 1995: 69–94) and provide direct evidence for a more mobile economy and the movements of peoples throughout this area.

Maikop-related peoples may also have moved south into northwestern Iran. Six of eleven surveyed kurgans, collectively referred to as Sé Girdan, which were excavated in 1968 and 1970, were laid out in a straight row running northwest to southeast and situated roughly west-southwest of the southwestern corner of Lake Urmia in northwestern Iran. O. W. Muscarella, who originally had excavated the kurgans, dated them initially to the Iron Age III period (seventh to sixth centuries BC), but recently he has accepted the criticisms of other scholars (Deshayes 1973; Trifonov 2000) and radically revised his interpretation, now dating them to the second half of the fourth millennium on parallels with Maikop remains from the northwestern Caucasus. Muscarella (2003: 126–130) provisionally accepts the interpretation that Maikop-related peoples from the northwestern Caucasus entered northwestern Iran during the second half of the fourth millennium BC, essentially prior to the expansion of Early Transcaucasian or Kura-Araxes peoples into northwestern Iran towards the end of the fourth millennium.

This interpretation is plausible but in need of additional archaeological confirmation from intermediate areas between the northern Caucasus and northwestern Iran. The parallels cited include aspects of the kurgans' constructions, such as the off-center location of the principal tomb, pebble floors and outer encircling stone revetments, and close similarities in arsenical copper/bronze artifacts, characteristic of the Caucasian Early Bronze Age, such as socketed axes with bent butts and blades with curved bases. It would be worthwhile to excavate one of the remaining kurgans to test this new, dramatically changed date through radiocarbon determinations from the skeletal remains.

The emergence of peoples burying their dead in raised kurgans in the Kuban basin of the northwestern Caucasus by the middle of the fourth and continuing into the third millennium is well established, but their subsequent spread farther east to the northeastern Caucasus and the western littoral Caspian plain is less well documented. Unfortunately, many kurgans on this coastal corridor have been leveled during the past fifty years with intensive modern settlement and agricultural exploitation. The Caspian littoral plain once was dotted with kurgans dating to various periods, but very few have been excavated. Maikop-related materials have been found in a handful of kurgans in Daghestan, such as at the Large Miatli kurgan along the Sulak River and at Torpakh-kala along the coastal plain south of Velikent.

This evidence is hardly conclusive but has been cautiously interpreted as documenting a northwest to southeast movement of Maikop peoples during the final stages of this culture's existence (cf. Magomedov 1991:34–35). If possible, one should locate partially destroyed kurgans through the study of earlier aerial photos and systematically excavate several of them. These movements still require more extensive archaeological documentation, but the hypothesis of prolonged north-to-south movements beginning possibly as early as the late fourth millennium BC is theoretically testable through selected excavations of the remaining kurgans. In any event, it is likely that such postulated movements did not represent sudden events, such as armed invasions, so much as protracted processes, consisting of cattle herders moving south with their families on oxen-driven wagons in search of better pastures for their animals.

THE KURA-ARAXES CULTURAL-HISTORICAL COMMUNITY (*OBSHCHNOST'*) OF TRANSCAUCASIA – THE HISTORY OF ITS RESEARCH AND THE DISTRIBUTION OF ITS SETTLEMENTS DOCUMENTING THE INITIAL DENSE OCCUPATION OF DIFFERENT ALTITUDINAL ZONES THROUGHOUT THE SOUTHERN CAUCASUS AND ADJACENT REGIONS; THE NATURE OF THESE SETTLEMENTS AND EVIDENCE FOR SOCIAL DIFFERENTIATION; THE SPREAD OF KURA-ARAXES PEOPLES INTO THE NEAR EAST IN THE LATE FOURTH TO MIDDLE THIRD MILLENNIUM BC

Very recognizable, black- and red-burnished, hand-made ceramics now attributed to the "Kura-Araxes" or, in the Western literature, "Early Transcaucasian" culture were first discovered in the Gyandzha region of Azerbaijan in the nineteenth century. The initial recognition of their significance and the fact that such ceramics were found often in the lowest levels of many later Bronze Age sites, some of which had cyclopean stone fortifications, is due principally to the work of B. A. Kuftin in the 1930s. He coined the term "Kura-Araxes" to describe these materials because at that time all the sites with these materials that were known to him were found in the greater catchment areas of the Kura and Araxes basins. We now know their distribution extended far beyond Transcaucasia itself, spreading at some point southeast along the eastern slopes of the Zagros at least as far as west central Iran (e.g., at the Godin IV settlement, see Weiss and Young 1975) and southwest across Anatolia and northwestern Syria as far as northern Palestine/Israel during the Early Bronze III period, where the pottery is known as Khirbet Kerak ware (Amiran 1968).

Kuftin also mistakenly attributed the Kura-Araxes culture to the Chalcolithic period, a conclusion that had to be revised thanks to the analytical work conducted initially by I. R. Selimkhanov in the 1950s on their metals, work that showed that they were not pure copper but contained significant amounts of arsenic, possibly from deliberately alloying arsenic with copper to produce arsenical copper/bronzes. Calibration of radiocarbon dates from Kura-Araxes sites (Kavtaradze 1983; 1999: 73–74; a partial list appears also in Kushnareva 1997: 52; *n.b.*, these last mistakenly listed as "B.C." when actually "B.P." and *uncalibrated*) pushes back the beginnings of the culture towards the middle of the fourth millennium, or slightly later than the sudden appearance of the Maikop culture (cf. Appendix).

The internal periodization of the Kura-Araxes "phenomenon" *within* Transcaucasia has been worked out most thoroughly by Kushnareva (1997: 53–54), who divides it into four sub-periods (E. B. I–IV), extending from ca. 3500–2300 BC. Although most Transcaucasian specialists would agree with her general periodization and relative chronological positioning of excavated sites, it still must be emphasized that much guesswork is involved and that the internal sequence requires additional refinement and corroboration. The vast majority of excavated materials have not been adequately published, and the best excavated and published sites, such as Khvatskhelebi (Djavakhishvili and Glonti 1962) in Shida Kartli, Georgia, are small villages with relatively thin cultural deposits (e.g., 1.7 m. of deposit for the Early Bronze levels B and C at Kvatskhelebi). It is doubtful that they would have been occupied for the entire 1000-year-plus period attributed to the culture.

Kura-Araxes sites are found throughout all areas of Transcaucasia, except for the subtropical Colchidean basin of western Georgia, and are located in markedly different environments at different altitudes. Not surprisingly, sites found high in the Great and Lesser Caucasus ranges or on highland plateaus are characterized typically by stone architecture and have relatively thin cultural deposits (sometimes barely exceeding 1 m.). Sites farther south on the fertile Ararat plain of southern Armenia and Nakhicevan, or in the eastern piedmont between the Guru and Kandalan Rivers in southeastern Azerbaijan (at Garakapektepe, cf. Ismailov 1983), or even farther south in northwestern Iran (e.g., Geoy Tepe, Yanik Tepe, and Tappeh Gijlar), or in eastern Anatolia (e.g., Pulur [10 m.] and Karaz [9 m.]) are often multiperiod tells formed by the decomposition of mud-brick architecture with very thick cultural deposits, at times exceeding 10 meters (at Tappeh Gijlar, for example, which is located west of Lake Urmia in northwestern Iran, the unmixed Kura-Araxes levels [period B] are nearly 11 m. thick [Belgiorno, Biscione, and Pecorella 1984: 241; see Fig. 3.14]).

It is very difficult to correlate precisely such differently formed settlements. Thus, Kushnareva (1997: 49) suggests that the initial dispersal of the Kura-Araxes culture is to be found in "the flatlands of the southern Caucasus" (i.e., on the Ararat plain and farther east in the interfluve between the Guru and Kandalan Rivers of southeastern Azerbaijan) and sees a movement from these plains into the highlands, associated ultimately with a productive agricultural economy and consequent population increase (ibid., 55, 74). Possibly, but the reverse process could also be argued on the basis of the archaeological evidence (earliest sites located possibly in Shida Kartli [cf. Sagona 1984] or even in higher areas) and is more consistent with the historical pattern of mountain valleys becoming overcrowded and sending their surplus population down onto the plains; for example, the Ossetians are known to have moved down from both sides of the Greater Caucasus and into the broader valleys of central Georgia during relatively recent historical times. Current evidence does not allow us to resolve this problem.

It is useful to recall that modern political borders rarely define prehistoric culture areas, and regions immediately adjacent to southern Transcaucasia (i.e., to the south and west of the Middle Araxes River or northeastern Anatolia and farther to the north and east into southeastern Daghestan) should also be seen as part of the formative area for this culture. To add further ambiguity to the situation, whereas some areas exhibit a break in material culture remains, others, such as Sos Höyük near Erzurum (Sagona 2000), show continuity from earlier so-called Chalcolithic into later Early and Middle Bronze times. Though never densely occupied with Early Bronze remains, the Erzurum region in northeastern Anatolia most likely lies within the original formative region of the Kura-Araxes "cultural-historical community," and, consequently as such, did not experience the later dispersal or intrusion of Kura-Araxes peoples into this area. Calibrated C14 dates suggest that the initial occupation of Sos Höyük, its period Va, occurred ca. 3500 BC or approximately at the same time that many other Kura-Araxes-related sites in distant regions, such as the Caspian coastal plain of southeastern Daghestan, were first occupied. The terminology here may be confusing: the Late Chalcolithic and initial Early Bronze designations refer to the same period and macrohistorical pattern of development.

The Kura-Araxes culture seems to have emerged in different places – northeastern Anatolia, the broad area of Transcaucasia drained by the Upper and Middle reaches of the Kura and Araxes Rivers, and the Caspian coastal corridor and adjacent mountainous regions of northeastern Azerbaijan and southeastern Daghestan (cf. below) – exhibiting different regional features at approximately the same time, towards the middle of the fourth millennium BC. The characteristic red-and-black burnished wares, one of the hallmark features of Kura-Araxes material remains, may actually have originated at sites, such as Sos Höyük, in today's northeasternmost Anatolia (Palumbi 2003, n.d.; Kiguradze and Sagona 2003) and subsequently spread east into Transcaucasia as conventionally defined. There seems to have been fairly rapid intra- and intercultural communication among these different contiguous regions, leading relatively quickly to the emergence of a recognizable Kura-Araxes *koine* or broadly defined "cultural-historical community."

Figure 3.14. Tappeh Gijlar, northwestern Iran – stratigraphic profile, showing thickness of Early Bronze deposit (adapted from Pecorella and Salvini 1984, pl. XXXIX).

Even within this broadly defined area, some thicker multiperiod tells that contain earlier pre–Kura-Araxes Chalcolithic levels show a gap or period of abandonment between the latest Chalcolithic and earliest Kura-Araxes occupations (e.g., at Kyul'tepe I in Nakhicevan), and other multiperiod tells with thick Kura-Araxes deposits (e.g., Dzhraovit and Mokhra-Blur on the Ararat plain or Garakepektepe in Azerbaijan) are inadequately published, and work on them has only preliminarily, if at all, plumbed the earliest Kura-Araxes levels. That is, we know little about the beginnings of these latter settlements.

Problems of interpretation are farther exacerbated by the distinct regional variants of this "cultural-historical community." This pronounced regional diversity (summarized by Kushnareva 1997: 54–73; cf. also Sagona 1984) may, of course, also be explained in part chronologically and suggests that this "culture" (or, perhaps better, "phenomenon" or "bloc of cultures") was quite heterogeneous, never representing a single unity or polity. The postulated movement over time of surplus populations from the restricted mountain valleys onto the plains is consistent with the original local formations of this culture – quite literally, northeastern Anatolia and in the high Caucasus mountains – and such movements in search of more arable land may constitute one of the mechanisms driving the peoples out of Transcaucasia and south into Iran, farther west in Anatolia, and into the upper Euphrates and beyond.

Some Kura-Araxes sites are located near steep ravines or in fairly inaccessible settings (e.g., Garni), and some (e.g., Shengavit, Mokhra-Blur) appear to have been fortified (Kushnareva 1997), though it must be emphasized that the dating of such fortifications to the Kura-Araxes occupation has not been established in all the claimed cases. Many sites, including those most carefully excavated, such as Kvatskhelebi in central Georgia and Karnut in northwestern Armenia, were not fortified but represent simple open villages with separate or clustered one-room houses with central hearths, often set at the southern foot or along the lower slope of a local large hill (e.g., the sites of Satkhe and Amagleba in southern Georgia [Isaac et al. 1994]). Certainly the Kura-Araxes settlements and their accompanying materials exhibit far less emphasis on militarism and defense, reflective of politically insecure and unstable times, than that characteristic for the later Transcaucasian Late Early and Middle Bronze and, particularly, Late Bronze/Early Iron periods (from the second half of the third through the beginnings of the first millennium BC).

Our understanding of the Kura-Araxes "phenomenon" is incomplete, and surprises, like the already mentioned burial of the "Signore di Arslantepe" with his rich array of weapons (Frangipane 1997, 1998, 2000), still await us. It is also possible that much larger Kura-Araxes settlements lie buried beneath more massive Late Bronze and Early Iron deposits (e.g., possibly at Metsamor, cf. Kohl 1992). The recently discovered site of Agarak in Armenia is reported to extend over 200 ha. and to have a substantial Early Bronze occupation. It also, however, is clearly a multiperiod site that was occupied intermittently into historic times; until the site is more thoroughly excavated and adequately published, it is impossible to evaluate the extent or nature of the Early Bronze settlement at the site.

Based on the currently available published evidence, however, most Kura-Araxes settlements in Transcaucasia are small (rarely exceeding 5 ha. in size) and show very little evidence of internal social differentiation. The dwellings in the largest sites, such as Arich (12 ha.) on the southern edge of the Shirak plain in northwestern Armenia, or Amiranis-Gora (approximately 4 ha.) near Akhaltsikhe in southern Georgia, a site which shows evidence of deliberate terracing, are quite dispersed, not densely packed together. At most, they can be considered large villages – not towns or cities – and do not constitute evidence for a sharply differentiated three-tiered settlement hierarchy (*contra* Kushnareva 1997: 74, 78). Thus, for example, the Early Bronze occupation at the site of Arich, which is located on a naturally fortified promontory drained by a stream flowing down from the northwestern slope of Mt. Aragats, is surrounded by

Late Bronze/Early Iron dwellings and burials and even later (Classical?) fortifications that cover the approximately 12-ha. area of the site. It is very difficult to estimate the extent and density of its Kura-Araxes occupation; it is misleading, therefore, to refer to the Early Bronze settlement at Arich as qualitatively different or larger than other Kura-Araxes villages or, at best, small towns.

Although the mortuary evidence is fragmentary and unexpected discoveries, like the rich burial at Arslantepe, may occur and alter our understanding, the currently available record does not suggest that the Kura-Araxes societies in Transcaucasia were torn apart by internal social divisions. In this sense, the Kura-Araxes materials contrast strongly with those of the Maikop culture to the north, or with what appears in Transcaucasia during the immediately succeeding late Early Bronze period or the time of the monumental "chiefly"/"royal" kurgans. Individual flat-grave burials have been excavated both within settlements and in cemeteries outside the settlements, as well as small kurgans or barrows associated with or in immediate proximity to Kura-Araxes settlements (e.g., at Satkhe in Djavakheti, cf. Kohl, Carson, Edens, and Pearce 1993). None of these Transcaucasian burials has yielded evidence for an accumulation of wealth comparable with that seen in the burial at Arslantepe or in those of the northern Caucasus. The metal assemblages of the Maikop cultural community in the northern Caucasus and the Kura-Araxes cultural community in Transcaucasia and eastern Anatolia also differ (Compare the Kura-Araxes metals from Transcausasia in Fig. 3.15a and the metals from Arslantepe VIA and VIB in Fig. 3.15b, on the one hand, with the Maikop metals illustrated above, on the other.).

The available evidence does unequivocally show that all areas of Transcaucasia (again excepting the distinct region of western Georgia bordering the Black Sea) were occupied during the initial Early Bronze period in the second half of the fourth millennium. Kura-Araxes settlements, now numbering in the hundreds (Kushnareva 1997: 44), are found throughout the region, even at very high altitudes, suggesting possibly seasonal occupations and some form of transhumance, and their association with terraced agriculture in some mountainous areas seems well established. These "peoples of the hills" – to use Burney and Lang's (1971) apt phrase – knew how to adapt to different altitudinal zones, settling in high mountain valleys, on broad volcanic uplands, or on lower-lying fertile plains. Given their occupation of these different altitudinal zones, it is not surprising that the materials used in the construction of their houses varies from stone and wattle-and-daub with wooden post structures in the intermontane valleys and higher plateaus to circular and subrectangular mud-brick structures sometimes with stone foundations in the lower plains. We know that they herded sheep and goats and, to a lesser extent, cattle, and it is hypothesized that some flocks may have been driven to higher pastures during the summer by transhumant pastoralists as occurs today on the passes into and on the plateaus of Djavakheti from the Adzhari and Imereti regions.

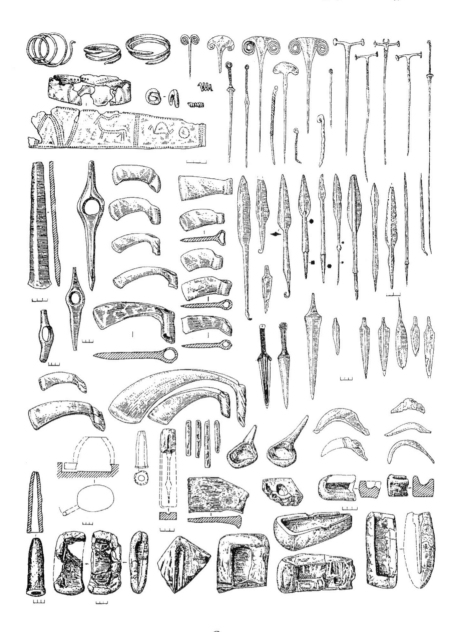

a

Figure 3.15. (a) Kura-Araxes metal tools, weapons, ornaments, and metal-working artifacts from Transcaucasia (after Kushnareva and Markovin 1994: 40, table 12); and (b) metal objects from Arslantepe; 1–5 from period VIA public area; 6–19 from period VIB "royal tomb" (after Frangipane 2000: 471, fig. 17).

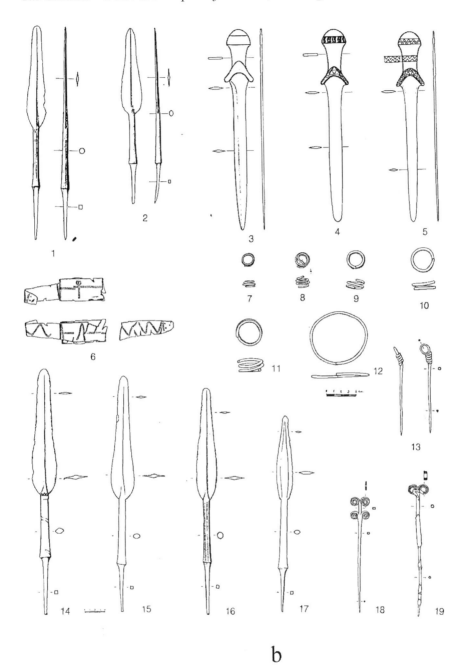

b

Figure 3.15 (*continued*).

Figure 3.16 Uncultivated terraces, mountainous Daghestan (picture taken by P.L. Kohl).

Kushnareva (1997: 182–196) provides a very complete summary of what currently is known of agricultural and herding practices, listing the domesticated species of plants and animals that have been documented on Kura-Araxes and Kura-Araxes related settlements. They cultivated soft (common) wheat and barley, including specific club or dwarf forms (such as *Triticum vulgare antiquorum, Hordeum sphaerococcum*), and grew grapes probably to make wine. Wild fruit trees are abundant in the Caucasus, and it is surmised that their fruits were collected during this period, though fruit pits are not well documented in the archaeological record. Apparently, apricot pits were recovered at the site of Garni in Armenia (ibid., 186).

What is uncertain is how intensive their agricultural practices were. Again, it is misleading to speak of a single adaptation given the different ecological zones that were occupied. It is very difficult to date the beginnings of terraced agriculture in mountainous areas, such as Djavakheti in southern Georgia or Daghestan to the northeast, though most scholars are inclined to date their initial construction back to this period when there is substantial evidence for permanent settlement. Conclusive evidence in the form of artifacts recovered from excavated artificial terraces at the site of Verkhniy Gunib in Daghestan have shown that they were constructed at least during the subsequent Middle Bronze period, and it is reasonable to place their beginnings even earlier (Aglarov 1986: 57–58; Kushnareva 1997: 187–189). The terraces that they constructed on steep hill slopes could have been built by related families or small

Figure 3.17 Model of a cart, Arich, Armenia (adapted from Khachatryan 1975: 77, fig. 37).

corporate kin groups and extended over some period of time. They do not necessarily suggest any form of centralized authority involved in their construction and maintenance, though they probably do indicate new forms of land ownership and attachments to the land and, correspondingly, transformed agrarian relations (Aglarov 1986; Fig. 3.16).

Similarly, no state hierarchies were needed for the probable construction of the small irrigation systems with dykes and canals in lower-lying, flatter regions, such as the Ararat plain where such dykes have been documented, for example, at Mokhra–Blur. In most areas such modifications of the natural landscape were not required, and it is in these areas where it is difficult to assess how intensive the agricultural practices were. The incredible profusion of small Kura–Araxes settlements throughout Transcaucasia and northeastern Anatolia may reflect both population increases over time and the periodic settlement of new areas suggestive of a form of extensive shifting cultivation, an interpretation consistent with the apparent sudden abandonment of several Kura–Araxes settlements. Kura–Araxes houses, such as those uncovered at Karnut on the Shirak plain of northwestern Armenia, often contain large complete artifacts, such as storage jars and the characteristic, distinctly modeled andirons or figured portable hearth supports. It appears almost as if the people had planned to return to the settlements that they had mysteriously and suddenly left.

Metal sickles have been recovered from several Kura–Araxes settlements (Kushnareva and Chubinishvili 1970: 118, fig. 42, nos. 27–31), though the sheer quantity of characteristic toothed flint sickle inserts suggest that basic agricultural activities continued to rely on chipped stone tools. There is some direct evidence for the use of wooden and antler light plows, such as the one recovered from Kvatskhelebi (Djavakhishvili and Glonti 1962: pl. XXXIII, no. 11), and the use of traction animals are at least suggested by depictions on clay plaques and models (Kushnareva 1997: 184). Models of solid-wheeled clay carts, presumably pulled by oxen, are attested at the site of Arich (Fig. 3.17).

Cattle, sheep, goats, and pigs are all documented on Kura–Araxes settlements, though quantitative counts of faunal assemblages, assessing their relative importance, are fragmentary or largely unavailable. The raising of sheep and goats seems to have been more significant than cattle or pig-herding, a dominance also suggested by the recovery of numerous figurines of rams and their depictions on andirons (Kushnareva 1997: 193; Fig. 3.17). Cattle may have assumed an increasing importance as they were harnessed to carts and used to plow fields, though more evidence is available for such uses at the end of the Early Bronze period with the appearance of the large "royal" kurgans and the direct recovery of oxen-driven wheeled vehicles. Given the location of Kura-Araxes settlements and later ethnographically and historically attested practices, it is assumed that some form of herding took place that brought the flocks of sheep and goats and even, to some extent, the herds of cattle to higher mountain pastures during the summer. The winter quarters for the animals may have been directly associated with the settlements (ibid., 194).

Whether it was the search for more arable land to support their burgeoning populations and/or their displacement with the arrival of new groups from the north with four-wheeled, oxen-driven wagons, the Kura-Araxes peoples moved over some extended period beginning towards the end of the fourth millennium far to the southwest across the Anatolian plateau to the Amuq plain and beyond to today's northern Israel, and to the southeast into northwestern Iran, along the Zagros mountains, and onto the Iranian plateau as least as far as Kermanshah. This spread of "Early Transcaucasian" settlements has long fascinated archaeologists (see, for example, the map in Roaf 1990: 80), many of them speculating on the ethnic/linguistic identity of these migrants and interpreting them as ancestral to Hurrians, Hittites, or other later historically attested peoples (e.g., Woolley 1953: 31–37). A. Sagona (1984) has published the most complete list of Kura-Araxes sites and sees the movement of these colonists first out of central Georgia (Kvemo and Shida Kartli) to the south followed by the development of distinctive regional traditions (Armenian, Upper Euphrates, Khirbet Kerak), and then a subsequent spread to the northeast (Daghestan) and southeast into western Iran. Others have placed the beginnings of the Kura-Araxes cultures along the Middle Araxes valley on the Ararat plain and in Nakhicevan, with its subsequent spread first to the north and then south.

As reviewed above, the "homeland" of this culture is elusive or difficult to pinpoint precisely, a fact that may suggest that there is no single well-demarcated area of origin, but multiple interacting areas including northeastern Anatolia as far as the Erzurum area, the catchment area drained by the Upper Middle Kura and Araxes Rivers in Transcaucasia, and the Caspian corridor and adjacent mountainous regions of northeastern Azerbaijan and southeastern Daghestan. Though broadly (and somewhat imprecisely) defined, these regions constitute the original core area where the Kura-Araxes "cultural-historical community" emerged. Kura-Araxes materials found in other areas are intrusive in the local sequences. Indeed, many, but not all, sites in the Malatya area along the Upper Euphrates drainage of eastern Anatolia (Norsuntepe, Arslantepe) and western

Iran (Yanik Tepe, Godin Tepe) exhibit a relatively sharp break in material remains, including new forms of architecture and domestic dwellings, and such changes support the interpretation of a subsequent spread or dispersal from this broadly defined core area in the north to the south. The archaeological record seems to document a movement of peoples north to south across a very extensive part of the Ancient Near East during the first half to the middle of the third millennium BC. Although migrations are notoriously difficult to document on archaeological evidence, these materials constitute one of the best examples of prehistoric movements of peoples available for the Early Bronze period. This dispersal needs to be restudied intensively. Here only a few general observations can be made.

Firstly, calibrated radiocarbon dates are beginning to yield a consistent picture for the timing of this dispersal. The relevant VIB period at the extensively excavated site of Arslantepe near Malatya dates ca. 2900–2700 BC, a date which is supported essentially by evidence from neighboring sites such as Norsuntepe (Di Nocera 2000: 75–76). It is also apparently consistent with sites in the Ezerum region farther east (Sagona 2000: 333). Related Khirbet-Kerak materials from northern Israel have been dated roughly from 2700 to 2450 BC (de Miroschedji 2000: 258), suggesting an initial dispersal into the Upper Euphrates basin at the very beginning of the third millennium (and after the collapse of the Uruk expansion), followed by a subsequent movement to the southwest in the second quarter of the third millennium. The chronological gap between the appearance of Khirbet Kerak (or Red-Black Burnished [R. J. Braidwood and L. S. Braidwood 1960]) ware on the Amuq plain and its appearance in the southern Levant may have been somewhat overestimated. New relevant radiocarbon dates from the southern Levant suggest that Khirbet Kerak ware may first have appeared ca. 2800–2700 BC, or almost simultaneous with its appearance farther north (Philip and Millard 2000: 284). The overall pattern seems reasonably clear: an initial spread across eastern Anatolia to the Upper Euphrates basin at the very end of the fourth and beginning of the third millennium, followed by a relatively rapid diffusion (during the course of a century or so?) farther southwest and ultimately to the eastern Mediterranean coast.

Sites in the Urmia basin with relevant materials (e.g., Geoy Tepe and Yanik Tepe) seem to have been occupied already in the last centuries of the fourth millennium (Voigt and Dyson 1992, vol. II: 137). "Early Transcaucasian" materials appear to be intrusive in this region; that is, they represent a break with earlier Chalcolithic remains on these sites, but this movement appears to predate the spread into the Upper Euphrates area. One can only speculate that the lack of an Uruk presence in northwestern Iran may have facilitated this earlier movement to the east. Their spread farther south into central-western Iran occurred later, though precisely how much later is still unclear. Carbon dates are unavailable for the beginning of the relevant Godin IV period, though the excavators (Weiss and Young 1975: 2) believed that there was only a short break in the sequence between this period and the underlying Godin V period that can be dated to the last centuries of the fourth millennium and "significant percentages" of recognizable Kura-Araxes wares first appear in the final Godin V levels (Badler 2002: 83, 107, fig. 17). The assumption is that the Godin IV period with its very distinctive Early Transcaucasian-related ceramic assemblage began in the early third millennium BC. Here too one wonders whether there is some causal relationship: the collapse of the "Uruk outpost" at Godin V (Algaze 1993: 60), accompanied by the protracted arrivals of Transcaucasian settlers from the north.

Second, these "peoples of the hills" seem to have consciously avoided certain regions, including large settled areas on the northern Mesopotamian plain. Less than a handful of Kura-Araxes sherds, for example, have been found at Tell Brak (J. Oates, personal communication), although apparently the ongoing excavations may have revealed more substantial evidence for Kura-Araxes related remains in previously uninvestigated areas. Movements across the Anatolian plateau and into northern Mesopotamia and regions farther west were undoubtedly very complex and involved more than just these dispersals from Transcaucasia. Other groups may have crossed the Caucasus from the northwest and then intermingled with both the local peoples and the Transcaucasians with whom they came into contact. A chain reaction was set in motion, with incoming groups successively displacing one another.

There also remained relatively empty places that the Transcaucasians could easily settle. They possibly destroyed or overran some settlements, whereas others they avoided or left alone, presumably because the polities that occupied them were more powerful. Although our knowledge of the distribution of the sites containing Kura-Araxes materials is obviously dependent on the nature and extent of the surveys conducted throughout these different regions, which manifestly are not commensurate with one another, it also seems clear that not all contiguous zones were equally affected by these dispersals. The spread was not continuous and there are clear gaps in the distribution of sites containing these materials, such as the dense concentration of Early Transcaucasian sites in the Malatya region of eastern Anatolia (Fig. 3.18) or the gap in known sites with Early Transcaucasian/Khirbet Kerak ceramics in Syria and Lebanon between the Amuq plain and northern Israel, a break possibly to be explained by coastal rather than overland contacts and movements of peoples (Philip and Millard 2000: 287–288, 292, fig. 1; also cf. De Miroschedji 2000: 278, fig. 7). Despite the uneven coverage, these gaps to some extent must reflect the historical reality that the newcomers from the north occupied only certain selected regions.

It is obvious also that for the most part these dispersals do not represent armed military invasions and that the movements involved considerable assimilation with preexisting local traditions, exacerbating the archaeologists' task of

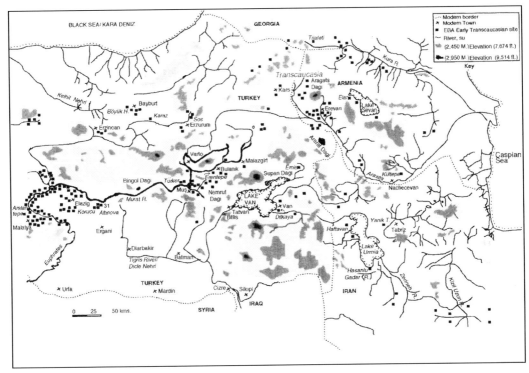

Figure 3.18 Distribution map of Early Transcaucasian/Kura Araxes settlements in Transcaucasia, eastern Anatolia, and northwestern Iran (after Rothman 2003: 96, fig. 4.1).

recognizing them. Populations expanded and intermingled with one another. In these processes, social structures obviously must have changed. It is an archaeological truism today to note that pottery styles do not equate with peoples, and the temptation to do so must be resisted. Nevertheless, the very frequency of distinctive, seemingly intrusive ceramics and other items of material culture, such as the highly specific figured andirons (Figs. 3.19 and 3.20), suggest that this phenomenon, however short-lived, must have been reasonably substantial. At Beth Shean, for example, the Khirbet Kerak pottery constitutes more than 60% of the total ceramic assemblage in levels 11–9 before dropping off to 38% in level 8 and essentially disappearing in level 7 (as summarized in De Miroschedji 2000: 259). At the type site of Khirbet-Kerak (Beth Yerah), these wares constituted 20–30% of the sherds found on the site. The site itself is 20–25 ha. in size (Albright 1926), or considerably larger than any known Kura-Araxes site in Transcaucasia. Site size too, as we have seen with the gigantic Tripol'ye settlements, cannot simplistically be equated with social complexity. The data, however, is suggestive that the "peoples of the hills" transformed themselves as they spread across large areas of the Ancient Near East.

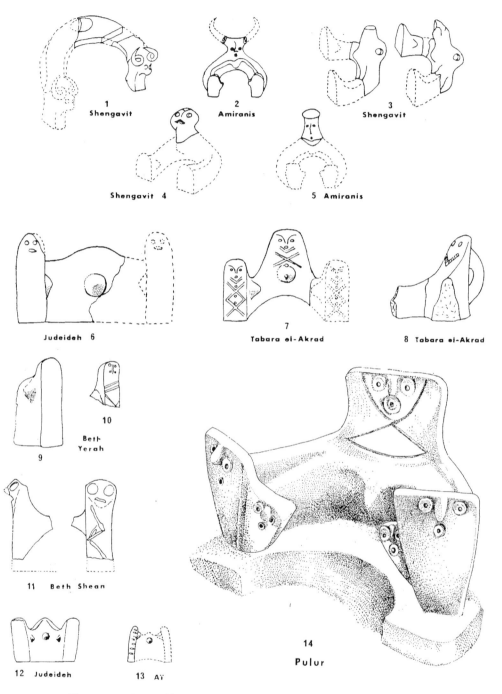

Figure 3.19 Figured hearth supports from Transcaucasia, eastern Anatolia, and Syria-Palestine (adapted from De Miroschedji 2000: 276, fig. 5).

Figure 3.20 (a) Figured andiron or hearth support from the Early/Midddle Bronze Age site of Marki *Alonia* in Cyprus (adapted from Frankel and Webb 2000: 763, fig. 3); (b) Anthropomorphic andiron from Zveli, southern Georgia, with obsidian eye insets (courtesy Akhaltsikhe museum).

It is unclear what was driving these dispersals. Possibly, the peoples involved were in search of new sources of metal in Jordan or, more convincingly, in Cyprus (cf. the recently excavated, Kura-Araxes-like hearth stands and evidence for migrants from southwestern Anatolia at the Early Bronze Age site of Marki *Alonia* [Frankel 2000; Frankel and Webb 2000; Webb and Frankel 1999], Fig. 3.20a). It should be noted, however, that anthropomorphic-figured hearth stands for what are interpreted as altars in sanctuaries have been found also on much earlier and seemingly unrelated Cucuteni-Tripol'ye sites (Lazarovisi and Lazarovisi 2003: 422, 484, figs. 143–144); nevertheless, because anthropomorphic representations are always, to some extent, going to resemble one another (insofar as they are remotely naturalistic), the question of the specificity of the parallel must always be addressed before suggesting a meaningful historical connection. The resemblance in this latter case may be fortuitous.

The settlers from Transcaucasia may have been skilled metallurgists, but why leave a metalliferous region like the Caucasus for unknown sources? Moreover, Khirbet Kerak materials are not found in the metal-bearing Wadi Feinan area south of the Dead Sea (De Miroschedi's 2000: 264). Perhaps they were simply in search of more and better arable land with natural population increases, replicating on a much larger scale the movements from the highlands to the plains that we thought may have characterized the initial spread of Kura-Araxes settlements within Transcaucasia? Possibly, but why did they move and not others? Another factor may also have been at work: people were not only moving south out of the Caucasus, but also may have been moving into Transcaucasia from the north – at least at some point beginning towards the middle of the third millennium (see the new calibrated dates for the "early kurgan cultures" of Transcaucasia, Kavtaradze 1999: 81).

It is hard to distinguish cause from effect here: did peoples move into the rich Alazani and Kura valleys because others had moved out, or were the Kura-Araxes peoples moving south because of the incursions of peoples from farther north? Before examining the materials from the late Early and Middle Bronze kurgan cultures of Transcaucasia, let us briefly review evidence for occupation of the Caspian littoral plain during the second half of the fourth and third millennia BC.

THE CASPIAN COASTAL PLAIN OF SOUTHEASTERN DAGHESTAN AND NORTHEASTERN AZERBAIJAN – THE VELIKENT EARLY AND MIDDLE BRONZE "COMPONENT" OF THE KURA-ARAXES "CULTURAL-HISTORICAL COMMUNITY"; THE SEQUENCE FROM VELIKENT AND RELATED BRONZE AGE SITES, CA. 3600–1900 BC

Soviet archaeologists have long recognized the presence of Kura-Araxes traits on Early Bronze Age sites in the northeastern Caucasus, referring to the Daghestan "variant" of this culture (for a classic exposition, see Munchaev 1975: 172–191). It is also clear that this "variant" had very specific features, many of which can be traced back directly to so-called Chalcolithic remains from mountainous Daghestan, particularly as documented at the site of Ginchi (Gadzhiev 1991: 34–78), and these Chalcolithic settlements in turn had their own ancestral roots in local Neolithic and Mesolithic developments, as documented at the site of Chokh (ibid., 110–126; Amirkhanov 1987). The Daghestan "variant" of the Kura-Araxes cultural tradition, thus, contains specific distinctive features related to these local roots that distinguish it from the more "classic" Kura-Araxes settlements in Transcaucasia to the south. Moreover, the Early

Bronze materials from Daghestan exhibit parallels with Maikop remains to the northwest and with materials also found farther north on the western Eurasian steppes, particularly in terms of metals and polished stone weapons, such as shaft-hole axe/hammers (battle axes) and perforated mace heads. The architecture on Early Bronze coastal plain sites varies from circular mud-brick free-standing architecture (e.g. at Serker-tepe in northeastern Azerbaijan) to deeply dug oval and circular pit-houses and even sunken, multi-roomed structures (e.g., at Velikent in southeastern Daghestan).

It may even be somewhat misleading to refer to the highly syncretic Early Bronze remains from the northeastern Caucasus as a "variant" of the Kura-Araxes culture – whatever that means. These remains seem sufficiently distinctive to warrant renaming them after the most extensively excavated Early and Middle Bronze Age site in the northeastern Caucasus, namely, that of Velikent on the Caspian plain of southeastern Daghestan. The temptation to define a new culture, however, must be resisted because there already exist too many archaeological cultures distributed across southern Russia (cf. the discussion in Chapter 1); to continue this proliferation only compounds the problem. Here reference will be to the Velikent "component" of the Kura-Araxes cultural-historical community, a less than satisfactory term that acknowledges the basic similarities in ceramics and portable hearth supports within the Kura-Araxes tradition, but also emphasizes the regionally distinctive and steppe-like features of the material remains most thoroughly documented at Velikent. Scores of Velikent component sites are known from both the coastal plain south of Izber-bash, Daghestan roughly to Divichi, northeastern Azerbaijan and in the immediately adjacent piedmont and mountainous regions to the west (Fig. 3.21).

As described earlier, the Caspian littoral plain forms the only unimpeded corridor around the Great Caucasus Mountains, linking the steppes to the north with Transcaucasia and the Anatolian and Iranian plateaus to the south. Peoples moving into Transcaucasia from the north would almost certainly have traveled down this corridor, encountering the settlements existing there. Preliminary survey reconnaissances to the south of Velikent and in northeastern Azerbaijan, as well as limited excavations on sites to the north at least as far as the contemporary town of Izberbash, have shown that sites with materials similar to those from Velikent were relatively densely distributed on this section of the coastal plain during Early Bronze times (Gadzhiev 1991: 128; Gadzhiev et al. 2000: 47–56; Khalilov et al. 1991). Early Bronze sites in mountainous Daghestan, such as Mekegi, Galgalati, and Chirkei, as well as in Chechnya to the northwest, such as Serzhen'-Yurt, contain materials closely related to those from Velikent (Gadzhiev 1991: 140–163), though obviously architectural traditions differ between the two zones with fairly simple one-roomed standing stone structures being characteristic in the mountains and mud-brick and pit-houses being typical on the coastal plain.

In other words, this Velikent "component" of the Kura-Araxes culture has a reasonably widespread distribution throughout the northeastern Caucasus.

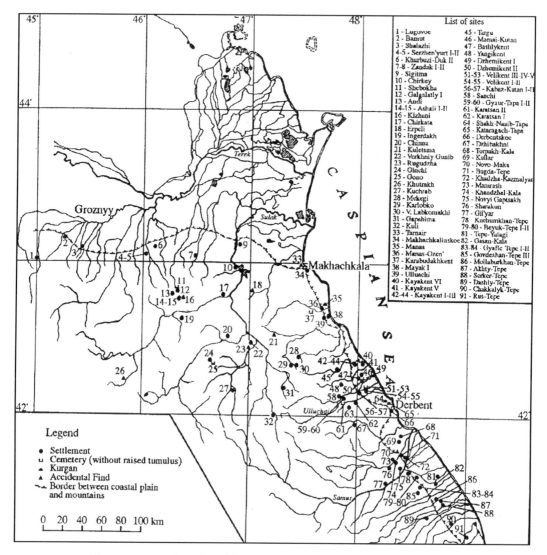

Figure 3.21. Early and Middle Bronze Age Velikent component sites of the Kura-Araxes cultural-historical community in the northeastern Caucasus (map compiled by R.G. Magomedov).

There is practically no earlier evidence for Chalcolithic sites on the littoral plain, as there is in the mountains, suggesting that the coastal plain was first settled during the middle of the fourth millennium BC, or slightly later than early Maikop sites to the northwest and roughly contemporaneous with the initial appearance of Kura-Araxes sites to the south. The essentially simultaneous emergence of the different components of the Kura-Araxes cultural-historical community seems to coincide roughly with the so-called Uruk expansion up the Euphrates and onto the eastern Anatolian plateau.

Velikent

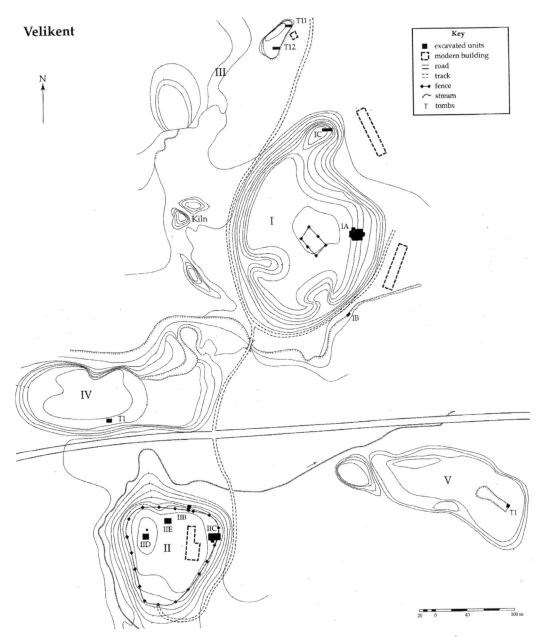

Figure 3.22. The cemetery and settlement terraces at Velikent on the Caspian coastal plain (adapted from Kohl, Gadzhiev, and Magomedov 2002: 115, fig. 7.3).

The Early Bronze Age site of Velikent was occupied from the mid-fourth to the early second millennium BC (or ca. 3600–1900 BC as based on a series of calibrated radiocarbon determinations). Its cultural remains, which consist of separate burial and settlement areas set on the top of five natural clay terraces, extend intermittently over approximately 28 ha. (Fig. 3.22). Excavations at the type site of Velikent have been the most extensive and have yielded the most materials, particularly from its collective catacomb burials, where hundreds of metal and polished stone objects and complete ceramic vessels have been recovered. Large circular dwellings with internal features such as hearths and benches and made of dried mud-bricks, some of which were occasionally fired, characterized the earliest building horizon (Gadzhiev et al. 2000: 63). Subsequently, the architectural tradition changed, and deeply dug pit houses became the norm. An even later multi-roomed building, which had been extensively burned, was excavated above a series of these deep circular pit-houses, though the rooms of this building, which were reinforced with wooden posts, flat river boulders, and even columns of stones set on top of one another reinforcing the corners (ibid., 76–77), were dug down into the natural clay terrace and not built-up as in the first building horizon. This multi-roomed burned building was not a domestic structure but served some public function, possibly associated with ceramic production and storage.

Thus, there was a very significant shift in building traditions not long after Velikent had been initially settled. The earliest horizon has numerous parallels with Kura-Araxes materials from sites to the south, whereas the later levels, which are deeply dug down from the surface, may reflect more northern influences as well as represent a unique local adaptation to the dense clay terraces into which they were dug and into which they also dug their collective catacomb burials. The forms of the tombs with their attached entrance pits closely resemble or even consciously emulate the deeply sunken circular pit-house dwellings. Although one can trace strong continuities in the ceramics and stone and bone tool industries from the earliest to latest levels at the site, it is unclear whether the site was continuously occupied or periodically abandoned, possibly owing to transgressions and regressions of the Caspian Sea (M. Martín Sánchez, P. López Garcia, and J. A. López Sáez 2000). The initial settlers at the site arrived with metal-working skills, for arsenical copper/bronzes and ceramic molds for casting objects appear in the earliest levels.

They also initially produced very fine, highly fired ceramics with impressed designs that probably were turned on a wheel. These "high-quality" wares, which constitute approximately 10% of the total ceramic assemblage in the early levels (Fig. 3.23), are also found at the site of Serzhen-Yurt to the north-west in Chechnya (Munchaev 1975: 340, fig. 76) and also distantly resemble "Uruk-related" fine ceramics with impressed designs from northern Syria (Lyonnet, personal communication). Their quality of manufacture bespeaks more a connection with the south (northern Mesopotamia?) than with the ceramics from the steppes to the north, despite superficial similarities in terms of the impressed designs. These "high-quality" wares were not found in the multi-roomed building or in the latest excavated pit houses on the northern settlement mound at Velikent; that is, they disappear at some point during the occupational sequence at the site.

Figure 3.23. "High-quality," apparently wheel-turned ceramic from Velikent – present at beginning of occupation of site, found as far west as Serzhen-Yurt in Chechnya and as far south as Serker-tepe (Borispol-tepe) in northeastern Azerbaijan.

A wealth of materials has been recovered from the salvage excavations of fifteen collective catacomb tombs at the site (Fig. 3.24). It is unclear how long such tombs were in use, and materials from them can be seriated into earlier and later groups. Two calibrated dates, taken from two separate tombs, almost perfectly overlap and date roughly 2850–2400 BC (Gadzhiev et al. 2000: 88, note 22), suggesting that burials were being interred in them during the first half of the third millennium. It is possible, if not likely, that some continued to be used during the latter part of the third millennium or Middle Bronze times and show clear relations with (or form part of?) the so-called later Middle Bronze Ginchi culture of mountainous Daghestan and Chechnya (Magomedov 1998; *n.b.,* this culture should not be confused with the previously mentioned Chalcolithic site of Ginchi, which is also located in mountainous Daghestan).

A few highly burnished, occasionally incised vessels and fragments have been recovered from these collective tombs that closely resemble so–called Bedeni vessels found in the large early kurgans in the Kakheti and Kvemo Kartli regions of eastern Georgia (Gadzhiev et al. 2000: 88–89; Miron and Orthmann 1995: 233–236). These earliest pre-Trialeti kurgans will be described below; here it is relevant to note that specialists divide them into two chronologically successive groups: the earlier Martkopi and the later Bedeni phases, which are named after excavated clusters of kurgans from these two areas in Georgia. Bedeni materials also have been found in some of the kurgans excavated at Martkopi. Calibrated radiocarbon dates from these kurgans are not entirely consistent, as is also the case for the dates from the later Middle Bronze Trialeti kurgans (compare Kavtaradze 1999: 81 and 86). In general, however, the calibrated dates support a higher chronology, pushing the initial appearance of the Martkopi phase kurgans back towards the middle, if not into the early, third millennium BC. Thus, the presence of occasional Bedeni-like materials in the Velikent collective catacomb tombs is not surprising in chronological terms. The more interesting question is what their presence suggests in terms of the cultural and historical relations between these two regions.

Spectroscopic analysis of 195 metal artifacts from the first excavated collective tomb at Velikent showed that most were made of arsenical copper or bronze, but surprisingly 15 (or approximately 8%) of the total analyzed corpus proved to be deliberately alloyed tin-bronzes, representing some of the earliest tin-bronzes found in the Caucasus. Only ornaments, not tools and weapons, were made of tin-bronze at Velikent, possibly suggesting that the distinctive color of the exotic metal enhanced its value (for a more extended discussion of the cultural value inherent in the Velikent tin-bronzes and silver artifacts, cf. Peterson 2003: 34–37). The ornaments made of tin-bronze at Velikent also occur as arsenical copper/bronzes; thus, it is possible that the tin-bronzes were received in semiprocessed forms or as ingots (Gadzhiev et al. 1997: 191, fig. 8, no. 3), and then worked by the local smiths to produce distinctively colored, but immediately recognizable ornaments, particularly bracelets.

A few tin-bronzes occur on late Kura-Araxes sites in Georgia and Armenia (Kavtaradze 1999: 84–86; Tedesco, personal communication), but they begin to appear with any regularity only during this early kurgan period. According to Kavtaradze (ibid., 86), most of the bronzes from the Bedeni phase kurgans are tin-bronzes, containing 8 to 15% admixtures of tin. The source(s) of the tin are unknown, though not local, and lead-isotope analyses conducted on a few of the previously analyzed tin-bronzes from Velikent suggest that they could possibly be coming from the same eastern (?) sources that brought early tin-bronzes to Troy in northwestern Anatolia and, at a later date, tin-bronzes to Tell Abraq in the Arab Emirates (Kohl 2002a; Weeks 1999). This analytical evidence is more tantalizing than definitive, but it is consistent with the notion of the long-distance sporadic exchange of semiprocessed tin-bronzes and/or prestige goods that may have indirectly linked sites from as far west as the eastern Adriatic coast (Primas 2002: 304–305) to the northeastern Mediterranean across the Black Sea and/or west Eurasian steppes to the Caucasus and eastwards possibly to sources in southwestern Afghanistan or even farther east.

Most of the hundreds of bronzes artifacts from the collective tombs at Velikent represent fairly typical forms, such as awls, chisels, simple tanged

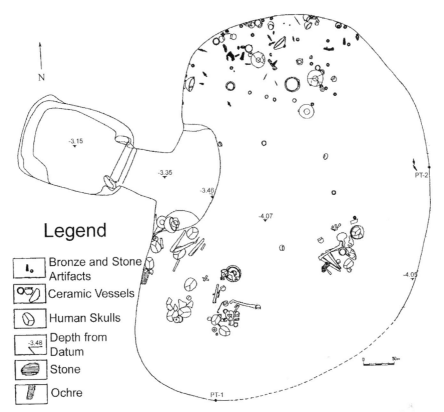

N

Legend

I.	Bronze and Stone Artifacts
	Ceramic Vessels
	Human Skulls
-3.48	Depth from Datum
	Stone
	Ochre

Figure 3.24. Plan of collective catacomb tomb 11 from Velikent (adapted from Gadzhiev et al. 2000: 84, fig. 38).

knives, flat axes/adzes, and heavy shaft-hole axes, characteristic of Chernykh's Circumpontic Metallurgical Province (Fig. 3.25). The metal ornaments from Velikent, such as the anchor-shaped pendants and the straight and crook-headed toggle pins perforated and flattened in the middle, are more distinctively characteristic of Velikent (Fig. 3.26), suggesting that they did not diffuse as widely as the tools and weapons; the circular bronze medallions with a characteristic bent loop for suspension, on the other hand, have been found repeatedly on the steppes, suggesting contact with that area (cf. Nechitailo 1991: cover illustration and 86–87). The ground polished stone industry includes circular, pear-shaped, and knobbed mace heads and ceremonial shaft-hole axe-hammers or battle axes that are frequently encountered in excavated kurgans found farther to the northwest, including burials of the Novotitorovskaya culture (Gei 2000: 156).

Clay models of wheels with projecting hubs have been found on the earlier settlement mound at Velikent and have been recovered from the surface of Velikent culture sites south of Derbent on the final coastal bay north of the Samur River and the border with Azerbaijan (Gadzhiev et al. 2000: 56, fig. 9). Such wheel models, which are typologically distinctive from the bone spindle whorls also found at Velikent, are frequently interpreted as evidence for the

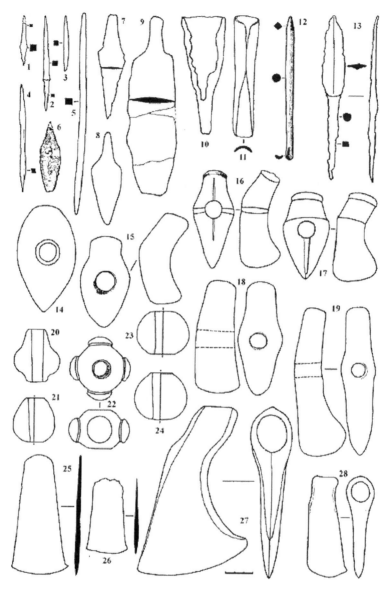

Figure 3.25. Characteristic metal (1–13, 25–28) and stone (14–24) tools and weapons from collective catacomb tombs at Velikent (drawn by R.G. Magomedov).

existence of wheeled transport, and current opinion suggests that it is roughly around the middle of the fourth millennium BC that wheeled transport first appears, stretching across a vast interconnected region from northern Europe to southern Mesopotamia (Bakker et al. 1999). The precise determination of which area or which archaeological culture first developed wheeled vehicles may prove impossible to document archaeologically simply because the technology diffused as rapidly as it did across this vast contiguous area. The question

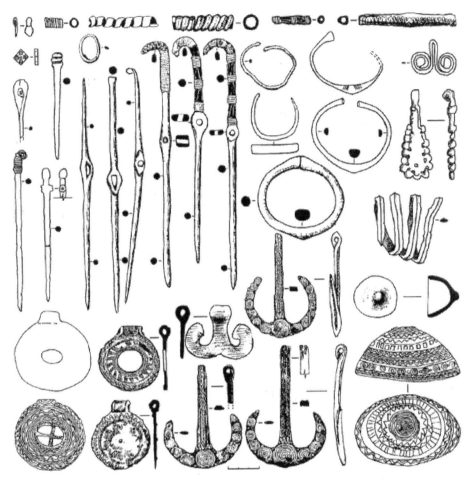

Figure 3.26. Metal ornaments from Velikent (drawn by R.G. Magomedov).

of origins, however, is much less significant than this phenomenon of convergence, this almost simultaneous evidence for the early use of wheeled vehicles stretching from northern Germany and southern Poland south across Anatolia to southern Mesopotamia, beginning ca. 3500 BC or immediately after the collapse of the gigantic Tripol'ye settlements.

Wheeled vehicles can be used for different purposes by different cultures (or different purposes by the same culture) across this interconnected area; they can serve military purposes, function to transport traded goods, such as semiprocessed metal ores and ingots, and facilitate the development of a new, more mobile way of life based principally on cattle herding. It is shortly after the introduction of wheeled transport that evidence for its massive utilization on the western Eurasian steppes is documented in the excavation of scores of kurgans containing wheeled carts with tripartite wooden wheels. These were not the chariots of a military aristocracy but the heavy, ponderous carts and

wagons of cowboys who were developing a form of mobile Bronze Age pastoral
economy that fundamentally differed from the classic Eurasian nomadism that
is later attested historically and ethnographically.

The actual existence of wheeled vehicles has been extensively documented
in Novotitorovskaya culture burials on the Kuban steppe to the northwest
(Fig. 3.31) and, less frequently, in the monumental early kurgan tombs of
Transcaucasia, both of which begin apparently during the first half of the third
millennium BC, or during the period when the catacomb collective burials,
occasionally with Bedeni-like vessels, were first utilized at Velikent. One does
not yet have comparable evidence from kurgans on the Caspian coastal plain,
many of which, unfortunately, have been leveled during the past fifty years
with the intensive modern settlement and utilization of the plain. The plain
once was dotted with kurgans dating to various periods, and it is now necessary
to locate and excavate the earliest of them, such as still remain.

Currently available settlement pattern evidence suggests that this part of the
Caspian plain extending south from Velikent to northern Azerbaijan may have
been largely abandoned at the end of the third or beginning of the second
millennium BC, though it is unclear whether the local inhabitants of the plain
retreated into the mountains to the west for ecological reasons and/or were
displaced south or north because of the periodic movements of peoples off
the steppes and down the coastal plain into Transcaucasia, movements that
may have begun roughly during the middle of the third millennium BC or
even earlier, if the revised dating and cultural identification of the Sé Girdan
kurgans in northwestern Iran is correct (cf. earlier discussion). Such postulated
migrations did not represent armed invasions so much as cattle herders moving
south with their families on oxen-driven wagons in search of better pastures
for their animals. They partially assimilated with the local Velikent and Kura-
Araxes peoples, as represented by continuities evident in the materials from
both cultures.

There was a sharp break in the distribution of settlements in Transcaucasia
that occurred during the late Early Bronze period, possibly beginning around
the middle of the third millennium; specifically, the dense distribution of Kura-
Araxes settlements was followed by a much more sparse distribution of known
settlements and a sharp increase in burial sites during the late Early and Middle
Bronze periods. This pronounced change in the material culture record, the
dramatic decline in settlements and increase in burial sites, unfortunately, is
not sufficiently emphasized in Kushnareva's otherwise excellent discussion of
Transcaucasia during the late Early and Middle Bronze periods (cf, her introductory comments to the Transcaucasian Middle Bronze Age 1997: 81); that
is, if one superficially compares the distribution maps of Kura–Araxes Early
Bronze remains in Transcaucasia with those of the subsequent Middle Bronze
period (ibid., 46–86), the marked discontinuity in settlement pattern would not
be immediately apparent. The difference, however, is striking: an abundance

of known settlements and a relative paucity of mortuary remains is followed by a precipitous decline in known settlements and the advent of essentially new, monumental raised burial mounds (cf. Dschaparidze 2001: 101–102).

Moreover, the post Kura-Araxes settlements that have been investigated, such as the site of Uzerlik-Tepe in Azerbaijan, are impressively fortified on a scale not characteristic of the earlier Kura-Araxes settlements, and there is more diversity evident in the material culture remains, as is evident in Kushnareva's delineation of five Middle Bronze overlapping archaeological cultures: Western, Trialeti, Karmirberd, Kizylvank, and Sevan-Uzerlik (Kushnareva 1997: 84–85). These supplanted the earlier, more homogeneous Kura-Araxes remains. What is the significance of such a sharp shift in settlement patterns?

THE EARLY KURGAN CULTURES OF TRANSCAUCASIA – THE ARRIVALS OF NEW PEOPLES, CHANGES IN SUBSISTENCE ECONOMIC PRACTICES, AND THE EMERGENCE OF SOCIAL COMPLEXITY

Some raised earthen burial mounds have been found in association with late Kura-Araxes settlements (e.g., at Satkhe in Djavakheti); they are not typical, however. Single, paired, and collective Kura-Araxes burials have been excavated both within settlements and in separate cemeteries adjacent to the settlements (e.g., at Amiranis-gora in Djavakheti). They are not typically mounded, but simple pits sometimes lined with stones. The mortuary evidence from Transcaucasia radically changes with the advent of the early kurgan cultures found initially in eastern and central Georgia. Georgian archaeologists distinguish two early phases of kurgan construction – Martkopi and Bedeni, which are named respectively after clusters of kurgans found immediately east and southwest of Tbilisi; other clusters of kurgans in the Alazan valley of eastern Georgia (e.g., at Tsnori) and some on the Tsalka plateau near Trialeti are also related to this period of the late Early Bronze kurgan cultures of Transcaucasia.

Absolute dating for the initial appearance of these large kurgans is somewhat contradictory, though most calibrated radiocarbon dates (cf. Kavtaradze 1999: 81) suggest that this process may have been underway at the end of the first half of the third millennium BC and then continuing into the second half of the third millennium. If this dating is basically correct, it suggests that the monumental early kurgans of Transcaucasia appear after the initial spread of Kura-Araxes peoples to the south, and that these kurgan cultures overlap chronologically with the latest phases of the Kura-Araxes culture in Transcaucasia (e.g., at Sachkere in Imereti). Mortuary remains continue to dominate the Transcaucasian archaeological record throughout the Middle Bronze Age, a period that traditionally continues – on the basis principally of synchronisms with the shaft-graves at Mycenae – down to the middle of the second millennium BC.

Unfortunately, very few settlement sites bridge the development from the Early Bronze Kura-Araxes culture to the regional Middle Bronze variants defined by Kushnareva. The important site of Berikldeebi (Glonti and Dzhavakhisvili 1987) along the left bank of the Kura River in Shida Kartli is an exception. This settlement has a ceramic sequence that extends from Late Chalcolithic pre–Kura-Araxes levels to the Late Bronze Age, including a well-defined occupation containing ceramics identical to those recovered from the early Bedeni kurgans. The site is small (0.5 ha.), badly pitted, and has a relatively thin cultural deposit (less than 2 m.). Berikldeebi's long, apparently continuous sequence is most important for the relative ordering of materials, but, on current understanding, it is also exceptional and can hardly be cited to justify a general continuity of occupation in the Caucasus from Late Chalcolithic to Late Bronze times.

Some materials from the later collective catacomb tombs at Velikent mound III and from the synchronous, later levels of the settlement mound II at Velikent suggest that occupation at this site and presumably at other Velikent culture sites on the Caspian littoral plain may have continued into the late third and possibly into the beginning of the second millennium BC. As already mentioned, occasional Bedeni ceramic "imports" have been recovered from the later collective tombs, strengthening the basic chronological link between these materials and those from the early kurgan cultures of Transcaucasia. But afterwards settlement on the Caspian coast appears at least to have been largely interrupted, not resuming on a major scale until possibly Early Medieval times.

These shifts in settlement patterns must reflect a fundamental change in subsistence practices and increased social differentiation during late Early and Middle Bronze times. Some of the monumental, so-called great early kurgans (e.g., no. 1 at Tsnori) are spread across nearly 3 ha., encompassing a greater area than most known Kura-Araxes settlements! Kushnareva (1997: 229–233) has attempted to reconstruct the total number of "man-days" of labor needed to construct the kurgans found at Bedeni, Tsnori, and Uch-tepe on the Mil steppe of Azerbaijan and has come up with a figure of 48,000 days of labor for the largest kurgan from the last group. Although such calculations may be inflated or, at best, provide only approximate estimates of the required work, they still give some idea of the organization and expenditure of energy needed to construct these monumental houses for the dead with their elaborate wooden structures covered by massive stone mounds that can exceed 100 m. in diameter and 20 m. in height. Some kurgans on the Tsalka plateau in Georgia have stone-lined "procession ways" stretching more than 100 meters and sometimes linking one kurgan to another (Litscheli 2001: 65; Puturidze 2003; Fig. 3.27).

A plausible case can be made for the occasional practice of human sacrifice on the basis of the presence of secondary burials without grave goods accompanying the principal, richly accoutered interment found in these tombs.

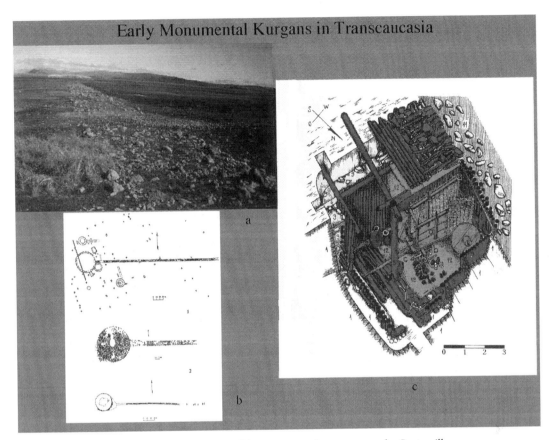

Figure 3.27. (a) Stone "procession way" between two kurgans near the Santa village, Tsalka (adapted from Litscheli 2001: 65); (b) Drawing of kurgans with stone-lined processional ways, Tsalka, Georgia (adapted from Puturidze 2003: 124, fig. 5.9); (c) Wooden "house of the dead," the great Bedeni kurgan 5 (adapted from Lordkipanidze 2001: 13; caption translated from German: 1) construction pit; 2) plank wooden floor; 3) threshold; 4) longitudinal beams; 5) posts; 6) transverse beams; 7) roof beam; 8) grave chamber wall; 9) wall fill comprised of stones, earth, and wood; 12) interwoven bast mat; b) four-wheeled wagon; c) grave inventory; d) skeletal remains; e) metal objects).

Materials found in these tombs include precious silver and gold vessels, figurines, jewelry, and decorated felts. Tin-bronze weapons and tools are regularly found alongside arsenical copper/bronzes, and four-wheeled wooden wagons with tripartite wheels of the type earlier found in the Kuban region of the northwestern Caucasus also regularly appear in the larger kurgans from the Bedeni phase through Middle Bronze times.

Social differentiation and unstable political conditions also are evident in the iconographic representations on some of the vessels. The famous silver goblet from the Middle Bronze Karashamb kurgan found north of Yerevan is most instructive in this respect. This goblet, which closely resembles one earlier

Figure 3.28. Karashamb silver goblet (adapted from Tiratsian 1992: 39).

excavated in Kurgan XVII in the Trialeti kurgans from the Tsalka plateau of southern Georgia, contains five bands of naturalistic and one band of geometric representations. The second and third bands from the top, which encircle the central body of the goblet, contain particularly vivid images (Fig. 3.28). A ceremonial banquet and procession scene occupies the second row with musicians playing behind a seated central figure, who is shown larger than the others and appears to be feasting on the various foods set on a table in front of him. This procession and feasting scene is then flanked by a row of fighting warriors. In the band beneath there appears a scene showing a warrior stabbing his opponent, followed by a lion, three standing headless figures, a feline-headed bird of prey of indisputably Mesopotamian or, more generally, West Asian inspiration, a fighter apparently decapitating a hapless victim or prisoner, and a seated figure holding a weapon before a column of disarticulated human heads set next to what can be interpreted as war booty: arrayed shields and metal weapons.

The representations are fascinating for their combination of local and more general, pan-West Asian traits, such as the feline-headed bird of prey and the processional scene with the central seated figure, feted by the musicians and the retainers serving him liquid and solid foods. Militarism, as reflected in the arrayed weaponry and depictions of combat and decapitation, appears endemic in the society. Social hierarchy and differential access to power are also clearly evident in these scenes.

The Karashamb goblet is unquestionably related to the earlier excavated silver goblet from Trialeti, the culture of which is dated traditionally to the Middle Bronze Age, or to the first half of the second millennium BC. Trialeti

Figure 3.29. Anchor-shaped, shaft-hole ceremonial axes from (a) Karashamb, (b) Bedeni, and (c) Kyurduluk (compiled from Pilipossian 1996: 65, no. 33 for the Karashamb axe; Dschaparidze 2001: 106 for the Bedeni axe; and Akhundov 2001: cover for the Kyurduluk axe).

black geometric designed and black-on-red painted wares can easily be distinguished from those from the earlier Martkopi and Bedeni kurgans, which are much more closely related to the preceding Kura-Araxes ceramic tradition. Similarly, there is a change in burial practice from the late Early Bronze monumental kurgans, with their principal interred and occasional accompanying individuals, to that of cremation in the Trialeti Middle Bronze kurgans. Possibly, such differences can be explained in terms of different ethnic groups who have successively crossed the Caucasus Mountains into Transcaucasia. It is true also that features of continuity can be observed and that the traditional division between late Early and Middle Bronze remains both on the western Eurasian steppes and in the Caucasus is imprecise, exhibiting considerable chronological overlap as based on calibrated radiocarbon determinations. At least some Middle Bronze sequences date to the third millennium BC (Chernykh et al. 2000: 41–42).

One striking illustration (Fig. 3.29) of chronological and typological continuity is provided by the anchor-shaped, shaft-hole ceremonial silver axe (Pilipossian 1996: 65, no. 33) that was found together with the silver goblet in the Karashamb kurgan. The highly distinctive shape of this axe is precisely paralleled by bronze axes from Idzhevan in northern Armenia (Kushnareva 1997: 107, fig. 45, no. 21), from kurgan 14 in the Kyurduluk cluster of kurgans just southwest of Sheki in northwestern Azerbaijan (Akhundov 2001: cover, and

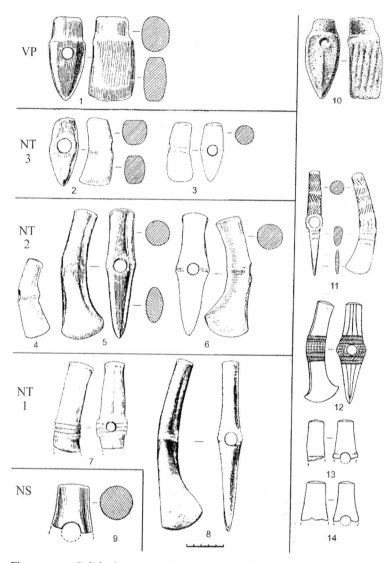

Figure 3.30. Polished stone axe-hammers (or battle axes) from Novotitorovskaya culture sites and comparisons with other steppe examples, Troy (no. 12), and Daghestan 13–14; cf. also stone axe-hammers from Velikent, Fig. 3.24, nos. 14–19 above (adapted from Gei 2000: 156, fig. 47).

295, pl. XXXV, no. 3), from kurgan 12 at Bedeni (Dschaparidze 2001: 106), and from private grave 691 in the Royal Cemetery at Ur (Woolley 1934, vol. I: pl. 224, type A 14). The last example suggests that this type of axe was initially produced at least sometime toward the middle of the third millennium BC. It also should be noted that this ceremonial axe from the Bedeni kurgan was made of tin-bronze with a 9.2% concentration of tin (Gambaschidze et al. 2001: 270).

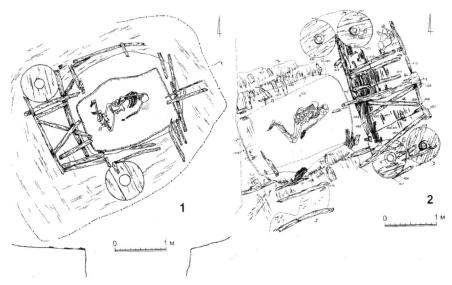

Figure 3.31. Wagons found in Kurgans of the Novotitorovskaya Culture (Lebedi 1, kurgan 2) (adapted from Gei 2000: 30, fig. 5).

Parallels from the early kurgans can be drawn also to materials found in Velikent "component" sites on the Caspian plain and in the steppes north of the great Caucasus range. Thus, a stone "battle-axe" of a type common in the northern Caucasus and southern Russia was found in one of the Martkopi kurgans (Dshaparidse 1995: 75), as were gold spiral pendants presumably worn about the temples or in the hair (ibid.), pear-shaped ground marble mace-heads (Miron and Orthmann 1995: 233), and perforated animal-toothed pendants (ibid., 228). Very similar materials are found in the collective catacomb tombs at Velikent (cf. Gadzhiev et al. 1997: 191; Gadzhiev et al. 2000: 91, 92), and the stone battle-axes are very typical for Novotitorovskaya culture remains in the Kuban region of the northwestern Caucasus (Gei 2000: 156; Fig. 3.30).

Most significant, of course, is the parallel appearance of oxen–driven wooden wagons in Novotitorovskaya kurgans and, more generally, in kurgans in the western Eurasian steppes from Novosvobodnaya, Pit-Grave, Early Catacomb, Kemi-Oba, and other related culture sites north of the Great Caucasus range and less frequently in the large kurgans of the Late Early Bedeni and Middle Bronze Trialeti–related cultures in Transcaucasia (Fig. 3.31). Gei (2000: 176–177) estimates that the remains of more than 250 wagons have been excavated in kurgans from the Kuban area and across the southeastern European steppes, 115 of them to be attributed to the Novotitorovskaya culture of the former region. The parallel appearance of similarly constructed wagons in both areas cannot be coincidental but must be historically related, possibly as suggested here through the continuous movement of cattle herders north to south around the great Caucasus range. One cannot fail to observe also the nearly simultaneous appearance of such oxen-driven wagons in the "royal" tombs of southern Mesopotamia, tombs that contain striking parallels in precious jewelry and bronze weapons with remains from the Caucasus. It should be emphasized, however, that many more wagons have been excavated north of the Great Caucasus Mountains suggesting possibly their more practical, every day use on the steppes than the apparently ritualistic/ceremonial purposes they principally performed south of the Great Caucasus.

The societies responsible for the construction of the large late Early and Middle Bronze kurgans in Transcaucasia were not egalitarian but must have been ruled by a paramount leader or chief who was capable of waging war and amassing labor on a significant scale to raise these monumental mortuary mounds. The number of known settlements decreased dramatically from the earlier time of the Kura-Araxes cultural community, and the later Middle Bronze settlements that have been excavated, such as at Uzerlik-Tepe, were heavily fortified, safely encircled behind massive stone walls, again reflecting unsettled, perpetually bellicose conditions. It is thought, though not yet conclusively demonstrated, that the earliest fortresses with cyclopean stone architecture, which typically are located in steep or relatively inaccessible locations such as the citadel of Schaori on top of a steep peak overlooking the western shore of Lake Paravani in Djavakheti (Litscheli 2001: 65), may first date to the Middle Bronze period. Later during the Late Bronze/Early Iron Age, such citadels became a characteristic feature of the Transcaucasian landscape (Badalyan et al. 2003).

Some of the early kurgan clusters, such as the Bedeni kurgans on the Tetri-Tskaro plateau, the Meskheti kurgans on the Niaili plateau, and the Trialeti kurgans on the Tsalka plateau, are found in highland areas more likely used as summer pasture lands than places of intensive agriculture. Others, located in the Alazan valley or on the Mil steppe, may have been areas where pastoralists drove their flocks and quartered themselves during the winter months. Kushnareva's reconstruction (1997: 230) is reasonable:

> The pasturing of herds of animals in the high mountains during the spring and summer seasons compels us to view those areas of the Mil steppe where kurgans were erected and the mountains of the neighboring Caucasus as a single cultural-economic region. And if the annual herding cycle was approximately the same in antiquity, it would seem logical that the building of the kurgans took place during the winter months with the slackening of herding activities, at a time when the herders had descended from the mountains.

Conversely, those kurgans found on the plateaus were most likely constructed during the summer months when the herders had driven their herds from the valleys and steppes onto these highland areas then covered with luxuriant grasses. Such annual movements of pastoralists are known ethnographically (e.g., herders wintering in the Alazan valley of eastern Georgia and then driving their flocks to the Djavakheti plateau for its summer pastures), and the physical separation of the kurgan clusters and the general lack of obvious agricultural settlements suggest that a similar pattern of annual movement had been established already by late Early and Middle Bronze times. This interpretation does not mean that agriculture had been abandoned or that the composition of the herds during this initial period was similar to that recorded ethnographically. More data on settlement patterns and subsistence practices needs to be gathered to determine these issues.

Cattle herding pastoralists, who habitually utilized ponderous oxen-driven wagons, gradually moved south from the western Eurasian steppes into Transcaucasia. As they came into contact with the remaining Kura-Araxes related peoples, their material culture and economic activities necessarily changed. Assimilation is evident in the continuities between Kura-Araxes and Bedeni ceramics, such as sharply carinated, highly burnished black vessels, and is to be expected in other aspects of material culture, including basic economic activities. This reconstruction is potentially testable. Over time, the immigrant cattle herders developed a more mixed economy with more varied compositions of their herds, including greater reliance on sheep and goats. Replacement was partial, not total, and the Early Kurgan and Middle Bronze cultures that emerged were hybrids exhibiting features both local and nonlocal in origin.

CONCLUSION – SOME LATER DEVELOPMENTS IN CAUCASIAN PREHISTORY AND SHIFTS IN THE PRODUCTION AND EXCHANGE OF METALS

Traditionally the Late Bronze period in Transcaucasia begins around the middle of the second millennium BC. Several different regional archaeological cultures (e.g., in Georgia, Iori-Alazan, Shida Kartli or Samtavro, Colchidean/Koban) are recognized. Settlements once more are documented on a large scale and include the fortified sites with cyclopean stone architecture perched on inaccessible, easily defended promontories or on the steep slopes of mountains, as well as more open settlements located in lower-lying plains. The Caucasus now appears even more densely settled than in Kura-Araxes times, with Late Bronze sites located in valleys and in piedmont regions "beneath nearly every contemporary village" (Abramichvili 1984: 46).

Cemeteries, which usually now consist of individual pits, stone-lined cist graves, or stone-ringed cromlechs, but not raised kurgans, are often associated with these settlements. Male burials typically contain a relatively standard assemblage of functional and ceremonial metal weapons, including somewhat later the famous engraved Colchidean/Koban axes (e.g., at the Tli cemetery [Tekhov 1980; 1981; 1985; 1988]). Special "sanctuary" sites of ritually deposited hordes containing literally thousands of functional and miniature-sized metal weapons, jewelry, figurines, and ceramic vessels also now appear and are particularly well-documented in eastern Georgia (Pizchelauri 1984). The record suggests that the times remained unsettled and that Transcaucasia had now filled up with different peoples armed with bronze weapons to defend the territories that they had staked out for themselves.

Tin-bronzes increasingly replaced arsenical copper/bronzes, though this process of replacement apparently took place in different areas at different times, occurring earlier, for example, in the Alazan-Iori plain than in Shida Kartli (Dschaparidze 2001: 114–116). Nevertheless, over time throughout the Caucasus, tin-bronzes became dominant and were readily available, despite the fact that there were no local sources of tin that were exploited at this time. During the Late Bronze and Early Iron periods, the Caucasus is one of the richest metalworking areas of the Old World, with tens of thousands of tin-bronze artifacts having been unearthed in clandestine and controlled excavations dating back to the nineteenth century.

E. N. Chernykh's discussion (1992: 275–295) of this later "Caucasian Metallurgical Province," which takes shape around the middle of the second millennium BC, refers extensively to the highly distinctive and isolated character of the bronzes produced in the Caucasus at this later time and contrasts its paradoxically isolated character with the range of metal products distributed across the contemporaneous vast "Eurasian Metallurgical Province" centered far to the northeast (Chernykh 1992: 192) and with the earlier role of Caucasian metallurgy in the late third and early second millennium for supplying metals over much of the western Eurasian steppes. What is perhaps even more paradoxical is that by the second half of the second millennium BC, the Caucasus was one of the most prolific metal-working areas of the Old World, and what it was dominantly utilizing were tin-bronzes, the tin of which had to be imported from sources lying far to the east (cf. Chernykh 1992: 194). If this picture is accurate, it is hard not to adumbrate the outlines of a structurally integrated, metallurgically linked, extensive *system* of production and exchange stretching across a vast area of Eurasia by the latter half of the second millennium BC.

BIOGRAPHICAL SKETCH

R. M. MUNCHAEV

Photo 3.1. R. M. Munchaev delivers remarks, while E. E. Antipina listens.

Rauf Magomedovich Munchaev was born in Zakataly, Azerbaijan on September 23, 1928. In 1949 he graduated from the Historical Faculty of the Daghestan State Pedagogical Institute (now Daghestan State University). In 1953 he defended his Candidate's Dissertation (first PhD) on *The Copper and Bronze Ages in the History of Daghestan (3rd to 2nd millennia BC)* [*Epokha medi i bronzy v istorii Daghestana (III-II tyc. do n.e.)*], and he finished his Doctoral Dissertation (second PhD) on *The Caucasus in the Aeneolithic and Early Bronze Age (5th to 3rd millennia BC)* [*Kavkaz v epokhu eneolita i rannei bronzy (V-III tys. do n.e.)*]. He began to work at the Institute of Archaeology, Academy of Sciences in Moscow in 1955, and he served first as Deputy Director of the Institute from 1968 to 1991 and then as Director from 1991 to 2003. He successfully led the Institute of Archaeology through the turbulent years that immediately followed the collapse of the USSR and the massive cutback in state support that drastically affected field-based sciences such as archaeology.

He has participated in archaeological field expeditions to the northern Caucasus, the Middle Volga, and Stavropol' regions, and to Bulgaria. He directed the Soviet expeditions to northwestern Iraq (1969–1984), where extensive excavations were conducted on pre-Hassuna, Hassuna, Halaf, and Ubaid settlements (several articles of which were translated into English in the edited volume *Early Stages in the History of Mesopotamian Civilization: Soviet Excavations in Northern Iraq* [Yoffee and Clark 1993]), and since 1988 he has led the Russian excavations to northeastern Syria, where they have exposed the monumental remains of a fourth–third millennium cult-administrative center at Tell Khazna I (Munchaev, Merpert, and Amirov 2004). He has been the editor-in-chief of the central journals *Sovetskaya Arkheologiya* and its successor *Rossiiskaya Arkheologiya* and was the deputy editorial chief of the multivolume *Arkheologiya SSSR* series. He has published more than 250 archaeological articles and monographs, including his extensive overviews to the Maikop culture that are cited frequently in our study (Munchaev 1975, 1994). Most recently, he is the coauthor with V. I. Markovin of a semipopular overview to the prehistory, early history, and contemporary material culture of the northern Caucasus (Markovin and Munchaev 2003).

In order to convey something of the integrated "international" character of Soviet/Russian archaeology, let me relate one personal anecdote. In late December 1987 I accompanied the well-known ancient historian, Dr. Muhammed A. Dandamaev, to New York to attend the annual Archaeological Institute of America meetings. Dr. Dandamaev had spent the previous two weeks with me in Wellesley, MA, painstakingly compiling the indices for his book (coauthored with V. G. Lukonin) *The Culture and Social Institutions of Ancient Iran*, which was published by Cambridge University Press in 1989. It was the height of the Gorbachev era and several leading Soviet archaeologists, including Rauf M. Munchaev, had been invited to New York to participate in a special session on the origin of the state. Dr. Dandamaev and I had also been invited to participate in these meetings, but when we arrived at the hotel in

New York, Muhammed, who is an ethnic Lakh born in mountainous Daghestan, asked me to find where his fellow Lakh, Dr. Munchaev, was staying. We
located Rauf's room, and I was delighted to observe the two Lakhs embracing
in this opulent setting. Rauf then opened the door of the desk where he had
been working and took out a recent Russian newspaper article, reporting the
activities of the Lakh Soviet cosmonaut who was then circling the globe. Two
of the eighty thousand or so still extant Lakhs happily celebrated the exploits
of their fellow countryman in the very incongruous surroundings of a fancy
hotel room in midtown Manhattan – a classic, unforgettable moment.

BIOGRAPHICAL SKETCH

M. G. GADZHIEV

Photo 3.2. M. G. Gadzhiev is pictured here on his
last visit to Wellesley, MA, spring 2002.

Magomed Gadzhievich Gadzhiev, an ethnic Avar, was born on December 1,
1935 in the mountain village (*aul*) of Okhli in the then Autonomous Soviet
Socialist Republic of Daghestan; he died after a short illness in the Daghestan
capital of Makhachkala on February 4, 2003. He was born into a family of
teachers who worked in the rural countryside, but he left the mountains to
study first in the regional center at Buinaksk and then in the Faculty of History
at the Daghestan State University in 1954. Four years later he was accepted
as a graduate student in archaeology at the Daghestan branch of the Russian
Academy of Sciences, where he continued to work for the rest of his life. From
1980 until his death in 2003, he directed the Archaeological Department of
the Institute of History, Archaeology, Ethnography of the Daghestan Scientific
Center, Russian Academy of Sciences and also taught courses in archaeology
as Professor in the History Department of the Daghestan State Pedagogical
University.

He was an extremely active field archaeologist, conducting both research and
salvage excavations on Chalcolithic and Bronze Age settlements and cemeteries, such as in the mountains at Ginchi, Irganai, Galgalatli, and Chirkei and on

the Caspian coastal plain at Gemi-Tyube, Mamai-Kutan, and Velikent. He even investigated several fortresses and settlements of Albanian-Sarmatian and Early Medieval times near his ancestral mountain village of Okhli. He was also the Daghestan Director of the Daghestan American Archaeological Expedition to Velikent (or DAV), which conducted excavations at the site from 1994 to 1998, or until the political situation in neighboring Chechnya temporarily halted this collaborative project. He was the author of more than 140 scientific articles and coauthored several fundamental works, such as the four-volume *History of Daghestan* (1967), the first volume of which was completely revised, appearing in 1996 as *Istoriya Dagestana s dreveneishikh vremen do kontsa XV v.* (with O. M. Davudov and A. P. Shikhsaidov). His expanded and revised doctoral dissertation (or second PhD) *Ranne-Zemedel'cheskaya Kul'tura Severo-Vostochnogo Kavkaza* appeared in 1991 and demonstrated clearly that the so-called Daghestan variant of the Kura-Araxes cultural community had not been introduced into Daghestan as part of the relatively later dispersal of this cultural community, but rather had local indigenous roots related to Chalcolithic settlements that dated back at least to the middle of the fourth millennium BC.

Magomed Gadzhiev's contribution to the archaeology of Daghestan and of the Caucasus, in general, was simply immense. Those of us fortunate enough to have worked with him also remember him as a wonderful, warm individual who treated everyone alike with the same unpretentious, caring manner. M. M. Mammaev, the editor of the recently published volume dedicated to his seventieth anniversary (2005: 5), sums up these unforgettable personal strengths:

> Being an uncommonly modest man, Magomed Gadzhiev never engaged in self-promotion or demanded special homage. He always maintained a Daghestan mountaineer's sense of moral virtue (*namus*), honor, and dignity. His straightforwardness and accessibility won him the deep respect of all those who knew and worked with him.

CHAPTER 4

TAMING THE STEPPE – THE DEVELOPMENT
OF MOBILE ECONOMIES: FROM CATTLE
HERDERS WITH WAGONS TO HORSEBACK
RIDERS TENDING MIXED HERDS; THE
CONTINUED EASTWARD EXPANSION
OF LARGE-SCALE METALLURGICAL
PRODUCTION AND EXCHANGE

> Although many present-day situations constitute valid analogues of ear-
> lier ones, it is possible that certain living strategies existed in the past for
> which no equivalent appears at present or for which modern equivalent
> may actually prove to be poor analogues.
>
> (Morales Muniz and Antipina 2003: 331)

Broadly defined, the Eurasian steppe consists of the belt of open grasslands
stretching latitudinally from Hungary in the west to Manchuria in the east,
the largest expanse of such open grasslands in the world (Frontispiece). Our
geographical horizons necessarily are more restricted, and our concern is principally to trace late prehistoric developments across the western Eurasian steppe,
or the belt extending north of the Black Sea (Pontic steppe) from the mouth of
the Danube east across the South Russian steppe beyond the Lower and Middle Volga to the southern trans-Urals region bordering western Siberia and
Kazakhstan. Throughout this area, the open grasslands of the steppe proper
are sandwiched between the more wooded boreal and broad-leafed forest and
then forest-steppe belts to the north and the highland zones of the Caucasus
and the Anatolian and Iranian plateaus west and south of the Caspian Sea,
and the Central Asian Kyzyl Kum and Kara Kum deserts east of the Caspian.
These latitudinal bands can be further subdivided north to south into distinct
vegetation zones consisting of forest, forest-steppe, steppe, desert-steppe, and
Artemisia and sandy desert zones (Hiebert 2000: 52–53; Figs. 4.1 and 4.2).

As mentioned earlier, the open steppe essentially encroaches on or meets
the Great Caucasus range west of the Caspian, although it is separated from
the mountain ranges of Central Asia and the complex Bronze Age societies
that developed in the foothills of the Kopet Dagh and in the low lying plains
of Margiana and Bactria by the Kyzyl and Kara Kum deserts. This physical

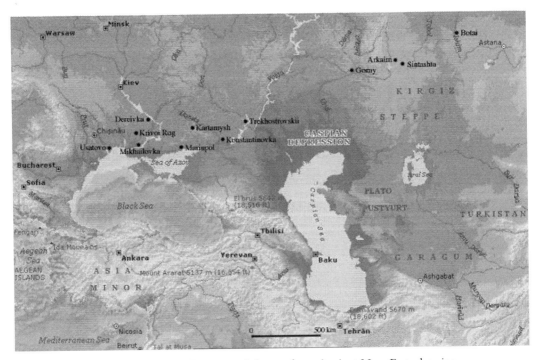

Figure 4.1. Western Eurasian Steppes and the northern Ancient Near East, showing approximate locations of selected archaeological sites.

separation constituted at least one factor in the relatively later development of sustained contacts between the Bronze Age steppe cultures and their neighbors practicing oasis irrigation agriculture east of the Caspian.

A series of consistent palynological studies have demonstrated that the forest-steppe and steppe belt of western Eurasia fluctuated markedly during Holocene times essentially between more humid and more arid phases (Kremenetski 2003). Although it is not always possible to distinguish anthropogenic changes from natural climatic shifts, the forest-steppe and, even more, steppe zones are marginal environments for the pursuit of productive agricultural and herding economies, and even relatively minor changes in precipitation patterns can have disproportionately large cultural effects.

Several large rivers that flow north to south into the Black and Caspian Seas bisect the Eurasian steppe west of the Urals; crossing this latter divide and east of the Ural basin, the major rivers of western Kazakhstan and Siberia then run south to north emptying into the Arctic Ocean. The climate generally becomes harsher and more continental as one proceeds west to east, and this pattern becomes particularly more noticeable and pronounced east of the Dnieper River of Central Ukraine, this river long functioning as almost a natural frontier dividing more agriculturally based societies to the west from more herding-based societies to the east.

This harsh continental climate affects cultural developments in at least two obvious ways: 1) the growing season for spring or early summer sown crops gets progressively shorter as one moves west to east, the availability of water also being a critical factor that varied during the Holocene; the relatively short growing season and limited supply of water effectively precluded the accumulation of large food surpluses characteristic of sedentary societies farther south; and 2) the severe winter also becomes progressively harsher with a deeper snow cover as one moves west to east, meaning that crops and/or fodder for animals needed to be stored or somehow procured during the long winter. Transport theoretically was less affected because major rivers, such as the Volga, and even the extremely shallow Sea of Azov freeze during the winter, thus making it possible to cross them without difficulty.

Most reconstructions of Bronze Age life on the Eurasian steppes have focused on the herding of livestock and the development of more mobile economies, as documented by the appearance of wheeled transport and ultimately horse riding. Animal herding and intensive gathering/cultivation typically constitute complementary activities; that is, theoretically one would expect to find a continuum of herding and collecting/agricultural practices that vary from period to period and area to area depending on technological and cultural developments and fluctuations in climatic and environmental conditions (cf. Bunyatyan 1997; 2003). What is surprising, therefore, is the lack of empirical evidence supporting the cultivation of domesticated cereals throughout nearly the entire duration of the Bronze Age (cf. Lebedeva 2005 and later discussion). A brief consideration of the historical development of steppe, largely "kurgan archaeology" reveals how our understanding of Bronze Age life on the steppes has changed with the accumulation of archaeological data and with the use of more nuanced and historically appropriate interpretive models.

ARCHAEOLOGY ON THE WESTERN EURASIAN STEPPES – A SHORT SKETCH OF THE RECOGNITION OF CULTURAL DIVERSITY AND ITS RELATIVE PERIODIZATION

In early 1901 Countess P.S. Uvarova invited V.A. Gorodtsov to investigate the relationship between the anthropomorphic carved *babi* stones and the raised barrows or kurgans scattered across the south Russian and Ukrainian steppes. This commission led to four months of intensive field investigations in the Kharkov province of eastern Ukraine in the northern Donets basin during which time Gorodstov surveyed and investigated several small Neolithic sites and excavated 299 burials from 107 kurgans, 264 of which he dated to the Bronze Age (Safonov 2001: 12). He published the detailed account of his work in 1905, presenting the basic typological and chronological sequential classification of kurgan burials – Pit Grave (*Yamnaya*), Catacomb (*Katakombnaya*), and Timber Grave (*Srubnaya*) – that is still used and accepted today. He recorded

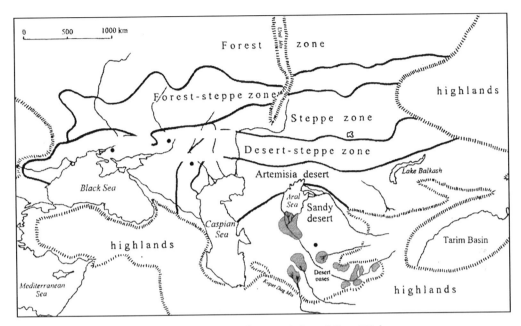

Figure 4.2. Central Eurasian Environmental Zones (adapted from Hiebert 2000: 52, fig. 14).

the type of tomb construction, the position and orientation of the skeleton, the stratigraphic position of burials within the kurgan, distinguishing particularly the initial interment from subsequent burials, and the accompanying grave goods of each burial.

For his time, Gorodtsov was a pioneer of archaeological methods in Russian and, indeed, world archaeology (Merpert 2001; Bochkarev 2001). His typological classificatory approach and focus on mortuary evidence continued to dominate steppe archaeology throughout the twentieth century, leading to the ever-finer chronological and regional classification of mortuary remains, and his use of the archaeological culture concept remains the basic model for distinguishing and explaining material assemblages. It is impossible to overemphasize his continuing influence in steppe archaeology. In short, while Gorodtsov's basic framework is still accepted, the process of developments on the steppes have been both extended chronologically into earlier Neolithic and Chalcolithic times and shown to exhibit considerable regional diversity, consisting of the coexistence of distinct "cultures" or "cultural-historical communities" in different areas at different times (e.g., the Sabatinovka and Timber Grave complexes at the beginning of the second half of the second millennium BC).

Although Gorodtsov's overarching model is maintained, the documentation of greater cultural diversity has not led to a universally agreed-on consensus as to the numbers (and even names) of Bronze Age archaeological cultures on the Eurasian steppes; often the same "culture" is referred to by different names by different scholars (cf. Gei 1999), the end result being a bewilderingly complex proliferation of archaeological cultures that we have already commented on in Section IV of Chapter 1. Part of the problem is intrinsic to the nature of the evidence: the lack of sharply defined differences among these cultures. E.N. Chernykh has emphasized the basic problem:

> There is no doubt that this lack of definition in the cultures and the indistinctness of their external manifestations was caused by the mobile way of life of the steppe peoples, which made contacts far easier. The constant exchange of people, things, and ideas was the most important feature of the steppe cultures. Cultures and the boundaries between separate groups seem to shade into one another.... It is for this reason that it is so difficult for archaeologists to distinguish individual cultures, draw clear boundaries between them, and ascribe individual sites to particular cultures. (Chernykh 1992: 101, 194)

The situation lacks a solution, and certainly no attempt will be made here to introduce greater clarity into the definition and periodization of these steppe cultures. Rather, we shall just trace broad Bronze Age developmental processes and how they have been interpreted in respect to the emergence of classic Eurasian mounted pastoral nomadism, a way of life so important and well documented for later historical periods.

With the accumulation of new evidence not only were new Bronze Age archaeological cultures or variants of larger cultural historical communities (*obshchnost'i*) defined, but also earlier Neolithic and Chalcolithic remains of food-producing economies on the Eurasian steppes, extending at least as far to the east as the southern Urals (Morgunova 1995). Documentation for the earlier occupation of the steppes led to a reinterpretation of the origin and development of the Early Bronze Pit Grave culture, beginning in the second half of the fourth millennium BC. In his classic study N.Ya. Merpert (1974: 153) defined nine regional variants of the Pit Grave culture, stretching from the Lower Prut to the Ural basin; the later discoveries subsequently made it clear that the entire steppe zone east of the Dnieper was not exclusively occupied by hunting and fishing groups, but more densely settled by intensive gatherers/incipient cultivators who also herded animals in the river valleys, a fact that seemingly better explained the emergence and apparently rapid spread of the Pit Grave culture from the South Russian steppes west towards the Balkans (cf. Merpert 1991: 36–38). Others have not been as impressed with the productive economies of these Neolithic steppe groups, noting the continuing high percentage of wild animals in the faunal assemblages, and suggesting a continued reliance on hunting, as well as fishing, and necessarily relatively small populations dispersed over broad areas (cf. Kuzmina's recent review 2003; and Rassamakin's assessment 1999: 133).

Chalcolithic developments on the steppes from the mid-sixth to the end of the fourth millennium are clearly formative for what occurred later during the Bronze Age but, unfortunately, are interpreted quite differently by different specialists, even including the definition and naming of specific archaeological cultures. The result, as Telegin (2002: 45) explicitly feared, is confusion, but the main issue is not one related to the name and number of archaeological cultures – some splitting, some lumping the archaeological evidence – but rather what were the basic processes of development for the emergence of the successive Bronze Age kurgan cultures. Such processes of development, in turn, are related to questions concerning whether the horse was domesticated and ridden on the Eurasian steppes during Chalcolithic times and whether successive migratory waves of mobile herders began moving east to west during this period (cf. Dergachev 2002 for a defense of Gimbutas's long enshrined invasion hypothesis).

The calibration of radiocarbon dates has, of course, extended the traditional periodization, leading to alternative "high" chronologies (cf. Appendix). Steppe materials can be related more confidently to remains from the Caucasus and southern Central Asia, and the latter, in turn, can be tied in to the radiocarbon *and*, in the best of cases, historical chronologies established for the Ancient Near East. Use of the high chronologies is justified on scientific grounds. Despite the protests of some scholars (e.g., Kuzmina 1994: 377), one cannot choose whether to calibrate or not calibrate the C14 dates. If such calibrated determinations change traditional chronological reconstructions, so be it. Greater objectivity is one of the theoretical virtues of the adoption of C14 analyses.

Nevertheless, certain problems typically emerge when calibrated dates are utilized. There are just so many millennia to fill with archaeological sequences. If one extends the chronologies of Chalcolithic and Early and Middle Bronze developments upwards, then either later blank periods emerge or the absolute dates for Late Bronze and Early Iron Age developments also must be raised and the blank periods somehow filled in. There are, however, typically chronological limits for so proceeding that are usually based on relatively firm ties to historical evidence. Thus, for example, when calibrated C14 dates suggested that the traditional Namazga sequence (see Chapter 5) in Central Asia needed to be revised upwards or extended, it became unclear as to how to conceptualize developments during the Namazga VI period or a period traditionally defined as the Late Bronze Age, which now apparently began during the last centuries of the third millennium BC and overlapped on the Bactrian and Margiana plains with the Namazga V or Middle Bronze period that had been defined for southern Turkmenistan (cf. Chapter 5). Subsequent work revealed that a complex sequence of successive stages could be established for a longer Late Bronze period, corresponding to the development and decline of the Bactria–Margiana Archaeological Complex (or BMAC), and that the beginnings of the Central Asian Early Iron period could also be extended towards the middle of the second millennium BC. In this case the gaps disappeared.

Such a solution is not yet apparent for the high, calibrated C14-based chronologies proposed for steppe and Caucasian materials. This problem is clear when one reviews the sequence of developments proposed by V.A. Trifonov (2001; Appendix), most of whose field investigations have been in the north-western Caucasus or at the interface between the world of the Caucasus and that of the steppes. Trifonov's periodization is very detailed and based on the most systematic and standardized lists of dates that he is continuing to compile. Although it is imperative that the essential works of Trifonov, Chernykh, and others to establish an absolute chronological framework continue, it should nevertheless be noted that these calibrated radiocarbon-based periodizations still must be seen as preliminary, raising almost as many problems as they solve.

Thus, for example, seemingly firm parallels to historically secure remains, such as those linking Trialeti-related "Middle Bronze" Transcaucasian materials to early second millennium Kultepe II in central Anatolia or even later remains from Mycenae (cf. Gogadze 1972; Rubinson 1977), must be rethought and/or the Middle Bronze Transcaucasian sequence must be extended into the first half of the second millennium BC. Similarly, the Sintashta horse-driven "chariots" and bronze weaponry suggest parallels farther west, with more securely dated remains from Mycenae and Late Bronze Age sites dating towards the middle of the second millennium BC, and yet the use of the still-limited number of calibrated radiocarbon dates for Sintashta and Sintashta-related sites places the beginnings of this culture at the end of the third/beginning of the second millennium BC (D.G. Zdanovich 2002: xvi; Kuzmina 2003: 222–225). How does one explain this discrepancy except by postulating a chronological horizon sloping fairly sharply east to west?

Thus, absolute chronological correlations on the steppes (and in the Caucasus and in southern Central Asia) are far from being resolved now despite an impressive compilation of calibrated dates. Eventually, one can reasonably hope for a more secure, more finely tuned periodization, probably along the lines proposed by Trifonov or Chernykh and his colleagues. At the moment, however, it seems fair to admit that the problems resolved by the application of calibrated radiocarbon dates generally refer to discrepancies of roughly 300–500 years or more (e.g., the traditional mid-third millennium date for Maikop compared with its now seemingly convincing beginning dates in the second quarter to the middle of the fourth millennium), although those inconsistencies that are less than roughly 200–300 years in duration remain uncertain, and relative comparisons based on even indirect ties to more historically grounded materials must be utilized alongside the "absolute" calibrated dates, if at all possible.

NEW PERSPECTIVES ON PRE–PIT GRAVE INTERCONNECTIONS ON THE WESTERN EURASIAN STEPPES

Scholars have long recognized Neolithic and Chalcolithic intercultural connections stretching from the Carpathian basin across the North Pontic steppe east at least as far as the Lower Volga and southern Urals area. As discussed earlier, the movement of metals west to east from the Balkans to the Lower Volga has been demonstrated analytically (e.g., Pernicka et al. 1997) and forms the basis for the concept of an early Carpatho-Balkan Metallurgical Province dating back to the sixth millennium BC (Chernykh 1992: 48–53; Fig. 2.7). Unambiguous connections can also be traced with other archaeological materials, including stone axe-hammers, mace heads, various stone, bone, and copper ornaments, and abstract and animal-headed stone scepters. What differs markedly is the interpretation of such material correspondences. One group of scholars, perhaps most notably and consistently articulated earlier by M. Gimbutas (1977, 1979, and 1994; Dergachev 2002), postulates on the basis of such evidence successive migrations east to west of early horse-riding nomads who destroy "Old Europe" or the agriculturally based Chalcolithic cultures of the Balkans and western Ukraine and who introduce large-scale stockbreeding and eventually the so-called kurgan cultures of the Bronze Age across this vast region.

Others, such as A. Häusler (1985, 1995, 1998) have adamantly rejected these reconstructions as fanciful and anachronistic, conjuring up much later historical phenomena to explain very different remains. Simplifying these starkly opposed interpretative models, one can say that the first group sees the basic direction of movements or cultural impulses even before the beginnings of the Bronze Age as proceeding east to west, whereas the latter group reverses the arrows and essentially interprets developments on the Pontic steppes and farther east as ultimately dependent on innovations that were associated with the sedentary agricultural societies first of southeastern Europe, including the Cucuteni-Tripol'ye culture, and the mixed agricultural/transhumant societies of the Caucasus.

Yu. Rassamakin (1994, 1999, and 2002) has recently documented this latter thesis in considerable detail in a series of articles that have appeared in English, and his views have been sharply criticized by proponents of the theory of waves of migrations from the east (e.g., Telegin et al. 2001; Telegin 2002; Dergachev 2002). Unfortunately, much of the debate has misleadingly – if tellingly – focused on Rassamakin's attempt to highlight newly defined archaeological cultures, such as a Skelya culture developing in the Don-Dnieper interfluve during the second half of the fifth millennium, as responsible for introducing cultural developments on the Pontic steppes. The debate, however, should not be concerned principally with the validity of these newly defined cultures, but rather with the mechanisms used to explain the remains of nonindigenous, exotic materials on the steppes. Rassamakin (1999:103) sees their presence as due to the development of a luxury trade or exchange of prestige goods associated with the emergence of local elites and the development of metallurgical production and the long-distance distribution of copper.

Emphasis is placed on the breakup of the Tripol'ye culture and the immediately subsequent development of oxen-driven wheeled transport, which is

also associated with this collapse and with the development of more mobile
economies and the emergence of the Maikop-Novosvobodnaya cultural community in the northwestern Caucasus. The sources of innovations are to
be found with agricultural, not pastoral, societies, even including developments in ritual monumental architecture, that is, the emergence of raised kurgans (Rassamakin 2002: 66). Most importantly, Rassamakin, Levine (1999),
and others (e.g., Benecke and von den Dreisch 2003) question the evidence
for Chalcolithic horse domestication and riding, a basic tenet, of course, of
the advocates of successive waves of migration from the east. Early so-called
"cheekpieces" from Dereivka are interpreted as tools and dismissed as evidence
for the domestication and riding of horses (cf. also Dietz 1992, 2003):

> It is quite clear the claimed presence of cheekpieces at Dereivka was dictated
> exclusively by the abundance of horse bones at the settlement. This pro-
> duced completely unwarranted inferences concerning riders, cheekpieces
> and battle-hammers, on which basis the image of Sredny Stog mounted
> warriors was created – horsemen who presented a military threat and
> destroyed the Tripol'ye settlements. . . . [rather] the horse represented one
> of the main species of animal used for meat, and was obtained through
> hunting. (Rassamakin 1999: 147)

For Rassamakin, there is even no convincing evidence for horse domestication
and riding during the subsequent Early Bronze Age or Pit Grave period (ibid.,
153, 155).

Before discussing the problem of horse domestication in more detail, let us
briefly consider how best to interpret the real parallels in material remains that
can be traced across the western Eurasian steppes during Chalcolithic times.
Do they constitute evidence for a system of luxury exchange linking nascent
elites or local leaders whose existence has long been recognized on the basis
of the differential distribution of mortuary goods (e.g., Makarenko 1933: 139)?
Or are such parallels better viewed as documenting the movements of peoples
east to west?

Consideration of the abstract and animal-headed stone scepters is instructive
in this respect, particularly because some scholars have used them to document
the early presence of domesticated horses. These so-called "scepters," which
were carved out of hard stones and hafted in some fashion, have long been
recognized in the archaeological literature and have stimulated considerable
discussion and debate despite the fact that their exact function is uncertain and
that the total number of such finds is remarkably small (only thirty-three being
listed in the recent catalogue of Govedarica and Kaiser [1996], despite their
initial discovery more than 100 years ago, hardly a robust corpus). Nevertheless, they are clearly related to one another, are distributed over a broad area
stretching from the Balkans to the Volga, and are found both in Chalcolithic
graves and settlements and as isolated finds (Figs. 4.3, 4.4, and 4.5).

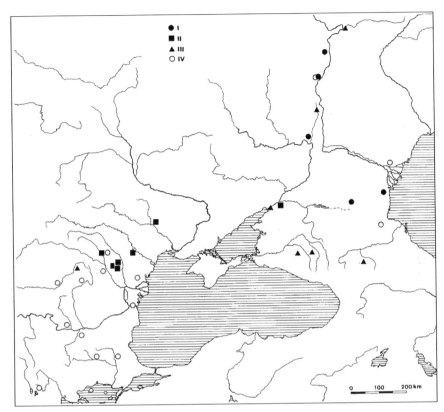

Figure 4.3. Distribution of Abstract Scepters (adapted from Govedarica and Kaiser 1996: 60, abb. 1); I – grave find; II – settlement find; III – isolated find; IV – distribution of zoomorphic scepters.

They can be divided into two basic types: oval or elliptically shaped abstract (i.e., nonrecognizable) forms and those that are clearly zoomorphic, depicting animals that in some instances are plausibly seen as horses (Fig. 4.5). What is their significance? Can they be used to document movements of early horse-riding nomads across the steppes from the Volga to the Danube? Such interpretations seem fanciful, not really supported by this evidence. The animals on the zoomorphic scepters are not depicted naturalistically and their identification as horses is often uncertain. Moreover, the zoomorphic scepters occur with greater frequency in the Balkans and western Ukraine than farther east, a pattern that is reversed for the abstract scepters. This distributional evidence alone seemingly contradicts their interpretation as evidence for migratory waves of horse-riding nomads east to west.

Occam's razor needs sharpening. A more parsimonious explanation views them as evidence for the very occasional exchange of luxury exotica and the gradual emergence of local elites who accumulated such symbolic goods as they gained power and prestige. The same pattern applies to the general

Figure 4.4. Distribution of Zoomorphic Scepters (adapted from Govedarica and Kaiser 1996: 61, abb. 2); I – grave find; II – settlement find; III – isolated find; IV – distribution of abstract scepters.

distribution of metals throughout the Carpatho-Balkan Metallurgical Province: their basic fall-off west to east from the metal-producing and metal-working areas of the Balkans to their more sporadic acquisition farther east. Rassamakin (1999: 102) refers to the recent discovery of two copper necklaces, a Varna-like gold baton, and copper bracelets, rings, and an awl from the Krivoi Rog cemetery west of the Dnieper in central Ukraine or on the western border of his newly defined Skelya culture (Figs. 4.6 and 4.7). Clearly, these finds bespeak relations with their more developed neighbors to the west in terms of both their acquisition and probably conscious emulation. His conclusion (1999: 112) is straightforward:

> The Early Eneolithic saw not warlike migrations of steppe peoples – a first kurgan wave – from the Volga or Caspian region, but rather the emergence of a mutually beneficial system of exchange between the steppe populations and the production centres of the agricultural world. . . . The steppe world now emerges as a distinct yet well-integrated part of the prestige-trade network that existed in Southeast Europe. (ibid., 112)

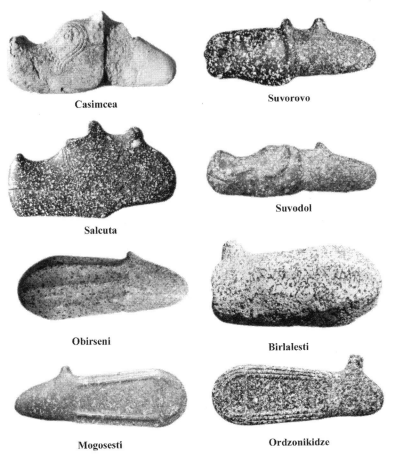

Figure 4.5. Zoomorphic and Abstract Scepters (adapted from Govedarica and Kaiser 1996: 96, abb. 21 and 22).

Many specifics of this postulated exchange are uncertain and/or remain archaeologically invisible. What did those steppe folks exchange for their copper beads and gold batons? That story needs to be told. Nevertheless, it is clear that there were connections across this vast area throughout the Chalcolithic period, and there is no reason anachronistically to postulate invasions of mythical mounted warriors from the East, particularly when hard evidence for the domestication and riding of horses during Chalcolithic or even Early Bronze times is at best ambiguous, a contentious subject to which we now turn.

HORSE DOMESTICATION AND THE EMERGENCE OF EURASIAN MOUNTED PASTORAL NOMADISM

Experts are sharply divided on when horses were first domesticated and first ridden and even theoretically on whether one can intensively herd horses

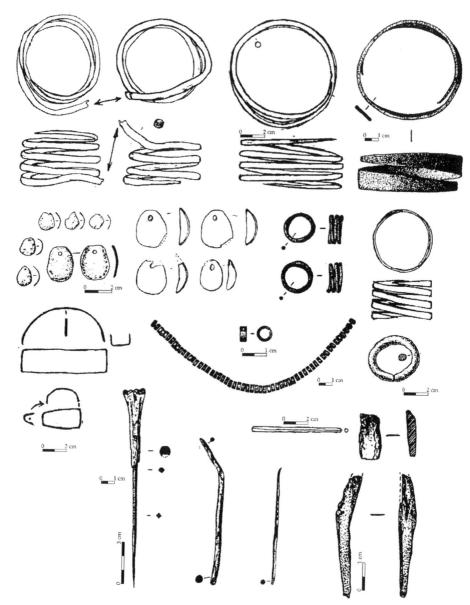

Figure 4.6. Copper ornaments from burials of the so-called Skelya culture (adapted from Rassamakin 1999: 82, fig. 3.15).

without riding them. The literature on this topic is vast and widely open to debate (cf. the contradictory articles in *Prehistoric Steppe Adaptation and the Horse* [Levine, Renfrew, and Boyle 2003]). We will not attempt to resolve these issues but only briefly review them in the light of our overall discussion of innovations and interconnections linking the Eurasian steppes with more agriculturally based societies to the west and south. Part of the problem relates

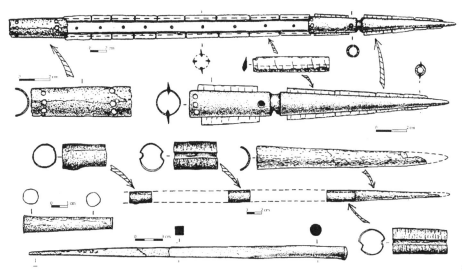

Figure 4.7. Ceremonial weapons and scepters of the so-called Skelya culture (adapted from Rassamakin 1999: 84, fig. 3.17).

to the difficulty in skeletally distinguishing wild from domestic horses. Given this analytical problem, conclusions as to whether the horse bones from a site come from domesticated or wild animals typically are based on indirect evidence or even theoretical considerations. Thus, Benecke and von den Dreisch (2003) review the equid remains from mid-fourth millennium Botai culture sites in western Kazakhstan as evidence for the intensive year-round hunting of wild horses. Their nonselective kill pattern, their age composition and subsequent replacement with domesticated sheep, goat, and cattle remains from comparative assemblages in central and northern Kazakhstan, and their lack of size reduction and of variability all suggest to Benecke and von den Dreisch that the horses at Botai culture sites were wild, the products of intensive and specialized hunting.

Olsen (2003) reviews this same evidence, emphasizing the presence of entire skeletons (which would have to have been hauled back from some distance to the site if hunted), their discovery in ritual contexts and in association with dog remains, and the presence of numerous worked horse mandibles that are interpreted as thong smoothers or tools meant ultimately to facilitate the control of horses. For her, the evidence for early horse domestication on these Botai culture sites is "compelling" (ibid., 101). She admits that most of the horse bones from these sites were products of the hunt, but uses this fact to explain away the lack of diagnostic changes recorded by Benecke and von den Dreisch; most of the horses were hunted – but by riders on horseback.

Anthony and Brown (1991, 2000, and 2003) have recorded significant beveling on the second lower premolars of horse teeth from Chalcolithic sites across the Eurasian steppes from Ukraine to Kazakhstan and view this evidence as conclusive proof that horses were bitted at this time, even probably initially controlled with organic bits and bridles that have not been preserved in the archaeological record. Other specialists view such beveling as a pathological condition that occurs naturally on horses with bad occlusion. Anthony and Brown (2003: 64–65) ironically observe that the presence of such beveling on Middle and Late Bronze horse teeth found with cheekpieces is considered as evidence for bitting, whereas the beveling on Chalcolithic horse remains found without such cheekpieces is categorically dismissed as too early.

Efforts to record pathological damage to the thoracic vertebrae of horses as evidence for riding (see Levine 1999) may ultimately help resolve these issues, though currently such work must be considered at a preliminary stage still lacking definitive results. Similarly, one could envision a future research project that would examine systematically the femora from human skeletons in Chalcolithic to Iron Age burials for bowing and other distortions and stress associated with habitual riding, such as seen recently in a Bronze Age female burial in southeastern Kazakhstan (M. Frachetti, personal communication). One potential problem with both these latter studies will be the interpretation of negative evidence: does the lack of vertebrate pathologies in horses or femoral bowing in humans conclusively demonstrate that horses were not ridden? It is too early to know, but regardless such studies should be conducted and may help ultimately resolve these contentious issues.

There is another way to view this issue: to separate the question of origins from that of use and significance. Horses, like donkeys and camels, can be used as pack animals; they can be hitched to wagons, ploughs, or other devices to utilize effectively their remarkable speed and power (Fig. 4.8); and they can be ridden. Perhaps, horses were initially "domesticated" on the Ukrainian steppes in the fifth millennium or in western Kazakhstan by the mid-fourth millennium BC, but, if so, the effects of such horse domestication were not felt throughout the greater Ancient Near East and Europe until much later, probably not initially until the late third millennium BC. The use of horses probably did not constitute a decisive factor in transportation, mobility, and did not transform draft and military activities until later in the second millennium, if not during Early Iron Age times. Christopher Columbus discovered America, not Leif Eriksson, despite the latter's presence on Vinland in northeastern North America four centuries before Columbus. There is no question that some of the Chalcolithic inhabitants of the Eurasian steppes from eastern Ukraine to western Kazakhstan intensively hunted horses from at least the fifth millennium. In order to do this more efficiently, some may have ridden early tamed or "domesticated" horses. Evidence for such activity is ambiguous, but what is clear is that there were no immediate major social consequences from such practices; no mounted Chalcolithic warriors wreaking havoc on their sedentary neighbors as they pressed westwards and southwards to destroy "Old Europe," or eastwards and southwards to carry their

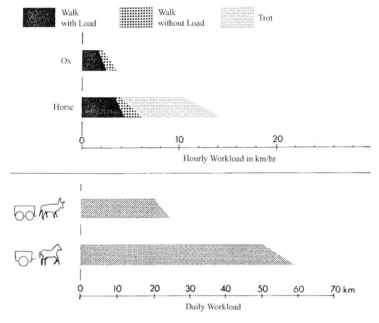

Figure 4.8. Horse/Ox Comparison in terms of draft capacity and speed (adapted from Bökönyi 1991: 553, abb. 4).

Aryan heritage ultimately into northern India and to the western border of China.

Cattle were domesticated and oxen probably harnessed to sledges and then solid-wheeled wagons long before horses were so utilized, and, on the basis of the Egyptian and western Asian evidence, so were donkeys and the donkey/onager hybrid or *kunga*; in fact, the first Ur III or end-of-the-third-millennium cuneiform reference to horses refers to them as "asses of the mountains" (Oates 2003: 117). Whereas horses as draft animals are considerably superior to cattle or oxen, particularly in the area they can cover in a given unit of time (Fig. 4.8), unequivocal evidence for their use as such occurs later and postdates the harnessing of oxen, donkeys, donkey/onager hybrids, and even possibly mules and Bactrian camels.

A. Sherratt (2003) imaginatively hypothesizes that horses were initially domesticated to produce mules to drive wagons laden with metals and other trade goods and that their domestication was intimately linked to Childe's second Urban Revolution and may have first occurred off the steppes proper in the Caucasus or on the greater Near Eastern periphery. His "interactionist" model remains speculative and considers nearly every innovation, including the appearance of oxen-driven ploughs, as developing initially on the surplus temple estate economies in the Mesopotamian heartland, but he does nicely show that the harnessing of oxen to wheeled transport precedes evidence for the practical utilization of horse power and sees the latter as ultimately linked to the harnessing of donkeys and other equid hybrids as part of the same interrelated process.

In other words, there is something "out of sync" with an early Chalcolithic domestication of the horse on the Eurasian steppes. If this had happened as early as Anthony and others have argued, its effects should have been more visible throughout the increasingly interconnected late prehistoric/early historic greater Eurasian world, and this demonstrably is not the case (cf. discussion in concluding chapter).

Dietz (1992, 2003) has convincingly demonstrated that none of the claimed Chalcolithic cheekpieces are likely to have functioned as bridle elements. Bitless bridles with rigid nosebands are likely to have preceded the complicated bitted bridles that were later introduced, probably during the late Early and Middle Bronze Age, and that became standardized only during Late Bronze times. Because harnessing preceded riding, it is likely that horses were initially used for draft purposes and for pulling wagons and were only later regularly ridden:

> Without any doubt, horseback riding requires less equipment than does driving. . . . On the other hand horseback riding, especially wild horses, requires specific knowledge of equine behavior. . . . Moving slowly, the horse working as a beast of burden or hitched to a heavy vehicle was easy to lead. *Knowledge and equipment used for driving or guidance developed from the tradition of hitching cattle.* (Deetz 2003: 197, italics added)

In other words, there is a logical connection or technological relationship between the harnessing initially of cattle and then later of equids and the Bactrian camel.

The pictorial representations from greater Mesopotamia, which depict equids – donkeys, the donkey-onager hybrid, and possibly mules and horses – harnessed to wheeled vehicles, become relatively abundant only from the middle of the third millennium BC on, and the occasional depictions of horses actually being ridden begin to appear subsequently in Akkadian and post-Akkadian times. They show riders precariously perched on the backs of the equids trying to control the animals with reins attached to nose rings, devices more appropriately suited to harnessing cattle (cf. Oates 2003: 116–119). Equids and the Bactrian camel are similar in that they have long necks and cannot have the yoke set immediately above the shoulders in the same fashion as oxen so that it is possible, if not likely, that the harnessing of equids and camels was a technologically interrelated development.

The importance of Bactrian camels as draft and pack animals also should not be overlooked in discussions on the initial control and utilization of horses. Clay models of Bactrian camels attached to wagons have been found in Early Bronze or Namazga IV levels (i.e., early to mid-third millennium BC) at Altyn-depe in southern Turkmenistan (Masson and Sarianidi 1972: 109, pl. 36), and camel skeletal remains have been found on a series of third millennium and even earlier sites in southern Central Asia and in eastern Iran (Compagnoni and Tosi 1978). It is possible that Bactrian camels were initially domesticated much earlier in Neolithic times farther east in Xinjiang and Mongolia (Potts 2004.) and diffused north onto the western Eurasian steppes only after their integration into the settled agricultural communities in southern Turkmenistan, though this process cannot yet be precisely traced and dated.

One also should remember the central importance of Bactrian camels (and later the Bactrian-dromedary hybrid) in the adaptation of historically documented mounted pastoral nomads to life on the Eurasian steppes. It is unclear exactly when camels started to assume this critical role, but it may not have been until the real emergence of mounted pastoral nomadism – during the Iron Age; camel remains are extremely rare in the Sintashta-related fortified settlements in the so-called "Country of Towns," and their presence there in the early second millennium BC is seen as evidence for contact with areas farther south, though not yet with actual camel breeding in the southern trans-Urals at that time (Gayduchenko 2002: 414).

In a famous study R.W. Bulliet (1975) documented how the use of camels as pack animals replaced wheeled vehicles throughout most of the Middle East during the third to sixth centuries AD, and how the latter largely disappeared throughout this region until modern times. Can one detect a similar inverse relationship on the steppes at the end of the Bronze Age? Unlike in the Middle East, wheeled vehicles never totally disappear on the steppes; they remain part of the historically and ethnographically documented material culture of classic mounted steppe nomads. But does their significance diminish as the herders become mounted nomads, riding horses and, at some point, keeping camels as pack animals? Utilizing both Neo-Assyrian cuneiform sources and archaeological evidence, D.T. Potts (2004) recently has suggested that Bactrian camels were crossed with dromedaries to produce the stronger and more useful first-generation hybrid by the end of the second and beginning of the first millennia BC. If correct, such a change would have revolutionized systems of transport across the steppe (and the Iranian plateau), resulting in practices similar to those well documented in later historical and ethnographic sources.

But again, such a change occurs at the end of the Bronze and beginning of the Iron Age and, presumably, was not in place or adopted on a large scale during earlier times. Wheeled vehicles seem to lose their ritual social significance during the later Bronze Age; that is, they are not found with such regularity in Late Bronze burials, as in Early and, particularly, Middle Bronze times. Why? Is it no longer so prestigious to own an oxen-driven cart when more social value and importance is attached to riding horses? With the advent of iron, new, widely distributed sources of ores were exploited that still needed to be exchanged, but they were moved now by more mobile systems of transportation in which horses and probably Bactrian and/or hybrid camels may have played critical roles.

The initial development of more mobile herding economies and the opening up of the steppe beyond the confines of narrow river valleys involved two distinct steps: the first was associated with the introduction of heavy oxen-driven wheeled carts and wagons, a process that certainly was underway by the end of the fourth millennium BC; and the second, which may have occurred during the second half of the third millennium BC, was associated with the possible riding and harnessing of horses to lighter vehicles, developments that greatly enhanced the mobility of the herders occupying the steppes from the trans-Ural region in the east to the Danube basin in the west. This latter process of horse harnessing and possible riding is first convincingly attested archaeologically across this area by the appearance of disk-shaped cheekpieces in the east and then slightly later rod-shaped cheekpieces farther west, beginning in late Middle Bronze Age times (Boroffka 1998; Teufer 1999; Fig. 4.9).

As based on the density of such finds, this development may have begun in the Don–Volga forest-steppe zone (Priakhin and Besedin 1999: 40), though this problem of origins may prove as insoluble as that previously discussed for the development of wheeled vehicles. Once developed, the technology may have spread so rapidly that its precise origins will be incapable of archaeological determination, but again what is more significant is that this innovation was almost immediately adopted across the western Eurasian steppes and then rapidly diffused to the west, south, and east.

BRONZE AGE LIFE ON THE STEPPES: PIT GRAVES TO TIMBER GRAVES – MAJOR PATTERNS OF DEVELOPMENT AND CHANGES IN WAYS OF LIFE

Ethnologists have recorded a range of herding practices from mixed agricultural/pastoral economies to various forms of transhumance to so-called pure (and consequently "poor," according to O. Lattimore) nomadism where the nomadic group largely, if not exclusively, subsists totally on its pastoral products. Many question the reality of this last form of nomadism or consider it very exceptional, limited to specific historical and geographical conditions. Was such a "pure" form of nomadism present in Pit Grave times during the latter fourth and third millennia BC when the archaeological remains consist principally of raised kurgans or mortuary remains, not settlements, and the evidence for agriculture in the form of charred palaeobotanical remains or, less directly, agricultural implements is scarce to nonexistent? Can one trace a process of gradual sedentarization or movement toward a greater territorial differentiation between collecting/agriculture and stock-breeding activities from Pit Grave to Timber Grave/Sabatinovka culture times?

The general pattern is clear. Earlier Chalcolithic settlements and typically flat cemeteries disappear across the steppes, and, from the beginnings of the Bronze Age and well into much later historical periods, the most common

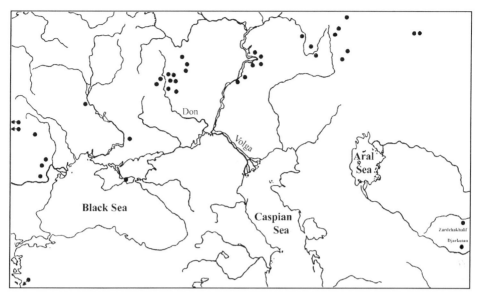

Figure 4.9. Distribution of disk-shaped cheekpieces (adapted from Teufer 1999: 70, abb. 1).

archaeological sites on the steppes are raised barrows or kurgans, tens of thousands of which have been excavated since the time of Gorodtsov. It should be noted also that occasional pre–Pit Grave Chalcolithic kurgans have been excavated in eastern Ukraine and southern Russia at least as far east as the Lower Volga basin, some of these even being catacomb-shaped and containing exotic trade goods, like long obsidian blades possibly from the Caucasus (e.g., the Aksai, Mukhin II, kurgan 5 burial near Rostov [Bespalyi 2002; Fig. 4.10]). Very few settlements have been recorded during Pit Grave times, though this is disputed – at least for Kalmykia and may in part be due to the dispersed and temporary nature of the Pit Grave settlements (cf. Otchir-Gorieva 2002 and later discussion).

   This absence is traditionally explained as due to a reliance on herding or on an incipient form of pastoral nomadism, a shift attributed to increased aridity, the development of dairy farming, and the use of wheeled transport, providing greater mobility and yearly exploitation of greater areas at this time. Grain impressions of millet, wheat, and barley on Pit Grave ceramics are scarce but do occur, and occasionally implements, like grinding stones and horn mattocks, have been found in Pit Grave kurgans that presumably were used in some form of agricultural activity. Pit Grave peoples supposedly were not exclusively herders, but are supposed to have engaged in "sporadic agriculture," entire communities moving in yearly cycles, principally along river valleys avoiding the so-called open steppe (Bunyatyan 2003: 276; for a critical evaluation of the concept of the "open steppe," see Otchir-Gorieva 2002: 122–123).

Subsequently, an ever-increasing number of settlements are recorded from Catacomb through Timber Grave/Sabatinovka times, and these become increasingly larger and presumably permanent by the Late Bronze Age. Burials contain more grave goods, and appear richer by comparison with Pit Grave remains, though, in general, Bronze Age evidence on the steppes for the accumulation of wealth and social differentiation is meager relative to what is documented in the Caucasus or in other areas where agriculture dominated farther south, particularly during Late Early and Middle Bronze times, and, of course, Bronze Age steppe grave goods cannot compare with the riches recovered from later "royal" Scythian or Sarmatian burials on the steppes. Attempts (e.g., Pustovalov 1994) to see the emergence of a nobility and separate classes or castes and proto-state formations as early as Catacomb Middle Bronze times are not convincing, though it must also be admitted that the nature of the archaeological evidence with its primary focus on mortuary remains hinders the reconstruction of social organization, a problem that becomes more acute during Late Bronze times when there is evidence for greater specialization and for the near industrial-scale extraction of metal ores. How such extraction and production was organized and directed remains unclear (see later discussion).

The steppes east of the Dnieper at the end of the third/beginning of the second millennium BC can be divided into several distinct cultural communities: 1) the multi-cordoned ware culture (or *KMK: kul'tura mnogovalikovoi keramiki*) that developed out of earlier regional variants of the Catacomb culture; 2) the Abashevo community farther east in the forest-steppe zone of the Middle Don and the Don-Volga interfluve; 3) the Potapovka culture along the Middle Volga and along its left bank; and 4) the Sintashta/Arkaim (or Sintashta/Arkaim/Petrovka) community east of the southern Urals.

Two hundred or more settlements of the KMK have been documented, some of them with cultural deposits approximately 1 m. thick (e.g., Babino III, see *Arkheologiya Ukrainskoi SSR.* 1985: 451), and nearly two dozen planned fortified settlements, similar to Arkaim and Sintashta, are dispersed evenly and define a Middle Bronze "Country of Towns" (or "Cities" – in Russian *gorodov*) that stretches over a 400 × 150 km. area along the eastern slopes of the southern Urals (Zdanovich 1997: 59; 1999; Figs. 4.11) or essentially along the watershed between the left bank tributaries of the Ural River, which flows through Orenburg to the Caspian, and the left bank tributaries of the Tobol River, which joins the Irtysh and Ob Rivers before ultimately flowing north to the Arctic Ocean. The Abashevo and Potapovka formations are known principally from mortuary remains, though some settlements (e.g., the Shilovskoe settlement on the Don) also have been documented. Notably, disk-shaped studded antler and bone cheekpieces have been found in all these communities and attest to the harnessing, if not riding, of horses at this time across a broad interconnected area of the western Eurasian steppes.

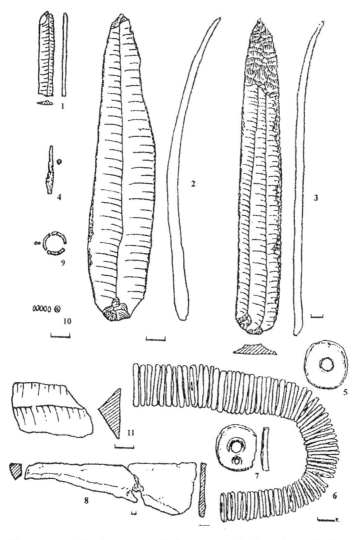

Figure 4.10. Exotic grave goods from catacomb-shaped pre–Pit Grave
kurgan near Rostov: Aksai Mukhin II, kurgan 5, burial 9 (adapted from Bespalyi 2002:
fig. 59); 1,2, 11 – flint; 3 – obsidian; 4, 9, 10, copper; 5–7 – shell; 8 – bone.

The well-known materials from Sintashta are particularly informative in
this respect. A planned, protected, and possibly fortified settlement was partially uncovered in salvage excavations at Sintashta during the 1970s and 1980s
together with several flat cemetery areas and raised barrows or kurgans that contained collective and individual burials, as well as what has been reconstructed
as an attached wooden beamed nine-tiered pyramidal "temple-sanctuary,"
24 m. in diameter at its top. Reasonably complete descriptions of these discoveries are available in English, including the resume in the site report (cf.
Gening, Zdanovich, and Gening 1992; also Anthony and Vinogradov 1995;

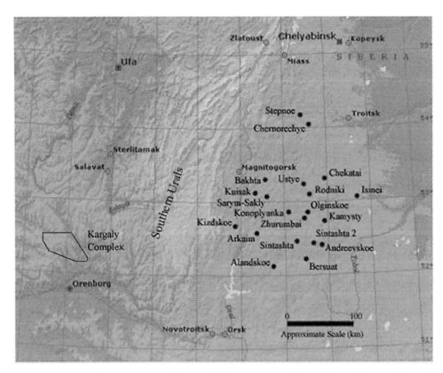

Figure 4.11a. The "Country of Towns" (*Strana Gorodov*) with southern Urals and Kargaly Complex shown (adapted from Zdanovich and Batanina 2002: 122, fig. 1).

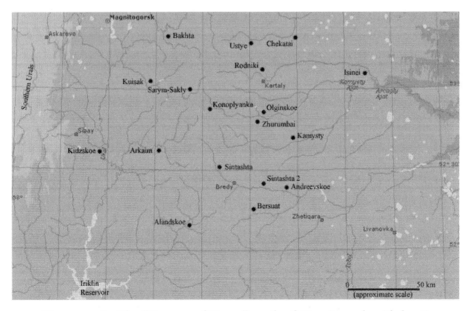

Figure 4.11b. The "Country of Towns" south of Magnitogorsk with location on tributaries of the Ural and Tobol rivers.

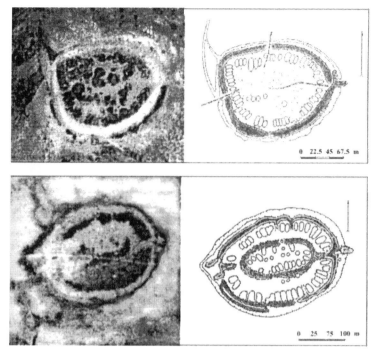

Figure 4.12. Oval Settlements of the "Country of Towns" (adapted from Zdanovich and Batanina 2002: 127, fig. 3).

Lamberg-Karlovsky 2002: 68; and Jones-Bley and Zdanovich 2002). Our discussion here will be more general.

The settlement was only partially preserved and excavated. Twenty-four trapezoidal rooms/dwellings (90–140 sq. m. in area) were arranged, "like the spokes in a wheel" (Gening et al. 1992: 378). They formed a circle roughly 136–140 m. in diameter with their back walls abutting the outer "fortification" wall and sharing walls with the adjacent dwellings on either side. The remains of an additional six dwellings were partially uncovered and seemed to form part of a comparably laid out inner circle of dwellings. Roughly similarly laid out concentric circles of twenty-nine trapezoidal shaped dwellings were excavated subsequently at the neighboring site of Arkaim. The pattern of inner and outer rings or groups of dwellings abutting the inner and outer walls can be considered a characteristic architectural feature of the "Country of Towns," though the sites themselves may be circular, oval, or rectangular in plan (Zdanovich and Batanina 2002; Figs. 4.12 and 4.13).

The Sintashta settlement was destroyed by fire, though this is seen as the result of deliberate, possibly ritual burning, and not violent conquest. Such arson is not unique to the "Country of Towns"; the gigantic Tripol'ye settlements, for example, are thought to have been similarly burnt and abandoned. Most of the dwellings contain storage pits, hearths, and facilities interpreted as metal

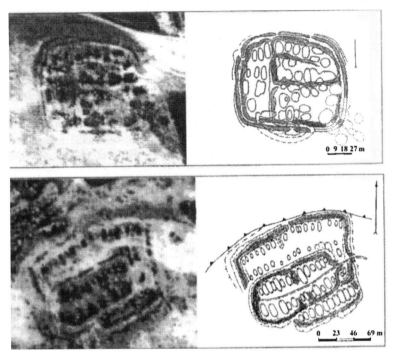

Figure 4.13. Rectangular Settlements of the "Country of Towns" (adapted from Zdanovich and Batanina 2002: 134, fig. 5).

furnaces. Evidence for metal working is pervasive, and the wealth of metal objects, particularly bronze weapons but also ornaments, including gold-leafed hair or temple rings, silver chest plates, and bronze bracelets from the burials at Sintashta is impressive, whereas the ceramic corpus from these same burials (roughly 100 vessels recovered from 40 graves, containing 60–65 burials at the large flat SM cemetery) is relatively poor.

Materials recovered from the planned settlements are less striking. Only 9000 sherds from roughly 300 vessels, for example, were recovered at Arkaim, despite excavating roughly 40% of the entire planned settlement (Zdanovich 1997: 51); by comparison, a single collective catacomb tomb from Velikent in the northeastern Caucasus contained more than 500 complete vessels. The relative paucity of the archaeological materials from Arkaim is also striking when one compares its total remains, including evidence for metal working, with those from the later, specialized Late Bronze metal-producing settlement of Gorny near Orenburg (Chernykh 2002c: 10–11); roughly ten times the number of sherds and 200 times the number of animal bones were recovered from an excavated area nearly ten times smaller at Gorny. Such figures should be kept in mind when one tries to assess the significance of the "Country of Towns" settlements and to reconstruct its social organization.

Figure 4.14. Horse Skull with Studded Disk-Shaped Cheekpiece, Sintashta Burial 11 (adapted from Gening et al. 1992: fig. 22).

Sintashta is most famous for the discovery of the remains of light, two-wheeled (spoked) "battle chariots" in five graves along with a series of disk-shaped studded cheekpieces, two of which are shown *in situ* resting on the sides of a horse skull (SM, burial 11, Gening et al. 1992: 157, illus. 74 and fig. 22; Fig. 4.14). Today, the remains of twenty-one such "chariots" have been recovered from nine cemeteries of the Sintashta-Arkaim culture and the slightly later Petrovka culture on the steppes between the Ural and Ishim rivers (Anthony n.d.). Partial remains, consisting of the heads, jaws, and feet, and complete animal skeletons of horses, cattle, rams, and dogs were sacrificed and placed in the pits or in coverings above the burial chambers. The quantity of such sacrifices varied substantially. In one case six horse skeletons were recovered, and no sacrifices were found in the burials of young girls. Both adult male and female burials contained grave goods, such as a few ceramic vessels, and bronze knives, adzes, and awls, and male burials are said to have frequently contained bronze and flint arrowheads.

The scale of some of the burials and presumably accompanying funeral feasts is impressive. The Sacrificial Complex 1 at the Sintashta SM cemetery contained the skulls and leg bones of six horses, four cattle, and two rams, laid in two rows around a single overturned vessel. Anthony (n.d.) estimates that this single sacrifice could have provided roughly 2700 kg of meat, or enough to provide nearly a kilogram of meat to 3000 participants in the funeral feast (3000 being the number of man-days of labor estimated to build the so-called Bol'shoi Kurgan situated slightly to the north of this complex). Given the size of the Sintashta settlement, such a feast must have drawn its participants from neighboring communities settled elsewhere in the "Country of Towns." Some differential accumulation of wealth is also documented in the burial goods. Burial 7 from the small flat cemetery SII, for example, was considered particularly rich; the male was buried with a quiver containing bronze and flint arrowheads, a bronze spearhead, and a stone mace head.

Other evidence is more ambiguous or open to alternative, more skeptical and restrained evaluation. Some consider the excavated remains insufficient to divide the population into distinct social strata (cf. Epimakov 2002), whereas others (e.g., Bockharev 1995a: 23) have interpreted the burials with chariots as documenting the existence of a chiefly or higher-ranked elite, a possibly lineage-based collective, leading stratum in the society. The uniform architecture of the dwellings and the lack of craft specialization (every unit showing some evidence of metal working) suggests otherwise: a relatively homogeneous or undifferentiated population. It simply is unclear how the settlements were planned and constructed or, more fundamentally, what basic functions they served beyond simple habitation and the working of metals.

There have been no lack of hypotheses, however (cf. the articles in Jones-Bley and Zdanovich 2002), and the undoubted significance of these discoveries has been sensationalized in part because they are seen as directly ancestral to the formation of the Andronovo cultural community, a Late Bronze phenomenon that seemingly spreads far to the south and east. As this culture underlies the beginning of the so-called Andronovo "cultural-historical community" of the Late Bronze Age, it is also associated ultimately, according to many specialists, with the spread of the Indo-Aryans (Kuzmina 1994), or movements that are considered important for understanding cultural processes in the Iron Age, including the formation of the first nomadic empires. From this perspective, Sintashta and Arkaim comprise part of the original Aryan "homeland," a connection that has been consciously promoted and that has turned the site of Arkaim at least into a center for tourism and pilgrimage (cf. G.B Zdanovich 1995; D.G. Zdanovich 1995; and, more critically, Shnirelman 1998, 1999). We will return to this quest for ethnic/linguistic identification later (at the end of Chapter 5), but now we must try to disentangle the archaeological significance from the rhetorical hyperbole.

The settlements show evidence of planning with closed double walls, built from blocks of pressed clay, wooden frames, and stone, and are surrounded by outer ditches. The encircled areas range in size from 0.6 to 3 ha. and contain projections and other features that safeguard passage into and out of the settlements. Their small size, however, undercuts the concept of a "Country of Towns" (or even worse, "Cities"). They are more accurately described as villages, probably containing several hundred inhabitants at most. As we have seen, there is substantial evidence at the Sintashta-Arkaim sites for local metal working in the form of metal slag, crucibles, molds, and numerous bronze artifacts,

though these cannot compare in quantity with those recovered from the principally later specialized copper ore extracting settlement at Gorny on the other
side of the Urals. The mortuary remains, particularly the animal sacrifices, are
indeed lavish, suggesting some degree of social complexity and the ability to
organize and feed significant numbers of people. Neo-evolutionary formula-
tions, such as chiefdoms – individual or collective – may prove enlightening or
helpful, but they seemingly do not correspond with the overall, relatively even
distribution of the burial goods or the architectural uniformity of the settlements. The concept of some form of military democracy capable of coalescing
into a more extensive confederation seems at least as appropriate.

Horse-harnessing to light two-wheeled carts with spoked wheels is unequivocally attested, and such finds suggest qualitative, if not revolutionary, advances
in transportation and probably warfare. As reconstructed, the carriages on these
vehicles are small, either square or rectangular in shape roughly 1 to 1. 3 m
wide by 1 to 1.9 m long (Gening et al. 1992: 166–168; 204–206; 215–216),
though Anthony (n.d.) reports that nine "chariots" (four from Sintashta) have
now been excavated that extend at least 1.5 m. in track width (overlapping the
dimensions of later Egyptian war chariots) and could have carried both driver
and armed javelin-hurling warrior.

Are these two-wheeled horse-driven carts, then, battle chariots? If so, they
should not conjure up the image of Ben-Hur racing in Rome or an Assyrian
king hunting animals on his royal preserves. Some appear to have been too
small to have been used as effective weapons of war. The larger ones could
have accommodated both driver and warrior, but the quarters still would have
been somewhat cramped. The abundance of arrowheads found in the graves
at Sintashta suggests the increased importance of archery at this time. Individuals or materials could be transported quickly over longer distances using
such carts/"chariots," and their ownership and use probably conveyed social
prestige. Certainly, the numerous weapons (Figs. 4.15 and 4.16), such as socketed spearheads, axes with secondary blades on projecting butts, tanged knives,
stone mace heads, flint and bronze arrowheads, and longer projectile, possibly
javelin, points (4–10 cm. in length) are eminently functional, not just prestige ceremonial items, and imply increased militarism, a trend that continues
throughout the Late Bronze into the Iron Age and is not only characteristic
of the steppes, but also of the Near East. It should also be noted that bronze
fishhooks and bent sickle-like knives are also found on the settlements, the
latter of which indirectly attest to the harvesting or intense collecting of plants
or cereals (cf. later discussion).

Besides the horse sacrifices and the horse-driven wheeled carts, the most
striking discoveries were the planned settlements themselves. Such early sym-
metrical architecture had not previously been recorded on the steppes and, consequently, was unexpected, creating the initial sensation. Do the circular walls
enclosing these settlements constitute monumental architecture, fortifications

Figure 4.15. Bronze knives, axes, and spearheads from Sintashta (adapted from Gening et al. 1992: 195, fig. 100).

with buttresses and towers, surrounded by moats? Possibly, but it helps to have an overly active imagination. Such fortifications certainly seem quite flimsy and markedly less monumental than the impregnable, inaccessible Late Bronze citadels with cyclopean stone architecture that are found throughout Transcaucasia from at least the mid–second millennium BC to the advent of the Urartian Iron Age kingdom (Smith 2003; Badalyan, Smith, and Avetisyan 2003; Litscheli 2001: 64–65).

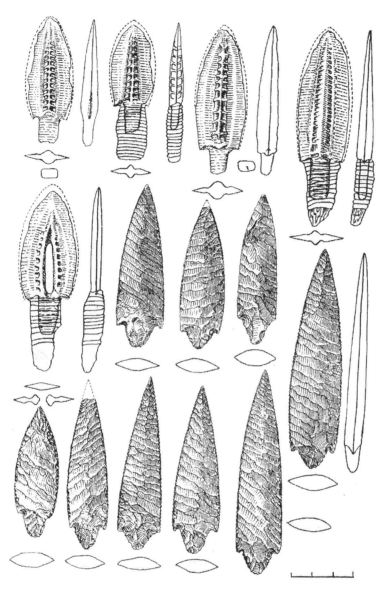

Figure 4.16. Bronze and flint arrowheads from Sintashta (adapted from Gening et al. 1992: 321, fig. 185).

From its inception, steppe archaeology has focused on the raised kurgans and not concentrated on locating settlements, the cultural deposits of which are thin and not clearly visible from the surface. This problem is compounded by the fact that dwellings typically consisted of semisubterranean pit houses that were dug into the ground, and these too are hard to locate. The Sintashta-Arkaim settlements are for the most part not distinctly visible from the ground; most were discovered through the use of aerial photos, confirmed subsequently by helicopter flyovers.

Recently, the transitional Late Bronze to Early Iron Age planned settlement of Ciça, with multiple concentric rings of dwellings extending over roughly 8 ha., or more than two times larger than the largest Sintashta–Arkaim sites, was found farther east in the Irtysh–Ob interfluve between Omsk and Novosibirsk in western Siberia (Molodin et al. 2002). The site was discovered utilizing magnetometer measurements. Similarly, more than seventy Late Bronze/Early Iron Age settlements, which are distributed over a 20 × 30 km. area, have recently been discovered in the Kislovodsk basin in the northern Caucasian piedmont through the use of aerial photography (Korobov and Reinhold n.d.); some of these later North Caucasian settlements superficially at least resemble the Sintashta–Arkaim sites of the trans-Urals "Country of Towns." One can only wonder how many more settlements – habitation and special purpose sites – of various periods will be discovered across the steppes through the use of aerial photography and more sophisticated remote sensing technologies and geophysical explorations.

Despite the bias against locating settlements, the general trend throughout the Bronze Age consists of an increase in the size and number of settlements over time, culminating with the Sabatinovka culture on the Lower Dnieper and west of the Azov Sea in the late second millennium, with reportedly more than 700 settlements documented alone for the northwest Pontic area, ranging up to 27 ha. in size (Bunyatyan 2003: 281; for their distribution, see Gershkovic 1999: Tafel 1). Metals – both weapons, such as spearheads and socketed axes, and harvesting/collecting implements, including notably sickles – were increasingly utilized and had clearly become essential for the practice of basic economic activities; that is, their use no longer was principally related to social status and exchange, a process already visibly underway in the Sintashta–Arkaim settlements or roughly at the end of the third millennium BC. Apparently "agriculture" was considerably less developed farther to the northeast where the Timber Grave communities flourished, though they also worked and utilized metals on an extremely substantial scale.

The question of the nature and extent of cereal cultivation for Timber Grave and Andronovo-related sites on the steppes during the Bronze Age remains uncertain, though the largely negative evidence that has been recovered suggests minimal to nonexistent cultivation of West Asian cereals (wheats and barley). Flotation studies of charred macrobotanical remains, conducted on forty-nine Middle and Late Bronze Age settlements from the Lower Danube to the Trans Urals region, have yielded very little indication of deliberate cultivation (Cernych et al. 1998; Lebedeva 2005: 52–53, 65); excluding the results from the westernmost settlement (Coslogeni) on the Lower Danube, only 23 of 316 flotation samples taken from sites stretching from the left bank of the Dnieper to east of the Urals yielded any macrobotanical charred remains of cultivated plants; samples from the Middle Bronze and early Late Bronze (LB1) sites produced no evidence for cultivated plants. All the cultivated remains that were recovered came from the second and final phases of the Late Bronze period (LBA-2, 3–4). The palynological analyses that have been undertaken, such as those at the Gorny mining settlement in Kargaly, have discovered very few pollen grains identified as Cerealia type, but their significance and interpretation is unclear (Martínez-Navarrete, personal communication.). Among other factors, one must always remember that the Gorny site was a highly specialized mining community (cf. later discussion), and whatever agriculture may have taken place could have occurred relatively far from the site itself.

For Anthony and his coworkers (Anthony et al. n.d.), the negative results of the flotation studies undertaken at the permanently occupied Late Bronze Krasnosamarskoe site in the Samara Valley are striking and suggest that grains were not cultivated in that area during the first half of the second millennium; their subsistence economy correspondingly is characterized as composed of animal herding and the intensive gathering or collecting of wild plant foods, such as species of *Chenopodium* (goosefoot) and *Amaranthus* (amaranth). Related species of these two families were also intensively collected/incipiently cultivated in prehistoric eastern North America before the introduction of maize, as were the related so-called pseudo-cereals, *quinoa* and *cañigua*, deliberately grown in the Andes at altitudes where maize was not cultivated (Hernández Bermejo and León 1994). Perhaps a similar intensive collection/cultivation of these Eurasian species of Chenopodium and Amaranthus independently developed on the western Eurasian steppes during the Bronze Age? Later at the site of Russkaya Selit'ba II, barley (*Hordeum vulgare*), wheat (*Triticum dicoccum* and *compactum*), and millet (*Panicum miliaceum*) grains were recovered, suggesting their introduction in the final phase of the Late Bronze Age (Anthony et al. n.d.).

Although difficult to evaluate, the absence (or relative absence) of unequivocal evidence for cereal cultivation in Timber Grave and Andronovo-related sites is striking and can be contrasted to later Iron Age practices where the cultivation of cereals is definitely attested even far to the east in southeastern Kazakhstan (e.g., Benecke 2003). The largely negative evidence recorded so far seems to suggest little, if any, cultivation of West Asian cereals during all but the final phases of the Bronze Age. Paradoxically, agriculture seems to have become well established throughout the steppes only during the subsequent Iron Age, or the time when true mounted Eurasian pastoral nomadism also finally emerges.

Farther west, north of the Black Sea by the second half of the second millennium BC, the climate had ameliorated and had become wetter and more humid, making possible cultivation even on the "open steppe." Herding likewise intensified at the same time and may have assumed a territorial differentiation in which part of the community focused on agriculture and part on herding, coming together during the winter and keeping herds in special dispersed sites where they were sheltered and supplied with forage (Bunyatyan 2003: 283). Cultivation had intensified but, even at its maximum Bronze Age extent, still represented an extensive, possibly shifting field or swidden system with a long fallow cycle. Gershkovich (2003:315) summarizes the evidence:

> The Sabatinovka culture shows evidence of dairy-centred animal husbandry, sheep and goat breeding, the presence of different breeds of horses. This culture occupied the steppe zone and practiced transhumant animal husbandry, together with swidden agriculture in which fields were periodically shifted. . . . During the Late Bronze Age in the Northern Pontic area, efforts were made to change to a more effective form of animal husbandry. Subsequently, nomadism was established during the Early Iron Age.

It seems clear that Late Bronze Age subsistence economies were mixed and varied across the steppes with increasingly greater, if not exclusive, reliance on herding as one moved west to east into Kazakhstan and western Siberia. There was also a general increase in the size and number of recorded settlements and in the widespread use of effective bronze tools and weapons from Pit to Timber Grave times.

BRONZE AGE HERDING VS. EURASIAN MOUNTED PASTORAL NOMADISM

Ethnologists distinguish different types of nomadism based essentially on two criteria: the extent of animal husbandry relative to agriculture in their economy and the typical species composition of their herds and environmental/climatic conditions to which they have to adapt. The animals herded and the environments in which they are herded are also used to separate types of nomadism by large geographic or cultural areas. Thus, in a very accessible and illuminating study Barfield (1993) distinguishes among East African pastoralists, desert Bedouin nomads, pastoral tribes of Southwest Asia, Eurasian steppe nomads, and high altitude pastoralists in Tibet. Khazanov's (1994: 40–69) types are essentially similar. For Barfield each type is characterized principally by its focus on a specific animal that is accorded great economic and cultural value. For the classic Eurasian steppe nomads, that animal is the horse (Barfield 1993: 131–138), though both he and Khazanov correctly emphasize that this form of nomadism really specializes in two species: horses and sheep.

Large stock, principally cattle, are less important, though more so than in Near and Middle Eastern types of nomadism, their significance varying according to two rules: "in steppe regions there were more large stock [i.e., cattle] than there were in desert regions; and the greater number of large stock the more important the role of agriculture in the general balance of the economy" (Khazanov 1994: 47; cf. also Benecke 2003: 79). Semisedentary peoples, like the Karakalpaks in the region south of the Aral Sea, kept greater numbers of large stock than their more nomadic neighbors to the north (Khazanov 1994: 48). The percentage of cattle on Scythian "seminomadic" settlements is likewise considerably higher than on those Scythian sites considered to be principally nomadic; on the former cattle are calculated to comprise 43–55% of the herd (with horse ranging from 26 to 34%, sheep roughly 18%, and pig 2–5%), whereas on the latter cattle constitute approximately 24%, horses 42%, and sheep 32% of the herd (Gavrilyuk 1999: 154).

Eurasian steppe nomadism has also been termed multi-animal nomadism (Bacon 1954: 46) because it herded together different species of animals – sheep, goats, horses, cattle, Bactrian camels – some of whose value lay principally in transportation and riding. Eurasian nomadism had to adapt to severe continental climatic conditions: a short but very hot and intense summer and a much longer, bitterly cold winter during which time pastures were often covered with thick deposits of snow. Crops can be grown, but, as we have seen, direct palaeobotanical evidence for any form of intensive cultivation on the steppes during the Early, Middle, and beginning of the Late Bronze Age is largely negative. Whatever practices were adopted, the growing season had to have been very short, particularly relative to what was possible farther south in Transcaucasia and in southern Central Asia.

The continental conditions became more severe, of course, as one crossed the Urals and moved deeper into Eurasia. Horses, Bactrian camels, and, to a lesser extent, sheep were particularly valuable for the fact that they could uncover grass covered with snow by kicking at it with their hooves; apparently horses could reach grass in this manner that was buried up to a half meter in snow (Khazanov 1994: 50). Pastures so uncovered could, to some extent, be utilized by other less well-adapted species, thus eventually leading to the mixed herds characteristic of Eurasian nomadism. Another solution to this problem was to grow fodder and store it for the winter season when it was less available; this solution must have archaeological consequences that are still largely unrecorded, except, as we have seen, in the reconstruction of Sabatinovka winter farmsteads.

Another problem on the "open steppe" was the availability or accessibility of water, underground water sources sometimes being available; thus, not surprisingly, many of the migratory cycles of recorded nomadic groups followed the river valleys, moving meridian-wise north possibly into the forest-steppe zone in the summer and south into warmer, less snow-covered climes in the winter; such a pattern would bring herders in the Volga and Ural river basins annually down towards the northern Caspian Sea. Ultimately, their increasing presence would successively displace other herders and cultivators farther south in a kind of chain reaction, until peoples began to traverse the Kyzyl and Kara Kum deserts to reach more hospitable conditions. N. Shishlina (2003: 360–363) believes that the "open steppe" was only progressively occupied. In Pit Grave times at the end of the fourth and beginning of the third millennium, the movement of the herders was largely confined to the river valleys and immediately surrounding grasslands; the real "open steppe" was occupied only

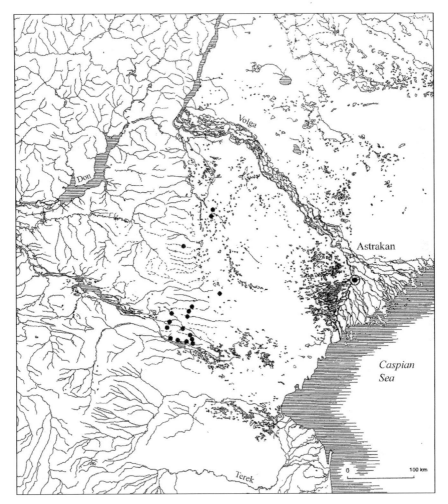

Figure 4.17. Kurgan groups with more than 75% Early Iron and Medieval Burials in Kalmykia (adapted from Otchir-Gorieva 2002: 115, abb. 1).

during subsequent Catacomb grave times out of necessity (increased aridity and overexploitation of the neighboring grasslands) and owing to their increased mobility and mastery of the horse (cf. also Shishlina and Hiebert 1998).

In a recent study Otchir-Gorieva (2002) uses different data to alter this model, arguing instead for mixed herding and agricultural practices during Pit Grave times – at least in Kalmykia. She (2002: 122, 126) emphasizes that dozens, if not hundreds, of settlement points or stations have been recorded on the left banks of the Lower Volga, though they have rarely been excavated or intensively studied, and argues that theoretically Pit Grave settlements can be expected to be small, dispersed, and over time subject to erosion, that is, difficult to discover archaeologically. She compares the location of Pit Grave and Catacomb burials on the right bank and south of the Lower Volga with the late

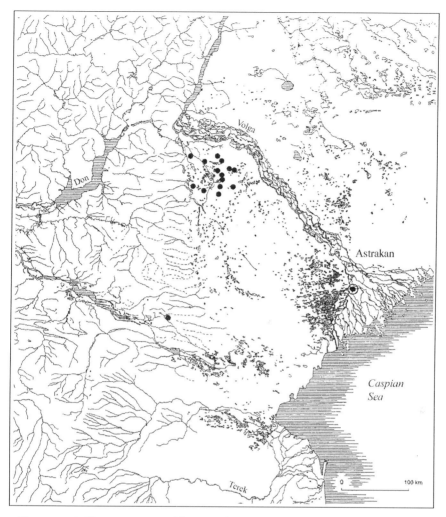

Figure 4.18. Kurgan groups with more than 75% Bronze Age Burials in Kalmykia (adapted from Otchir-Gorieva 2002: 116, abb. 2).

nineteenth-century settlements of Russian colonists, who depended principally on agriculture, and contrasts this distributional evidence with the location of Early Iron and Medieval nomadic burials (contrast Fig. 4.17 with Figs. 4.18 and 4.19). The location of the nomadic Early Iron and Medieval kurgans differs sharply from the distribution of the Bronze Age kurgans and of the settlements of the nineteenth-century Russian colonists who practiced agriculture (though the sites of these latter two also differ; contrast Fig. 4.18 with 4.19) and is used to bolster her argument for a mixed herding and cultivating Bronze Age economy. Whether or not this locational evidence confirms her claim, the contrast between the locations of the Bronze Age and Iron Age/Medieval kurgans is striking and supports our basic distinction between Bronze Age herding (Fig. 4.18) and historically documented classic Eurasian nomadism (Fig. 4.17). Historically mounted pastoral nomads moved seasonally from the lower left bank of the Volga, which provided ideal summer pastures after spring flooding, to the higher right bank in winter, which provided shelter against the severe cold and snow. The Bronze Age cattle herders stayed on the right bank of the Volga and exhibited less mobility. She also considers the cultic importance of cattle in Bronze Age sacrifices as a nonnomadic practice because cattle – unlike sheep, horses, and camels – assume no such sacral significance among true nomads (ibid., 127).

Whether her model is compelling in all its features or whether it works for regions other than Kalmykia is unclear. The basic point for us is that her reconstruction coincides with those of other scholars we have cited in her emphasis on a fundamental disjunction or qualitative difference between Bronze Age cattle herding and the later mounted pastoral steppe nomadism that focused principally on maintaining flocks of sheep and riding horses. This latter classic form of Eurasian nomadism, as known to us historically and ethnographically, is *not* archaeologically attested during the Bronze Age. Morales-Muñiz and Antipina's exhaustive review (2000, 2003; Antipina and Morales 2005) of the faunal evidence from the steppes from Chalcolithic through Bronze Age times records very little presence of sheep and goats, except at some post–Tripol'ye Usatovo sites, and a continuing focus on cattle that seems to increase significantly only during the Late Bronze Age, an increase that they intriguingly suggest may be related to the development of horse riding for cattle herding purposes, the emergence of more mobile cowboys on the "Wild East" of the Eurasian steppes.

If Bronze Age steppe pastoralism or pastoralism supplemented by cultivation is not the same as historic Eurasian mounted pastoral nomadism, then it is misleading to anachronistically envision hordes of marauding nomads sweeping down off the steppes with their chariots and advanced bronze weaponry to invade and subjugate established agricultural societies to the south. Rather, more mobile seminomadic economies utilizing oxen-driven carts and wagons, and herding principally cattle spread across the western Eurasian steppes during the second half of the fourth and third millennium. At some point they began to ride horses and develop lighter vehicles and new techniques for harnessing horses to them. Their way of life was never fully nomadic, though obviously successful.

As this way of life spread farther east into more continental, colder areas, these cattle herders must have experienced a continuous pressure to move farther south into warmer climes more suitable for raising their livestock. This process would have been gradual, but relatively continuous, leading to the movements or, perhaps better, successive displacements of cattle herders north to south ultimately into areas where permanently settled, often irrigation-based agriculture had been practiced for millennia. As we have seen, west of

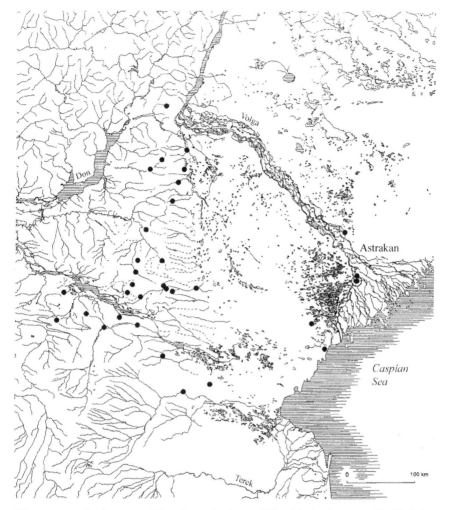

Figure 4.19. Settlements of Russian colonists in Kalmykia in the second half of the nineteenth century (adapted from Otchir-Gorieva 2002: 118, abb. 3).

the Caspian this process seems to have been underway at least by the middle of the third millennium BC with the advent of impressively large kurgan burials in Transcaucasia. East of the Caspian this process was delayed for several centuries, a chronological discrepancy that can also be partially explained by the greater physical separation of the steppes from the cultivated oases of southern Central Asia.

The role of sheep and goats in the herding economies of the steppes also varied over time and must be determined directly from the archaeological record. Sheep and goats have been herded since Early Neolithic times in the Ancient Near East, and they diffused onto the steppes during at least the Late Neolithic, probably independently via Central Asia and the Balkans, and possibly slightly

Figure 4.20. Kyrgyz winter encampment with sheep enclosure (note prevalence of Bactrian camels), Wakhan corridor, northeastern Afghanistan (adapted from Michaud and Michaud 1978: pl. 14).

later from the Caucasus. Bones of *"melkyi rogatyi skot"* certainly constituted typical burial offerings in the countless kurgan cultures of the Bronze Age, but how significant was their contribution to stock-raising practices during this period? What was the role of sheep and goats in the overall herding strategies of the Bronze Age? One needs settlement, not mortuary, data to answer the question, and here this latter evidence is unfortunately limited, particularly for Early and Middle Bronze times. Following again the analyses of Morales-Muñiz and Antipina (2000, 2003), one can conclude that the role of sheep and goats varied regionally but, in general, was far less central than what was later characterized as classic Eurasian mounted nomadism.

Were sheep and goats kept principally for their meat or also for their dairy products and wool? When does what Andrew Sherratt (1981, 1983) termed the "Secondary Products" Revolution reach the steppes, a question that potentially could be answered by analysis of age composition data for faunal assemblages from Bronze Age settlements, not burials? For the moment, such questions must remain open, but it is useful to raise them in order to emphasize the contrast with what we later know to be characteristic of Eurasian mounted nomadism: heavy reliance on the "secondary products" – dairy and wool – provided principally by sheep and goats.

Sheep and the use of wool and felt are absolutely central to that latter way of life (Figs. 4.20, 4.21, and 4.22), but they appear far less pivotal on the steppes during Bronze Age times. Large-scale, almost industrial surplus

Figure 4.21. Heavy felt door covering to yurt, Wakhan corridor northeastern Afghanistan (adapted from Michaud and Michaud 1978: pl. 23).

production of woolen textiles of varying qualities was practiced in the temple and palace institutional economies of Mesopotamia, possibly from the late fourth or third millennium BC onwards (cf. the discussion in the next chapter). We know these textiles were traded widely throughout the Ancient Near

Figure 4.22. Kazakh women preparing felt for rugs and mats (adapted from Trippett 1974: 149).

East during the Bronze Age. Did such exchange reach the steppes and/or did knowledge of such production stimulate their ever-increasing utilization there, or was their ultimate use on the steppes the product of a totally independent process of development? What are the archaeological indices documenting such utilization?

Possible woolen rugs and felt mats and carpets have been documented in Early Bronze kurgans on the steppes and in Transcaucasia (Barber 1991: 169–170, 220–222; Kushnareva 1997: 92, 231), but how widespread was their use at this time? Years ago, Berthold Laufer (1930: 2; cited in Barber 1991: 221–22) observed:

> Eliminate felt from Chinese, Greek, and Roman civilizations, and they would still remain what they are, not being in the least affected by this minus. Eliminate the same element from the life of the nomadic populations, and they would cease to exist, they would never have come into existence.

Similarly, Basilov and Naumova (1989: 101) emphasize:

> It is hard to imagine the daily life of the nomadic and seminomadic peoples without carpets and felts. Convenient to handle and transport, they were indispensable to the nomads.

The Bronze Age herders of the western steppes also raised nearly all the animals kept by later Eurasian mounted nomads, save perhaps Bactrian camels. It is the relative frequency of the different species, particularly the striking dominance of cattle and the markedly secondary presence of ovicaprines and horses that are distinctive and suggestive of a fundamentally different way of life. The multi-animal nomadism of later times was a tightly integrated system, highly adapted to coping with the rigorous conditions of life on the steppes, particularly the long cold winters. It essentially took the two-plus millennia of the Bronze Age to come up with the right combination of animals and the development of technologies for maximizing their control and utilization. There clearly is still much to be learned about stock herding and the utilization of animal power and products on the Bronze Age Eurasian steppes.

THE TRANSFORMATION AND EASTWARD EXPANSION OF METALLURGY DURING THE LATE BRONZE AGE; ACCOUNTING FOR ITS SOCIAL ORGANIZATION – THE CONTRASTIVE HIGHLY CENTRALIZED "GULAG" OR FLEXIBLE/OPPORTUNISTIC "GOLD RUSH" MODELS

Throughout our study we have utilized E.N. Chernykh's concept of a metallurgical province or large area, comprising numerous distinct archaeological cultures, which are linked together through a shared tradition of producing and working metal artifacts into a limited number of related types of tools and weapons. According to Chernykh, the first such province – the

Carpatho-Balkan Metallurgical Province (CBMP) – emerged in the northern Balkans and Carpathian mountains and expanded northeastwards across the western Eurasian steppes at least as far east as the Lower Volga, supplying semifinished and finished metal products to regions either lacking in ores or having minor or less accessible ore deposits. This province was then supplanted by the even more extensive Circumpontic Metallurgical Province (CMP) in the mid to late fourth millennium BC. According to the model, many of the metals, now dominantly arsenical copper/bronzes, were mined and worked in the southern Caucasus and exported north onto the steppes, though it is also recognized that other areas, including the western Urals, were also centers of primary ore extraction and reduction at this time.

Ukrainian archaeologists, such as V. I. Klochko (1994) and L. Cernych (2003), have criticized the generally held assumption that most of the Early and Middle Bronze Age arsenical copper/bronzes originated in the Caucasus. They emphasize the considerable evidence for metal working in the form of bellow nozzles, molds, crucibles, hammer stones and pounders, and founder's burials containing such remains that are found throughout the North Pontic area from Chalcolithic times onwards. Metallographic studies have confirmed the distinctive, relatively primitive (by comparison to Balkan) metal-working techniques of early Tripol'ye smiths, suggesting that they produced the objects themselves, having received the metal possibly as semifinished ingots (a point also admitted by Chernykh, compare Klochko 1994: 145 with Chernykh 1992: 40–41). Such practices of locally producing widely shared metal types continued throughout the Early and Middle Bronze periods, or throughout the existence of the postulated CMP.

L. Cernych (2003: 53–55) emphasizes the limits of spectrographic analysis for identifying ore sources, questioning in particular the axiomatic identification of arsenical copper/bronzes as Caucasian; she believes that many of these could have come from other known sources, including Ukraine, particularly the Donbass region in the east. Fingerprinting archaeological artifacts to specific source deposits is notoriously difficult whether one uses compositional spectrographic or lead-isotope analyses. The lack of specificity and internal variability of the sources themselves make such identifications hazardous, as does the continual reprocessing of metals possibly from different sources by the ancient smiths.

Arsenical-bearing copper ores are quite common and were commonly exploited in antiquity both in the Old and New Worlds. H. Lechtman (1996: 477, cited in Weeks 2003: 109) further explains:

> In both the Old World...and the Americas, copper-arsenic alloys were produced over a vast area, from Russia to Great Britain and from Chile to Mexico. This production was made possible by the relatively large number of metallic mineral species that contain arsenic, by their geological co-occurrence with ores of copper, and by the widespread association of these ores in the earth's crust.

Such association makes it impossible to distinguish absolutely whether the arsenic present in an artifact was deliberately alloyed, the product of co-smelting copper and arsenic-rich ores or of just smelting arsenic-rich copper ores (Weeks 2003: 113–118). Because this determination is not certain, we have consistently used the admittedly awkward, ambiguous phrase – arsenical copper/bronzes.

E. N. Chernykh (personal communication), however, is convinced that in most instances the addition of arsenic was deliberate, an intentional alloy that was added in controlled amounts to facilitate the production and functional use of the objects. He claims that only about 10 arsenic-copper deposits, 2 or 3 of which are Caucasian in origin, have a sufficiently high concentration of arsenic for the consistent production of arsenical coppers of the more than 500 copper and polymetallic deposits that he has examined throughout Eurasia from the Balkans to Mongolia. Certainly such arsenic-rich copper deposits existed throughout the greater Ancient Near East (e.g., southeastern Arabia, central Iran, etc.) and were exploited during the Bronze Age. Most of the known arsenical copper/bronzes found farther south did not originate in the Caucasus, and it is unclear how distinctive or "fingerprintable" Caucasian arsenical copper/bronzes are, that is, whether or not they can be readily distinguished analytically from other Old World arsenical copper/bronzes.

Regardless, a general eastwards extension and dramatic expansion of metal production, distribution, and utilization are evident with the advent of the Late Bronze Age, beginning possibly in the first half of the second millennium BC. This extension and expansion are reflected in the emergence of several coexisting "metallurgical provinces," according to Chernykh, or "hearths of cultural genesis" in which "blocs of cultures" formed, according to Bochkarev (1990, 1995b). These provinces include a Eurasian Metallurgical Province (EAMP), divided into Asiatic and European zones (Chernykh 1992: 246); a European Metallurgical Province (EMP); and Caucasian, Irano-Afghan, and Central Asian provinces, the last of which extended east to Mongolia and northwestern and northern China (Chernykh 1992: 264). Connections in metal types and shared technologies can be traced across much of Eurasia, though some extremely rich metal-producing and consuming areas, like the Caucasus, seem to be more isolated or set apart than in the Early and Middle Bronze Ages (see our earlier discussion in Chapter 3).

Though metal-producing and metal-working technologies have clearly spread west to east across the steppe and forest-steppe belts, a pattern that began in Chalcolithic times, it is now possible to detect movements of materials in the opposite direction, or east to west. Such a pattern possibly is first represented by the enigmatic Seima-Turbino horizon or "transcultural phenomenon" in which highly distinctive socketed axes, spearheads with forked shanks, and curved daggers often with figured hilts, many of which are made of tin bronzes apparently originating in the Altai, are found in cemeteries

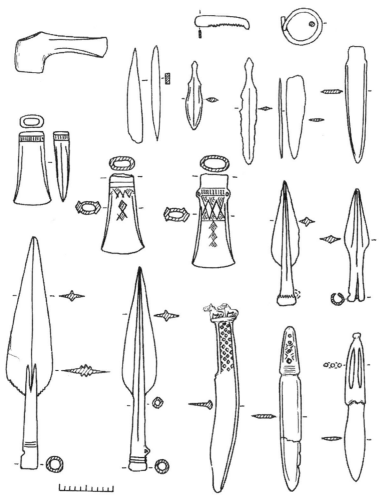

Figure 4.23. Distinctive copper and bronze artifacts from the Seima cemetery (adapted from Chernykh 1992: 219, fig. 73).

stretching from western Mongolia to Finland (Chernykh 1992: 215–233; Figs. 4.23 and 4.24). It is unclear how best to account for these geographically disparate but obviously related mortuary remains. They may trace the actual movements of a people or even of mounted warriors (?) across northern Eurasia at the end of the Middle and beginning of the Late Bronze Age, or, alternatively, they may record some system of elite prestige exchange that is difficult to model given the incomplete, exclusively mortuary nature of the evidence.

What is clear is that during the Late Bronze Age peoples from more areas are extracting more ores and producing more metal tools and weapons of related types on a greatly expanded, nearly industrial scale across most of Eurasia. Some of these peoples, such as those living in the western Urals, may have first prospected for and extracted ores during the Early Bronze Age, whereas others, such as those possibly at Kartamysh and related sites in the Donbass region of eastern Ukraine (Tatarinov 2003), may have begun to exploit their local ores only during Late Bronze times. Nevertheless, there was a dramatic expansion in metallurgical production reflected in the discovery of tens of thousands of metal artifacts from hoards, particularly in Europe, burials, and settlements. This expansion in production, in turn, is clearly related to increased utilization for agricultural and military purposes, as represented by the countless metal sickles and very effective and obviously functional weapons, such as socketed axes, spearheads, and knives. They are no longer principally luxuries, but necessary items for conducting basic economic, social, and political activities.

Tin-bronzes also begin to be utilized on a much more extensive and regular basis, though their dominant use is characteristic only of certain areas, such as those occupied by Andronovo-related cultures east and south of the Urals or in various parts of the Caucasus, such as Kakheti or eastern Georgia (Dschaparidze 2001: 103, 114; Inanischwili 2001: 147), representing in this latter case a greatly expanded pattern of utilization of tin-bronzes that began during the late Early Bronze period. Other areas, such as those occupied by Timber Grave related communities, like the western Urals and the Don-Volga interfluve, continued to use principally arsenical copper/bronzes or even "pure" copper artifacts throughout the Late Bronze Age. The increased utilization of tin-bronzes implies greatly expanded systems of exchange and probably the exploitation of new sources of tin both far to the south and east, such as in the Zeravshan valley and Rudny Altai, and probably also to the west in central Europe.

Currently, the expansion of metallurgical production during Late Bronze times is best documented by recent archaeological (1991–2002) investigations of the massive Kargaly complex that encompasses a roughly 500 sq. km. area principally in the Ural basin west of Orenburg (Fig. 4.25). More than 30,000 surface mine workings have been documented in different zones across the Kargaly region (Fig. 4.26 and Fig. 4.27), though it is unclear whether all, or even most, of such surface workings can be dated to Late Bronze Timber Grave times. This complex was also one of the principal sources for the copper mining and smelting industry of imperial Russia during the eighteenth and nineteenth centuries AD, accounting for roughly one-quarter of copper production at this time. Minimally the later Russian miners extended and considerably deepened the Bronze Age mining shafts, though they used similar tools and dug similar-looking shafts, making it essentially impossible to distinguish the earlier Bronze Age from imperial Russian exploitation.

Nevertheless, explorations of these surface workings and shafts have frequently recovered Bronze Age materials, such as Timber Grave ceramic fragments, and it is likely that hundreds of kilometers of interconnected galleries were first opened during Late Bronze times. The scale of Bronze Age copper ore extraction at Kargaly, which has been estimated to consist of the extraction

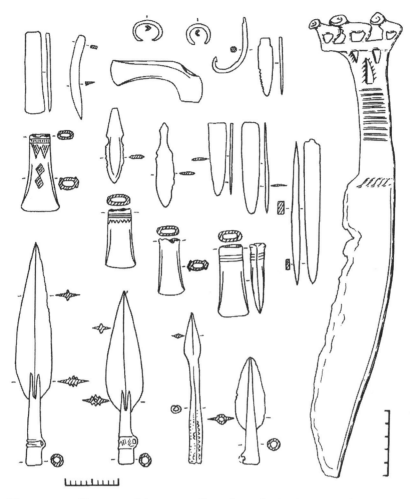

Figure 4.24. Copper and bronze artifacts from the Turbino I and II cemeteries (adapted from Chernykh 1992: 220, fig. 74).

of several million tons of copper minerals and possibly the production of 100,000 or more tons of copper, is staggering, even though its total extent can never be precisely calculated, given this much later massive exploitation during the eighteenth and nineteenth centuries AD.

Excavations, which were conducted during the 1990s at the Gorny settlement within the Kargaly complex, support this interpretation of large-scale specialized mining production. An unsuccessful prospecting shaft was opened at the site probably towards the middle of the third millennium BC (Chernykh 2002d: 136–138; 2004: 293–294), and then the site was revisited and metal production began, as represented by an earlier phase of clusters of small pit-houses or burrows dug deeply (some more than 2 m.) into the soil that are thought to have been occupied seasonally, probably during the summer.

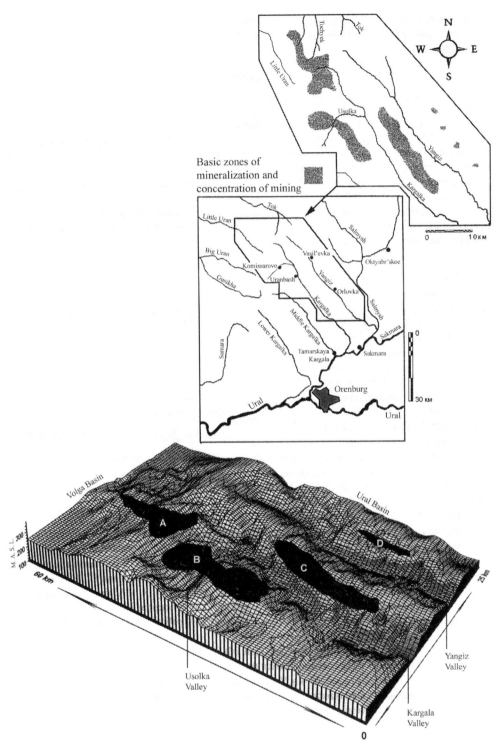

Figure 4.25. Kargaly ore field: basic zones of mineralization and concentration of mining works (adaped from Chernykh 2002a: 11, figs. B.2 and B.3); translated from the Russian. Relief of the Kargaly region (computerized reconstruction) and basic zones of mineralization.

Figure 4.26. The Kargaly landscape: traces of different mining shafts and dumps (adapted from Chernykh 2002a: 29, fig. 2.7).

A series of calibrated radiocarbon dates determined that the main period of occupation (phase B) extended from the seventeenth through the fourteenth centuries BC. During this period the settlement expanded considerably with individual "housing/production complexes" extending over roughly 200 sq. meters, consisting of different parts: dwellings, metallurgical and ore yards, garbage pits, and underground "sacral" galleries imitating mining shafts. On the basis principally of their size (Chernykh 1997a: 37), these dwellings are thought to have been occupied year-round or permanently by miners who were principally, if not exclusively, engaged in the extraction and, to a lesser extent, smelting of the local copper ores and production of tools for continued

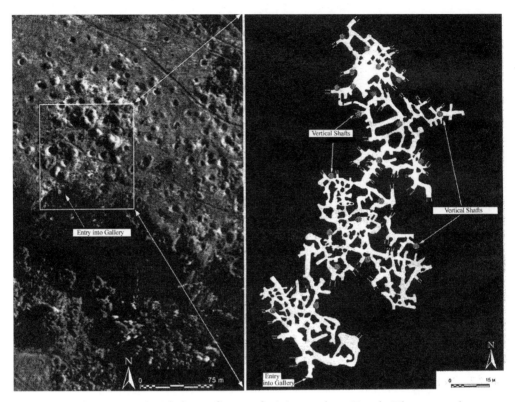

Figure 4.27. Aerial photo of traces of mining works at Kargaly. The rectangular area delimited in white corresponds to the mapped labyrinthine mining shafts and corridors roughly 10–15 m. beneath the surface shown on the right (adapted from Chernykh 2002a: 30, fig. 2.8); translated from the Russian.

local metal working purposes. More than 3000 metal artifacts, 174 fragments of molds, and approximately 20 kg. of metallurgical slag were recovered from the excavations at the Gorny settlement.

A very systematic and methodologically rigorous palynological study by Spanish archaeological collaborators (Díaz-del-Río et al. 2006) determined that the Late Bronze vegetative landscape essentially resembled the present day open steppe surrounding the site, making it difficult to sustain the large-scale smelting of copper ores using only locally available woods as fuels. This fact coupled with the relatively primitive metallurgical technology (Rovira 2004 and 2005) and relatively small amount of recovered slag and smelted copper has led Chernykh (2002f: 88; 1997: 66–68) to believe that the specialized Bronze Age miners at Kargaly were principally involved in the primary extraction of copper ores, not the production of smelted processed copper. These ores were then exported far to the west – at least as far as the Middle Volga basin. He further speculates that the miners received livestock (principally cattle) in exchange for their copper ores.

Figure 4.28. Faunal remains from the cultural levels at the Gorny settlement; more than 2,000,000 animal bones were recovered from these excavations. E.E. Antipina sits in the middle of the hill of animal bones surrounded by other members of the Kargaly project (adapted from cover Kargaly III volume).

One of the most unexpected discoveries at Gorny was the incredible number of recovered animal bones: roughly 2.3 million bones and bone fragments comprising a volume of about 24 cubic meters were recovered from an excavated area of approximately 1000 sq. m. and represented the remains minimally of tens of thousands of animals (Antipina 2004; Fig. 4.28). This mountain of bones consisted almost exclusively of domesticated animals (99.8%), principally cattle (roughly 80%), followed by sheep and goats, horses (2%), and pig (.3%) (Antipina 2002). Most animals, undoubtedly, were eaten, but some, including embryonic calves, pregnant cows and mares, and dogs, were deliberately buried in ritual contexts, associated with underground tunnels or passages on the site that seemed deliberately to imitate the mining shafts and galleries. Many bones were split and processed as tools, including the shoulder blades and long bones of cattle, some of which were used as "throwaway" shovels, chisels and picks/wedges for opening mining shafts and ore extraction (Figs. 4.29 and 4.30); that they could have been so utilized for opening and extending the mining shafts was demonstrated experimentally.

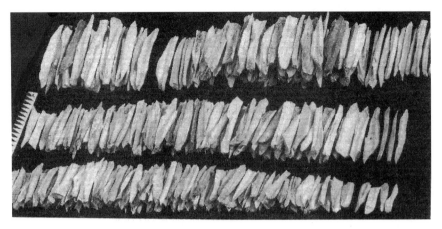

Figure 4.29. Series of mine-shaft opening bone wedge-shaped pointed tools from the Gorny excavations (adapted from Antipina 2004: 197).

This incredibly large collection of bones from a relatively small excavated area is difficult to explain; it seems to represent an almost deliberate stock-piling of the animal remains. As reconstructed, the variability in the sex, age, and size composition of the cattle remains, in particular, suggests that they came from different herds. In most archaeological contexts, the faunal remains represent only a small sample of the total number of animals that once had been herded, stalled, and ultimately consumed by the humans who controlled them. One assumes the same must have been true at Kargaly. Such sizeable herds require substantial grazing land that must have extended far beyond the area immediately surrounding the Gorny settlement. Thus it is argued that herders brought their livestock to Gorny to exchange them for metal ores; the miners then, according to this theory, were able to survive the entire year at the site by slaughtering the animals and freezing their meat during the long, snow-covered winter. Chernykh (1997a: 69–71) hypothesizes that the Gorny phase B miners lived at the site and consumed meat, and presumably milk products, year-round and that they exchanged the extracted copper ores for the livestock.

It is hard to envision exactly how such a system was organized and coordi-nated. As already noted, cattle in particular are not very able to feed themselves during long winters with deep snow covers, and the number of horses relative to cattle is quite small and there is little or no evidence for the use of camels (who are also able to dig beneath the snow for pasture). These animals could have also provided dung for fuel to keep the miners warm during the winter, though there is no direct evidence to support the use of dung as fuel for warmth and/or smelting and other mining-related operations. Oxen could have been used to haul wagons laden with copper ores, though again no direct evidence has been found (or is likely to be found) to confirm this aspect of the model. Despite these uncertainties, what can be said unequivocally is that the materials

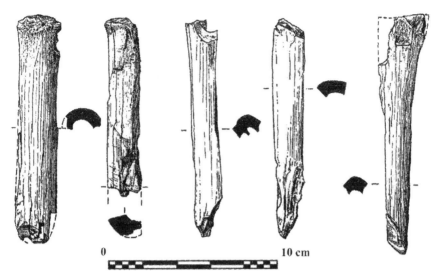

Figure 4.30. Bone wedge-shaped pointed tools for mining work, showing traces of work (adapted from Antipina 2004: 232, fig. 7.29).

from the Kargaly complex, particularly the Gorny settlement, represent something specialized both in terms of mining operations and livestock utilization; both specializations should be interrelated and form part of a larger whole that is not yet documented archaeologically, or satisfactorily reconstructed.

Metal-working technologies diffused across the steppes already in Chalcolithic times, initiating a tradition of metal working on the steppes that was already millennia old by the Late Bronze Age. One of the most striking features of Late Bronze settlements across the steppes is the pervasive evidence for local metal working, as shown by the recovery of slag, nozzles, molds, crucibles, and metal tools and weapons. Nearly everyone seems capable of working metals, at least to some extent. How were metals brought to these sites, many of which were far removed from ore sources? Were the production, distribution, and consumption of metals coordinated activities directed by an overarching social and political system, that is, a Late Bronze despotic totalitarian state or a less centralized confederacy of related interdependent groups?

The miners at Kargaly must have led miserable lives, working and living underground for a considerable part of, if not the entire, year, enduring hot short summers and possibly long cold winters. Did they do this willingly or were they compelled to do so by some despotic state, forming the bottom rungs on a gulag-like labor camp system? The specialization in mining activities evident at the Gorny site seemingly supports this "gulag" model, but, unfortunately, there is little else recorded for the Timber Grave "cultural-historical community," besides an occasional ritual site, like the monumental Three Island (*Trekhostrovskoi*) fired wooden stepped or pyramidal structure above the Middle Don northwest of Volgograd (D'yachenko et al. 2004; Skripkin et al.

2004), to suggest additional specialization or complex hierarchically coordinated activities.

Thus, perhaps, an alternative model is more likely: prospectors occupying known or recently discovered ore sources, exploiting them with relatively primitive extraction procedures, and hauling the ores away on their sturdy oxen-driven wagons to work elsewhere during other times of the year – the "gold rush" model. Mining and herding activities were more broadly shared and freely engaged in by different groups within the broader Timber Grave "cultural-historical community." Possibly – despite the substantial habitation structures – the Gorny miners occupied the site only seasonally, living during the winter in relatively small, dispersed, self-contained settlements, perhaps resembling in their ubiquitous working of metals those of the somewhat earlier Sintashta-Arkaim villages immediately across the Urals to the east.

These latter settlements are located typically on the first terraces of marshy, meandering streams, perfectly situated winter encampments to provide winter forage for their livestock (Anthony n.d.), though it is also probably the case that such well-watered locations were attractive places for settlement throughout the year. As we have seen, nearly every excavated structure or house of the excavated "Country of Towns" settlements contains evidence for the processing of metals. Was this a supplementary activity conducted during the long winter months, whereas during the summer some groups intensively extracted metal ores? In other words, is it possible that the "Country of Towns" settlements – or, more precisely, their later descendants, who presumably resembled them in their broadly shared metalworking activities – provide the complement to what is missing at Kargaly?

In this alternative model, Kargaly is occupied during the summer by herders who also engage in the extraction of ores, minimally process them there, and then haul the ores home with them to work during the long winter months (and keep warm in the process). Some mining specialists, such as those at Gorny, may continue to occupy mining sites year-round, but others, presumably with whom they are culturally related and/or politically affiliated, will retreat with their cattle herds to live elsewhere during the long snow-covered winter where, among, other activities, they will continue to work metals in their densely packed and enclosed settlements. Perhaps confederacies of related tribal groups were distributed across the Bronze Age steppes, providing enough coordination to procure and distribute the ores that were extracted on an increasingly intensive scale over time. This suggestion or alternative model, of course, is speculative, lacking, at least at the moment, convincing archaeological confirmation. Highly specialized activities, even on the immense scale of ore extraction evident at Gorny, seem somehow to have taken place without the coercive presence of an overarching centralized state.

Paradoxically, if anything, the Late Bronze archaeological record for the western Eurasian steppes documents relations that are more egalitarian and less

Figure 4.31. Oxen-driven wagons carrying a yurt and furnishings on the open Kazakh steppe (adapted from Trippett 1974: 145).

stratified than what is known for the Early and Middle Bronze periods. At the end of the Bronze Age, burials in flat cemeteries typically replace raised kurgan burials. Chernykh (1992: 191) observes:

> The magnificent Caucasian kurgan tombs of the Early and Middle Bronze Age also became a thing of the past. Differentiation between burials was still present, of course, but was rather more subtle. The general appearance of all of the northern Eurasian cultures was more 'egalitarian' during the LBA than it had been during the MBA and EBA.

This picture, of course, changes again dramatically with the advent of the "royal" kurgans of the Iron Age, a development beyond the scope of this study.

How do ever-improving systems of transportation affect these metal-producing and metal-working activities? Specifically, what are the consequences of increased reliance on riding horses, as opposed to harnessing them to wagons or "chariots," during the Late Bronze Age? Unlike in the Middle East (cf. Bulliet 1975), wheeled vehicles never totally disappear on the steppes; they remain part of the historically and ethnographically documented material culture of classic mounted steppe nomads (Fig. 4.31). But does their significance diminish as the herders become mounted nomads, riding horses and, at some point, keeping camels as pack animals? Wheeled vehicles seem to lose their ritual social significance during the Bronze Age, that is, they are not found with such regularity in Late Bronze burials, as in Early and, particularly, Middle Bronze times. Why? Is it no longer so prestigious to own an oxen-driven cart when more social value and importance is attached to riding horses?

Ultimately, with the advent of iron, new, widely distributed sources of ores were exploited that still needed to be exchanged, but they were moved now by more mobile systems of transportation in which horses and probably Bactrian camels may have played critical roles. Even earlier during the Late Bronze Age, steppe peoples had become more mobile and capable of spreading their technological skills in the new areas into which they moved and opened up far to the east. They also moved south into areas occupied by peoples principally engaged in agricultural activities, some of whom lived in state-structured societies far more socially complex than anything known on the steppes during Late Bronze times. How did they interact with the peoples with whom they came into contact, and how were they transformed in the process? These questions will be addressed in the next chapter as we turn our gaze further south and review the archaeological record from southern Central Asian and the Indo-Iranian borderlands during Late Bronze (traditionally Namazga VI) times, or from the late third through the first half of the second millennium BC.

BIOGRAPHICAL SKETCH

N. YA. MERPERT

Photo 4.1. A young N. Ya. Merpert at Novgorod in 1947.

Photo 4.2. Still digging (and drawing) at the site of Tell Khazna I, Syria 1998.

Nikolai Yakovlevich Merpert, who was born in Moscow on November 26, 1922, celebrated his fifty-fifth year of work at the Institute of Archaeology,

Russian Academy of Sciences in 2002 (Munchaev 2002). After finishing high school Merpert served on the northwestern front in the early months of World War II after the German invasion in June 1941. He was wounded several times, receiving medals for his bravery, and was released from the Red Army as a wounded veteran in 1942. Later that year he entered the Faculty of History at Moscow State University and began to study archaeology under many famous Russian archaeologists, including A. V. Gorodtsov.

His early work was on classical and Scythian remains and on later Slavic kurgans near Moscow, and he participated in the Soviet excavations to Mongolia in 1948 and 1949, later coauthoring its final published report *Drevnemongol'skie Goroda* (Moscow: Nauka 1964). Immediately thereafter in 1950, he began to work in the Volga region near Samara (or Kuybyshev from 1935 to 1991), excavating scores of Bronze Age kurgans and Timber Grave settlements. He continued to investigate Chalcolithic and Bronze Age developments on the Eurasian steppes, publishing his famous doctoral dissertation (second PhD) on the Yamnaya Pit Grave culture-historical community *Drevneishie skotovody volzhsko-ural'skogo mezhdurech'ya* (*Ancient Herders between the Volga and Ural Basins*) in 1974. His studies on the Eurasian steppes have continued throughout his long and distinguished career. Perhaps most notably, he has founded his own "school" of highly trained specialists working on the western Eurasian steppes, supervising nearly forty candidate and doctoral dissertations and lecturing frequently on the archaeology of the steppes at Moscow State University (Munchaev 2002: 7, 9).

He has also excavated at the site of Serzhen Yurt in the northern Caucasus, at Ezero in Bulgaria, and on salvage work and reconnaissance surveys in Egypt and northwestern Sudan. He participated in the first Soviet/Russian expedition to Mesopotamia that excavated a series of Neolithic and Chalcolithic settlements in northern Iraq from 1969 to 1984, and at Tell Khazna I and II in northeastern Syria from 1988 till the present. He is the author of more than 300 scientific publications. The recipient of many medals and honors, N.Ya. Merpert today lectures on biblical archaeology at a private university in Moscow, serves as a corresponding member of the editorial board for *Rossiskaya Arkheologiya* and *Vestnik Drevnei Istorii,* and directs the group of archaeologists who are working on expeditions abroad at the Institute of Archaeology in Moscow.

CHAPTER 5

ENTERING A SOWN WORLD OF
IRRIGATION AGRICULTURE – FROM THE
STEPPES TO CENTRAL ASIA AND BEYOND:
PROCESSES OF MOVEMENT, ASSIMILATION,
AND TRANSFORMATION INTO THE
"CIVILIZED" WORLD EAST OF SUMER

> The infiltration process of Andronovo tribes to the south was relatively
> slow. There are no traces of violent ends of farming settlements . . . The
> contacts between steppe and farming tribes were of a peaceful character,
> thereby promoting an exchange of agricultural products and crafts from the
> south and copper and tin from northern regions. In this case settling down
> and 'dissolution' of steppe population into that of farming oases could take
> place.
>
> (Vinogradova 1994: 46)

Central Asia usually refers to the extensive area south of the steppes and east
of the Caspian Sea, stretching east across Xinjiang and the Dzungar Basin to
the Gobi Desert of southern and Inner Mongolia nearly to the upper reaches
of the Huang Ho River in Kansu province of western China proper. It is
divided physically by the separate drainage systems formed by the knot of the
Pamir and Tien Shan mountains into western and eastern halves, often referred
to as western and eastern Turkestan. Our concern here will be principally
with Middle and Late Bronze developments in western or formerly Soviet
Central Asia, which today comprises the independent states of Turkmenistan,
Uzbekistan, Tadjikistan, and Kyrgyzstan together with the neighboring regions
of southern Kazakhstan, northern Afghanistan (north of the Hindu Kush), and
Khorassan and eastern Mazanderan provinces of northeastern Iran. We will
consider briefly Bronze Age developments in eastern Central Asia (principally
in Xinjiang or today's westernmost China) when we discuss problems with
archaeologically based ethnic and linguistic identifications at the end of this
chapter.

Western Central Asia can be defined as the lands drained by the Amu Darya,
Syr Darya, their present and former tributaries, and the rivers and streams
flowing north towards the Amu Darya from the Hindu Kush mountains of

Figure 5.1. Eastern Iran ("Turan") and adjacent regions, showing approximate locations of selected archaeological sites.

Afghanistan or west and north towards the Caspian from the Elburz and Kopet Dagh mountains of Iranian Khorassan and eastern Mazanderan, as well as the smaller streams flowing north from the Kopet Dagh mountains into the Kara Kum desert. This vast area, which contains distinct ecological zones ranging from high intermontane valleys to piedmont and alluvial plains, can be characterized in general as a land of interior drainage with its waters flowing either into the landlocked Aral and Caspian basins or terminating in the Kara Kum and Kyzyl Kum deserts (Fig. 5.2).

R. Pumpelly (1908: xxvii), who conducted systematic excavations at the site of Anau in southern Turkmenistan at the beginning of the twentieth century, referred to the entire area as a "cemetery whose graves are the wasted and half-buried mounds of vanished cites" (cf. Fig. 5.1 and Fig. 5.2). His description is apt, though the location of such vanished cities varies greatly from one period to another. Our concern here is not to detail this long history of development

from the Neolithic to the Iron Age, an evolutionary sequence that has been
summarized and revised in English several times (e.g., Masson and Sarianidi
1972; Kohl 1984, 1992b; Dani and Masson 1992), but rather to discuss evidence
for sustained contacts between western Central Asia and the Eurasian steppes
to the north, processes that increasingly intensify from the end of the third into
the first half of the second millennium BC. First we will review the history
of archaeological explorations in western Central Asia and describe briefly the
physical features of its different regions.

ARCHAEOLOGICAL EXPLORATIONS IN WESTERN CENTRAL ASIA FROM THE EXCAVATIONS AT ANAU TO THE DISCOVERY OF THE BACTRIA-MARGIANA ARCHAEOLOGICAL COMPLEX (OR "OXUS CIVILIZATION") – THE EVOLUTIONARY HERITAGE OF SOVIET AND WESTERN ARCHAEOLOGY IN CENTRAL ASIA

The Russians conquered Central Asia in the second half of the nineteenth century, taking Tashkent in 1865, Samarkand in 1868, and southern Turkmenistan
only later in the 1880s. They occupied the area militarily, occupying principally
cities, like Tashkent. They did not intensively colonize it with agricultural settlers as they had the plains abutting the northern Caucasus or the steppes of
western Siberia and northern Kazakhstan. The first archaeological excavations
were conducted in the last decades of the nineteenth century by Russian military officers and included early explorations of the important historical city
of Merv and General Komarov's extensive trench that nearly bisected the earlier northern mound of Anau in southern Turkmenistan. The American R.
Pumpelly continued the work at Anau in 1904, investigating its two mounds
more systematically on a much smaller scale. Pumpelly's work, which was published in 1908, brought Central Asia to the attention of Western scholars who
were trying to synthesize later prehistoric developments throughout the greater
Ancient Near East. Ironically, this Western attention later waned as the area
became politically inaccessible, while Soviet archaeologists, particularly after
World War II, uncovered many more sites and considerably expanded overall
understanding of its later prehistory. Beginning in the 1930s, Soviet scholars
established a series of complex interdisciplinary expeditions covering different
regions throughout the area (Kohl 1984: 18–23), and relevant research institutions also were founded under the aegis of the Soviet Academy of Sciences for
each of the Central Asian Republics.

   Three of these interdisciplinary expeditions should be mentioned here: 1)
the Khoresmian Archaeological Ethnographic expedition, initially directed by
S.P. Tolstov, began in 1937 systematically to explore the historically important
area of ancient Khoresmia, or the area surrounding the Aral Sea, particularly
to its south along the extensive deltas formed by the lower courses of the Amu
Darya; 2) The Southern Turkmenistan Complex Archaeological Expedition

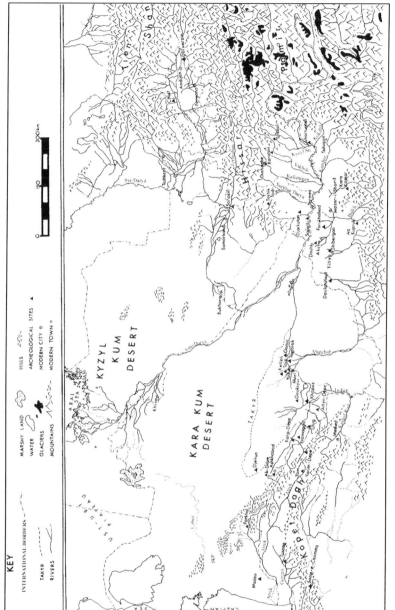

Figure 5.2. Western Central Asia with selected archaeological sites (adapted from Kohl 1984: 16, map 1).

(or *Yu.T.A.K.E.*) began its work in 1946 under the direction of M.E. Masson, and in 1952 B. A. Kuftin conducted a series of deep soundings at the site of Namazga-depe that established the basic Chalcolithic to Late Bronze sequence (Namazga or NMG I-VI) still used today; and 3) The Soviet-Afghan Archaeological Expedition surveyed and excavated sites in northern Afghanistan or southwestern Bactria from 1969 to 1979, and included the extensive Late Bronze Age excavations of V.I. Sarianidi in the Dashly oasis, which together with the work of the Uzbek scholar A. Askarov in northern Bactria at Sapalli-tepe from 1968 to 1973, initially defined the Middle and Late Bronze cultural complex now most commonly referred to as the Bactria-Margiana Archaeological Complex (BMAC), or what the French archaeologist H.-P. Francfort (1984a: 174) has dubbed the "Oxus civilization." Subsequently, V.I. Sarianidi's excavations of monumental architectural constructions, particularly in the Gonur and Togolok oases of historical Margiana or the lower course of the Murghab river in southeastern Turkmenistan, uncovered the western or Margiana component of this newly recognized Bronze Age civilization. Despite the upheaval associated with the collapse of the Soviet Union in 1991, archaeological investigations continue in all these areas except for northern Afghanistan and today often include international collaborative projects bringing archaeologists trained in different national traditions of research.

Most of the past and even current archaeological investigations in Central Asia have emphasized internal evolutionary developments (cf. Götzelt 1996), even while acknowledging movements of peoples into the area or the establishment of intense exchange relations with neighboring regions to the south and west. Initially, this emphasis was given a Marxist twist. Thus, S.P. Tolstov (1962: 5, 12) initiated his Khoresmian project in part to demonstrate that the pre-Islamic peoples of Central Asia had passed through a slave-holding socioeconomic stage or formation, and M.A. Itina (1977: 236–237) stressed the progressive overall development of society and growth in productive forces from the Neolithic to the Iron Age despite the continuous arrival of Andronovo-related herders from the steppes and their supposed destruction of urban life in southern regions at the end of the Bronze/ beginning of the Iron Age. The sequence established for the Kopet Dagh piedmont strip of southern Turkmenistan, which was first definitively established by the soundings at Namazga-depe and then elaborated by numerous *Yu.T.A.K.E* directed excavations of neighboring multiperiod tells, such as Altyn-depe (Masson 1988), was interpreted principally in terms of internal development, a product of natural growth from small Djeitun Neolithic villages with largely undifferentiated single-roomed houses to the advent of true cities with monumental public and ritual architecture, such as stepped terraces or ziggurats, craft specialization, and elite and impoverished residential quarters.

Western archaeologists, who have studied these materials, have placed them in a broader geographic context that relates them more directly to complex "protourban" formations or "civilizations," such as those documented in the Helmand basin at Mundigak in western Afghanistan and Shahr-i Sokhta in eastern Iran or at Harappa and Mohenjo-daro in the Indus Valley, but the story is still to be explained principally in terms of local growth and adaptation leading to the nearly contemporaneous, albeit related, emergence of these complex formations in the second half of the third millennium BC or during this proto-urban/urban phase. These perspectives are valuable and reinforce the basic theme of broad interconnections and shared processes that are stressed throughout our study, but they also sometimes result in the expectation that everything *must* happen simultaneously across vast regions. Thus, for example, H.-P. Francfort (1984b: 262) asserts:

> ... il devient absurde d'imaginar une Bactriane et une Margiane demeurées isolées et sous-dévelopées au milieu de regions 'urbanisées' d'Iran, de Turkménie, de l'Indus, du Baluchistan, et du Sud de l'Hindu-Kuch ... on voit que toute l'Asie centrale, à des degrees divers, a fait partie d'un trés vaste ensemble urbain entre 2500 et 1800 environ.... [All sites of varying size throughout this area] ont été touches par cette phase.

Similarly, the lack or extreme scarcity of recorded Chalcolithic and Early Bronze remains on the plains of Bactria and Margiana or occupations prior to this urban phase is explained as due to alluviation (i.e., their burial) coupled with insufficient research (cf. Salvatori 1998: 52). If the piedmont skirt or *atak* of southern Turkmenistan records all these phases, then they *must* also be present in Bactria and Margiana.

Perhaps future work will confirm this perspective, but a point that must be emphasized here and one to which we will return is that different local regions, including some that were historically most significant in Central Asia, such as Khoresmia, Fergana, and the lower Zeravshan Valley, exhibit markedly different records of development during late prehistoric times, as reflected in the very archaeological terminology and sequences themselves that jump directly from the Neolithic into the Bronze Age. What is fascinating about Central Asia is this uneven record of development and how best to explain it, but before doing so we need to sketch in greater detail the physical and environmental features of this area.

PHYSICAL FEATURES OF THE LAND – DESERTS, MOUNTAINS, AND SOURCES OF WATER; ENVIRONMENTAL CHANGES AND ADAPTATIONS TO ARID ENVIRONMENTS; IRRIGATION AGRICULTURE AND EXTENSIVE HERDING AND SEASONAL TRANSHUMANCE

Today most of western Central Asia, save for its high mountain valleys to the south and east, is an arid area in which it is necessary to irrigate fields in order to raise crops. Russian specialists (e.g., contrast Lisitsina 1978 with Dolukhanov 1981) differ sharply as to the extent of climatic changes that have occurred during Early and Middle Holocene times. Certainly, some areas, such as limited regions of the piedmont skirt or *atak* of southern Turkmenistan, may have changed little or have always depended on the relatively stable groundwater discharges feeding the small rivers and streams flowing down from the northern slopes of the Kopet Dagh mountains. On the other hand, soil analyses and archaeological data in the form of numerous recorded stations of hunters and fishermen from other areas, such as the hilly region of salt lakes in the inner Kyzyl Kum desert, suggest considerable desiccation and aridization, long-term processes that intensified particularly towards the end of the third millennium BC (ca. 2200 BC) and have been recorded elsewhere both on the steppes to the north and in the Ancient Near East to the south and west (Hiebert 2000). Although it is difficult to generalize about the entire area, given marked differences in local conditions, it seems reasonable to conclude that the area became even drier during the Middle and Late Bronze Age, or that period that witnessed a considerable expansion of permanent settlement, supposedly based on irrigation agriculture (Lisitsina 1981: 62–63), both on the Margiana and Bactrian plains and presumably on the terminal branches of the Lower Zeravashan and in the Akcha Darya delta of the Amu Darya or ancient Oxus River south of the Aral Sea.

The lower courses of the major rivers of western Central Asia have often retracted, such as the Lower Zeravshan that once flowed into the Amu Darya, and/or have exhibited considerable hydrological instability over time, sometimes even changing direction, such as the lower Amu Darya that at times flowed towards the Caspian, not into the southern Aral Sea. These "Seas" are both landlocked basins, fed principally in the case of the Caspian by the Volga and Ural Rivers that flow into it from the north, and in the case of the Aral by the Amu Darya and Syr Darya that flow into it respectively from the south and northeast. The overexploitation of these latter two rivers and diversion of their waters for irrigation purposes principally to produce the "white gold" crop of cotton during Soviet times is a principal reason for the current "death" or severe ongoing shrinkage of the Aral Sea. Presently, the much-reduced Aral Sea (approximately 51–53 m. above sea level) lies at an absolute elevation roughly 80 m. above that of the Caspian (roughly 28 m. above sea level), though the latter also has experienced a complicated history of periodically rising and transgressing or spreading west across the low-lying steppes of northern Daghestan and then retracting back.

The area contains two "Mesopotamias" or lands between rivers: 1) the first consisting of the area drained by the Amu Darya (approximately 2500 km. long with numerous tributaries forming a catchment area of roughly 300,000 sq. km.) and the Syr Darya (stretching nearly 3000 km. from the source of its parent Naryn river and draining more than 200,000 sq. km.), both of which today flow into the Aral Sea; and 2) the much smaller "little Mesopotamia" formed by the Tedjen (roughly 1150 km. long with a catchment area of approximately 70,000 sq. km.) and the Murghab (roughly 1000 km. long, draining approximately 50,000 sq. km.), both of which terminate in the Kara Kum desert of southern Turkmenistan (for more detail, see Kohl 1984: 25–34). Both rivers peak in early spring, being fed by snow melt from the mountains of northwestern Afghanistan and, in the case of the Tedjen, also the Khorassan highlands of northeastern Iran.

As far as is currently known, the upper and middle courses of the Amu Darya and Syr Darya were not directly exploited (i.e., their waters not diverted for irrigation) in the Bronze Age (Hiebert and Kohl 2000), although numerous settlements are recorded along the tributaries of the Amu Darya or ancient Oxus River in the highland valleys of southern Tadjikistan and the contiguous Bactrian plains of southern Uzbekistan and northern Afghanistan through which the river flows, justifying the appellation "Oxus civilization" (Francfort 1984a). The terminal deltas of the lower courses of these rivers were diverted for irrigation purposes during the Late Bronze Age, but by peoples, such as the bearers of the Tazabag'yab culture, whose remains, particularly ceramics, resemble Andronovo-related materials from the Trans Urals region to the north, suggesting some protracted process of movement into the area and assimilation with the local post-Kelteminar or Neolithic population of the area.

Except for the practice of irrigation agriculture and metallurgy, the Late Bronze sites on the Lower Zeravshan, Lower Amu Darya, or Lower Syr Darya Rivers exhibit none of the cultural complexity seen farther south on sites of the Bactriana-Margiana Archaeological Complex (BMAC). Unlike the big Central Asian "Mesopotamia," the land between the lower courses of the Tedjen and Murghab Rivers was exploited by oasis irrigation agriculturalists as early as Late Chalcolithic times, and the Margiana plain formed by the Lower Murghab constituted one of the principal foci of elaborate cultural developments during the Middle and Late Bronze Age.

The *atak* or piedmont "skirt," which is drained by nearly fifty small rivers and streams flowing north from the Kopet Dagh mountains into the southern Kara Kum desert, provided the setting for the long development of permanent settlements practicing irrigation agriculture, a process that began possibly as early as the late seventh millennium BC. This fertile strip – approximately 80 km. wide by 600 km. long – is characterized by a relatively stable discharge or flow of waters and by the relative lack of huge flooded areas and destructive mudflows during the spring high water period. Today many underground *karez* or *qanat* systems cross this strip, which tap the high water table and groundwater sources, a practice that may initially have been introduced in late prehistoric times, though more research is needed to determine exactly when these systems were first developed. The southern

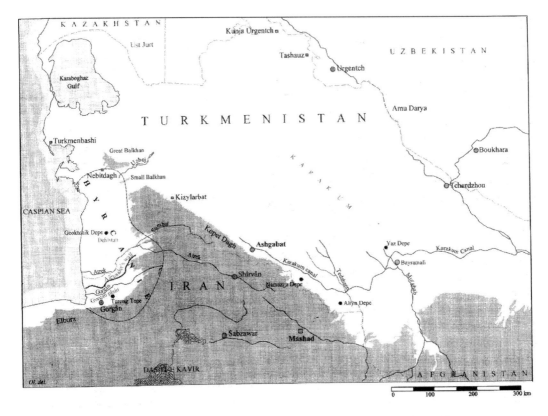

Figure 5.3. Southwestern Turkmenistan and northeastern Iran (adapted from Lecomte 1999: 136, fig. 1).

Turkmenian *atak* is dotted with multiperiod tells of the characteristic Ancient Near Eastern type, some of which contain cultural deposits more than 30 m. thick.

Finally farther west, the Atrek and Gorgan Rivers drain the northeastern Iranian plateau and the eastern Elburz and western Kopet Dagh mountains, running parallel in their lower courses before flowing into the southeastern corner of the Caspian Sea (Fig. 5.3). The contiguous Gorgan and Misrian plains formed by these rivers are extremely fertile when watered and comprised the important classical region of Hyrcania. Today, they are divided by the international border between Iran and Turkmenistan, a political reality that has precluded their systematic investigation as a single region as well as their conceptualization as a naturally integrated region or province within western Central Asia. The Gorgan plain in Iran, like the *atak* strip of southern Turkmenistan, is dotted with scores of multiperiod tells (Arne 1945; Kiani 1982; Shiomi 1976, 1978), documenting a sequence that extends throughout late prehistoric times, whereas the drier Misrian plain to the north in western Turkmenistan is, on current understanding, only first extensively occupied

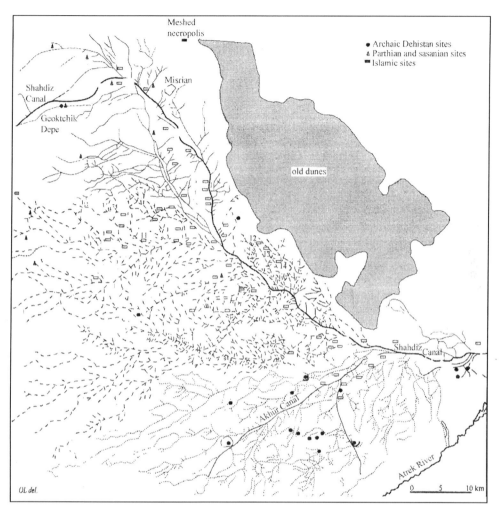

Figure 5.4. Map of sites on Misrian Plain with major irrigation canals (adapted from Lecomte 1999: 139, fig. 2).

during the Iron Age by the very large sites (some exceeding 200 ha. total area) of the Archaic Dehistan culture, possibly beginning towards the end of the second millennium BC.

These latter sites emerged only after the construction of an elaborate system of irrigation canals, the main branch of which extended from the lower Atrek across the plain to the northwest for roughly 130 km. (Kes', Kostyuchenko, and Lisitsina 1980; Lecomte 1999; Fig. 5.4). It is also to be noted that the so-called Alexander Wall, which may have initially been constructed in Parthian times and then extended and strengthened by the Sasanians (Keall and Roaf 2000), stretches more than 150 km. from the southeastern corner of the Caspian to the northeast, running south of today's international border and paralleling the Gorgan River that flows to its south. This wall was built to stem the incursions of mounted nomads coming down from the north to plunder the towns and cities of the Gorgan plain and the northeastern Iranian plateau. It formed part of the extensive system of Sasanian long wall fortifications (*limes*) on both sides of the Caspian that were constructed for this same purpose (Aliev et al. n.d.).

THE TWO WORLDS OF WESTERN CENTRAL ASIA: "CIVILIZED" AND "BARBARIAN"; ARCHAEOLOGICAL TRANSFORMATIONS – MOBILE CATTLE HERDERS BECOME IRRIGATION AGRICULTURALISTS; THE MULTIPLE ORIGINS, FLORESCENCE, AND COLLAPSE OF THE BACTRIA-MARGIANA ARCHAEOLOGICAL COMPLEX

Russian archaeologists have long recognized the presence of steppe Bronze Age materials, particularly handmade coarsely incised ceramics, in western Central Asia and have interpreted their presence as documenting movements of stock breeding "nomads" north to south from the Eurasian steppes into the irrigated oases and highland valleys of Central Asia. Most researchers today see such movements as protracted processes occurring over centuries and not as sudden events, and most stress their largely peaceful character, involving gradual assimilation with the already established, culturally more complex agriculturally based populations of the region (e.g., Itina 1977; Kuzmina 1994; P'yankova 1993, 1994, 1999; Vinogradova 1994, 2004; Kutimov 1999; Shchetenko 1999). Certain materials and technologies may have diffused south to north, whereas the primary movements of herders from the steppes, who are thought to have spoken a different language(s), proceeded in the opposite direction (Itina 1977: 235–236). Processes of assimilation are recognized, but the contrasts between the "barbarian" herders of the steppes and the "civilized" irrigation agriculturalists of the oases are emphasized and find direct reflection in a series of material culture traits.

"Barbarian" western Central Asia exhibits a markedly different sequence of developments from "civilized" Central Asia: a protracted and fairly primitive Neolithic horizon in which fishing and non–food-producing activities remain considerably important but suddenly change or are interrupted seemingly by the arrivals of new peoples from both the north and the south, and this transformation leads to the construction of irrigation networks along the terminal deltaic fans of the Lower Amu Darya and the beginnings of their Bronze Age (Fig. 5.5). Irrigation technology, wheel-turned ceramic imports, and possibly wool-producing flocks of sheep and goats as well as Bactrian camels diffuse south to north or indicate contact with the southern "civilized" world, whereas large semisubterranean pit dwellings, crude incised pottery, horses, and evidence for local metal-working activities suggest contacts to, if not also actual

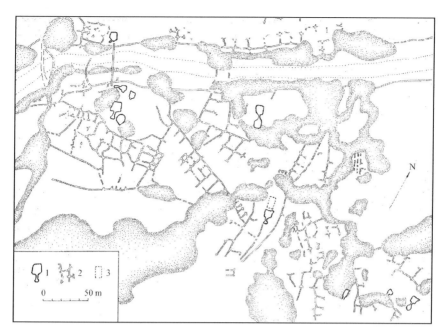

Figure 5.5. Kokcha 15 settlement, Tazabag'yab culture, in the Akcha-darya delta, Khoresmia (northern Turkmenistan, south of Aral Sea): irrigation networks with semisubterranean pit-houses (adapted from Itina 1977: 46, fig. 4); legend: 1 – houses; 2 – traces of irrigation network; 3 – borders of surface dwellings.

movements of peoples from, the north, from either side of the southern Urals on the western Eurasian steppes.

Clearly, if we were to draw the borders of the Namazga-related cultures and subsequent civilization or BMAC, they would not only differ substantially from the borders that define the contemporary nation-states of the region, but also they would fluctuate and expand over time, incorporating, for example, new regions, such as Margiana, Bactria, and possibly the Lower Zeravshan and the narrow mountain valleys of southern Tadjikistan during the Middle and Late Bronze periods. Peoples from the steppes principally herded animals and produced relatively coarse incised and immediately recognizable handmade ceramics (Fig. 5.6). They often continued to live in large semisubterranean pit houses, even when they had settled permanently and practiced irrigation agriculture (Itina 1977: 44–103; Fig. 5.5). They utilized wheeled vehicles and probably rode horses, and they cast sophisticated and also diagnostic and highly functional tin-bronze weapons and tools (Fig. 5.7).

The southern farmers, on the other hand, continued to extend their systems of irrigation agriculture, a tradition that began through the diversion of the largely rain-fed streams that flowed down from the Kopet Dagh mountains and that by the Middle Chalcolithic (NMG II) period included the construction of larger canals paralleling the terminal streams from the deltaic fans of the

Figure 5.6. Andronovo-related "steppe" ceramics from the Kangurttut settlement, southern Tadjikistan (adapted from Vinogradova 2004: 144, fig. 25).

Lower Tedjen and then by the Middle Bronze period the Lower Murghab and tributaries of the Middle Amu Darya and rivers flowing onto the northern and southern Bactrian plains. The long prehistoric Namazga sequence of cultural development from Neolithic through Late Bronze times in southern Turkmenistan was related or interconnected in some way with developments taking place in neighboring regions of northern Iran, as documented, above all, on the densely settled Gorgan plain at sites such as Shah-tepe, Tureng tepe, and Yarim tepe, and on the Iranian plateau proper at sites, such as Hissar at Damghan or the Nishapur-P sites near Nishapur (Hiebert and Dyson 2002).

Similarly, Anau or Namazga-related materials have also been found in the Upper Atrek Valley at sites such as Yom tepe and on the Darreh Gaz plain, which is nestled between the Iranian plateau proper and the northern piedmont strip or *atak* of southern Turkmenistan, at sites such as Yarim Tepe (or DG 2, Kohl and Heskel 1980; Fig. 5.8). Systematic surveys, which currently are being undertaken in northeastern Iranian Khorassan by Iranian archaeologists (Yazdi 2004; Garazhian 2004) are recording many related multiperiod tells and more extensive single-period sites both in the intermontane valleys of Khorassan and farther south bordering the great Dasht-e Kavir desert of the central Iranian plateau. Undoubtedly, more Namazga-related sites eventually

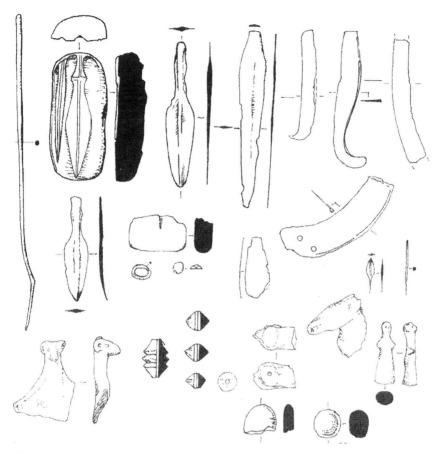

Figure 5.7. Bronze tools and weapons, including stone-casting mould, and clay fig-urines and spindle whorls from the Kangurttut settlement (adapted from Vinogradova 2004: 145, fig. 27).

will be documented along the Kashaf Rud stretching through the Meshed plain east to join the Tedjen River at Serakhs. In other words, the Kopet Dagh mountain range

> never acted as a barrier, but rather as a corridor where an intense cultural exchange took place. The material evidence of cultural traits shared on both sides of the Kopet Dagh is large, widespread and precise . . . and covers the cultural sequence from the Neolithic to the Iron Age. At a certain point in time, two cultural regions, a western and an eastern one, can be detected both encompassing the two sides of the Kopet Dagh. (Salvatori 2003: 7; cf. also Kohl, Biscione, and Ingraham 1981)

By the late third millennium, these sedentary farmers fired elegantly propor-tioned wheel-turned ceramics, including diagnostic footed vases and inverted

Figure 5.8. Multiperiod prehistoric mound of Yarim Tepe on the intermontane Dar-reh Gaz plain of northeastern Iran (picture taken by P. L. Kohl, November 1978)

conical cups; they lived in above-ground, mud-brick houses often in planned fortified settlements with monumental public architecture that are described on analogy to Mesopotamia as "temples" and "palaces" (Sarianidi 1986: 64; 1998a: 83; Fig. 5.9), and they produced a range of prestige crafts, some made from exotic materials, such as lapis lazuli, steatite, and alabaster, that had to have been imported onto these plains and some, such as grooved stone columns and long tapering staffs, that apparently were used principally for ritual or cultic purposes. They also worked copper, copper-lead, and copper-arsenic metals, and over time they made tin-bronzes, producing distinctive vials with applied wands with thickened ends or pins sometimes capped with figured animals, mirrors, and elaborate ceremonial shaft-hole axes with flaring tails (cf. Hiebert 1994b for an overview of BMAC craft production).

Notably, possibly from as early as Late Chalcolithic fourth millennium times (as represented by a figured stone cylinder seal from Sarazm (Isakov 1994: Fig. 10; Fig. 3.2b above), they also had seals or devices for securing the contents of vessels and rooms for administrative purposes, including highly diagnostic metal and then stone compartmented seals with elaborate geometric and figured representations. Occasional spectacular finds – such as "royal" burials (Fig. 5.10) with four-wheeled wagons, one of which may have been driven by a Bactrian camel (Fig. 5.11), a classic Harappan stamped seal depicting an elephant with Indus script (Fig. 5.12a), a Trans-Elamite-like cylinder seal (Fig. 5.12b), gold and silver vessels, some depicting Bactrian camels (Fig. 5.12c), and bullae with seal impressions (Fig. 5.13a) and a Sargonid (?) cylinder seal with a

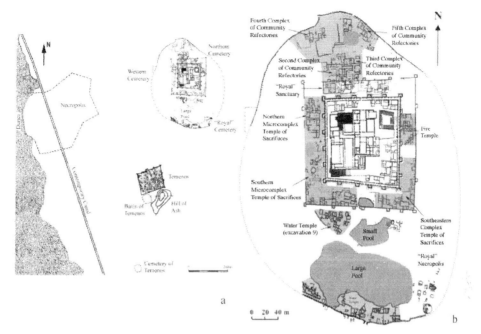

Figure 5.9. Gonur-depe: (a) general plan of temenos and north mound (adapted from Kosarev et al. 2004: 230, fig. 2); and (b) palace-temple complex of Gonur north (adapted from Sarianidi 2005: 31).

Figure 5.10. "Royal" Burial 3225 with remains of four-wheeled wagon (adapted from Sarianidi 2005: 240).

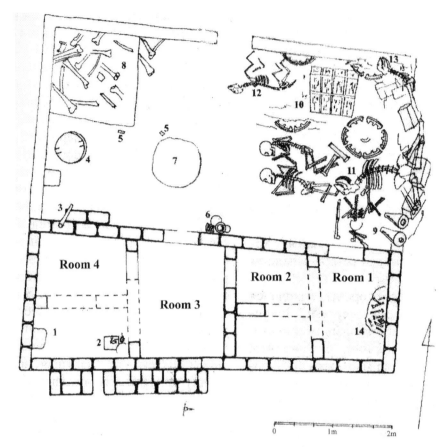

Figure 5.11. Plan of Burial 3200, northern edge of "Royal Cemetery" Gonur-depe north "Palace-Temple" complex; 1 – concentration of valuable funereal gifts; 2 – two fragments of mosaics with "carpet" ornamentation, silver cosmetic flask, tiny cosmetic shovel-shaped applier, toggle pin with its head in the form of a lying calf, iron toggle pin with its head in the form of a gold eight-pointed star, a half-moon, and a standing golden gazelle and a crouching turquoise lion; 3 – a two-meter-long stone staff with its end in the form of a horse's hoof; 4 – stone disk of marble limestone; 5 – bronze objects of uncertain significance; 6 – two open bronze "censers" and a ceramic vase on a raised hollow foot with decoration; 7 – a patch of red-fired sand; 8 – concentration of bones of an adult camel; 9 – two large ceramic vessels with narrow bases; 10 – a four-wheeled wagon; 11 – the skeleton of an adult camel lying in correct anatomical order; 12 – the complete skeleton of a dog in correct anatomical order; 13 – a strongly disturbed skeleton of a young horse; and 14 – the strewn accumulation of disarticulated bones of four individuals.

cuneiform inscription (Fig. 5.13b) at the Gonur-depe north "palace-temple" complex and adjacent "royal cemetery" (Sarianidi 2002, 2005; Kosarev et al. 2004; for a criticism of the identification of the public architecture at Gonur and the hypothesized proto-Zoroastrian rituals that are supposed to have been

Figure 5.12. (a) Harappan seal with inscription from Gonur-depe north "Palace-Temple" complex, "water temple" (excavation 9), room 19; (b) trans-Elamite-like seal from Gonur-depe, north "Palace-Temple" complex, northern "Temple of Sacrifices," western façade, near an "altar" (adapted from Kosarev et al. 2004: 239, 241); (c) Silver goblet with Bactrian camel, Gonur-depe "royal" burial 3220 (adapted from Sarianidi 2005: 236).

conducted in them cf. Francfort 2005: 276–285) – all bespeak some form of extensive interregional relations, such as mercantile exchange or the establishment of political alliances, with other late third/early second millennium states of the Ancient Near East (cf. later discussion).

The basic pattern is clear. "Civilized" western Central Asia of southern Turkmenistan, Margiana, and Bactria interacted, probably principally through the exchange of raw materials and finished prestige goods (Lyonnet 2005; n.d.a.), with other "civilized" centers of the ancient Near East in eastern Iran, Baluchistan, the Indus Valley, the Elamite realm of southwestern Iran, and greater Mesopotamia. "Barbarian" western Central Asia, which at this time included Khoresmia, the Fergana Valley, and possibly the Lower Zeravshan Valley and the narrow intermontane valleys of southern Tadjikistan, witnessed relatively sudden changes or transformations of their local cultural sequences marked by the appearance of steppe ceramics, distinctive architecture, and decentralized metal-working practices that produced functional tin-bronze tools and weapons (Vinogradova 1994: 40, 42–44) with direct parallels to Andronovo-related sites from the southern trans-Urals region and adjacent steppes of western Kazakhstan and Siberia.

Numerous "steppe" burials are now being recorded in the Middle Zeravshan Valley (Tosi, personal communication), suggesting that settlement from the north into Central Asia became relatively substantial at some point during the later Bronze Age. Such archaeologically attested "steppe" material remains have most plausibly been interpreted as evidence for the gradual movements of peoples from farther north into the Lower Amu Darya region south of the Aral Sea and across the Kyzyl and Kara Kum deserts first into "barbarian" and ultimately into "civilized" western Central Asia. When did these movements begin and how do they compare with the previously discussed north to south movements of peoples with oxen-driven wheeled wagons from the western Eurasian steppes across and around the Caucasus?

Whereas the Eurasian steppes directly abut the northwestern Caucasus and the settled agricultural communities of Transcaucasia, the Kyzyl and Kara Kum deserts separate the steppes from the "civilized" southern plains of western Central Asia. These deserts functioned as a more effective cultural barrier until roughly the end of the third millennium BC, when the semisedentary cattle herders in the Volga and Ural river basins and even farther east were regularly able to cross these extensive arid expanses by developing ever more mobile means of transportation with the help of horses and, most likely, Bactrian camels, which had earlier been harnessed to wagons and probably used to haul goods and worked for draft purposes in southern Central Asia and eastern Iran. It is therefore not surprising that contacts between the western Eurasian steppes and the Ancient Near East developed earlier on the western side of the Caspian since the steppes and the Caucasus mountains, particularly in the northwest along the Kuban River, were directly contiguous with one another, not separated by waterless deserts, the only problem being how to get around or over the high Caucasus mountains. The mobile cattle herding economy of the Bronze Age steppes, which developed after the breakup of the gigantic Tripol'ye settlements in central Ukraine, also initially spread west to east reaching the Caucasus before emerging in the Don and Volga basins and east of the Urals. Thus, peoples on the steppes moved south of the Caucasus before entering southern Central Asia for easily understood natural physical and historical reasons.

The precise beginnings of the gradual but continual movements of cattle herders north to south east of the Caspian Sea are uncertain owing to the somewhat floating, unanchored chronology of Bronze Age steppe remains, particularly for sites located east of the Urals. The earliest evidence suggesting form of connection with the steppes to the north may be the rich Afanasievo-like burial from Sarazm I, dating at least to the late fourth millennium BC, although this constitutes a unique, isolated example of such contact at that time (Lyonnet, personal communication). Much later, early Andronovo ceramics with Abashevo and Petrovka elements in association with Sarazm IV ceramics were excavated at Tugaï along the right bank of the Zeravshan river immediately

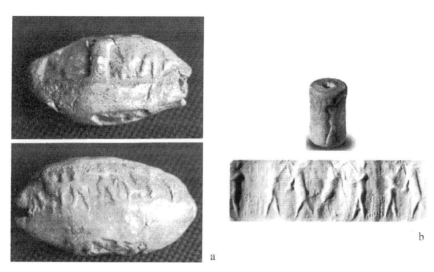

Figure 5.13. (a) Bullae with impressions of cylinder seals found within Gonur "temenos" (adapted from Sarianidi 2002: 195); (b) Cylinder seal with cuneiform inscription from Gonur-depe necropolis (adapted from Sarianidi 2002: 326).

east of Samarkand (Avanessova 1996), suggesting that more substantial contacts had been established by the middle of the third millennium, though Parzinger (2003: 270, 280) argues convincingly that the Tugai settlement was occupied subsequent to the final occupation of Sarazm or during the second half of the third millennium. Interestingly, the limited salvage work at this site also yielded considerable evidence for metal working (crucibles, kilns, slag, etc.), a characteristic practice of the later Andronovo-related groups that moved south into Central Asia at the beginning of the second millennium and worked the tin mines of the Zeravshan Valley (Alimov et al. 1998; Parzinger and Boroffka 2003).

The evidence for a steppe presence in southern Central Asia becomes more substantial after the emergence of the Bactria Margiana Archaeological Complex (BMAC), the latter process already being underway by the late third millennium BC (cf. chronological discussion in Section IV). Archaeologically, the arrival of these newcomers from the north is recorded by the discovery of scatters of "nomadic" or "incised coarse ware" sherds in the Murghab delta, as well as by their occasional occurrence in the excavations of the public buildings in the major centers in the Togolok, Gonur, and Dashly oases.

We will not review in detail here all the features of the BMAC, nor exhaustively review problems of its origins, chronology, and geographical extent. These topics are fundamentally related to current understanding or the state of research and are extremely complex and sharply debated by specialists working on these materials (for a general accessible summary, cf. Lamberg-Karlovsky 1996: 194–217). The use of the term BMAC itself is debated, referring either to settlement on these plains in both Middle (Namazga V) and Late (Namazga VI) Bronze Age times or just exclusively the latter. Salvatori (personal communication) believes that the term BMAC should be reserved for the Late Bronze Age because many substantial changes occurred between Middle and Late Bronze times, including shifts in settlement pattern (from centralized to acephalous), defensive architecture (square to circular towers), stamp seals (from metal compartmented seals to stone stamp seals), figurines, and so forth. According to him, most of the plundered, truly spectacular BMAC materials from Bactria – as well as now the properly excavated ones from the Gonur necropolis, particularly the newly recognized "royal cemetery" in Margiana (Figs. 5.9–5.13) – date to his urban phase or Middle Bronze Age, that is, to the last centuries of the third millennium BC (cf. his discussion and list of new calibrated C14 dates, Salvatori 2000: 97–103; cf. also the list of calibrated C14 dates for Central Asia in Vingogradova 2004: 290–297), and contemporary with the final Namazga V occupation at Altyn-depe and other contemporaneous sites in the piedmont strip of southern Turkmenistan.

Kircho and Popov (2005: 528–541) have recently defended the basic outlines of the traditional or "younger" Soviet/Russian chronology and published more than two hundred C14 dates from Central Asia, including seventy-one analyzed from Altyn-depe alone. Although many dates from the same sites and levels vary widely (cf. our discussion in Chapter 4 on the uncertainties of C14 dates) and some clearly cannot be correct, the overall late prehistoric Central Asia chronology remains uncertain, "floating" over at least 300 years that allows for alternative younger and older systems of dating. More works needs to be done and more reliable dates still need to be compiled to resolve this uncertainty. Here we follow the Western or "older" system and accept Francfort and Salvatori's concept of an "urban phase," the beginnings of which date to the last centuries of the third millennium BC and which would include both the earliest materials from Gonur North and the final remains from Altyn-depe, traditionally assigned to the Namazga V phase. In any event, materials from this "urban phase" predate any significant evidence for the arrival of northern herders from the steppes.

Most archaeologists of the former Soviet Union initially seized on the obvious parallels in ceramics and figurines between the BMAC materials, on the one hand, and those found on multiperiod tells in the Kopet Dagh piedmont strip of southern Turkmenistan, on the other, to argue for a strong formative influence from this latter region; indeed, the very fact that BMAC remains were first described by Soviet scholars as Namazga VI underlies their belief in this basic genetic connection to the millennia-long developmental sequence established by Soviet archaeologists in southern Turkmenistan. Not surprisingly, some Western scholars have observed similarities with other areas and in other materials, including earlier stone and metal seals and public architecture, from sites located to the south in eastern Iran, Afghanistan, and Pakistani Baluchistan to suggest southern roots for the BMAC from these regions, if not also from the Indus Valley itself. Undoubtedly, the BMAC had diverse origins and both these perspectives can be maintained; they are not mutually exclusive or, as B. Lyonnet (n.d.: 48) observes, the BMAC represents "une culture nourrie des deux poles, 'turkmène' et 'indien'."

Over time during the Late and Final Bronze periods the BMAC complex or phenomenon became even more of a hybrid with the continuous arrival of cattle herding pastoralists from farther north. These newcomers settled down on the watered plains of Bactria and Margiana and changed their way of life, adopting and transforming the material culture of the agriculturalists with whom they came into contact. The central thesis here is that current archaeological evidence, as limited and problematic as it is, documents precisely the assimilation process described above; that is, the later northern component of the Late and Final Bronze Age manifestation of the BMAC, has been detected archaeologically. What has been found is just what one would expect to show the gradual, but continuous infiltration and assimilation of cattle herders into the established sown world of irrigation agriculturalists that becomes increasingly substantial in the last phases of the Bronze Age, particularly towards the middle of the second millennium BC.

Although incomplete and problematic, settlement pattern data for southern Central Asia (cf. the calculations and caveats in Kohl 1984: 143–146, 151–154, and 159–160; and also now the more systematic work in the Murghab delta [Gubaev, Koshelenko, and Tosi 1998]) supports minimally the following conclusions: 1) there is scant evidence for occupation of the lowland plains of Margiana prior to the Middle Bronze period or prior to the second half of the third millennium and later periods (Salvatori 1998: 52); 2) the total known occupied area for the plains of Margiana and northern and southern Bactria during Middle and Late Bronze Age times considerably exceeds the known occupied area for earlier Chalcolithic and Bronze Age remains from the piedmont strip of southern Turkmenistan or even also from northeastern Iran (excluding the Gorgan plain), a fact that seems to preclude the possibility of deriving the former exclusively from the latter, as has been postulated (e.g., Biscione 1977); and 3) the most notable disjunction in the settlement pattern data in terms of location, size, and nature of settlements from southern Central Asia from Neolithic through Iron Age times or throughout later prehistory occurs precisely during this initial major occupation or settling of the lowland plains of Bactria and Margiana beginning in the second half of the third millennium BC.

The lowland plains watered by the Lower Tedjen River and its terminal branches and the Lower Murghab were occupied during Late Chalcolithic times (e.g., the Geoksyur oasis and scattered Namazga III materials in the Kelleli oasis of Margiana), probably by settlers from southern Turkmenistan, but this occupation was restricted as the recent survey work has demonstrated. Evidence for an earlier occupation of the Bactrian plains west of the Kunduz Valley or west of eastern Bactria (where such occupation has been documented at Shortughaï and other settlements on the Ai Khanum and Taluqan plains, see Lyonnet 1997: 68–71) is even less apparent, save for the scatters of "Early Neolithic" lithic materials found in the sands north of the Bronze Age oases of northwestern Afghanistan (Vinogradov 1979).

It is impossible to calculate precisely the increase in settled area and its overall extent during BMAC times. One major unresolved problem is the contemporaneity of the occupation of the various oases. If Russian archaeologists, like Sarianidi, are correct in arguing for the sequential occupation of the oases and the general movement of settlement in Margiana upstream over time (from Kelleli to Gonur to Togolok to Takhirbai), then the total occupation in any specific period correspondingly would be reduced (cf. Lyonnet n.d.: 53–54). It is unclear to what extent this perspective is correct or to what extent it simplifies a much more complex reality (e.g., Gonur-depe north was occupied during at least two, if not three, periods; see Hiebert 1994: 36–38; Salvatori, personal communication). Nevertheless, the very rough calculations that can be made suggest a substantial increase in settlement, comparing the data available for southern Turkmenistan in the Early Bronze period with that for the Middle and Late Bronze BMAC settlements. It is difficult to consider such a marked increase in settlement as solely the product of a local developmental process.

The BMAC synthesis is highly original, even if some of its practices (e.g., diverse mortuary rituals, use of seals) find their roots farther south in Baluchistan and eastern Iran (trans-Elamite) or west in southern Turkmenistan. However one interprets the planned public architecture on BMAC sites (cf. again the criticisms of Francfort 2005: 276–285), its distinctive, easily recognizable character is apparent (Fig. 5.9). Most BMAC sites are at least to some extent fortified, a feature that was not characteristic for many earlier settlements in southern Turkmenistan, and the very presence of such fortifications suggests, of course, that the settling of these plains was not an entirely peaceful process. The conflict may not have been so much between steppe and sown as later arrivals ousting or displacing earlier peoples who had moved into the area; sometimes the new immigrants may simply have occupied settlements that had earlier been abandoned.

Many BMAC sites, such as the Dashly 3 "fortress" (Sarianidi 1977) or the later "fort" at Gonur south (Sarianidi 1998a: 115), record later occupations by peoples who significantly alter the preexisting architecture and often contain considerable evidence for metal working (Sarianidi, Terekhova, and Chernykh 1977: 35). A "fortress" (Sarianidi 1977: 33) rose above the earlier Dashly 3 "palace," and its third and fourth final periods of occupation consisted of reusing earlier rooms and constructing new, less substantial rooms within the former "palace" courtyard. A clay crucible, slag, and copper ingots also were recovered from this final, almost squatter-like occupation.

Sites in the Kopet Dagh piedmont strip of southern Turkmenistan typically form multiperiod tells that were occupied in some cases for millennia. Though the larger excavated sites in Margiana exhibit a cultural sequence and were occupied for some period of time, the total depth of cultural deposit on the BMAC sites never approaches that of the larger tells in southern Turkmenistan or northeastern Iran. The "deep sounding" of a stratified midden at Gonur North extended down 3.5 m before reaching virgin soil (Hiebert 1994a: 30), whereas the total depth of the cultural deposit at Altyn-depe was estimated as at least 30 m. (Masson 1981: 75) and that of Yarim-depe on the Darreh Gaz plain possibly even greater (Kohl and Heskel 1980; Fig. 5.8). BMAC sites exhibit planned, highly symmetrically arranged architecture; by comparison, the proto-urban settlement at Altyn-depe, with its winding streets and distinct residential and functional areas (Fig. 5.14), seems to have evolved organically over time; it was not preplanned in the same way as the major BMAC settlements, including even the smaller sites such as Sapallitepa (Askarov 1973), obviously were. This contrast of BMAC features with other areas could be extended, the point being that the BMAC represents something original, a unique blend of diverse cultural elements.

How convincing is the empirical support for the thesis of a gradual continuous movement into and settling of the Margiana and Bactrian plains by northern cattle herders? Do a total of 336 incised coarse ware sherds from 34 "nomadic camp sites" (Cerasetti 1998: 67; or 75 such sites, according to Salvatori [personal communication]) constitute sufficient proof for such postulated movements? Evidence for the Indo-Aryans — if that is the correct ethnic/linguistic identification for these cattle herders (see later discussion) — has never seemed so meager and puny. Or does it? What would one expect to find archaeologically to document the process of gradual but continuous movements of cattle herders onto the lowland plains of Margiana and Bactria?

The plains these settlers entered were not empty but already occupied by peoples practicing a form of irrigation agriculture that they had developed over preceding millennia. As the northern settlers entered these plains, their way of life changed; they focused more on irrigation agriculture, adopting and assimilating the preexisting material culture of the neighboring peoples they encountered. The process is the inverse of that already adumbrated for the collapse of the gigantic Tripol'ye settlements; there agriculturalists who also herded became pastoralists, adopting an ever more mobile and extensive economy; here cattle herders settled down and began to cultivate crops more intensively than they had previously practiced farther north. This process undoubtedly was very complex and protracted.

The peoples living in Tazabag'yab culture settlements, which have been excavated in the Akchadarya delta of the Lower Amu Darya south of the Aral Sea, clearly practiced irrigation agriculture (Itina 1977: 44–45; Fig. 5.5). Their practice may or may not reflect influence or even some initial colonization from the south (ibid., 229–231), but this culture also exhibits clear links to the steppes farther north and represents a rapid transformation from the earlier Neolithic Kelteminar culture documented throughout the area. The "steppe" or "coarse incised" ceramics of the Tazabag'yab culture are those most typically found in Margiana and Bactria, suggesting that these peoples were those first displaced farther south; they already knew how to survive in the new environment that they entered.

Later movements may have been more direct with ever more mobile pastoralists moving from the southern Urals and other areas on the Eurasian steppes into the settled oases of southern Central Asia. The important point is that initially at least these movements did not represent armed invasions but gradual, largely peaceful, continuous infiltrations and encounters with earlier established cultures, the product being the further development of a distinctive archaeological culture or phenomenon, the later or Late and Final Bronze manifestation of the BMAC, with its diverse multicultural roots.

The archaeological and early historical record is replete with such processes of assimilation and emulation of more culturally complex societies by less developed ones. Mexica origins, for example, are likewise somewhat obscure and mixed, but when mobile Chichimec groups came into the valley of Mexico from the north they consciously adopted and emulated the high Toltec culture that they encountered. Smith describes the hybrid origins of the Mexica:

> Native historical descriptions of the Atzlan migrants contain contradictory information on the cultural sophistication of these peoples. In some accounts they are said to have lived in caves, made their living by hunting with bows and arrows, and wore animal skins for clothing. These traits describe peoples known as Chichimecs (barbaric peoples from the north)...Contrasting with this picture of the migrants as barbaric Chichimecs are descriptions of complex economic and cultural activities such as the planting of maize, the construction of temples, and the use of the ancient Mesoamerican 52-year calendar.... The presence of these contradictory traits among the Aztlan migrants is part of the dual conception of the cultural origins of the Aztecs, who believed themselves descended from both savage Chichimecs and civilized Toltecs. (Smith 1996: 40–41)

In mixing with the local peoples and in transforming their way of life, they created a new distinctive culture with obvious roots in the Mesoamerican cultural tradition.

Numerous other historical processes of movement into an area followed by assimilation into or even absorption by the local preexisting culture could be cited to support this model (e.g., the Mongols in China over time becoming

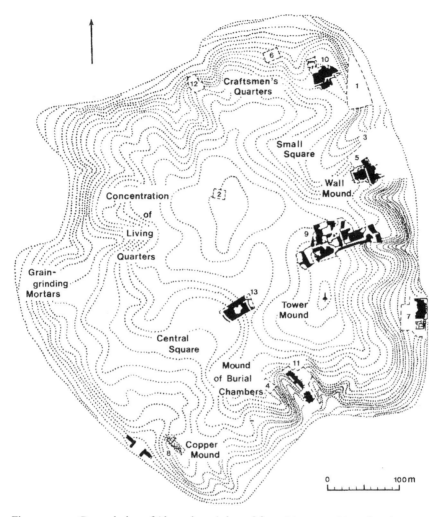

Figure 5.14. General plan of Altyn-depe (adapted from Masson 1988: 5, fig. 1).

Chinese). Each would differ in terms of specific features, such as the number of migrants versus the number of local inhabitants, and such features would clearly affect the final outcome of the assimilative process, for example, the language adopted, the degree of continuity or change evident in religion or social and political institutions, and so forth. Such a process of assimilation obviously affects material culture, but theoretically one can expect that such changes are going to be muted or difficult to interpret. In other words, the archaeological signature of assimilation and emulation is likely to be indistinct or hard to decipher, much less clear than, say, a rapid and disruptive military incursion or a sudden colonization (e.g., the establishment of Greek colonies in Sicily). This theoretical expectation of an ambiguous material record may not be comforting to the archaeologist, but it is realistic in terms of what is known historically and ethnographically.

Theoretically as well, there should be some relatively distinct instances of mixed "steppe" and "sown" character. Where the economy can reasonably be reconstructed as more extensive with a greater reliance on herding, steppe elements should dominate; where the way of life is obviously more dependent on some form of intensive agriculture, one would expect the reverse: the dominance of material features not present on the steppe that are either novel or can be linked to the cultures of neighboring areas to the west and south. Current archaeological evidence supports these theoretical expectations.

Incised and ornamented "steppe" ceramics occur in small proportions on many BMAC sites that can reasonably be interpreted as permanent irrigation agricultural settlements. Recently, two sites were partially excavated southeast of Takhirbai 3 containing complete incised coarse "steppe" ware vessels stratigraphically associated with Takhirbai Final Bronze ceramics. These excavations uncovered grain storage and processing facilities and semisubterranean rectangular pit houses similar to those documented for Tazabag'yab culture sites farther north in Khoresmia; that is, these excavations presumably record sedentary villages of "steppe" peoples who had moved south to practice irrigation agriculture on the Murghab plain (Salvatori 2003: 13); similar evidence has also been recovered for southern Uzbekistan (Avanessova 1996).

Salvatori (2003: 12) believes the "steppe" presence in Margiana significantly increases during the Late and particularly Final Bronze periods, or towards the middle of the second millennium, and associates their more substantial presence with an environmental crisis: increased aridization and sanding up of the delta resulting in a general contraction of settlements at the end of the Bronze Age. As life gets more difficult, steppe peoples presumably settle down and occupy now partially abandoned and formerly more intensively cultivated lands. The process is not one of development, but of breakdown or regression, though it is unclear how much is human and how much is naturally induced.

The steppe element in "civilized" southern Central Asia is suggested not only by the ceramics, but also by metals, such as characteristically bent knives and sickles (Vinogradova 1994: 43, fig. 8; Fig. 5.7), and by direct evidence for metal working (ibid., 45, fig. 10). Such evidence increases over time and is more visible in areas, such as the relatively narrow mountain valleys of southern Tadjikistan, where pastoralism formed a greater component of the economy (Mandel'shtam 1968; Litvinskii and Solov'ev 1972). The recently published salvage Zardchakhalif burial (Bobomulloev 1999) from the narrow Upper Zeravshan Valley near Pendjikent classically illustrates the process of mixture or hybridization. This grave contained two bronze bits, a bronze toggle pin capped with the figurine of a horse, and disc-shaped bone cheekpieces identical to those found farther north on the steppes (Fig. 5.15). The bits and

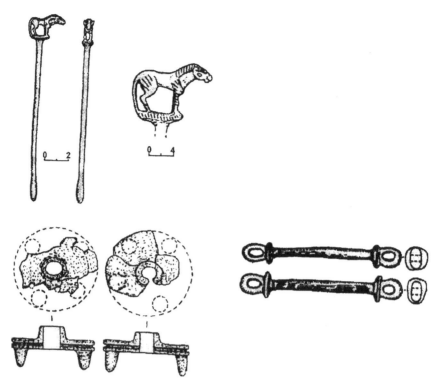

Figure 5.15. Selected artifacts from Zardchakhalif burial near Pendjikent, Tadjikistan (adapted from Kohl 2002b: 189, fig. 9).

cheekpieces, obviously, document horse harnessing, and the studded cheekpieces in particular, which have now also been recovered at the Late Bronze site of Djarkutan in southern Uzbekistan (Teufer 1999: 88, fig. 13, 4), clearly attest to a northern connection to the steppes where numerous cheekpieces essentially identical in form have been found (cf. Teufer 1999 for a complete list and also Boroffka 1998; and Fig. 4.8 above).

Toggle pins capped with animal figures are a relatively characteristic BMAC item, but the depictions of horses are quite rare on these toggle pins (Ligabue and Salvatori 1988: pl. 82), as they also are on the much more numerous seals and amulets from Margiana and Bactria (cf. Sarianidi 1998b: nos. 112, 1397, 1398, 1405, 1444, 1445, 1446, 1486, 1487, 1488, 1496), particularly relative to other animals, such as sheep, snakes, eagles, and even Bactrian camels. The horseman buried at Zardchakhalif had mixed origins, relating both to the steppe and the sown. Solid-wheeled wagons (Figs. 5.10 and 5.11) have also been discovered in some of the "royal" graves at Gonur-depe, and may have been driven by different animals – oxen, Bactrian camels, and even horses. A "horse burial" lacking a skull has been excavated in the early Middle Bronze cemetery at Gonur-depe (Sarianidi 2001), though questions have been raised as to its precise context, date, and significance (Salvatori 2003: 11).

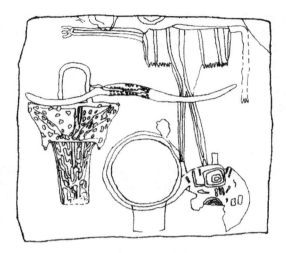

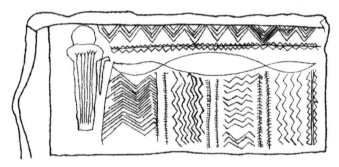

Figure 5.16. Depictions of the composite bent bow from a Novosvobnaya tomb (adapted from Shishlina 1997: 56, fig. 2).

Composite bent bows, which are attested possibly from Novosvobodnaya times in the northwestern Caucasus (Fig. 5.16) and in slightly later Middle Bronze (or Catacomb) times on the western steppes (Shishlina 1997: 57–58), also appear on a silver goblet, lacking certain archaeological provenience but presumably from Bactria (Francfort 2003: 45–49; Fig. 5.17). Such a development in bentwood technology may ultimately be associated in some way with the treatment of wood to produce the heavy tripartite wooden-wheeled vehicles, but Shishlina (2003: 363) emphasizes its social significance and apparent relationship with the harnessing and riding of horses, equating its development with the appearance of mounted warriors. That may be true, but the Bactrian archers shown fighting with the same weapons, possibly defending their flocks of sheep and goats, are not shown riding, but releasing their arrows from bent knee positions. The scene – if genuine – records either the diffusion of the bent bow technology from the steppes to Bactria and/or, possibly, the transformed way of life of a settler from the steppes.

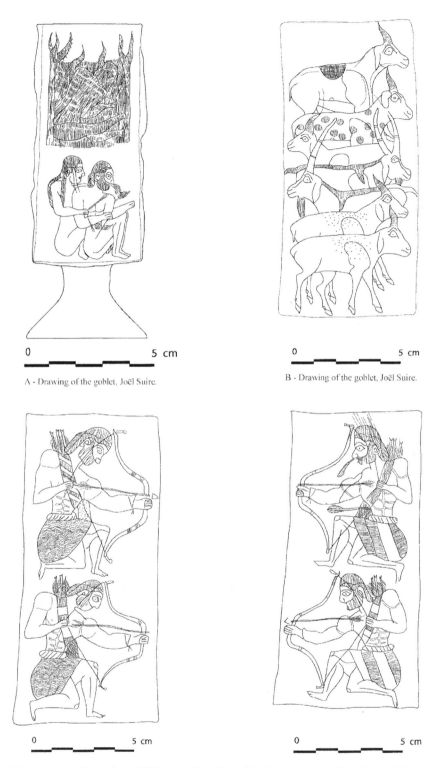

A - Drawing of the goblet, Joël Suire.

B - Drawing of the goblet, Joël Suire.

Figure 5.17. Silver footed "Bactrian" goblet with skirted archers fighting and dying and images of sheep and goats (adapted from Francfort 2003: 49); translated from the French.

Similarly, the well-known depictions on two other BMAC-related silver vessels also visually record this same process of settling down and transforming the mixed economy of their forefathers into one increasingly reliant on irrigation agriculture. The vehicles depicted are not chariots engaged in a hunt, as Amiet (1990b: 161) suggested, but more plausibly form part of a train of oxen-driven wagons and carts with their heavy wooden wheels that are strikingly similar to scores of examples found on the western Eurasian steppes particularly from Novotitorovskaya and Catacomb culture times onwards. The wagon trail of cattle herders, the cowboys of the Wild East, in search of more reliable pastures, had by the middle of the second millennium BC increasingly infiltrated the lowland plains of Margiana and Bactria. As they changed their way of life, they emulated the material culture of their settled neighbors and helped farther transform the already established, highly original, and culturally diverse phenomenon known as the Bactria Margiana Archaeological Complex (Fig. 5.18).

The BMAC, in turn, does not exhibit a continuous pattern of growth, but rather records an initial or proto-urban Middle Bronze period of florescence in which a common cultural *koine* stretched from the northern and southern plains of Bactria to Margiana and on to the piedmont strip of southern Turkmenistan, followed by a Late Bronze period of fragmentation and decentralization. It is estimated that Gonur-depe north was the economic and political center of Margiana during the earlier "urban phase," reaching a size of roughly 40 ha. and possibly exhibiting similar social complexity and performing similar functions to the contemporary NMG V proto-urban sites of Namazga-depe and Altyn-depe in southern Turkmenistan. The settlement data suggests "some form of integrated territorial hierarchy or political administrative dominance by the centre in Gonur" (Salvatori 1998: 58) at the end of the third millennium. This situation collapses during the subsequent Late Bronze period, when the occupation at Gonur-depe south is estimated only at about 5 ha, and there is no single political administrative center for the area (for the contrastive rank size index graphs for Middle and Late Bronze settlements in Margiana, cf. Salvatori 1998: 65, figs. 8 and 9).

Comparable data does not yet exist for Bactria to the east, though it is possible that a different pattern may prevail. Djarkutan in northern Bactria is a later and much larger site than Sapallitepa, and the still later (?) site of Farukhabad 1 in northern Afghanistan is estimated to have covered nearly 90 ha. (cf. Kohl 1984: 159–160). Additional excavations and surveys need to be conducted throughout Bactria to determine whether the pattern parallels or contrasts with that documented for Margiana.

What caused the apparently political breakdown of the proto-urban Middle Bronze phase in Margiana and southern Turkmenistan? Was the continuous infiltration of herders from the steppes partially responsible for this collapse? Or, perhaps more consistently with current archaeological evidence, does the

a

b

Figure 5.18. Settling and cultivating the plains of Bactria and Margiana (adapted from Kohl 2002b: 190, fig. 10).

movement of herders from the north qualitatively increase in intensity and scale only after the breakdown of this integrated, proto-urban phase? In the Caucasus we have seen that the movements of the builders of the early monumental kurgans occurred probably sometime after the principal dispersal of Kura-Araxes peoples from Transcaucasia, earlier movements in turn that seem to have occurred immediately in the wake of the abandonment of Uruk-related settlements in eastern Anatolia and western Iran. Similarly perhaps, the cattle herders from the north only significantly settled in southern Central Asia after a collapse of centralized political control.

Possibly, but the quality of the archaeological evidence makes it difficult, if not impossible, here to disentangle cause from effect. What other contributory factors may have led to the breakdown of the Middle Bronze BMAC polity? This question forces us to consider briefly the early civilizations or complex states that arose and flourished east of Sumer during the second half of the third and into the early second millennium BC. We refer to them as secondary states because they developed after Sumer and were economically integrated through networks of exchange and political and military relations/domination by the truly urban centers and urbanized societies of southwestern Iran, Mesopotamia, and Syria throughout their period of florescence; they were incorporated into a larger interacting world in which materials and peoples continuously circulated.

SECONDARY STATES EAST OF SUMER CA. 2600–1900 BC –
CYCLES OF INTEGRATION AND COLLAPSE; SHIFTS IN
PATTERNS OF EXCHANGE AND INTERREGIONAL RELATIONS
FROM THE LATE CHALCOLITHIC THROUGH THE MIDDLE
BRONZE AGE

Numerous archaeological and historical studies document the long-distance
exchange between Mesopotamia and lands to the east of Sumer both along
the Gulf and across the Iranian plateau to Afghanistan and the Indian subcontinent (for example, Oppenheim 1954; Muhly 1973; Adams 1974; Larsen
1976; Amiet 1986; T.F. Potts 1994; Lamberg-Karlovsky 1996: 128–217; Lyonnet 2005, n.d.a..; Aruz 2003a; Weeks 2003; Ratnagar 2001, 2004; for a very
accessible, up-to-date and principally archaeological overview to this extensive
topic, cf. Possehl 2002: 215–236). Our review here is selective and limited to
consideration of how movements of peoples from the steppes affected later
Bronze Age developments in Central Asia, possibly facilitating a breakdown in
integration or possible collapse of a centralized polity in Margiana and Bactria,
and how this process resembled and differed from other transformations occurring throughout the Ancient Near East from the end of the third to nearly the
middle of the second millennium BC or essentially overlapping with the rise
and fall of the BMAC.

Several years ago G. Dales (1977) commented on "Shifting Trade Patterns
between the Iranian Plateau and the Indus Valley in the Third Millennium BC."
At that time, Western scholars were focused on recent discoveries far to the
east of Sumer at sites such as Shortughai, Shahr-i Sokhta and Tepe Yahya and
were just beginning to appreciate the significance of Soviet discoveries on the
Bactrian plain of northern Afghanistan; the principal discoveries in Margiana
were still to be made. In this context, Dales observed what he thought was
a shift in long-distance relations from one principally focused on overland
exchange across the Iranian plateau to the borders of Afghanistan and Pakistan
to a maritime trade along the Arabian Sea through the Gulf to southwestern
Iran and Mesopotamia. The latter was associated with the emergence of the so-
called Indus Valley or Harappan civilization and the famous historically attested
trade between Mesopotamia and the lands of Dilmun (principally Bahrain,
though also for a time probably the little island of Tarut and adjacent regions
of the eastern Arabian mainland), Magan (northern Oman, the Arab Emirates,
and possibly coastal southeastern Iran and Baluchistan principally abutting the
entrance to the Gulf [Tosi n.d.]), and Meluhha (usually identified with the
Indus Valley civilization, which, of course, extended far beyond the confines
of the Indus Valley itself, including an intrusion west along the Makran coast
at least as far as Miri Qalat; see Fig. 5.29).

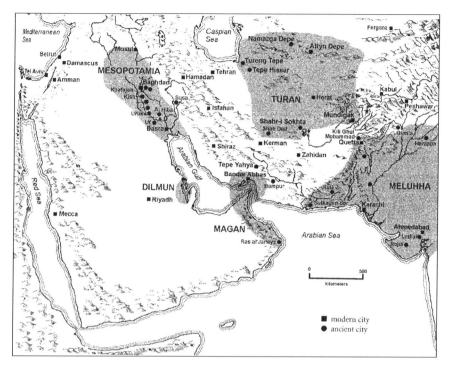

Figure 5.19. Archaeological sites and culturally related regions in G. Possehl's Middle Asian Interaction Sphere (adapted from Possehl 2002: 215, Fig. 12.1).

Dales referred to this latter period as an incipient urban or proto-urban phase linking the cities of Sumer with those of the Indus Valley. He conveyed a sense of excitement associated with the then recent discoveries in Bactria and at Shortughai, and in the same volume M. Tosi (1977) defined the emergence of early civilization in Turan or eastern Iran, an extensive area encompassing southern Turkmenistan, the Atrak Valley, the eastern Elborz mountains, the Helmand Valley, and Bactria and Margiana (ibid., 47), a definition still employed by Possehl for delineating his heuristically useful Middle Asian Interaction Sphere (2002: 215, 228; Fig. 5.19).

Although Dales' study today is dated in part because of the more recent discoveries in Margiana and now in the Jiroft or Jaz Murian basin of southeastern Iran (see Section V), many scholars, such as H.-P. Francfort and S. Salvatori, still utilize the concept of an integrated "urban phase" in the second half of the third millennium extending across much of the Ancient Near East and western Central Asia during the second half of the third millennium BC. In the lands east of Sumer, this urban phase did not continue to develop but devolved into a less integrated, less centralized era of localization (Kenoyer 1998:24–27), an "eclipse of the East" in terms of an overall collapse in urbanism and social complexity that some scholars have associated with the arrival of Indo-Iranians

onto the Iranian plateau and Indo-Aryans into the Indian subcontinent beginning sometime during the second millennium BC (Lamberg-Karlovsky 1996:
243–250). For us, Dales' study remains seminal for attempting to discern larger
patterns of interregional interaction, implicitly associated with political competition and attempts to expand their alliances, networks of exchange, and even
to establish political hegemony and control.

Today additional, even earlier patterns of interregional exchange and political expansion are discernible. As we have seen, the Uruk expansion, first
defined by G. Algaze (1993), refers to the movement of peoples and establishment of colonies from southern Mesopotamia north up the Euphrates
into Anatolia and east into western Iran beginning roughly in the middle
of the fourth millennium. This possibly imperial expansion into neighboring areas collapsed towards the end of the fourth millennium, and its decline
may have facilitated the movements of Kura-Araxes or Early Transcaucasian
peoples west across Anatolia and south into Syria and Palestine and southeast
into western Iran during the end of the fourth and beginning of the third
millennium BC. Subsequently during the first centuries of the third millennium, a new political and economic expansion of proto-Elamites spread from
southwestern Iran eastwards across the Iranian plateau to occupy sites in central and eastern Iran (cf. Alden 1982; Amiet 1986; and Lamberg-Karlovsky
1996: 108–127), a process that is principally defined by the discovery of proto-
Elamite tablets throughout these regions. Thus, painting a very broad canvas,
we can identify an Uruk expansion principally to the north, followed by a
proto-Elamite expansion emanating from southwestern Iran principally to the
east, and then a shift to maritime exchange and the emergence of the Indus
Valley civilization overlapping with and rapidly followed by the appearance
of proto-urban sites throughout Turan or a very extensively defined eastern
Iran.

The broad picture is clear, but is it possible to shade more details into this
canvas, particularly during this "urban phase?" There is really no acceptable
blanket term for all the complex polities that emerged east of Sumer during the
second half of the third millennium BC. The concept of Turan encompasses
too many diverse regions, and terms like eastern Iran or western Afghanistan
are, at least, implicitly anachronistic in their reference to areas defined by
the borders of contemporary nation-states. The concept of an Indus Valley
civilization likewise contains implicit assumptions, some of which – such as the
occurrence of Indus remains far beyond the lands actually drained by the Indus –
are only partially correct at best. There is no agreement on whether the Indus
Valley represented a "state" in neo-evolutionary terms or some less rigorously
defined "archaic complex society" (Possehl 2002: 5–6, 56–57), and we are
not certain whether this "civilization" comprised a single or multiple polities,
though it is interesting that the major urban centers of Harappa, Mohenjo-daro,
Ganweriwala, Rakhigari, and Dholavira occupy distinct regions encompassed

Chronological/"Cultural" Distinctions and Shifting Political/Economic Alliances: patterns of interaction east of Sumer during the 3rd millennium BC

Multiple Complex Polities ("secondary states") in eastern Iran, the Gulf and eastern Arabia, Baluchistan and northwestern India, southern Central Asia, and Afghanistan c. 2500 - 1800 BC

Work to be done: How many separate polities? Co-existing or overlapping/sequential? Alliances between states? Attempts at hegemony (e.g. Indus intrusion in eastern Bactria (Shortughai) and Makran coast/interior Baluchistan)?

Some possible examples:

1) North-central to northeastern Iran to southwestern Turkmenistan - Damghan (Hissar), Gorgan plain (Tureng), and Lower Atrek and Sumbar (Parkhai) valleys, western Turkmenistan piedmont "skirt" (Ak-depe)

2) Upper Atrek (Yom) and Darreh Gaz (Yarim) valleys, prehistoric Nishapur and Kashaf Rud valley, South-central and southeastern Turkmenistan(Namazga, Altyn), Middle and Lower Tedjen, Margiana (Gonur, Togolok), Bactria (Sapalli, Djarkutan, Dashly) or BMAC (Bactria-Margiana Archaeological Complex)

3) Lower and Middle Helmand/Seistan/northern Kerman: Mundigak,Shahr-i Sokhta, Gardan-i Raig (SW Afghanistan) Shahdad with ties to group 2

4) Southern Kerman: Yahya, and Jiroft - Marhashi (?)

5) Southern Baluchistan, Makran coast: Bampur (?), Miri Qalat -- Indus "intrusion"(Sutkagen-Dor, Sotka-Koh)

6) Khuzestan and Fars (Susa and Malyan) - Elam

7) Central Iran (Sialk, Arisman, Veshnaveh)

8) The Indus Valley "Mature Harappan"/Meluhhan polity (polities ?)

9) Others - Oman and Lower Persian Gulf (Magan?) and Bahrein and Upper Persian Gulf (Dilmun ?)

Figure 5.20. Complex polities or secondary states east of Sumer: towards a political geography of eastern Iran/Turan in the late third to early second millennia BC.

by this early "civilization," suggesting some degree of coordination of activities, or perhaps overarching unity based on their roughly equidistant spacing (cf. Kenoyer 1998: 49–50). The concept of a politically unified, hierarchically integrated Indus Empire (e.g., Rao 1972: 4–6), analogous to much later South Asian empires, on the other hand, scarcely seems credible.

Numerous diverse "states" or "archaic complex societies" emerged east of Sumer in distinct ecological settings. The concept of a culturally unified BMAC or cultural *koine* stretching from the plains of northern and southern Bactria to Margiana and southern Turkmenistan is consistent with the archaeological record, as is the well-enshrined concept of the Harappan or Indus Valley civilization, whether or not it was politically unified. We also have dense concentrations of Bronze Age settlements and/or large "proto-urban" socio-culturally complex sites emerging on the Gorgan plain (Tureng Tepe), the lower Hilmand basin (Shahr-i Sokhta and, farther upstream, Mundigak), central Iran near Kashan (Sialk), the western edge of the Dasht-i Lut (Shahdad), and the Jiroft or, better, the Jaz Murian basin of southeastern Iran (Konar Sandal A and B, and possibly Bampur; Fig. 5.20).

This list undoubtedly is partial. Many other areas, particularly in Pakistani Baluchistan, and western, southern, and northeastern Afghanistan, the real *terra incognita* of the Ancient Near East, can be expected to yield similar evidence for

Secondary States East of Sumer: shared features

- 1) Secondary states are secondary in the historical sense that they emerge in a context of pre-existing states and complex systems of expansion, dispersal, and interregional interaction

- 2) The secondary states east of Sumer are less nucleated and densely populated (i.e., urban) and less socially differentiated than 3rd millennium Mesopotamia

- 3) Origins in a local Neolithic/Chalcolithic sequence (e.g., Djeitun/Namazga I-III for BMAC; Merhgarh for Indus)

- 4) Reliance on intensive but technologically simple irrigation agriculture in lands of interior drainage (e.g., lower Helmand for Shahr-i Sokhta, Lower Murghab for Margiana, Middle and Lower Halil Rud for "Jiroft")

- 5) Shared features of monumental, possibly religious architecture (stepped terraces or "ziggurats") with shared architectural features (e.g., stepped niches)

- 6) Shared meaningful iconography of fantastic beings (e.g., lion-headed eagles, bearded bulls, eared serpents, scorpion men)

- 7) Circulation by some means (e.g., political/military/marital alliances, elite gift exchange, war booty, commercial trade) of finished and unfinished metal artifacts, jewelry, stone vessels, and precious raw materials

- 8) The secondary states collapse or "devolve" primarily during the 1st half of the 2nd millennium BCE

Figure 5.21. Secondary states east of Sumer: shared features.

"archaic complex societies" with remains dating to this same "proto-urban" or "urban phase," though, as argued earlier, some areas may have remained outside the "civilized" world of interregional interaction and/or were incorporated into it relatively late. These blank spaces on our archaeological maps always must be considered, even if there is no immediate possibility of filling them in or documenting their participation in broader historical processes.

While their scales and settings differ substantially, certain common elements can be discerned (Fig. 5.21). Nearly all emerge from their own separate cultural developmental sequences from Neolithic or Chalcolithic times to the Bronze Age and reach their maximum extent during the second half of the third millennium, though some, such as Shahr-i Sokhta, devolve or become less hierarchically integrated earlier than others. Nearly all these "proto-urban" formations collapse or become radically less centralized principally during the first half of the second millennium BC. Many, like the sites in Margiana and Bactria, along the lower Hilmand River in Seistan, and in the Jaz Murian depression, are situated in lands of interior drainage where similar forms of intensive, though technologically simple, irrigation agriculture could have been practiced. The *political* geography of an extensively defined eastern Iran or Turan undoubtedly was very complex and changed over time during the late third and early second millennium BC.

The different regional polities or secondary states clearly interacted with one another, and some shared many elements of material culture, including

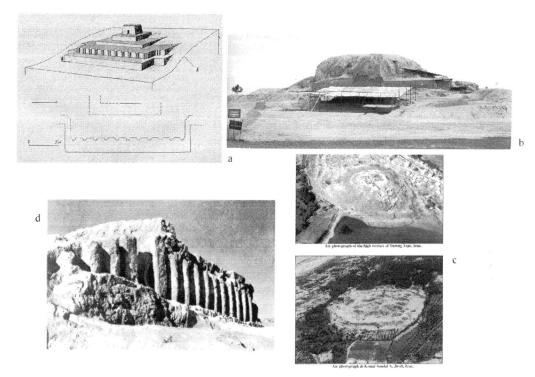

Figure 5.22. Stepped or Terraced Monumental Architecture in the Secondary States East of Sumer (from upper left clockwise): (a) Altyn-depe; (b) Sialk South Hill (adapted from Shahmirzadi 2004: 205, abb. 7); (c) Tureng Tepe and Konar Sondal A, Jiroft (courtesy of E. Leone and M. Tosi); (d) Mundigak (Tepe A, period IV 1).

monumental, probably religious or sacred architecture at certain centers in the form of imposing ziggurat-like stepped or terraced structures (e.g., at Tureng Tepe, Altyn-depe, Mundigak, Sialk, and Konar Sandal A) and specific architectural features, such as distinctive stepped niches and sagging lintels reminiscent of the designs on the carved Intercultural Style chlorite vessels (Figs. 5.22 and 5.23). Although these sites flourished at roughly the same time towards the end of the third and beginning of the second millennium BC, future work undoubtedly will refine our understanding and may make it possible to see the emergence of these regional secondary states as sequentially staggered or overlapping, that is, not perfectly coincidental, reflecting subtle shifts in the formation of political alliances and the conduct of military campaigns and interregional exchange. If Meluhha – while it flourished – dominated maritime long-distance trade along the Arabian Sea, Gulf of Oman, and into the Gulf, these regional secondary states or kingdoms east of Sumer may have directed and controlled exchange along northern (BMAC, Gorgan, Sialk?) and southern (initially Shahr-i Sokhta then Jaz Murian, Shahdad?) overland routes.

Figure 5.23. Shared "Ritual" (?) Architectural Features on Sites in Eastern Iran/Turan. (a) and (b): stepped niches in platform hearth from Burned Building /1/ at Tappeh Hesar (Hissar) (adapted from Schmidt 1937: 165, fig. 93 and Dyson and Howard 1989: 95, fig. 22); (c) "crescent-shaped"/ "sagging lintels" niches at Tapeh Hesar (Hissar) (adapted from Dyson and Howard 1989: 80, fig. 5); (d) stepped niches at Altyn-depe, excv. 5, level 6 (adapted from Masson 1988: plate I); both features recall stepped terrace/ziggurat and hutpot motifs on carved chlorite vessels (cf. Fig. 5.24b).

The system of exchange in which they were caught up was not only one of unfinished or semiprocessed materials arriving in the urban centers of Mesopotamia, Syria, and southwestern Iran where they were further worked into highly crafted tools, weapons, containers, and ornaments. It also consisted of the movement of finished products between these regions, a system of exchange most clearly seen in a corpus of widely distributed and elaborately carved soft stone, so-called Intercultural Style vessels (see, for example, Aruz 2003c; Majidzadeh 2003; Perrot 2003), produced principally in southeastern Iran. These carved vessels had a distinct, recognizable iconography with a highly specific symbolic content that was shared by different cultures, suggesting that ideas and possibly belief systems were also exchanged or diffused over large parts of western Asia during the late third and early second millennia BC. Finished luxury goods were exchanged among the elites of these secondary states and farther west throughout the Ancient Near East. Such goods included jewelry, precious vessels, *and* ceremonial weapons. This last category deserves more critical scrutiny because the luxury trade in ceremonial weapons over time changed into the more systematic procurement of metals and ultimately the exchange of functional bronze tools and weapons.

There is a relationship between the emergence of these secondary Bronze Age states during the second half of the third and first half of the second millennia BC and the long-distance exchange first of luxuries and then increasingly of utilitarian tools and weapons. Undoubtedly, over time – particularly during the Late Bronze period – different sources of tin were exploited: from the Iberian peninsula, the Erzgebirge of central Europe, Cornwall, the Zeravshan Valley of Central Asia (exploited by Andronovo-related peoples from the trans-Ural and Khoresmian regions at the end of the third and beginning of the second millennia BC [Parzinger and Boroffka 2003]), central Kazakhstan, and even farther east. But the initial elite and then functional use of tin-bronzes, so nicely documented by the cuneiform tablets from the early second millennium Old Assyrian trading colony at Kanesh, may have received their tin from one or more of the numerous reported tin sources of western, southern, and north-eastern Afghanistan, sources that are located essentially in archaeological *terrae incognitae*. These poorly investigated regions sometimes contain tin deposits, such as those in the Sarkar Valley of western Afghanistan (Pigott 1999a: 118; Lyonnet 2005), that are associated with Bronze Age mounds. Others, even less well investigated, are nevertheless encircled by regions that we know were interacting with each other and with far distant regions during the Bronze Age (Fig. 5.24).

Different forms of gift exchange probably operated alongside commercial, market-driven trade, as attested in the Old Assyrian trading network. In either case – commercial or gift exchange – the Sumerians and the elites of these eastern states must have produced their own commodities or surplus goods to participate in such exchange networks, though, unfortunately, most of the evidence for Mesopotamian surplus production, above all of woolen textiles, remains archaeologically invisible. Fortunately, cuneiform texts correct for the deficiencies of the archaeological record and reveal the staggering scale of the Mesopotamian surplus production of woolen textiles on the centralized temple and palace estates of individual city-states in the late third millennium BC (cf. Adams 1981: 147–151; D.T. Potts 1997: 91–95).

Utilizing cuneiform documents, Adams, for example, has calculated that herds of more than 2.35 million sheep were kept in southern Mesopotamia during the centralized Ur III period, whereas his archaeologically based estimates for the human population of the southern alluvium are between 500,000 to 1,000,000; such figures reverse the known figures from the 1952–53 Iraqi agricultural census when 1.5 million sheep and goats (90% sheep) helped support roughly 2.5 million people. Clearly a different dynamic prevailed in Bronze Age Mesopotamia, and much of this difference is explained by the production of five different qualities of textiles by tens of thousands of dependent, largely

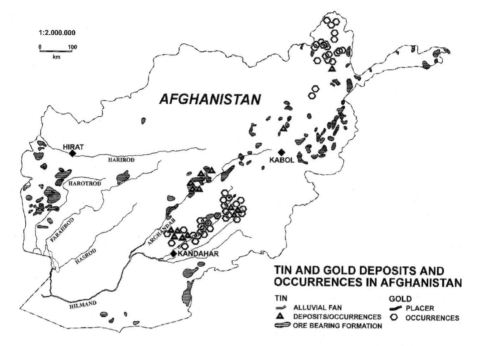

Figure 5.24. Reported tin and gold deposits in Afghanistan (adapted from Pigott 1999a: 117, fig. 9).

female workers, who plucked and sheared the sheep and wove the textiles to be used not just for internal consumption but to support foreign trade. The finest wool was obtained from a variety of fat-tailed sheep (*udu-gukkal*) kept principally at Lagash, whereas other highland varieties yielded lower quality wool.

Mesopotamia may have experienced a "fiber revolution" during the fourth or perhaps principally during the third millennium when it shifted from chiefly cultivating flax to herding wool-bearing sheep to produce textiles. This development may have led to qualitative transformations in land-working and land-holding relationships, freeing prime agricultural land from flax cultivation for additional cereal cultivation and utilizing more marginal or adjacent lands for pasture to support the dramatically increasing flocks of sheep, a process that McCorriston (1997) terms "agricultural extensification." Ultimately, such a shift may have fueled the development of the temple and palace estates, the heart of the Mesopotamian political economy, culminating in the attachment of dependent workers, largely women and children, who spent much of their time weaving woolen garments. Faunal remains from several Uruk sites, such as Tell Rubeidheh in the Jebel Hamrin region of eastern Iraq, show an increase in mature and robust sheep, suggesting specialized wool production by the late fourth millennium and possibly driving the Uruk expansion northwards and eastwards in search of more extensive lands for pasture (McCorriston 1997: 521, 534).

Like other obviously useful innovations, the breeding of robust, wool-bearing sheep may have spread quickly, revolutionizing the herding practices of more simply structured societies on the periphery of the Ancient Near East and ultimately helping to make possible the emergence of true Eurasian pastoral nomadism, a way of life that was not fully in place until the Iron Age. Indeed, it is impossible to define the initial cradle of this development and the directions of its subsequent, rapid spread. The earliest fragments of wool have been identified together with fragments of linen and a cotton-like fiber from Novosvobodnaya kurgans of the Maikop "cultural-historical community" (Shishlina et al. 2003), and the faunal remains from Arslantepe show a dramatic increase in sheep between period VII (Late Uruk) and period VI (Early Bronze I), the latter presumably associated with the arrival of Kura-Araxes or Early Transcaucasian peoples (Liverani 1997: 536) from the northeast. Were deliberately bred, fine wool-bearing sheep first raised in and around the Caucasus, diffusing from there to Mesopotamia to help jump-start their urban revolution, or the reverse? Such origin questions rarely can be answered unambiguously from the archaeological record alone; much more interesting is their rapid adoption among societies already interacting through the ongoing circulation of materials and/or peoples.

The diffusion of wool-bearing sheep into other areas of Eurasia is also a story that needs to be told to account more completely for the appearance of mounted pastoral nomadism (Barber 1991: 27–30). Although based on a very limited sample, Moore (1993: 165) has analyzed the age composition of the sheep and goat bones from Gonur-depe and concluded that the "residents of Gonur would have been full time herders of sheep and goats, eating meat, drinking milk and using other milk products, and spinning and weaving textiles." Similarly, Meadow (personal communication) has suggested the presence of a different larger, presumably wool-bearing sheep in the Indus Valley by the Mature Harappan period, and similar evidence has been recovered from other areas (e.g., at Kastanas in northern Greece, Boroffka, personal communication), suggesting the widespread, if not universal, adoption of larger, more productive breeds of sheep by at least Middle and Late Bronze times.

Finally, all of these "secondary states" emerged *after* the "urban revolution" had transformed Mesopotamia and *after* the initial Uruk expansion had profoundly affected the neighboring societies that directly experienced this process of colonization. In this sense, these late third millennium "states" east of Sumer were *historically* secondary, and they also qualitatively differed in overall scale, degree of urbanization, and social differentiation and complexity from Sumer. The "elites" in these secondary states east of Sumer were hardly the peers of their urban contemporaries in Mesopotamia. There is little evidence for striking social differentiation on the Mesopotamian (or even more Egyptian) scale at sites such as Shahdad and elsewhere in eastern Iran, Afghanistan, the Indus borderlands, and Central Asia, though the elaborate "royal burials" currently being excavated at Gonur-depe north (Figs. 5.9–5.13), including some resembling "houses of the dead" with wheeled vehicles, now appear to qualify this generalization.

In some respect, the social differentiation evident in the mortuary remains of these secondary states east of Sumer (save for Gonur) is even less than that of the roughly contemporaneous monumental kurgan cultures (Martkopi, Bedeni, Trialeti, etc.) of Transcaucasia, particularly in terms of the labor invested in their construction. On the other hand, there is no comparable settlement data for Transcaucasia at this time: no cities, no monumental nonmortuary architecture; and essentially no complex administrative practices, as suggested by the recovery of seals or tablets. Such contrasting records make it difficult to compare the chiefs (?) of Transcaucasia with the rulers (kings?) of the secondary states east of Sumer. Neither, however, were the peers of Sargon. When it is to their advantage to do so, of course, royal elites can overlook such status distinctions and treat their inferiors as equals; thus, the Mesopotamian references to the "kings" of Magan and of other areas east of Sumer. The exchange of luxuries among such "royal" personages explains, at least in part, the broad distribution of carved vessels, jewelry, ceremonial weapons, and other such finished commodities.

Nevertheless, it is not necessary to conjure up a Bronze Age world system or refer here to cores and peripheries supposed to characterize modern times. By any objective measure or scale – save the incredible geographic extent of the enigmatic Indus Valley civilization – Mesopotamia and Old Kingdom Egypt qualitatively differed from neighboring regions with whom they interacted. The evidence for Mesopotamian preeminence has been convincingly summarized by S. Ratnagar (2001: 358):

> Mesopotamia, with its levels of population and subsistence output, its use of materials from as far west as the Mediterranean and as far east as India, its metal technology, its recording systems, calendar, mensuration systems, and writing, and the fact that its more powerful kings seized booty and exacted tribute from several neighboring regions, was obviously the pre-eminent centre.

The secondary states east of Sumer were likewise not commensurate with one another. Some, like the Harappan (Meluhha), were huge or at least displayed a strikingly uniform material culture over an incredibly extensive area. Others were more spatially restricted, although exhibiting considerable sophistication in craft specialization and the production of luxury goods and metals; they represented local kingdoms or regional polities, some of which are

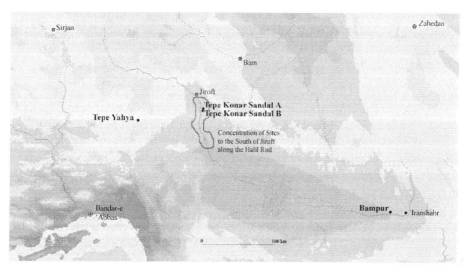

Figure 5.25. The Jaz Murian depression, southeastern Iran: the setting for the newly discovered Jiroft polity or secondary state, showing concentration of settlements along Halil Rud and locations of Tepe Yahya and Bampur.

mentioned in the cuneiform sources. To illustrate some of the common features of these secondary states east of Sumer and the difficulty of constructing an appropriate *political* geography for eastern Iran/Turan, it is useful to examine one of these states in greater detail. Let us look briefly at the most recently recognized secondary states and one that is currently being excavated in the Jaz Murian depression of southeastern Iran (Fig. 5.25).

JIROFT/HALIL RUD: A NEWLY DISCOVERED REGIONAL POLITY OR SECONDARY STATE EAST OF SUMER IN SOUTHEASTERN IRAN

Waters from several seasonal streams or wadis and two rivers – the Bampur River, flowing east to west for roughly 315 km and the Halil Rud (Kharan or Zar Dasht River in its upper reaches), carrying more water and flowing from the north/northwest for about 360 km – drain into the Jaz Murian depression, culminating in low-lying marshlands and the intermittently inundated Jaz Murian Lake (or *Hamun-e Jaz Murian*). This marshy shallow lake lies at an altitude of only about 300 meters or far lower than the high mountains ringing it, such as the Kuh-e Laleh Zar (4734 m.), to the northwest. The *Hamun-e Jaz Murian* is dry for most of the year but at least partially fills with fresh water during the winter because of precipitation. It is a distinct physical region extending northwest to southeast just beyond the south easternmost extension of the Zagros Mountains. Today the city of Jiroft along the Halil Rud is the

main administrative center to the north and Iranshahr, just east of the famous
Bronze Age site of Bampur, is the major city along the Bampur River to the
east (Fig. 5.25).

Sir Aurel Stein initially traversed the area in spring 1932, test excavating several prehistoric sites particularly along the smaller Bampur River, but recording
only later historic sites in the then dry depressed basin between the Lower
Bampur and Lower Halil Rud. He concluded that, because they did not
yet utilize *qanats* or underground canals that he considered essential for its
occupation, the late prehistoric inhabitants did not occupy the intermediate
area (Stein 1937: 35–36); only future, more systematic surveys and excavations
will test the accuracy of this observation. When water is continuously available, agriculture flourishes and the area is renowned for its produce, including
its dates and melons. Many of the recurrent figurative motives, such as date
palms, snakes, and scorpions, on the soft-stone vessels that have been clandes-
tinely pillaged from cemeteries along the Halil Rud accurately reflect the flora
and fauna of this extremely hot, and, when watered, extremely productive
region.

Numerous large Bronze Age settlements and cemeteries have recently been
located along the middle to lower course of the Halil Rud south of Jiroft, and
some of the latter have been illicitly plundered, yielding thousands of spectacular carved stone and metal artifacts, some immediately recognizable in style,
others previously unknown (Madjidzadeh 2003; Perrot 2003). Excavations have
commenced at some of the settlements, such as Konar Sandal A and Konar
Sandal B, and are already documenting considerable social complexity in the
form of monumental architecture and administrative practices (e.g., numerous
sealing impressions). These ongoing excavations along the Halil Rud south of
Jiroft are certain to clarify the contexts of the wealth of carved stone vessels
and other luxury exotica plundered from there.

Although some – given the lack of recorded context – may not be genuine (Muscarella n.d.), many of the carved soft-stone chlorite vessels, both in
forms and carved motives, constitute classic examples of the so-called Intercultural Style (Kohl 1978). They could easily have been produced in the workshop at Tepe Yahya, the well-known site nestled at the southeastern end of
the Zagros Mountains roughly 95 km. west/southwest of the town of Jiroft
(Fig. 5.26). Other objects, such as flat inlaid zoomorphic statues or plaques
(Madjidzadeh 2003: 131–136), footed goblets (some of which also are carved
and inlaid [ibid.: 11–12, 18–33, 49–50; Fig. 5.27]), and double-sided lapis lazuli
amulets or "stamp seals" (some of which have copper/bronze handles and
fairly elaborate bronze artifacts, such as tools and figurines, including a raised
or high relief bird of prey within a shallow bowl [ibid.: 169–174, 151–157;
Fig. 5.28]) are unique or have less certain parallels. The relative abundance
of lapis lazuli suggests connections farther east, probably with the mines of

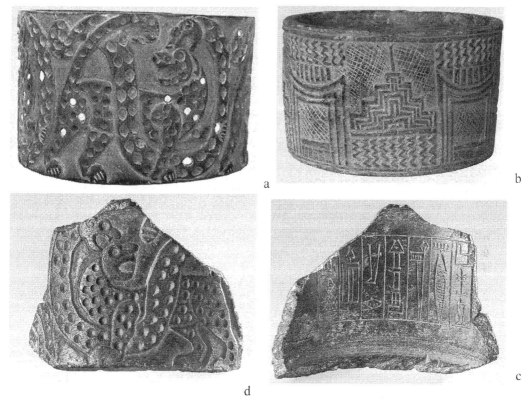

Figure 5.26. Carved Intercultural Style chlorite vessels from plundered graves along the Halil Rud, south of Jiroft: (a) Combatant serpent and feline motif (adapted from Madjidzadeh 2003: 81); (b) hutpot (or sagging lintel) and stepped terrace motif (ibid., 71); (c) and (d) Berlin vessel with combatant serpent and feline motif (exterior) and inscription of the Akkadian ruler Rimush (interior) (adapted from Aruz 2003c: 336, fig. 233).

Badakhshan in northeastern Afghanistan, and the footed goblets recall BMAC ceramic forms, as well as more remotely a footed carved steatite/chlorite goblet from the necropolis at Gonur-depe in Turkmenistan (Aruz 2003c: 340, fig. 237a).

In short, the dense concentration of early cemeteries and large settlements suggests a regional florescence of a recently discovered complex Bronze Age polity or secondary state stretched along the Halil Rud south of Jiroft and located in the same catchment area and necessarily connected or in some form of contact with the documented late third-millennium cemeteries and settlements that are found along the Bampur River that flows into the Jaz Murian basin from the east (De Cardi 1970: 260, fig. 13). It may be premature to speculate too broadly on how to draw the political borders of this Bronze Age

Figure 5.27. Figured chlorite footed goblet and inlaid flat zoomorphic plaque from plundered Jiroft graves (adapted from Madjidzadeh 2003: 20 and 131).

Figure 5.28. Double-sided figured lapis lazuli seal or amulet with copper/bronze handle and bronze bowl with raised bird of prey from plundered Jiroft graves (adapted from Madjidzadeh 2003: 170, 156).

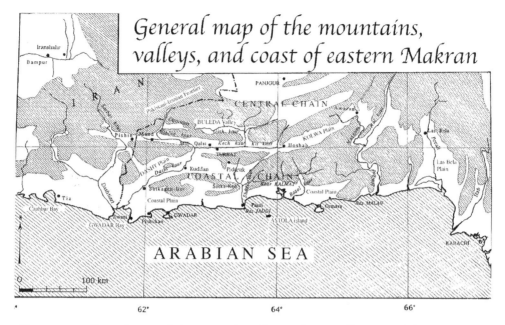

Figure 5.29. General map of the mountain valleys and coast of eastern Makran, north of the Arabian Sea, showing Bampur, Miri Qalat, Sutkagen-dor, and Sotka-koh (adapted from Besenval 1997: 6, fig. 1).

polity. Only future work at Bampur itself or at other prehistoric sites along the Bampur River will reveal whether this area was more tightly integrated with the Halil Rud Valley to the west or linked more closely to the intrusion of Harappan settlements along the Makran coast (Sotka-koh, Sutkagen-dor) and other inland sites farther east, such as Miri Qalat in the Kej Valley (Besenval 1997; Fig. 5.29). Historically, during the Achaemenid period this region represented the border between Karmania and Gedrosia, and today it divides Kerman province from Iranian Baluchistan. Presumably it could have functioned as such a frontier zone or marchland during much earlier Bronze Age times (Tosi, personal communication).

Similarly, the soft-stone workshop at Tepe Yahya, a site located at the terminal southeastern extension of the Zagros immediately west, southwest of Jiroft, seems on the basis of these recent discoveries to represent a highland component to this Halil Rud complex polity, though conceivably Yahya could also have been more closely tied to Anshan and Elam farther west. The recently discovered remains from the Jiroft suggest that many of the soft-stone vessels carved at Yahya were produced principally for the local consumption of peoples living in the Jaz Murian basin, though it is impossible to determine on current evidence whether they were destined solely for the local elite or interred in a more egalitarian pattern; that is, distributed relatively uniformly throughout the society, as exhibited, for example, in the excavated cemetery at Shahdad (Hakemi 1997), another secondary, presumably independent state located farther north on the western edge of the Dasht-i Lut, or principally deposited in "royal" tombs akin to those found at Gonur-depe north.

Conversely, Bampur's relationship with the settlements in the Halil Rud may have been less intense, judging by the dominance of incised grey ware imitations of the chlorite vessels and the paucity of the carved stone vessel themselves. This distributional difference could be chronological, political, or even just fortuitous, an accidental by-product of the very limited excavations that have been conducted at this large, important, and strategically situated site (cf. De Cardi 1970: 241–241); only much more systematic and much larger-scale excavations at Bampur will determine whether the entire Jaz Murian basin was politically integrated during the second half of the third millennium BC or, as seems more likely, whether it was divided politically into western and eastern halves.

Regardless, these spectacular recent discoveries along the Halil Rud do not represent, as claimed, evidence for "the earliest Oriental civilization" or the legendary "State of Aratta" (Madjidzadeh 2003: 12) but for another secondary, albeit quite important and prosperous, state east of Sumer that emerged during the "proto-urban" or "urban phase" of interregional exchange, political alliances, and military campaigns during the second half of the third millennium BC. More specifically, the Halil Rud or, possibly, Jaz Murian polity can be plausibly identified with the kingdom of Marhashi, known from numerous cuneiform texts, including boasts recording the depredations of Akkadian rulers, such as on an inscription on the back of a carved soft-stone Intercultural Style vessel (Klengel and Klengel 1980; Steinkeller 1982; Aruz 2003c: 336; Fig. 5.26 c and d). D.T. Potts (n.d.; cf. also 2005) has convincingly made this identification, succinctly summarizing the historical evidence for the land of Marhashi:

> [Marhashi's] army and generals fought against Sargon, Rimush and Naram-Sin; its ruling family intermarried with the élite of Agade and Ur, exchanging diplomatic gifts; a contingent of its soldiers served the royal house of Ur; and its stones, most probably in the form of finished vessels, were familiar in Mesopotamia as well. . . . Marhashi was a real place, with real soldiers, fighting real battles and a ruling élite who were inter-married with two of the most powerful dynasties in the ancient world.

As we have emphasized, Marhashi/Halil Rud/Jiroft was only one such state east of Sumer that flourished in the second half of the third millennium and then collapsed sometime during the first half of the second millennium. Distinct local factors certainly affected such collapses and varied from one state to another. Thus, for example, the continuous arrival of "cowboys" with wheeled vehicles, horses, and tin-bronze weapons and tools from the steppes must have disrupted – particularly at some point as their numbers increased – sedentary life throughout the low-lying irrigated plains of "civilized" southern Central Asia, and this disruption must have been felt throughout this integrated system of interregional interaction throughout eastern Iran and beyond. The smaller fortified manors or *qalas* that dotted Margiana at the end of the Bronze Age bespeak unsettled times.

Many theories also, for example, have been advanced to explain the collapse of the famous Indus Valley cities, including the now-discredited and archaeologically unattested conquest by invading Indo-Aryan warriors. One intriguing hypothesis focuses on the introduction at the end of the Mature Harappan period of sorghum and millets from Africa (possibly via Oman) and rice and millets from Asia that led to double-cropping or the adoption of summer-sown, fall-harvested (*kharif*) cereals to complement the winter-sown, spring-harvested (*rabi*) crops of wheat and barley. More or less simultaneously, new species of domestic animals, such as the camel, horse, and donkey, were also introduced, the first two presumably from the north. These changes in basic subsistence practices opened up new agricultural lands east of the Indus alluvium and led to new zones of occupation within the alluvium, ultimately resulting in a more dispersed pattern of settlement within the alluvium itself (Meadow 1993); an archaic complex society always dominated by small settlements or villages abandoned its few urban centers, turning in on itself, a sort of Bronze Age example of agricultural involution (Geertz 1963).

The basic point is that many different explanations can be advanced to explain specific developments within each secondary state. Nevertheless, what is perhaps most striking are the *roughly contemporaneous* collapses of most of these states. Why did everything fall apart in the lands east of Sumer towards the end of the third or during the first centuries of the second millennium BC? This pattern of political collapse and de-urbanization was actually even more general and soon affected Mesopotamia itself, where Adams (1981: 138, table 12; 139, fig. 25) estimates that total settled urban area (defined as 40+ ha) declined from a peak in Early Dynastic II/III times of 78.4% (with a corresponding 10% nonurban or settled area less than 10 ha) to 50.2% in Old Babylonian times (with 29.6% nonurban) to 30.4% during the Kassite period (with 56.8% nonurban) and 16.2% in the Middle Babylonian period (with 64.2% nonurban).

Although Adams admits discrepancies in the quality of the data from period to period, the overall pattern is consistent and striking; it must reflect a real decline over time in the urbanization of the Mesopotamian heartland. To account adequately for this decline, broader explanations also must be considered, such as the large redirection of political and military campaigns, metals procurement and interregional exchange, and ultimately the growth of secondary Middle and Late Bronze states farther west in the eastern Mediterranean basin. Some of these developments were structural, occurring over some extended period of time; others were more immediately political but nevertheless had far-reaching consequences, such as Susa's rebellion against Ur at the end of the third millennium, its emergence as a major urban center and powerful state closely tied to highland Iran, and the redirection of the tin and tin-bronze trade through Elam to central Mesopotamia and the kingdom of Mari on the Euphrates (Ratnagar 2000: 123). Subsequently, the rise of Hammurabi and his conquest of Mari and the Middle Euphrates region may have had even longer-lasting consequences, ultimately diverting the long-distance trade in needed metals farther west, a change that marked the permanent decline of these Bronze Age secondary states east of Sumer.

Citing the works of Potts (1990: 226) and Crawford (1998: 155), Weeks insightfully observes:

> Hammurabi's actions simultaneously decimated Mesopotamia's major point of access to the Gulf trade, led to a widespread depopulation of southern Mesopotamia, and opened up routes to alternative copper sources in Anatolia and the Mediterranean. It is perhaps no coincidence that a text from the fifth year of the reign of Hammurabi's successor, Samsu-Iluna, bearing the first cuneiform reference to copper from Cyprus (Alashiya), also contains the last reference to Dilmun copper. (2003: 17)

In other words, broader patterns of interaction were redirected, and such a shift fundamentally undermined the viability of these secondary states and even ultimately of urban settlement in southern Mesopotamia.

Herders from the steppes played a part in these developments, even though they only faintly resembled the marauding mounted nomads of later historical periods. As we have seen, peoples crossed the Caucasus from the steppes as early possibly as the fourth millennium BC and had densely settled Transcaucasia by the beginning of the Late Bronze Age or roughly by the middle of the second millennium BC; peoples throughout Transcaucasia now lived in inaccessibly situated, fortified settlements ringed with massive cyclopean stone walls. On the other side of the Caspian Sea, movements from the steppes into southern Central Asia occurred later but were more prolonged and increased continuously in scale throughout the Bronze into the Early Iron Age.

Earlier complex "proto-urban" states collapsed, and newly arrived and indigenous peoples apparently lived together in smaller fortified sites, seemingly not integrated into larger, hierarchically structured polities. The ethnic and linguistic composition of the peoples of the Caucasus and southern Central Asia must have been profoundly affected by these movements that in turn transformed the ethnic and linguistic breakdown of adjacent regions farther south as peoples subsequently moved into the areas formerly controlled by the secondary states east of Sumer. The mute archaeological record only dimly records these disruptions in settlement patterns and tells us nothing directly about the ethnic changes and linguistic shifts that occurred in their wake.

Such absence of information, however, has not kept linguists and archaeologists alike from attempting to reconstruct these changes, and we conclude this chapter with some reflections on these efforts and on the uncertainties of archaeologically based ethnic and linguistic identifications, particularly as have been made for Proto-Indo-Europeans, Indo-Iranians, Indo-Aryans, and Tocharians – that is, for the peoples who are often credited with directing these changes.

ARCHAEOLOGY, LANGUAGE, AND THE ETHNIC IDENTIFICATION OF MATERIAL CULTURE REMAINS – PITFALLS AND LESSONS

Traditionally, archaeologists have considered the second millennium BC as the period when new peoples ancestral to the Iranians entered the Iranian plateau from the north and east. Successive waves of migration were postulated bringing first Indo-Europeans, then Medes, and finally Iranians into their later homeland (cf. Ghirshman 1954: 60–63, 73–77). The archaeological evidence supporting such movements consisted principally of the apparent abandonment or break in occupation at a series of archaeological sites particularly in northern Iran, such as Hissar, Tureng Tepe, and Sialk. Some interpreted this evidence boldly, tracing the seemingly successive appearance of diagnostic types of greywares as evidence for the migration of Iranians from the northeast into the western Zagros (Young 1967); others interpreted the evidence more cautiously, questioning the existence or extent of the so-called hiatus of settlements and suggesting internal developments within northern Iran during the second millennium (Dyson 1973).

More recently, striking similarities in the material remains from closed burial complexes at sites like Shahdad, Khinaman, and Sibri with those found in Bactria and Margiana were interpreted as evidence for the movements of Central Asians, presumably here Indo-Aryans, into eastern Iran en route to the Indian subcontinent (Hiebert and Lamberg-Karlovsky 1992); others have viewed this same evidence as suggesting BMAC traders and smiths living in one of the neighboring states with whom they habitually exchanged materials (Salvatori 1995: 48–51).

E. E. Kuzmina (1994) has consistently identified the Andronovo "cultural-historical community" (*obshchnost'*), which she believes emerged in the southern trans-Urals northeast of the Caspian Sea in the early second millennium (or late third on the basis of calibrated C14 determinations) and which she later divides into several chronological and regional tribal variants, as ancestral to the historically attested Aryans. According to Kuzmina, these Andronovo peoples moved in several successive waves throughout the second millennium far to the north/northwest and south/southeast (i.e., nearly in all directions; cf. the map on the inside of the front cover of her 1994 monograph) from their presumed homeland in the southern Urals.

Even more recently, the discovery of late prehistoric "Caucasoid" (i.e., apparently white "Europeans") mummies in Xinjiang China led to their tentative identification as Tocharians, an Indo-European speaking people known to have lived on the western border of China at the end of the first millennium AD (Mair 1998). This identification is made – despite the two millennia or longer chronological discrepancy between the archaeological and linguistic evidence – on the assumption that language and physical type correlate perfectly with one another.

Numerous other examples could be cited in which inherently ambiguous archaeological data are interpreted to fit supposedly firm linguistic or physical anthropological evidence, resulting in the ethnic/linguistic identification of the archaeological culture/cultural community concerned. Specific identifications must be evaluated separately on the basis of the evidence supporting them. Some may be quite convincing or at least plausible, others less so, but all are problematic and some – as the history of such identifications and theories show – may be dangerous. Theoretically, of course, a cardinal difficulty consists in the conflation of the independently varying concepts of "race," language, and culture; today many physical anthropologists deny the existence of distinct physical types or at least emphasize the great biological variation within populations and recognize their clinal distribution – that is, the merging or blending of adjacent groups resulting in a continuous spectrum of human populations exhibiting intermediate physical characteristics and no division of the species into discrete clearly defined "races." Language is culturally learned, not physically inherited. Because people generally (though not necessarily!) breed with partners with whom they can speak, there is typically a strong positive correlation between language and culture. Nevertheless, they must be distinguished. Caucasoid peoples do not necessarily speak Indo-European languages, nor are speakers of Indo-European necessarily "Caucasoid" in terms of their physical appearance. Culture, too, is obviously not found in our genes, but consists of learned behavior transmitted from one generation to the next.

Moreover culture, including eminently the material culture with which archaeologists grapple, is porous or capable of being adopted by other groups, resulting over time in the fact that few traits or features are uniquely and constantly specific to a given group (e.g., see Haüsler's cogent critique [1998] of the concept of an Indo-European burial). Many ethnic groups share similar material cultures, but simply identify themselves – and are so identified by their neighbors – as distinct. This critically important feature of ethnic self-identification is not directly observable in the archaeological record. Archaeological cultures only occasionally correspond to actual, self-recognized human groups. Finally, the always-problematic ethnic or linguistic identification made on archaeological evidence is necessarily also exclusionary. These Andronovo remains are Indo-European, not Turkic, and the Andronovo trans-Urals "homeland," consequently, is ours, not theirs. Other Aryan homelands, of course, have been and/or are still postulated for politically motivated reasons in central Europe, Ukraine, Turkey, and northern India.

This study has consistently emphasized the movements of peoples as one of the principal means in later prehistory for the establishment of interregional connections and the diffusion of technologies. On the basis of current evidence, one could update the hypothesis of an Indo-Iranian migration into western Iran and support the movement of Indo-Aryans into eastern Iran and northwestern India. The former may have initially "germinated" on the densely settled Gorgan/Misrian plain of northeastern Iran/southwestern Turkmenistan as steppe peoples from farther north gradually entered this settled agricultural area and emulated and assimilated with the indigenous population and its long distinctive grey ware tradition. The ancestors of the Indo-Aryans may have initially entered the plains of "civilized" Central Asia from the north and likewise adopted the culture of the original BMAC peoples who had first colonized the Margiana and Bactrian plains from farther south; then, as the BMAC Middle Bronze polity or "secondary state" collapsed, some assimilated BMAC peoples of steppe origin moved south – as Hiebert and Lamberg-Karlvosky (1992) argued – into the eastern Indo-Iranian borderlands. Both processes were largely peaceful and protracted, continuing throughout most of the second millennium BC.

Such reconstructions are not implausible and indeed may be correct, but they are almost impossible to demonstrate conclusively. The basic problem concerns the nature of these Bronze Age migrations: largely peaceful, protracted processes involving assimilation into the local, often well-established cultures. Unlike later invasions or colonizations, such as the establishment of Greek settlements in Sicily during the seventh century BC, these movements were not sudden events, leaving a very obvious material culture trail in their wake. J.-F. Jarrige (1985: 63) has understood this difference in relation to the supposed Indo-Aryan invasion of the Subcontinent:

> Those who postulate contacts between groups from the Eurasian steppes and those from the northwestern parts of South Asia, however, must not overlook the intermediary or filtering role played by the peoples of southern Central Asia. Given the existence of these cultures it seems unlikely . . . to find a continuous line of sites from the Eurasian steppes to the Ganges valley all with 'typical' gray ware or 'steppe-style' pottery which could be used to map the movements of Indo-Aryan populations. . . . Indeed, the expectation that such a chain of evidence would exist is based on a misconception of the way that population movements actually occurred.

Similarly, Lamberg-Karlovsky (2002: 74) has observed that "not a single artifact of Andronovo type has been identified in Iran or in northern India" and that, although BMAC materials can be found in eastern Iran on sites dating to the late third and early second millennium, it is "impossible . . . to trace the continuity of these materials into the first millennium and relate them to the known cultures of Iranian-speakers – the Medes or the Achaemenids (or their presumed Iron Age ancestors . . .)." The material culture trail vanishes, and the linguistic identification remains tenuous.

The same uncertainty even more obscures the larger linguistic identifications implicit in the canvas that we have sketched in this study. If there is a direct historical connection between the terminal Tripol'ye gigantic settlements in central Ukraine and the development and spread of mobile cattle herding societies west to east across the Eurasian steppes, culminating in the emergence of the Andronovo "cultural-historical community," then, at first glance, it seems possible to reconcile the linguistic/ethnic identifications of C. Renfrew (1987) and T. V. Gamkrelidze and Vya. Vs. Ivanov (1984), on the one hand, and those of J. P. Mallory (1989) and E. E, Kuzmina (1994), on the other. The gigantic settlements of the terminal Tripol'ye culture represent the culmination of "Old Europe," an agricultural way of life whose origins can be traced back to the Balkans and, ultimately, to Anatolia. The spectacular Chalcolithic remains of the Balkans clearly emerged out of the earlier and equally spectacular Neolithic remains of Anatolia.

During the first half of the fourth millennium Tripol'ye cultivators became cattle herders and spread eastwards across the Eurasian steppes. Their focus on cattle herding, as opposed to the mixed herding later characteristic of the Eurasian steppes, only increased during the Middle and Late Bronze periods, and their way of life, which fundamentally revolved around their cattle, must have been reflected in all the material and spiritual aspects of their culture, the latter of which eventually find their reflection in the Avestan and Vedic traditions. Gradually and continuously they moved south and changed the ethnic and linguistic composition of the areas that they entered. The easily recognizable steppe elements in their material culture were transformed as they assimilated to the local greater or more "civilized" traditions. Wheel-made pottery replaced the coarsely incised hand-made pottery, though these peoples continued to exploit metal resources and produce increasingly sophisticated and effective tin-bronze tools and weapons. The Indo-Iranians entered Iran, and the Indo-Aryans entered the South Asian subcontinent, and the rest, as they say, is history.

Unfortunately, this reconstruction cannot be definitively documented from the mute, underdetermined archaeological record. One could easily tell a different, potentially less dangerous tale from the archaeological evidence. There was no single Indo-European or Proto-Indo-European "homeland" but just an ever unfolding historical process of development in which peoples not only continuously transformed themselves, including their basic livelihoods, and sometimes moved into new areas, but in which they also continuously borrowed and assimilated the technological innovations and cultural developments of other peoples with whom they always came into contact. The linguists' favorite metaphor of likening a family of languages to a tree with its trunk and diverging branches is misleading, for the trunk itself has roots resembling both branches and trunks that extend deep into the earth, perpetually intertwining with other neighboring trunks and branches. Perhaps a better metaphor acknowledging both the continual divergence *and convergence* of related languages would be overlapping networks of highways, coming together at busy intersections and then spreading apart to form a continuously developing, non-random interconnected system of movement and communication.

The specific origins of developments in metal working, wheeled vehicles, and horse riding may never be established precisely because of the rapid sharing and adoption of these incredibly useful and multifunctional innovations. What is more significant is the extent of the interconnections suggested by the huge area over which, for example, wheeled vehicles appeared – seemingly simultaneously. It is inherently unlikely that all these developments were the products of a single, particularly gifted ethnic or linguistic group. The herders who initially left the Eurasian steppes were not mounted warriors led by a chariot-riding aristocracy, but impoverished cowboys who also probably knew how to cultivate or at least intensively gather crops seeking a better life. They quickly learned how to irrigate their fields, adopting the practices of the new cultures with whom they came into contact.

Archaeological cultures, like the ethnographic cultures that they are often assumed mistakenly to represent, are never pure and unmixed but always contain elements from neighboring and/or earlier cultures. The origins of the Bactria-Margiana Archaeological Complex are not to be sought in a single place, but in southern Turkmenistan, eastern Iran, Baluchistan, the Indian subcontinent, and later, as this complex further developed – or, perhaps better – devolved, the Eurasian steppes. Like other cultural phenomena, it was a hybrid, the product of a unique convergence of different cultural traditions. The argument for cultural diversity is not based on political correctness, but on historical accuracy. Prehistoric processes are interconnected and shared among different peoples, and, for that reason, our reconstructions of them must be as inclusive as possible.

Similarly, the spread of Andronovo cultural community remains from the southern trans-Urals far to the southeast is indisputable, as reflected in the spread of immediately recognizable ceramics, metal weapons and tools, and productive herding economies utilizing wheeled vehicles and horses. The diffusion from this "homeland" may have initially involved peoples principally of "Aryan" origin, as Kuzmina has consistently maintained, though as this diffusionary process spread farther and farther east it is likely also to have involved peoples speaking unrelated languages and exhibiting different physical characteristics. The diffusion eastwards of metallurgy and Andronovo, Seima-Turbino and Karasuk-like metal weapons and tools is certain ((Mei Jianjun and Shell 1999; Linduff 2002: 608; Figs. 5.30 and 5.31) and officially acknowledged by Chinese specialists. An Zhimin (1998: 60), for example, concedes the basic diffusionary process, though he also notes that such technologies may spread

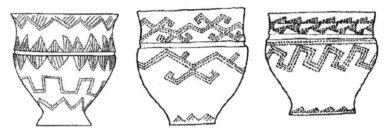

Figure 5.30. Pottery of Andronovo-type from Xinjiang (adapted from Mei Jianjun and Shell 1999: 572, fig. 3).

and be adopted without the large-scale movements of peoples and urges more fieldwork devoted to this problem:

> Cultural exchanges did not always result only from people's migrations, especially since metal implements of production were easy to be accepted as burgeoning productive forces by archaeological cultures in contiguous areas. It can be imagined that initially bronze and iron technology took its rise in West Asia, first influenced the Xinjiang region, and then reached the Yellow River valley, providing external impetus for the rise of Shang and Zhou civilizations. This means that Xinjiang was situated as the middle link in the eastward diffusion of metal culture, which constitutes one of the important problems worthy of thorough-going research.

One route of this diffusionary process was via northwestern and northern Xinjiang, a region that physically belongs to the steppes, not the irrigated oasis world farther south, and that during the Late Bronze Age formed "an integral part of the Andronovo cultural community" (Debaine-Francfort 2002: 57; Fig. 5.32).

Similar, albeit less striking, connections with Chernykh's Eurasian Metallurgical Province can be found in the metals from the late third- and early second-millennium BC Quijia and the slightly later Siba (1900–1600 BC) cultures from the Gansu province of northwestern China proper. More than 100 bronze artifacts were recovered from the Huoshaogu cemetery of the Siba culture, including distinctively shaped steppe-like circular earrings and bronze weapons together with jades, seashells, and agate and turquoise beads, and, significantly, horse sacrifices. Slightly later, or in the second quarter of the second millennium, in the last two levels at Ehrlitou on the Central Plain of China, there is increased evidence for alloying, the use of curved daggers similar to those from the steppes, and, most notably, the appearance of bronze footed vessels, the clear forerunners of the later elaborately cast figured ritual Shang Dynasty vessels. K. Linduff (2002: 608–609) aptly summarizes current understanding of this multifaceted diffusionary process:

> The movement of ideas about metal technology, artifacts or even peoples into the Gansu Corridor and across the Northern Corridor must have taken place via the valleys of the southern Altai bringing horse-herding, bronze

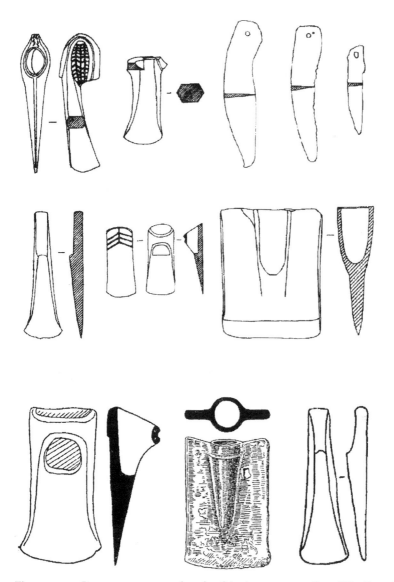

Figure 5.31. Bronze weapons and tools of Andronovo-type from Xianjiang (adapted from Mei Jianjun and Shell 1999: 574, figs. 4 and 5).

using peoples of Andronovo background. The whole region experimented with metals in the 3rd and early 2nd millennium BC, but by about 1700 BC different tracks were being followed. The emergence of state-level society, synonymous with bronze production took place in the Chinese Central Plain.... Where their methods of piece-mold casting were invented is yet to be found, but their restricted use of alloyed metals was apparent from at least as early as the upper strata at Erlitou.... Early metal technology in east Asia had both experimental and mature phases, was probably not independently generated, but emerged and was tempered in each area by local conditions, customs, and degree of receptivity.

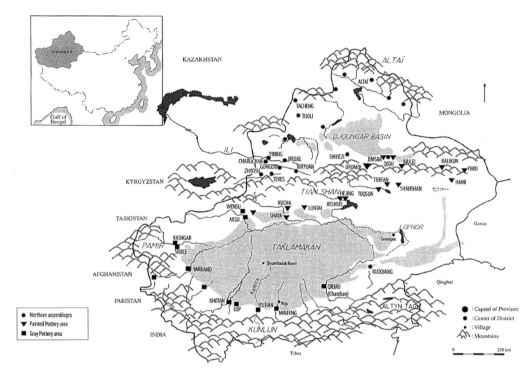

Figure 5.32. Bronze and Iron Age cultural areas in Xinjiang (adapted from Debaine-Francfort 2002: 58, fig.1).

Two additional points should be made. First, the spread of metal working west to east is associated at some level with the spread of productive, dominantly herding and horse-rearing economies that had also initially developed farther west and that can be associated at some level with a very generically identified Andronovo cultural tradition. The East Asian evidence is ultimately tied to the emergence of the Chinese Bronze Age early dynastic states, a process well underway by the middle of the second millennium BC. As this is true, the lower uncalibrated radiocarbon chronology for the Andronovo horizon and other western Eurasian archaeological steppe cultures cannot be correct. The use of calibrated dates, which now have been advanced by Trifonov, Chernykh et al., Rassamakin, and others and which we have utilized throughout this study, must now be universally adopted. Otherwise the causal arrows of direction documenting this process will have to be reversed, and that makes no historical sense.

Second, the diffusion west to east of metallurgy and horse rearing in no way constitutes a tale of civilization itself spreading from west to east, enlightening ultimately the indigenous inhabitants of China. Technologies and influences always spread in both directions, and there are many other tales to be told, including, probably, an early diffusion of sericulture and silks east to west. The early Chinese State may have received its metal technology, wheeled vehicles, and horses from the west, but they quickly adapted and improved on them for their own culturally defined purposes. The intricate, elaborately cast and figured bronze vessels for which the Shang Dynasty is so justly renowned have no direct parallels either in the way they were made or the uses to which they were put in western Asia. The "world" of West Asia was not united with the "world" of East Asia in a single interconnected "world system" during the Bronze Age (*contra* Frank 1993), despite the undeniable fact that both areas were in indirect contact with one another and that both borrowed and benefited from such contact.

BIOGRAPHICAL SKETCH

V. I. SARIANIDI

Photo 5.1. Three young members of the XIVth Brigade of the Southern Turkmenistan Archaeological Complex Expedition (Yu.T.A.K.E) take a break from their archaeological excavations in Turkmenistan during the mid-to late 1950s: V. M. Masson, V. I. Sarianidi, and I. N. Khlopin (pictured left to right).

V. I. Sarianidi studied archaeology initially at Central Asian (now Tashkent) State University under the direction of M. E. Masson, graduating in 1953. He then worked on a series of well-known sites that expanded and refined the prehistoric Neolithic to Iron Age (Djeitun, Namazga I–VI) sequence in southern Turkmenistan as a member of Yu.T.A.K.E. from 1955 to 1958. He also then worked in Margiana or along the Lower Murghab River, discovering Late Bronze Age settlements in the Auchin oasis that he would later investigate in greater detail from 1972 on. He completed his candidate's degree (first PhD) in 1963 on his excavations of Late Chalcolithic settlements in the Geoksyur oasis along a former delta of the Lower Tedjen River (published in 1965 as *Pamyatniki pozdego eneolita yugo-vostochnogo Turkmenistana*) and became a Senior Researcher at the Institute of Archaeology in Moscow, a position that he held until 2003. His doctoral dissertation was completed in 1975 and was based on his early investigations in northwestern Afghanistan (published in 1977 as *Drevnie zemledel'tsy Afghanistana. Materialy Sovetsko-Afganskoi ekspeditsii 1969–1974 gg.*). Throughout most of the 1970s he discovered and excavated Bronze Age sites both in northwestern Afghanistan and in the Kara Kum desert of southeastern Turkmenistan along former terminal deltaic extensions of the Lower Murghab River. This work led to the discovery of a new Bronze Age civilization dating towards the end of the third and the first half of the second

Photo 5.2. V. I. Sarianidi – the legendary "Lion of the Kara Kum" – shown in 2004, his seventy-fifth anniversary and after more than fifty years of archaeological investigations and sensational discoveries.

millennium BC: the Bactria-Margiana Archaeological Complex (BMAC), or what certain Western scholars refer to as the Oxus Civilization with its monumental public architecture, art, evidence for craft specialization, seals and other administrative devices, and now "royal" cemetery from Gonur-depe. He is the author of more than 250 articles, including roughly 30 monographs and popular scientific books. By a special decree of President S. Niyazov, he has been proclaimed a citizen of Turkmenistan, and with the support of the government of Turkmenistan, Greece, and various funding sources in western Europe and the United States, he continues to excavate the incredibly rich site of Gonur 1, the largest known Bronze Age "capital" settlement of Margiana.

It is no exaggeration to say that few archaeologists in the history of the discipline have made as many important and sensational discoveries as V. I. Sarianidi. How many archaeologists can claim to have discovered a totally new Bronze Age civilization? How many have uncovered – under extremely adverse, politically uncertain circumstances from late 1978 through the first half of 1979 – six "royal" Kushan period burials at the site of Tillya Tepe (the "golden mound"), containing more than 20,000 stunningly beautiful gold artifacts (which recently have reemerged unscathed after being hidden in bank vaults in Kabul)? It is almost as if he had worked in an earlier era, when pioneers like H. Schliemann and H. Carter uncovered Troy and King Tut's Tomb. Until his work in northern Afghanistan (1969 to 1979), some Western scholars, who had searched for decades in vain for Achaemenid period settlements, referred to the "Bactrian mirage" or absence of appropriately dated Iron Age sites in Bactria. Sarianidi arrived and soon discovered a series of Achaemenid sites, uncovering monumental architecture at the site of Altyn 10 in the Dashly oasis.

Some critics have considered him lucky, but such "luck" depended on extremely hard work, countless (and fearless) excursions across the arid Kara Kum desert and similarly barren landscapes of northwestern Afghanistan, and an incredible tenacity and sense of where to find and excavate archaeological remains. B. A. Litvinskii's (2004: 21) concluding assessment in his academic biographical foreword to the volume celebrating Sarianidi's seventy-fifth birthday is apt:

> Of course, not everything was peaceful in Sarianidi's relations with his colleagues. There were conflicts in which he not always played the role of the angel. But all this never interrupted his work. His work and expeditions were the chief goal of his life. . . . After half a century of the most persistent labors, he has had colossal results and made a whole series of epochal discoveries. He has uncovered new periods, previously unknown kingdoms, new civilizations, incredible architectural monuments, and a huge collection of fabulous works of art. . . . Viktor Sarianidi is now a famous world archaeologist, a genuine legend of Central Asian archaeology.

Generations of future archaeologists will refine and, in some cases, correct and modify our understanding of the discoveries made by V. I. Sarianidi. Such tasks, some of which should have been avoided, also will not be easily or quickly accomplished. The work will continue but it will always be based on the initial incredible discoveries of the "Lion of the Kara Kum." Several contributors to his commemorative volume fondly recount Sarianidi's acts of warm, almost spontaneous generosity and use the Turkmen word *adamchylyk* ("humaneness") to describe him. This word too is apt.

CHAPTER 6

THE CIRCULATION OF PEOPLES AND MATERIALS – EVOLUTION, DEVOLUTION, AND RECURRENT SOCIAL FORMATIONS ON THE EURASIAN STEPPES AND IN WEST ASIA: PATTERNS AND PROCESSES OF INTERCONNECTION DURING LATER PREHISTORY

> The Bronze Age was, however, unique even in ancient times in that the great river valley civilizations relied on metal for production and that metal (copper, tin, lead, etc.) was scarce and had to be procured from afar, from less developed regions. Thus trade involved not just luxuries but also basic requirements, interaction between societies at contrasting levels of technology and social organization, and organization by ruling elites . . . Bronze Age societies [however] were not inchoate versions of our own.
>
> (Ratnagar 2001: 351)

> Over against the processes of divergent development leading to the separation of distinct peoples – and confusion – can be traced no less clearly a process of convergence. . . . At least in the Old World the peoples accessible to archaeological study were constantly interchanging material objects, ideas and inventions. . . . What we call Civilization is the product of this collective tradition, transcending all national frontiers.
>
> (Childe 1933: 418–419)

This study has attempted to relate an interconnected story of developments from Chalcolithic through Bronze Age times that affected archaeologically defined peoples from the Balkans east to the borders of China. It has stressed the importance of contacts among different cultures and has emphasized the continuous circulation of materials, peoples, technologies, and ideas over long distances. At the same time it has inveighed against anachronistic reasoning, insisting that the dominantly herding economy that developed on the western Eurasian steppes during the Bronze Age qualitatively differed from the mounted steppe pastoral nomadism that emerged during the Iron Age and that is richly documented in later historical and ethnographic sources. There were no Bronze Age Genghis Khans or Timurs, but just cattle herders who utilized bronze tools and weapons and moved principally west to east across the steppes on wheeled vehicles from the late fourth millennium on and probably rode or at least harnessed horses by the late third millennium BC. Technologies – mining, metal working, wheeled vehicles, composite bent bows, woolen textiles and felts, cold-tolerant plants and animals, storage facilities and semisubterranean pit dwellings – diffused or were shared among different peoples; such peoples were not stationary but moved or migrated over time, seeking better pastures and more attractive conditions to cultivate crops or simply to live better. Materials were also exchanged over long distances – initially dominantly prestige goods, such as jewelry, exotic precious and semiprecious stones and metals, and ceremonial stone and bronze weapons, and later increasingly utilitarian goods, including functional metal weapons and tools.

MODELING THE "WORLD(S)" OF BRONZE AGE EURASIA

But how significant were these interconnections, and, more fundamentally, how can we even determine their significance? We should be consistent in our rejection of anachronisms. Bronze Age Eurasia was not structured systematically into cores, peripheries, and semiperipheries as postulated for the modern world from the sixteenth century AD on (Wallerstein 1974). There was no systematic development of underdevelopment, nor, with perhaps few exceptions, were dependencies deliberately created and consistently maintained as are supposedly characteristic of the modern world system. Globalization even more so is a phenomenon of contemporary times, not the Bronze Age. Cultivators and herders, not merchants and smiths, were the primary inhabitants of the Bronze Age. Most people most of the time were firmly rooted in their own soil, not setting off to far distant lands to exchange precious goods. Over time the Bronze Age cattle herding economy of the steppes became increasingly specialized, culminating in the emergence of true mounted pastoral nomadism with mixed herds of cold adapted horses, sheep, goats, cattle, and Bactrian camels at the beginning of the Iron Age. In a sense, with such a specialized development, the contrasting worlds of the steppe and the sown were driven even further apart in terms of their contrastive lifestyles. Rather than continuously integrated into a single "world system," the advent of iron also heralded the breakdown of the necessary interconnections for the procurement of copper and tin that were characteristic of the Bronze Age and, at least initially, may have led to a reduction in the scale of the intensive production and exchange of metal goods and to the emergence of more small-scale independent workshops engaged in iron production (cf. also McConchie 2004: 146–148, 163–166).

Two worlds – the "civilized" Ancient Near East with a primary, though by no means exclusive, focus on some form of intensive agriculture (terracing, irrigation, etc.) and the "barbarian" western Eurasian steppes with mobile herding economies and, presumably, some reliance on the intensive gathering, if not cultivation, of cereals (though its nature and extent remains unclear) – increasingly interacted both within and between each complementary region throughout Bronze Age times. Herding peoples moved along river valleys, as well as over the open steppe, constructing raised kurgans and exchanging prestige and ceremonial goods and increasingly functional tools and weapons. The Ancient Near East was interconnected through even more elaborate networks of exchange, as well as of political alliances and conquests or raids to achieve – however fleetingly – political hegemony and to procure exotic prestige goods and necessities: particularly, metal tools and weapons. These "worlds" were distinct yet interconnected not only through the exchange of materials, particularly metals, but also through the continuous movements of steppe herders into the sown agricultural world of the Near East, processes that we have tried to trace throughout this study.

This network of interconnections during the Bronze Age, however, did not constitute a single unit, an inchoate version of the modern "world system." Our models of the prehistoric past are necessarily partial and provisional; they should not assume a reality that they do not possess. Reference to a Bronze Age *world system* should enlighten, not mislead, our understanding of the extent of integration and interaction that was achieved during the fourth through second millennia BC. One of the strengths of this model is its focus on the relevant unit of analysis, that is, on the area that was integrated economically and politically to the extent that can be considered systemic so that changes in one part of the system affect changes or developments throughout the system. From this perspective, I would argue that Sumer and "the secondary states east of Sumer" during the last centuries of the third and beginning centuries of the second millennia BC constituted such a "world system," though the western and northern limits of this system are more difficult to define. The boundaries of the system also shift over time in a manner that reflects not simply continuous growth, but the conscious development of new areas of intense interaction, such as the eastern Mediterranean Basin, stretching into Central Europe, during the first half of the second millennium BC. Simultaneously, many of the "secondary states east of Sumer" collapse or devolve and – temporarily at least – seem to drop out of this "world system."

Is such a model useful or confusing? The utility of such an analogy between the Bronze Age and modern times may be more to reveal basic structural differences than to discover misleading, superficial similarities (Kohl 1989; Stein 1999). Unfortunately, archaeologists tend to overuse the models they develop. Advocates of the world systems model frequently become enmeshed in endless, essentially typological arguments over what areas constituted the cores, semiperipheries, peripheries, or other idiosyncratically postulated units of the defined system. Few want to work in peripheral areas, and most want to see their area as central to the whole. Ironically, such debates become exercises in classification, comparable to the neo-evolutionists' schema of labeling their societies as ever-refined and nuanced types of chiefdoms and early states (cf. the critical discussion in Sections I and III of Chapter 1). As this happens, whatever utility the world systems model has – dissipates.

Although the borders demarcating the civilized and barbarian worlds (not world systems) were porous, the differences in their overall structure and methods of interaction are striking. An "urban revolution" had occurred in Mesopotamia in which for awhile – particularly throughout the third millennium – more people seemingly lived in large nucleated cities than in the countryside (cf. the settlement data summarized in Section III of Chapter 5), and marked social stratification and specialization of the activities conducted by the population are evident both in the archaeological and cuneiform records. By the late third millennium this urban core had stimulated the rise of secondary states or complex regional polities to its east, and a complex network of exchange and shifting political alliances, established peacefully and forcefully, had emerged that united or integrated this entire area into an interlocking system across which materials, technologies, and symbols and ideas were broadly shared.

It is more difficult to construct the "barbarian" Bronze Age world of the steppes to the north, in good part because of the fact that it was illiterate, lacking historical sources to facilitate the reconstruction of its social features. The archaeological record that has been compiled, moreover, is deficient in its overemphasis on mortuary remains and relatively scant settlement data. This picture is changing, as settlements are being discovered through the use of more sophisticated remote-sensing techniques and excavated, although the picture in hand at the moment remains incomplete, with certain vital pieces missing to complete the puzzle. Different peoples interacted with each other not principally as traders, but as herders; that is, the mobile herding economies that were characteristic of the steppes brought different peoples into continuous contact with each other. This continuous contact stimulated political developments, both the formation and dissolution of large alliances or confederations of related peoples that presumably made possible the ever increasing large-scale extraction of metal ores and the nearly universally shared ability to produce and exchange metal tools and weapons.

Materials and technologies were shared or diffused across this vast world, and these processes are perhaps most clearly reflected in the spread of related types of metal tools and weapons within successively larger "metallurgical provinces." By the Late Bronze Age, metal ores were being extracted at specialized sites, such as the Gorny settlement at Kargaly, on a seemingly industrial scale. Settlements, such as those of the slightly earlier Sintashta-Arkaim so-called "Country of Towns" across the Urals, are small and relatively undifferentiated, certainly in comparison with the urban centers of the "civilized" Ancient Near East; the domestic houses resemble one another and the sites essentially lack public monumental architecture. What is striking, however, is the pervasive distribution and evidence for working metals at the Sintashta-Arkaim and other Middle and Late Bronze settlements. Nearly everyone seemingly could – at least at some level – fashion or rework his/her metal tools and weapons.

The broadly diffused metal-working technology of the Bronze Age Eurasian steppes contrasts with the more localized or concentrated evidence for metal-working in the Ancient Near East. The more egalitarian "barbarians" on the steppes were not technologically deficient in terms of their abilities to mine and work metals essential to their way of life; if anything, they were relatively advanced in this respect compared with their "civilized" neighbors to the south. In other words, the terms civilized/barbarian here do not carry their nineteenth-century connotations – the former supposedly being more progressive and superior, the latter more backward and inferior. Rather, the herders of the steppes were self-sufficient, organized into partially autonomous/independent kin-structured groups that were capable of forming and dissolving alliances with related groups, and increasingly worked metals for eminently practical purposes. In certain respects, such "barbarians" were more advanced than most of the peoples laboring in the "civilized" world to the south.

How was such large-scale mining organized? Was it our so-called "gulag" pattern, that is, one that took place under a despotic state organizing and controlling the extraction and distribution of ores? Or the contrastive "gold rush" pattern in which basically decentralized prospectors exchanged their raw materials with neighboring herders who, in turn, exchanged some of these ores with their neighbors in a down-the-line fashion? We lack essentially any evidence for the former, and yet it is hard to envision how the latter would have worked efficiently. Certainly, the "barbarian" world of the steppes was more egalitarian than the "civilized" Ancient Near East; sharp social distinctions on the scale of the latter are not seen in the mortuary remains or in the architecture of the settlements that have been excavated on the steppes.

Most likely kindred tribal groups periodically coalesced into larger confederacies to solve problems related to the procurement of materials or the acquisition of better pastures, such large-scale unions finding their dim reflection in the overall uniformity of the archaeologically defined cultures and the lack of sharp boundaries among them and the ubiquitous presence of countless raised kurgans, the continuous construction of which must have required considerable social coordination. Political and military unions of far less mobile Native Americans, such as the Iroquois (*Haudenosaunee*) confederation, are ethnographically attested as having successfully controlled vast regions, such as most of eastern North America, for centuries or relatively long periods of time. Perhaps broadly similar alliances characterized the Bronze Age Eurasian steppes, though it is difficult to envision how they will be convincingly documented archaeologically.

Nevertheless, trade and population movements continuously occurred throughout both these "worlds" during later prehistory, and this circulation of materials and peoples had far-reaching social and political consequences. Is this just an article of faith? How do we even recognize that long-distance exchange and movements of peoples actually occurred? The archaeological record is notoriously incomplete and difficult to interpret. Some areas are better investigated than others, or, stated negatively, some critical regions, such as the "tin belt" stretching from southwestern to northeastern Afghanistan (cf. Fig. 5.24), have benefited from very little sustained research and can essentially be considered archaeological *terrae incognitae*. Our interpretations are always conditioned by the uneven nature of archaeological research, a problem that compounds itself when we expand our spatial horizons.

Archaeologists who believe in the importance of far-reaching Bronze Age connections must emphasize the exceptional discoveries, such as the Uluburun shipwreck, that provide a rare glimpse into the scale and complexity of interregional exchange. From this perspective, such remarkable discoveries remind us how incomplete our understanding actually is and represent the tip of a massive iceberg of missing data to document such interconnections. Organic materials, such as textiles or various hardwoods essential for building boats and culturally valued aromatic substances, which we know historically from the cuneiform sources were important objects of exchange, rarely are preserved and, consequently, remain largely invisible in the archaeological record. They cannot be ignored. Awareness of them is essential, but it is extremely difficult, if not impossible, to assess accurately their scale and significance.

Similarly, we know that entire peoples migrated over long distances in early historic periods, and it is reasonable to assume that they did so in late prehistoric times as well, though they necessarily were conditioned by different technological and social constraints, such as the available means of transportation and the presence or absence of substantial polities throughout the areas they traversed. In many cases these movements can be detected only indirectly or dimly in the archaeological record. In the absence of written sources, it is doubtful that such movements are ever completely or accurately understood. Generally speaking, peoples moved into areas already occupied and assimilated with the cultures with which they came into contact. Total replacement rarely occurred, and thus changes in the archaeological record often remain somewhat ambiguous and open to equally plausible alternative interpretations as essentially internally or externally induced.

If this pattern of emulation and assimilation is dominant, as characterized the intrusion of steppe peoples into southern Central Asia during the Late Bronze Age, then its archaeological or material culture "signature" is going to be difficult to decipher. Such phenomena, however, should not be discounted because their detection is problematic. Somehow they must be accounted for or modeled, even though our interpretations are likely to remain partial and approximate, always subject to necessary revision based on the accumulation of new and more complete records of evidence.

Processual archaeologists working in the Anglo-American tradition largely rejected the concept of migration to explain changes in the archaeological record. Although overstated, this processual critique had a certain validity. There was no question that migration had been used too frequently or over-worked as an explanatory concept. New peoples were too often seen as the efficient causes to explain new material culture features, changes that often could be more efficiently interpreted as adaptations to local conditions. Migrations were also caricatured as unpredictable events, conveniently invoked *dei ex machina* to explain punctuated change in material remains. Migration, how-ever, is not a unitary phenomenon; peoples move for different reasons over different distances. What was needed was a typology of migrations, such as that proposed by D. Anthony (1990) in his sensible plea to reintroduce the concept of migration into Anglo-American archaeological discourse.

Here, we have focused principally on migrations that are not specific, sin-gularly occurring events, but protracted processes, taking place over centuries. In part, this focus also reflects the limitations of the evidence, particularly the lack of a firmly rooted and universally agreed-upon chronology, but it is also true that movements of peoples from one area to another can occur over extended periods of time, forming long-term patterns that are discernible in the archaeological record. Although life on the Eurasian steppes changed from the Bronze to the Iron Age and into later historical periods, the steppes always constituted the dominant "high-pressure zone" from which peoples moved into adjacent lower pressure regions, particularly to the south. This weather pattern was predictable, if occasionally stormy.

We have emphasized that these protracted movements from the steppes into the northern frontier of the Ancient Near East occurred during the Early and Middle Bronze Age in the Caucasus, possibly beginning in the late fourth mil-lennium, and only later began to affect profoundly the settled oasis agricultural areas of Central Asia, especially during the Late and Final Bronze Ages. Neither of these movements from the steppes resembled Iron Age and later historically documented movements from the steppes because the complex basic adap-tation of mounted steppe pastoral nomadism was not fully in place until the beginnings of the Iron Age. Nevertheless, it is important to distinguish the ear-lier cattle herding societies with oxen-driven wheeled vehicles that crossed the Caucasus from the later societies who also had harnessed horses and probably Bactrian camels pulling both heavy wooden wagons and lighter spoke-wheeled vehicles and rode horses, successfully traversing the Kyzyl Kum and Kara Kum deserts. The use of horses made a critical difference. S. Ratnagar (2000: 110) explains the significance of this development on the steppes by ca. 2000 BC:

> The herding of several animals, cattle, sheep, goat and also horses was done from horse back. Once the horse could be controlled by a rider the mounted herder could cover long distances in a day and scout for good pastures

and stray animals; this would ensure that flocks moved fast when necessary. This, in turn would make the tending of large herds possible. . . . In a positive feedback mechanism would arise yet more geographically extensive pastoral circuits and larger flocks. This coupled with geographic factors . . . would mean a precarious balance between people, animals, and the land, necessitating periodic outmigration.

Such recurrent, continuous movements north to south ultimately had profound consequences for the settled societies with whom they came into contact. Movements into the Caucasus were shorter lived, and the restricted mountain valleys of Transcaucasia quickly filled up with the arrivals of different peoples from the steppes, many of whom by the Late Bronze Age lived in inaccessible fortified settlements surrounded by roughly hewn and massive cyclopean stone walls.

Movements first into southern Central Asia and then subsequently onto the Iranian plateau and into South Asia were even more protracted and open-ended, continuing possibly throughout most of the second millennium BC. Here space was less restricted than in the Caucasus, and the irrigation-based agricultural societies with whom the steppe peoples came into contact were more "civilized" or had lived in more complex, hierarchically structured polities. Over time they continuously assimilated into the higher societies or Great Traditions that had developed in southern Central Asia, eastern Iran, and northwestern South Asia during the second half of the third millennium, and in doing so they became increasingly difficult to detect archaeologically. Changes in the ethnic and linguistic composition of the entire eastern Ancient Near East may have occurred in a manner broadly supportive of the reconstructions of most historical linguists (e.g., Mallory 1989). Unfortunately, this process is not directly observable or capable of definitive confirmation in the archaeological record.

Sudden intrusions or colonizations, such as the establishment of Harrapan sites in eastern Bactria and along the Makran coast or the Greeks' establishments of colonies throughout the Black Sea and western Mediterranean Basin in the eighth and seventh centuries BC, took place relatively quickly and left a striking, immediately recognizable archaeological signature. The more protracted movements of the Early Transcaucasians or Kura-Araxes peoples into western Iran, Anatolia, and ultimately parts of the Levant in the late fourth and early third millennium BC, as well as the subsequent movements of the builders of the early monumental kurgans into Transcaucasia from the adjacent steppes beginning roughly in the middle of the third millennium BC, also involved assimilation and acculturation with the preexisting cultures with whom they met. These processes leave a more attenuated material-culture trail but still, to a quite plausible extent, are observable archaeologically as population dispersals, taking place over some extended period of time. Historical linguists postulate more substantial movements of Iranians into Iran and Aryans into South Asia from an original Indo-Iranian homeland located somewhere farther north, but such movements occurred over several centuries and involved contact with more advanced settled complex societies. Theoretically, they should be more difficult to detect archaeologically, and, not surprisingly, they are so.

What other trends or patterned processes can we discern in the archaeological evidence we have reviewed? Let us briefly consider two of them: 1) the production, distribution, and consumption of increasingly functional metal weapons and tools, leading to increased militarism and ultimately the advent of the Iron Age and the breakdown of the earlier Bronze Age interregional connections; and 2) the cyclical pattern of evolution and devolution, social development and collapse as characteristic of the "barbarian" world of the steppes and the adjacent "civilized" world on the northern frontier of the Ancient Near East.

THE FUNCTIONAL USE OF METALS, RISING MILITARISM, AND THE ADVENT OF IRON

Two central theses of our study are that the herding of livestock had to have been intimately related to the production and exchange of metals during the Bronze Age and that classically attested Eurasian mounted nomadism truly emerged only during the subsequent Iron Age. What distinguishes one archaeologically defined Age from the other, and how do we explain the collapse of the Bronze and advent of the Iron Age? There are, of course, many explanations for the collapse of the Bronze Age, ranging from the depredations of the so-called Sea Peoples to changes in warfare (cf. Drews 1993). The extensive trade routes that crisscrossed the eastern Mediterranean in the second half of the second millennium BC were disrupted by such incursions and consequent political instabilities, possibly provoking an energy crisis, a shortage of copper and tin, that only was solved through the procurement and smelting of iron ores and the large-scale production of iron tools and weapons (cf., for example, Snodgrass 1971). Was a similar process underway to the east on the Eurasian steppes? The technology for producing iron tools and weapons also quickly diffused west to east, and this development too would have disrupted the elaborate large-scale exchange networks of copper ores, semiprocessed metals, and finished bronzes.

An inevitable consequence of the advent of iron would have been the collapse or transformation of these exchange networks and metallurgical provinces that had expanded since Chalcolithic times to spread less available ores and metals throughout most of Eurasia wherever food-producing economies had emerged. Principally, it is for this reason that S. Ratnagar (2001) pondered the question whether the Bronze – not Iron – Age represented a unique instance of a preindustrial "world system." Tin, the rarest important component of bronze, apparently was widely circulating in the eastern Mediterranean during the fifteenth to thirteenth centuries BC (Muhly 1980: 48), even though it had to have been imported over hundreds of kilometers both by land and by sea; a few hundred years later, it was no longer in such demand. Thus, paradoxically, whereas Iron Age cities and empires greatly surpassed in scale their Bronze Age predecessors, the interregional exchange of metals may have been reduced or replaced by the large-scale trade in other, less directly utilitarian goods.

We know that the introduction of iron tools and weapons, or the real advent of the Iron Age and not just a stage of archaeological classification, was a gradual process that occurred in the eastern Mediterranean from the twelfth through tenth centuries BC (Waldbaum 1978). By the time iron tools and weapons began to replace comparable bronzes, the latter were not only already widely available in the Late Bronze kingdoms of Mesopotamia and the eastern Mediterranean, but also extensively utilized throughout the "barbarian" realms of the northern frontier of the Ancient Near East and across the Eurasian steppes. And China, of course, was producing its own characteristic ritual vessels, ornaments, and weapons on a scale perhaps unmatched elsewhere. Childe popularized the view (1964: 191, 200) that commonly available

> cheap iron democratized agriculture and industry and warfare, too. Any peasant could afford an iron axe to clear fresh land for himself and iron ploughshares wherewith to break up stony ground. The common artisan could own a kit of metal tools that made him independent of the households of kings, gods, or nobles . . . With the new metal implements for breaking the ground, clearing it of trees and digging drainage channels, the small farmer might earn independence by reclaiming for himself a piece of waste; in any case, he could produce more.

Childe's thesis needs to be qualified. Stronger iron implements may ultimately have increased productivity, but by the late second millennium BC bronze tools and weapons were widely available and on the Eurasian steppes "democratically" utilized for many of the eminently practical purposes cited by Childe, including tilling the soil, harvesting the crops, building boats, composite bows, and wheeled vehicles (i.e., advanced carpentry), and killing one's neighbors.

The development of metallurgy in western Eurasia from the Chalcolithic through the Bronze and into the Iron Age is characterized by an overall increase in the scale of metallurgical production and in the functional utility of the objects produced. Chernykh's metallurgical provinces consistently expand in terms of their spatial extent from their Chalcolithic Balkan origins north into Europe and particularly east across the Caucasus, the Urals, and Kazakhstan to the borders of China. Over time more metal tools and weapons are produced, as is clearly reflected in the number of Late Bronze hoards in eastern Europe (Chernykh 1992: 252) or Late Bronze/Early Iron sanctuary deposits in eastern Georgia (Pizchelauri 1984), several of which contained thousands of bronze objects. The Caucasus, for example, produced an incredible number of metal tools, weapons, and ornaments, most often tin-bronzes, during Late

Bronze times. The State Historical Museum in Moscow alone contains tens of thousands of bronze objects plundered from the Koban cemetery of northern Ossetia in pre-Soviet times. Thousands more have been subsequently excavated throughout the Caucasus, mostly from cemeteries, such as the famous Tli cemetery (Tekhov 1977, 1980, 1988). There was no shortage of functional bronze tools and weapons at the end of the Bronze Age. Rather, they were increasingly available throughout the Ancient Near East and across the Eurasian steppes during the second half of the second millennium BC.

Throughout Chalcolithic and Bronze Age times, metals served both prestige and practical purposes. Most of the metals deposited in the graves at Varna were meant to exalt the social status of the deceased, as also were the ornaments found in the roughly contemporaneous hoards, settlements, and cemeteries of the Carpatho-Balkan metallurgical province stretching from the Balkans across the western Eurasian steppes to the Volga. Albeit on a small scale, functional copper daggers, knives, shaft-hole axes and hammer-axes, awls, and fishhooks are also found in Cucuteni-Tripol'ye settlements (e.g., Figs. 2.10 and 2.11), demonstrating the simultaneous practical uses of early copper objects. The Maikop culture of the northern Caucasus is most famous for its ceremonial use of precious metals – figured silver vessels, figurines, gold wands or staffs – but also contains large vessels (for communal feasts?), objects of indeterminate use such as the looped *psalia* and hooked kryuki (pitchforks?), and very functional daggers, spear heads, axes, adzes, and possibly hoes. Kura-Araxes metals include ornaments, such as hammer and double spiral-headed toggle pins and figured diadems, as well as again very usable weapons and tools, including curved bladed objects that most likely were sickles. The "royal" tomb from Arslantepe contained silver and gold ornaments, as well as numerous arsenical copper/bronze vessels, tools, and weapons (nine spearheads, two swords, two daggers, four axes and a knife). Possibly, four adolescents were sacrificed as part of the interment ceremony of the principal royal or chiefly person; human sacrifice likewise is most likely attested in some of the early monumental kurgans in Transcaucasia. Most graphically, the Karashamb silver goblet (cf. Fig. 3.28 and description), with its decapitation and stabbing scene together with stacked human heads and row of daggers, spearheads, and shields depicts the bloody purposes for which these weapons were made.

Similarly in Mesopotamia copper ceased being primarily an exotic luxury and was replaced by silver as a medium of exchange as copper became a widely available "necessity" in the middle of the third millennium (Edens 1992), and by the early second millennium bronze was regularly used for agricultural purposes as shown by the Old Babylonian hoards of tools from Tell Sifr and, supposedly, Ishchali (Moorey 1994: 262). Mid-second-millennium (or earlier?) Sabatinovka sites in southern Ukraine bordering the Black Sea practiced a much less intensive form of swidden cultivation, periodically shifting their fields and settlements, but broadly utilized bronze sickles to harvest their crops as shown by the recovery of numerous, repeatedly used stone sickle moulds (Gershkovich 2003: 311). Such examples could be multiplied.

Basically two interrelated trends are observable and characterize both the "civilized" Ancient Near East and its "barbarian" northern frontier and adjacent world of the steppes throughout the Bronze Age: the increasingly effective production of functional bronze weapons and practical use of bronze agricultural tools. From this perspective, the depredations of the Sea Peoples in the eastern Mediterranean were not accidental harbingers of new times, but the logical continuation of processes long underway in western Eurasia. Farther east on the Eurasian steppes, another factor also was at work: increased riding of horses, not just for herding cattle, but for raiding and military purposes. Mounted, militarized steppe nomadism was nearly in place and would soon impress itself on the consciousness of the Ancient Near East with the military incursions of the Cimmerians and Scythians.

From a cross-cultural comparative perspective, this functional application of metal technology for essential weapons and agricultural tools was not typical. The Harappan or Indus Valley "civilization" was a principal player in the interregional networks of exchange and complex polities that interacted with each other during the second half of the third millennium BC; they most likely regularly visited Oman (ancient Magan) to obtain copper. Yet their own practical use of copper/bronze seems impoverished by comparison with Mesopotamia or the Eurasian steppes. Their metal weapons, such as daggers and spearheads, lacked strengthening mid-ribs and were not terribly formidable; very few metal sickles have been recovered from Harappan sites, and metals clearly were not integrated into basic agrarian activities, as they were in the Caucasus or on the steppes (for a more detailed discussion, see Ratnagar 2000: 96–99). The same could be said for the metal assemblages of many of the secondary states east of Sumer where metals seemingly were used more for administrative (e.g., compartmented seals) or ceremonial/prestige (the elaborately cast figured, shaft-hole axes) purposes. This pattern applies even more to Bronze Age China, where tremendous effort and technological innovation characterized the piece-mould casting of ritual vessels, some of which were incredibly large and elaborate, yet stone sickles remained in use well into the Iron Age.

The conquests of the Spaniards in the sixteenth century cut short the indigenous use of metals in the Andes and in Mesoamerica. We will never know whether – given more time – the Andean and Mesoamerican peoples would have developed more functional bronze weapons and tools, analogous to those that developed in the Near East and Eurasian steppes. Nevertheless, it is impossible to refer to a Bronze, much less an Iron, Age in the New World, and most effort, which, of course, in the Andes was considerable with a history of metal production that extended back into the Early Horizon or late second millennium BC and in the south included the production of tin-bronzes, seems to have been devoted to producing copper-silver and copper-gold alloys (*tumbaga*) for luxury goods and for ceremonial/ritual purposes. The cultural value or technological style of gold- and silver-looking copper alloys seemingly inhibited the production of more functional weapons and tools (cf. Chernykh 2005), and "copper, through its alloys, . . . remained a handmaiden to gold and to silver: (Lechtman 1980: 295).

EVOLUTION AND DEVOLUTION IN BRONZE AGE EURASIA –
CULTURE HISTORY IN ARCHAEOLOGY AS THE SEARCH FOR
MACROHISTORICAL PATTERNS AND PROCESSES RATHER
THAN THE COMPILATION OF DATA; SOCIAL EVOLUTION
AS "WORLD" HISTORY

The archaeological narrative that we have related has shown that countless different cultures and peoples, who utilized very similar functional copper and bronze tools and weapons on an ever-increasing scale from the sixth through the second millennium and then quickly adopted even better and easier means to procure iron tools during the first millennium, were participants in a shared historical process that stretched from northwestern Europe to the borders of China, justifying C. Thomsen's original and prescient Three Age sequence. This process involved not only metals, but also other important shared technologies, such as means of transportation, including wheeled vehicles, ridden horses, and wind powered boats, and an assemblage of essentially the same domesticated species of plants and animals that were kept not only as sources of food, but for their fibers to produce textiles, and, for some important animals, their dairy products and labor power to plow fields and haul goods.

Some peoples *principally* grew crops, often investing considerable efforts in improving and modifying the land to support agriculture and expand its productivity, while at the same time maintaining animals with seasonal movements into the mountains or onto the plains. Others developed a different form of productive economy that concentrated *principally* on herding animals and necessarily involved large-scale systematic movements, often of the entire social group, to provide continuously pasture or fodder for their animals. These two ways of life complemented one another, and peoples frequently moved between them – some cultivators adopting a more pastorally mobile lifestyle and some herders settling down to practice agriculture. Technologies were shared; raw materials and semiprocessed and finished goods were exchanged or forcibly taken; and peoples moved in patterned, partially predictable ways to improve their lives. Technological advances proceeded in a logical and essentially cumulative fashion; or, to adopt a different terminology, the forces of production in society grew continuously over time.

The same cannot be said for the different forms of *society* we have encountered throughout this study. The gigantic, socially undifferentiated Tripol'ye settlements collapsed or were mysteriously abandoned sometime during the first half of the fourth millennium BC. Subsequent archaeological remains on the western Eurasian steppes markedly differ at least through Middle Bronze times; kurgans or burial remains now dominate the archaeological record and the few settlements that are known are much smaller than their Tripol'ye predecessors. The Early Bronze inhabitants of the Caucasus did not live in cities, but they worked metals on a substantial scale and precociously used them to cultivate and harvest crops. Towards the end of the fourth millennium, some of these peoples began to move south out of the Caucasus to occupy different parts of the Ancient Near East, whereas other peoples subsequently crossed or circumvented the Great Caucasus range and built large houses for the dead or monumental kurgans to inter the physical remains of what are reasonably interpreted as their chiefs and accompanying attendants. Later, peoples throughout Transcaucasia lived in inaccessibly situated and heavily fortified settlements that reveal little evidence for social differentiation or settlement hierarchy. Centralized regional kingdoms would emerge here only later during the Iron Age. Complex polities, reasonably termed "states" or even "civilizations," developed in parts of southern Central Asia and other lands east of Sumer during the second half of the third millennium, but they too collapsed or were abandoned during the first half of the second millennium BC, and the earliest Iron Age settlements in southern Central Asia, eastern Iran, and northwestern India seem much less complex and developed than the Bronze Age proto-urban or urban settlements that had flourished earlier.

Productive herding economies, focusing principally at first on raising cattle, spread throughout the vast belt of the Eurasian steppes, reaching the borders of western China. Eventually, they diversified the species of animals they kept, rode horses, and utilized lighter, faster, and militarily more effective wheeled vehicles. At least in parts of the western steppes, sedentary settlements reappear, becoming more numerous and larger over time, and metals are mined on an immense, seemingly industrial scale and distributed widely across the steppes, though it remains unclear exactly how these related processes of production and exchange were organized and coordinated. Later again during the Iron Age, mounted pastoral nomadic confederacies would emerge, interact peacefully and hostilely with settled societies to the south, and construct royal kurgans for their leaders that were laden with marvelously worked gold and silver ornaments, vessels, and other precious objects.

Is there any pattern to the developments described above? It certainly is not linear, progressing inexorably from the simple to the complex. Societies develop and collapse; devolution is as evident as evolution. Are these developments cyclical in any patterned manner, such as the oscillations between more integrated complex and more regionalized simple chiefdoms postulated by Koryakova (1996: 273) for temperate Eurasia from the Middle Bronze through the Iron Age? As our geographical horizons widen, it is hard to detect such regular developments, for one area may experience growth, such as the Caucasus with the sudden emergence successively of the Maikop and Kura-Araxes cultures, while another region, the Balkans to eastern Ukraine, declines.

Similarly in the early second millennium, societies in the eastern Mediterranean on Cyprus, Crete, the Greek mainland, and elsewhere flourished, participating in a complex marine-oriented exchange network in which exotic precious goods, semiprocessed and finished bronzes, and staples freely circulated, whereas elsewhere the complex regional polities east of Sumer had collapsed, these regions descending into an archaeological dark age populated increasingly by less "civilized" herders from the north. One area waxes and another wanes. Developments and declines in one area are distinctive from those in another, but they exhibit complementarities that are not fortuitous, but interrelated and systematic.

One detectable pattern is that centers of evolutionary development are not stationary, but shift or replace one another over time. The evolutionary "action" takes place in different areas at different times across the steppes and along the northern frontier of the Ancient Near East. In the Neolithic, cultural developments are most spectacular in Anatolia; in the Chalcolithic it is the Balkans, stretching across Romania, Moldova, and western Ukraine, then the Caucasus, southern Central Asia and eastern Iran, across the Urals and so forth. In this respect, later prehistory seemingly resembles the modern historical era with its consecutive shifts in world power from Portugal and Spain to the Netherlands, France, England, and, currently, the United States. . . . Political and economic hegemonies are never permanent but rise and fall principally as a result of ever-changing interconnected macrohistorical processes.

Such macrohistorical processes are impossible to detect archaeologically if one focuses on developments in a single region or over a relatively restricted chronological horizon of a hundred years or so. The basic task of the archaeologist as culture historian is not to compile and order new data and ceaselessly refine local chronological sequences, though those are both essential and necessary activities; the culture historian also must take advantage of the only real strength of the archaeological record: its coarse-grained, spatial and temporal macroperspective on the basic activities carried out by different groups, and then attempt to discern how these various activities relate to one another or are interconnected. As E. Wolf (1982) argued persuasively for the modern historical era, cultures continuously imbricate and get caught up in shared historical processes that extend far beyond the areas they occupy.

Cultural evolution does not proceed typically through internal developments and local adaptations to restricted environmental settings, but occurs as a product of these shared interconnections and experiences. Cultures are dynamic entities that can change dramatically over very short periods of time, particularly as they get caught up in larger historical processes that can overwhelm and transform them. Such large-scale processes, involving the development of new technologies and economies and the large-scale movements of materials through various forms of exchange and of peoples through their migrations, were at work on the Eurasian steppes during the Bronze Age and profoundly affected the countless archaeological cultures that have been defined throughout this vast area and adjacent lands farther south.

Cultural evolution is real in the sense that qualitative social and cumulative technological changes take place over time and can be traced. As discussed at the beginning of this study, evolution and history are not opposed, but complementary concepts. Social evolution is "world" history in the sense that evolution takes place on an interconnected scale in which different peoples differentially participate (cf. also Yoffee 2005: 197). The Mesopotamian "urban revolution" and the periodic rises and falls of the various states that continuously redefined Mesopotamian civilization for over three millennia cannot be viewed in isolation; rather, the emergence and early development of Mesopotamia must be placed within interacting "worlds" that stretched at least from the Balkans and the lands bordering the eastern Mediterranean in the west to the Eurasian steppes in the north to the Central Asian and Indus Valley Bronze Age urban centers in the east. Throughout these interconnected "worlds" developments in one area were associated with developments and declines in other areas.

Similarly as we discussed previously, the archaeological culture is a problematic concept with a checkered history of overuse. The fit between the archaeological culture and a specific group of people who viewed themselves as culturally distinct can never be assumed and rarely can be unequivocally demonstrated. The bewildering litany of archaeologically defined kurgan cultures on the Eurasian steppes is not just the product of a distinctive tradition of archaeological research, but more profoundly reflects the reality of mobile herding groups constantly meeting and mixing with their neighbors, each becoming the other or transforming themselves into something new. At the end of the Late Bronze Age some archaeological sites on the steppes reveal evidence for an extensive form of swidden or shifting fields cultivation; others lack such evidence. Are the former necessarily the remains of a different people from the Timber Grave herders farther north and east? Or were closely related groups or even the same people pursuing different subsistence activities in different contiguous areas? Finally, the attempt to identify such archaeological cultures as ancestral to much later, historically mentioned ethnic or linguistic groups is always a hazardous and, occasionally, dangerous enterprise, as perhaps is best illustrated in the endless search for the mythical Aryan "homeland."

The cultures that ethnographers study are not little homunculi born perfectly formed with all their distinctive features in place. As emphasized before, they are never made, but always in the making. The Maikop culture presumably originated in the northwestern Caucasus, but it is a product of influences both from the Eurasian steppes and from northern Mesopotamia. The Kura-Araxes culture is thought to have originated somewhere in Transcaucasia, but its "homeland" may actually extend into eastern Anatolia or even northwestern

Iran. As bearers of this cultural formation moved farther south, they changed and adopted some of the features of the peoples with whom they came into contact. Similarly the peoples from the steppes who subsequently moved into the southern Caucasus with their oxen-driven wagons and buried their dead in impressively large kurgans also assimilated and modified material features of those Kura-Araxes folks who stayed behind. The Andronovo-related herders who entered southern Central Asia settled down and adopted many material cultural traits of their new neighbors, becoming almost archaeologically invisible. Sudden shifts in the archaeological record need not necessarily involve the replacement of one people by another, but simply represent the transformation of the lifestyle of the same people. Some cultural traditions are extremely long-lived; others exhibit sharp discontinuities with the past, suggesting dramatic and sudden transformation.

Childe utilized two water metaphors to describe social evolution. One was that of a pool of collectively shared human experiences (1964: 180–181), the other that of a stream drawing in the waters of its tributaries to become a great river flowing into a common ocean:

> Prehistory and history do indeed show how culture grows more and more diversified through the differentiation of societies in response to special stimuli – geographical, technical, or ideological. What is, however, even more striking is the growth of intercourse and interchange between societies. If the streams of cultural tradition go on multiplying they nonetheless tend to converge more and more, and to flow into a single river. A main stream with ever-growing emphasis dominates the whole drainage system to canalize the waters of fresh springs. Cultures are tending to merge into culture. (ibid., 28–29)

Peoples engaged in different activities – herding, cultivating, mining, and trading – made both themselves and Bronze Age Eurasia, but they did so by interacting with one another, pooling together their knowledge and experiences, exchanging materials, and moving both continuously and periodically from one area to another. Processes of interconnection that developed in the Bronze Age have continued to accelerate and expand over time to our qualitatively distinct era of globalization. Both then and now peoples constantly engage in exchanging material objects, ideas, and inventions and learning from each other. Although differing in scale, structure, speed of communication, and technological level of development, the cultures of the Bronze Age and our own globalized era inevitably share this critical feature of interdependency.

APPENDIX

Towards an Integration of the "Absolute" Chronologies of the Eurasian Steppes, the Caucasus, and Western Central Asia during the Bronze Age

(based principally on Trifonov 2001)

Explanatory Key for Trifonov's Chronological Charts:

Number on chart	Culture/Site	Period	Region	quantity of C14 dates
1.	Arslantepe	VII	E Anatolia	6
2.	Arslantepe	VIA	E Anatolia	31
3.	Arslantepe	VIB1	E Anatolia	4
4.	Arslantepe	VIB2	E Anatolia	8
5.	Arslantepe	VIC	E Anatolia	7
6.	Arslantepe	VID2	E Anatolia	11
7.	Arslantepe	VID3	E Anatolia	5
8.	Ginchi		NE Caucasus	6
9.	Godin	3–4	NW Iran	1
10.	Dalma		NW Iran	1
11.	Dzhangar		Kalymykia	2
12.	Dinkha		NW Iran	2
13.	Dnepr–Donetskaya		Dnepr/N Donets	10
14.	Dolmen		NW Caucasus	25
15.	Dolmen	Final?	NW Caucasus	
16.	Karmir-Berd		S Caucasus	1
17.	Catacomb	Early	pri-Kuban	3
18.	Catacomb		Prut-Dnepr	34
19.	Catacomb		Lower Don/N Donets	25
20.	Catacomb		Kalymykia	49

(*continued*)

(*continued*)

Number on chart	Culture/Site	Period	Region	quantity of C14 dates
21.	Catacomb Baturinskaya		pri-Kuban	3
22.	Catacomb Predkavkazkaya		Stavropol'	4
23.	Kayakent-Khorochevskaya		NE Caucasus	2
24	Multi-Cordoned Timber Grave		pri-Kuban	5
25.	Kura–Araxes		NE Caucasus	17
26.	Kura–Araxes		S Caucasus	31
27.	Koruktepe/Norsuntepe	Early	Chalcolithic E Anatolia	8
28.	Leilatepe Culture		S Caucasus	
29.	Maikop		N Caucasus	14
30.	Darkveti-Meshoko		W Caucasus trans-Kuban	2
31.	Nal'chik		Central Caucasus	1
32.	Novotitorovksaya		pri-Kuban	4
33.	Pisdeli		NW Iran	8
34.	Pokrovsk-Potopova		Lower Don/Lower Volga	11
35.	Pokrovsk-Potopova-Sintashta L Don/L Volga/trans-Urals			27
36.	Poltavkinskaya		Lower Volga	2
37.	Predkatakombnaya		pri-Kuban	2
38	Protokolkhskaya		W Caucasus	15
39.	Protokolkhskaya	Final?	W Caucasus	
40.	Sabatinova		Prut-Dnepr	4
41.	North Caucasian		Stavropol'/Kalmykia	14
42.	North Caucasian		Kalmykia	
43.	Sredni Stog		Dnepr-Don	12
44.	Sredni Stog		Dnepr-Don	
45.	Timber Grave		Lower Volga	
46.	Timber Grave		N Don/N Donets/Lower Volga	18
47.	Timber Grave		Kalmykia	3
48.	Suskanskaya		Lower Volga	1
49.	Trialeti (Martkopi/Tsnori)	Early	S Caucasus	4
50.	Trialeti (Martkopi/Bedeni/Trialeti)		S Caucasus	14
51.	Tripol'ye A		Prut-Dnepr	22
52.	Tripol'ye B		Prut-Dnepr	24

Number on chart	Culture/Site	Period	Region quantity	of C14 dates
53.	Tripol'ye C I		Prut-Dnepr	11
54.	Tripol'ye C II		(Sofievskaya, Gorodskaya, etc.) Prut-Dnepr	12
55.	Usatova		Prut-Dnepr	12
56.	Haftavan	VI B (late)	NW Iran	1
57.	Khvalynsk		Lower Volga	9
58.	Shulaveri-Shomu		S Caucasus	17
59.	Chalcolithic burials		pri-Kuban	5
60.	Chalcolithic burials		Kalmykia	
61.	Pit Grave	Late	pri-Kuban	5
62.	Pit Grave		Lower Volga	8
63.	Pit Grave		Prut-Dnepr	165
64.	Pit Grave		N Don/N Donets	20
65.	Pit Grave		N Don	
66.	Pit Grave		Kalmykia	12
67.	Arslantepe, Hassek Hüyük, Habuba Kabira, Jebel Aruda, Tepechik, Judeidah, Gedekli	Late Chalcolithic Late Uruk	E Anatolia/N Mesopotamia	60
68.	Ur (Royal Cemetery), Abu Salabikh	Early Dynastic III	S Mesopotamia	6
69.	Selenkakh, Uruk-Warka, Nippur, Rimah	Akkadian/Ur III	Mesopotamia	5
70.	Early Bronze (Arslantepe VIB-C, Norsuntepe 26-19, Koruktepe S-E, Pulur, Tepechik, Hassek Hüyük, Korudzhu, Geoy K3, Yanik)	Kura-Araxes period I–II	E Anatolia/NW Iran	83
71.	Early Bronze Anatolia	periods I–III	E Anatolia/NW Iran	67

PERIODIZATION (SUMMARY ADAPTED AND MODIFIED FROM TRIFONOV 2001: 78–81, "ABSOLUTE" DATES BASED ON THE CALIBRATED C14 DETERMINATIONS):

Period 1: 5500–4700 BC – This Early Chalcolithic period includes Shulaveri-Shomu culture sites in Transcaucasia, the Nal'chik cemetery, and the beginnings of the Darkveti-Meshoko culture sites in the northern Caucasus.

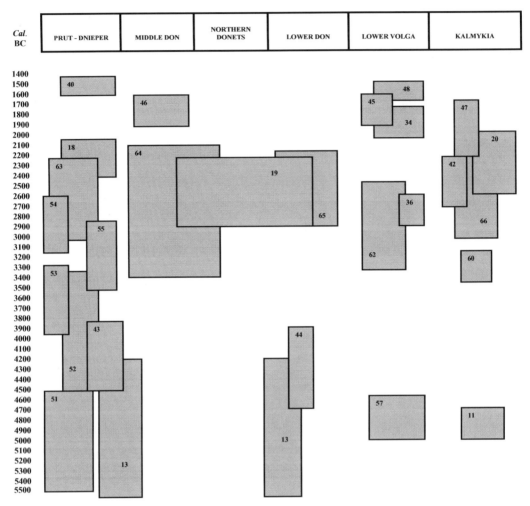

Figure Trifonov – left. – Chronology of the Chalcolithic and Bronze Age Steppes and Adjacent Regions, 5500–1500 BC (as based on calibrated C14 determinations), Chart 1 (courtesy of V. Trifonov, adapted from Trifonov 2001: 75, table 1).

Tripol'ye A and Dnepr-Donets culture sites are distributed on the steppes and forest-steppes from west to east to the Lower Don, and the Khvalynsk culture in the Lower Volga and the Dzhangar culture in Kalmykia appear at the beginning of the fifth millennium.

Period 2: 4700–3700 BC – This period corresponds to the end of the Shulaveri-Shomu culture in Transcaucasia, and the subsequent appearance of sites like Leila-depe (showing Late Ubaid influence) in Azerbaijan and Ginchi in mountainous Daghestan. Darkveti, Zamok, Svobodnoe, and Meshoko sites in the northwestern Caucasus continue to evolve locally under the influence of the East Anatolian cultural tradition. The Khvalynsk, possibly late Dnieper-Donets,

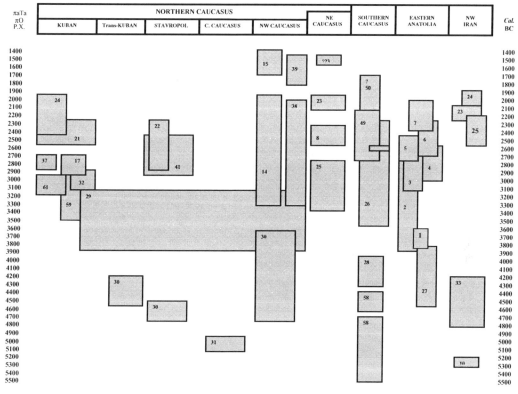

Figure Trifonov – right. – Chronology of the Chalcolithic and Bronze Age Steppes and Adjacent Regions, 5500–1500 BC (as based on calibrated C14 determinations), Chart 1 (courtesy of V. Trifonov, adapted from Trifonov 2001: 76, table 2).

Sredni Stog, and Tripol'ye B I /B II cultures are found on the steppes and forest-steppes to the north.

Period 3: 3700–3500 BC – This period marks the beginnings of the Maikop culture (Ust'-Dzhegutin stage) in the northern Caucasus and sites, like the lowermost level of Berikldeebi, of the Final Chalcolithic (or Sioni culture, according to Kiguradze and Sagona 2003) in the southern Caucasus and in eastern Anatolia. It would correspond also to the earliest occupation of the West Caspian littoral plain by Velikent culture sites. This period corresponds to a time of cultural collapse or hiatus in the Balkans and on the steppes, according to Chernykh, whereas Trifonov (2001: 19) considers the settlement pattern "still not clear" in certain regions, such as the Lower Volga. He also sees Sredni Stog sites as continuing and Repin culture sites on the Middle Don beginning during this period. Farther west, Tripol'ye B II ends and C I begins.

Period 4: 3500–3200 BC – This period marks the development and expansion of the Maikop culture with Maikop-related remains found farther north and east on the Lower Don and in Kalmykia. Late Uruk influence (presence?)

in eastern Anatolia also peaks at this time, as recorded at Arslantepe, and the Kura-Araxes culture sites begin to appear throughout Transcaucasia, except for western Georgia. Velikent culture sites continue to develop along the western coast of the Caspian Sea. This time represents the end of the Sredni Stog and late Konstantinovka cultures in the Northern Donets and Lower Don regions, and Repin sites are found along the Middle Don and Lower Volga areas farther east. Tripol'ye C I period sites continue much farther west in the Prut-Dnieper interfluve.

Period 5: 3200–3000 BC – The "Uruk Empire" collapses in northern Mesopotamia and eastern Anatolia, and the Kura-Araxes culture begins to expand or move farther south into northwestern Iran and eastern Anatolia. The Dolmen and proto-Colchidean (Ochamchira) cultures begin to develop in the western Caucasus, and the Maikop (Bamut stage) begins to contract on account presumably of the spread of the early Pit Grave cultures, which appear practically throughout the entire steppe zone stretching from the southern Urals to the Dnepr.

Period 6: 3000–2700 BC – Kura-Araxes culture sites flourish and reach their final phases of development in Transcaucasia, and the Dolmen and proto-Colchidean cultures continue to occupy the western Caucasus. Late Pit Grave sites develop into North Caucasian culture sites throughout the northern Caucasus stretching into southern Kalmykia. Presumably this is also the time of the development of the Novotitorvoskaya culture in the Lower Kuban region. Early Catacomb culture remains supplant Pit Grave sites on the Lower Don, northern Donets, and possibly Middle Don. Early Poltavka sites may begin to appear farther east in the Lower Volga region during this time.

Period 7: 2700–2500 BC – This period coincides with the appearance of the early monumental kurgans of the Martkopi-Tsnori type in the southern Caucasus, or, more generally, Kura-Araxes culture settlements begin to be replaced by early Trialeti culture sites. The western Caucasus does not change, while the North Caucasian culture extends only to the Central Caucasus since Early Catacomb remains are now distributed throughout the Stavropol' region into northern Kalmykia. These latter groups occupy a broad zone from the Lower Don-Volga interfluve to the Dnieper. Late Pit Grave cultures continue to exist farther west, while the Poltavka culture continues to develop in the Lower Volga region.

Period 8: 2500–2200 BC – The southern Caucasus Trialeti-related Middle Bronze cultures are closely linked with the Lake Van and Lake Urmia regions in eastern Anatolia and northwestern Iran, which, in turn, synchronize with the end of the Early Dynastic and Akkadian periods in Mesopotamia. The Dolmen and proto-Colchidean cultures continue in the western Caucasus, as does the North Caucasian culture. Most of the steppe zone north and west of the Caucasus, extending east to the Volga area, is occupied by different regional

Catacomb cultures (e.g., Baturin, Manysh, Bakhmut, Ingul', etc.). The Multi-Cordoned Ware culture possibly appears towards the end of this period in the northern Donets and Middle and Lower Don areas.

Period 9: 2200–2000 BC – This period sees the final development of the Trialeti Middle Bronze cultures of the southern Caucasus and related groups in Iran farther south (Haftavan VI B, Dinkha, Godin, etc.). The Kayakent-Khorochoi culture replaces the Middle Bronze Ginchi culture of the northeastern Caucasus. The Dolmen culture (Guam cave) and proto-Colchidean (Pichori) cultures continue to exist in the western Caucasus, while the Multi-Cordoned Ware cultural community spreads from the pri-Kuban region to the Dnieper. Catacomb cultures continue to exist only in Kalmykia, possibly extending to the trans-Kuban region.

Period 10: 2000–1800 BC – Cultural developments in the southern Caucasus in post-Trialeti times are sharply debated and unclear. Possibly the earliest materials from the Samtauro cemetery in central Georgia will prove fundamental for understanding regional developments during this period. The Multi-Cordoned Ware cultural community continues to exist from the pri-Kuban steppe to the Dnieper, extending even farther to the northwest. The Pokrovska and the Potapovka cultures are found farther east from the Lower Volga to the northern Donets regions. Sintashta culture sites are distributed farther east in the trans-Urals region and are synchronous with the A2 period of the Central European Bronze Age.

Period 11: 1800–1500 BC – The earliest remains from the Arich, Lchashen, and Samtauro cemeteries of the southern Caucasus date to this period and immediately precede the link established by Hurrite-Mittanian seals from Artik. Cultural developments in the northern Caucasus are unclear, though Timber Grave related cultures are distributed from the pri-Kuban steppe east to the Stavropol' area. Sites of the proto-Koban and proto-Meotskaya cultures are found in the foothills of the central and western Caucasus. Regional variants of the Timber Grave culture occupy most of the steppe between the Lower Volga and the Dnieper, though Sabatinovka culture sites may have begun to develop at this time farther west in the North Pontic area stretching from the Lower Danube to the Lower Dnepr (Gershkovich 2003: 308–309).

REFERENCES

Abibullaev, O.A. 1982. *Eneolit I Bronza na Terri-torii Nakhichevanskoi ASSR*. Baku: "Elm."

Abramishvili, R. 1984. Au pays du fer. *Les Dossiers Histoire et Archeologie* 88: 46–53.

Adams, R.McC. 1966. *The Evolution of Urban Society*. Chicago: Aldine.

Adams, R.McC. 1974. Anthropological perspectives on ancient trade. *Current Anthropology* 15: 141–160.

Adams, R.McC. 1981. *The Heartland of Cities*. Chicago: University of Chicago Press.

Aglarov, M.A. 1986. Terrasnoe zemledelie Daghestana (Voprosy genezisa, kul'turnoi tipologii i sotsial'noi roli sistemy). *Studia Prae-historica* 8: 50–62.

Akhundov, T. 2001. *Severo-zapadnyi Azerbaid-zhan v epokhu eneolita i bronzy*. Baku: "Elm."

Akhundov, T. 2004. South Caucasus in the Neolithic to Early Bronze Age: The Question of Epochs and Periods. In A. Sagona (ed.), *A View from the Highlands*, pp. 421–436.

Akhundov, T. n.d. Sites de migrants venus du Proche-Orient en Transcaucasie. To appear in B. Lyonnet (ed.), *Les cultures du Caucase*.

Albright, W.F. 1926. The Jordan Valley in the Bronze Age. *Annual of the American Schools of Oriental Research* 6: 13–74.

Alden, J.R. 1982. Trade and Politics in Proto-Elamite Iran. *Current Anthropology* 23: 613–640.

Algaze, G. 1993. *The Uruk Expansion: The dynamics of expansion of early Mesopotamian Civilisation*. Chicago: University of Chicago Press.

Aliev, A.A., M.S. Gadjiev, M.G. Gaither, P.L. Kohl, R.M. Magomedov, and I.N. Aliev. N.d. The Ghilghilchay Defensive Long Wall: New investigations. *Ancient West and East*, in press.

Aliev, N. and I. Narimanov. 2001: Kul'tura severnogo Azerbaidzhana v epokhu pozdnego eneolita Baku: "Agridag".

Alimov, K., N. Boroffka, M. Bubovna, Ju. Burjakov, J. Cierny, J. Jakubov, J. Lutz, H. Parzinger, E. Pernicka, V. Radililovkij, V. Ruzanov, T. Sirinov, D. Starsinin, and G. Weisgerber. 1998. Prähistorischer Zinnberg-bau in Mittelasien: Vorbericht der Kampagne 1997. *EurAnt* 4: 137–199.

Amiet, P. 1986. *L'âge des échanges inter-iraniens 3500–1700 avant J.-C.* Paris: Éditions de la Réunion des musées nationaux.

Amiet, P. 1990a. Elam and Bactria. In G. Ligabue and S. Salvatori (eds.), *Bactria: An ancient oasis civilization from the sands of Afghanistan*, pp. 127–140.

Amiet, P. 1990b. Antiquities of Bactria and Outer Iran in the Louvre collection. In G. Ligabue and S. Salvatori (eds.), *Bactria: An ancient oasis civilization from the sands of Afghanistan*, pp. 159–187.

Amiran, R. 1968. Chronological Problems of the Early Bronze Age. Early Bronze I–II: The City of Arad. Early Bronze III. The Khirbet Kerak Ware. *AJA* 72: 316–318.

Amirkhanov, Kh.A. 1987. *Chokhskoe poselenie*. Moscow: Nauka.

Andreeva, M.V. 1977. 'K voprosu o yuzh-nykh svyazakh maikopskoi kul'tury.' *Sovet-skaya Arkheologiya* 1: 39–56.

Anthony, D. W. 1990. Migration in Archaeology: The Baby and the Bathwater. *American Anthropologist* 92: 895–914.

Anthony, D.W. 1995. Nazi and eco-feminist prehistories: Ideology and empiricism in Indo-European archaeology. In P. L. Kohl and C. Fawcett (eds.), *Nationalism, Politics and the Practice of Archaeology*. Cambridge: Cambridge University Press, pp. 82–96.

Anthony, D.W. 1996. Bridling horse power: The domestication of the horse. In S.L. Olsen (ed.), *Horses through time*. Dublin: Roberts Rinehart Publishers for Carnegie Museum of Natural History, pp. 57–82.

Anthony, D.W. 1998. The opening of the Eurasian steppe at 2000 BCE. In V. H. Mair (ed.), *The Bronze and Early Iron Age peoples of eastern Central Asia*. Washington, DC: The Institute for the Study of Man, vol. 1, pp. 94–113.

Anthony, D.W. n.d. The origins of the Sintashta-Arkaim Culture: Climate change, warfare, and long-distance trade. Paper delivered at the "New Research Directions in Eurasian Steppe Archaeology: The Emergence of Complex Societies in the Third to First Millennia BCE" symposium, University of Pittsburgh, February 2006.

Anthony, D.W. and D. R. Brown. 1991. The origins of horseback riding. *Antiquity* 65 (246): 22–38.

Anthony, D.W. and D. R. Brown. 2000. Eneolithic horse exploitation in the Eurasian steppes: Diet, ritual, and riding. *Antiquity* 74: 75–86.

Anthony, D.W. and D. R. Brown. 2003. Eneolithic Rituals and Riding in the Steppes: New Evidence. In M. Levine, C. Renfrew, and K. Boyle (eds.), *Prehistoric Steppe Adaptation and the Horse*, pp. 55–68.

Anthony, D.W., D. R. Brown, E. Brown, A. Goodman, A. Kokhlov, P. Kosintsev, P. Kuznetsov, O. Mochalov, E. Murphy, D. Peterson, A. Pike-Tay, L. Popova, A. Rosen, N. Russell, and A. Weisskopf. n.d. The Samara Valley Project: Late Bronze Age Economy and Ritual in the Russian Steppes.

Anthony, D.W. and N.B. Vinogradov. 1995. Birth of the Chariot. *Archaeology* 48: 36–41.

Antipina, E.E. 2004. Arkheozoologicheskie materially. In E.N. Chernykh (ed.) *Kargaly Tòm III*, pp. 182–239.

Antipina, E.E. and E.Yu. Lebedeva. 2005. Opyt kompleksnykh arkhebiologicheskikh issledovanii zemledeliya i skotovodstva: Modeli vzaimodeistviya. *Rossiskaya Arkheologiya* 4: 70–78.

Antipina, E.E. and A. Morales. 2005. "Kovboi" Vostochnoevropeiskoi Stepi v Pozdnem Bronzovom Veke. *Opus: Mezhdistsiplinarnye Issledovaniya v Arkheologii* 4: 29–49.

An Zhimin. 1998. Cultural Complexes of the Bronze Age in the Tarim Basin and Surrounding Areas. In V. Mair (ed.), *The Bronze Age and Early Iron Age Peoples of Eastern Central Asia*, vol. I, pp. 45–62.

Archaeological Dialogues. 1998. Relativism, Objectivity, and the Politics of the Past. *Archaeological Dialogues* 5 (1): 30–53.

Arkheologiya Ukrainskoi SSR. 1985. Pervobytnaya Arkheologii, t. 1. Kiev: Naukova Dumka.

Arne, T. J. 1945. *Excavations at Shah Tepe, Iran*. The Sino-Swedish Expedition, Publication 27. Stockholm.

Aruz, J. (ed.). 2003a. *Art of the First Cities: The third millennium B. C. from the Mediterranean to the Indus*. New York: The Metropolitan Museum of Art.

Aruz, J. 2003b. Art and Interconnections in the Third Millennium B. C. In J. Aruz (ed.), *Art of the First Cities*, pp. 239–250.

Aruz, J. 2003c. "Intercultural Style" Carved Chlorite Objects. In J. Aruz (ed.), *Art of the First Cities*, pp. 325–345.

Aruz, J., A. Farkas, A. Alekseev, and E. Korolkova. 2000. *The Golden Deer of Eurasia: Scythian and Sarmatian Treasures from the Russian Steppes*. New York: The Metropolitan Museum of Art.

Askarov, A. 1973. *Sapallitepa*. Tashkent: FAN.

Avanessova, N.A. 1996. Pasteurs et agriculteurs de la vallée du Zeravshan (Ouzbékistan) au début de l'Age du Bronze: relations et influences mutuelles. In B. Lyonnet (ed.), *Sarazm (Tadjikistan) céramiques (Chalcolithique et Bronze Ancien)*. Paris: De Boccard, pp. 117–124.

Avilova, L. I. 2005. Metall Zapadnoi Azii (Eneolit-Srednii Bronzovyi Vek), *Opus: Mezhdistsiplinarnye Issledovaniya v Arkheologii* 4: 11–28.

Avilova, L.I., E.V. Antonova, and T.O. Teneishvili 1999: Metallurgicheskoe proizvodstvo v yuzhnoi zone tsirkumpontiiskoi Metallurgicheskoi provintsii v epokhu rannei bronzy. *RA* 1: 51–65.

Bacon, E. 1954. Types of pastoral nomadism in Central and Southwest Asia. *Southwestern Journal of Anthropology* 10 (1): 44–68.

Badalyan, R., P. Lombard, C. Chataigner, and P. Avetisyan. 2004. The Neolithic and Chalcolithic Phases in the Ararat Plain (Armenia): The View from Aratashen. In A. Sagona (ed.), *A View from the Highland*, pp. 399–420.

Badalyan, R.S., A.T. Smith, and P. S. Avetisyan. 2003. The Emergence of Sociopolitical Complexity in Southern Caucasia: An interim report on the research of project ArAGATS. In A.T. Smith and K. S. Rubinson (eds.), *Archaeology in the Borderlands*, pp. 144–166.

Badler, V. R. 2002. A Chronology of Uruk Artifacts from Godin Tepe in Central Western Iran and Implications for the Interrelationships between the Local and Foreign Cultures. In *Artefacts of Complexity: Tracking the Uruk in the Near East*. Iraq Archaeological Reports – 5. Wiltshire, England: Aris & Phillips, Ltd., pp. 79–109.

Bailey, D.W. and I. Panayatov (eds.). 1995. *Prehistoric Bulgaria*. Madison, WI: Prehistory Press.

Bailey, D.W. and D. Hofmann. 2005. Review of H. Todorova (ed.), *Die prähistorischen Gräberfelder*. *Antiquity* 79 (303): 220–222.

Bakker, J.A., J. Kruk, A.E. Lanting, and S. Milisauskas 1999. The earliest evidence of wheeled vehicles in Europe and the Near East. *Antiquity* 73 (282): 778–790.

Barber, E. J. W. 1991. *Prehistoric Textiles*. Princeton: Princeton University Press.

Barfield, T. J. 1993. *The nomadic alternative*. Englewood Cliffs, NJ: Prentice-Hall.

Barth, F. 1964. *Nomads of South Persia: The Basseri tribe of the Khamseh confederacy*. Oslo: Universitetsforlaget.

Basilov, V. N. and O. B. Naumova. 1989. Yurts, Rugs, and Felts. In V.N. Basilov (ed.), *Nomads of Eurasia*. Seattle: University of Washington Press, pp. 96–109.

Beck, L. 1986. *The Qashga'i of Iran*. New Haven: Yale University Press.

Belgiorno, M.R., R. Biscione, and P. E. Pecorella. 1984. Il Saggio E I Materiali Di Tappeh Gijlar. In P.E. Pecorella and M. Salvini (eds.), *Tra Lo Zagros e L'Urmia: Ricerche Storiche ed Archeologiche Nell'Azerbaigian Iraniano*, pp. 240–299.

Belinskij, A.B., A.A. Kalmykov, S.N. Korenevskij, and H. Härke. 2000. The Ipatovo kurgan on the North Caucasian Steppe (Russia). *Antiquity* 74 (286): 773–774.

Benecke, N. 2003. Iron Age Economy of the Inner Asian Steppe: A bioarchaeological perspective from the Talgar Region in the Ili River Valley (Southeastern Kazakhstan). *EurAnt* 9: 63–84.

Benecke, N. and A. von den Dreisch. 2003. Horse Exploitation in the Kazakh Steppes during the Eneolithic and Bronze Age. In M. Levine, C. Renfrew, and K. Boyle (eds.), *Prehistoric Steppe Adaptation and the Horse*, pp. 69–82.

Besenval, R. 1997. Entre le Sud-Est iranien et la plaine de l'Indus: Le Kech-Makran – Recherches archéologiques sur le peuplement ancien d'une marche des confines indo-iraniens. *Arts Asiatiques* 52: 5–35.

Bespalyi, E.I. 2002. Kurgannyi mogil'nik Mukhin. *Aksaiskie Drevnosti*. Rostov-on-Don: Archaeological Scientific Investigation Bureau.

Biehl, P. F., A. Gramsch, and A. Marciniak (eds.). 2002. *Archäologien Europas. Geschichte, Methoden und Theorien*. Münster: Waxmann.

Binford, L.R. 1972. Some Comments on Historical vs. Processual Archeology. In L.R. Binford, *An Archeological Perspective*. New York: Seminar Press, pp. 114–121.

Biscione, R. 1977. The crisis of Central Asia urbanization in II millennium BC and villages as an alternative system. In J. Deshayes (ed.), *Le Plateau Iranien et l'Asie Centrale des Origines à la Conquete Islamique*. Paris: CNRS, pp. 113–127.

Bobomulloev, S. 1991. Raskopki grobnitsy bronzogo veka na verkhnem Zeravshane. *Stratum Plus* 2: 307–313.

Bochkarev, V.S. 1990. Problemy drevnei istorii Severnogo Prichernomor'ya I Srednei Azii (epokha bronzy i rannego zheleza). Tezisy dokladov nauchnoi konferentsii. Leningrad.

Bochkarev, V.S. 1995a. Karpato-Dunaiskii i Volgo-Ural'skii Ochagi Kul'turogeneza Epokhi Bronzy. *Konvergentsiya i Divergentsiya v Razvitii Kul'tur Epokhi Eneolita-Bronzi Srednei i Vostochnoi Evropy*. Saint Petersburg, pp. 18–29.

Bochkarev, V.S. 1995b. Kul'turogenez i Razvitie Metalloproizvodstva v Epokhu Poznei Bronzy. In V. S. Gorbunov (ed.), *Drevnie Indoiranskie Kul'tury Volgo-Ural'ya (II tys. do n.e.)*. Samara, pp. 114–123.

Bochkarev, V.S. 2001. Periodizatsiya V.A. Gorodtsova v kontekste khronologicheskikh issledovanii evropeiskogo bronzovogo veka. In Yu. I. Kolev (ed.), *Bronzovyi vek vostochnoi evropy: Kharakteristika kul'tur, khronologiya i periodizatsiya*. Samara, pp. 8–10.

Bökönyi, S. 1991. Pferde-und Schafdomestikation bzw. -haltung in der frühen Kupferzeit Eurasiens. In J. Lichardus (ed.), *Die Kupferzeit als historische Epoche*, pp. 549–556.

Bolomey, A. and G. El Susi. 2000. The animals. In Marinescu-Bîlcu and A. Bolomey (eds.), *Draguseni: A cucutenian community*. Bucharest: Editura Enciclopedica, pp. 157–177.

Boroffka, N. 1998. Bronze-und früheisenzeitliche Geweihtrensenknebel aus Rumänien und ihre Beziehungen. Alte Funde aus dem Museum für Geschichte Aiud Teil 2. *EurAnt* 4: 81–136.

Boyle, K., C. Renfrew, and M. Levine (eds.). 2002. *Ancient Interactions: East and west in Eurasia*. Cambridge: McDonald Institute Monographs.

Braidwood, R.J. and L.S. Braidwood. 1960. *Excavations in the Plain of Antioch I: The Earlier Assemblages, Phases A-J*. Oriental Institute Publication 61, Chicago.

Brovender, Yu. M. and V. V. Otroshchenko. 2002. Ancient Mines in Seversky Donets Basin, Eastern Ukraine. In E.N. Chernykh (ed.), *Kargaly International Field Symposium – 2002, Earliest Stages of Mining and Metallurgy in Northern Part of Eurasia: Kargaly Complex. Proceedings of Symposium*. Moscow: Institute of Archaeology, RAN, pp. 55–56.

Bulliet, R.W. 1975. *The Camel and the Wheel*. Cambridge: Harvard University Press.

Bunyatyan, K.P. 1997. *Drevneishie Skotovody Ukrainskikh Stepei*. Nikolaev.

Bunyatyan, K.P. 2003. Correlations between Agriculture and Pastoralism in the Northern Pontic Steppe Area during the Bronze Age. In M. Levine, C. Renfrew, and K. Boyle (eds.), *Prehistoric Steppe Adaptation and the Horse*, pp. 269–286.

Burney, C. A. and D. M. Lang. 1971. *The Peoples of the Hills. Ancient Ararat and Caucasus*. London: Weidenfeld and Nicolson.

Carr, E.H. 1961. *What is History?* New York: Random House.

Casa, Ph. Della and M. Primas. 1998. La Production et la Circulation des Metaux sur la Côte Est de l'Adriatique d'après les Analyses Métallurgiques de Velika Gruda (Monténégro). In C. Mordant, M. Pernot, and V. Rychner (eds.), *L'Atelier du Bronzier en Europe du XXe au VIIIe Siècle avant Notre Ere*. Paris.

Cattani, M. 2004. Margiana at the End of Bronze Age and beginning of Iron Age. In

M.F. Kosarev, P.M. Kozhin, and N.A. Dubova (eds.), *U istokov tsivilizatsii*, pp. 303–315.

Cerasetti, B. 1998. Preliminary report on ornamental elements of 'incised coarse ware'. In A. Gubaev, G. Kosholenko, and M. Tosi (eds.), *The Archaeological Map of the Murghab Delta Preliminary Reports 1990–95*, pp. 67–74.

Cernych, E.N. 1978. Aibunar – A Balkan copper mine of the fourth millennium BC. *Proceedings of the Prehistoric Society* 44: 203–217.

Cernych, E.N. 1988. Frühester Kupferbergbau in Europa. In A. Fol and J. Lichardus (eds.), *Macht, Herrschaft und Gold: Das Gräberfeld von Varna (Bulgarien) und Anfänge einer neuen europäischen Zivilisation*. Saarbrücken: Moderne Galerie des Saarland-Museums, pp. 144–150.

Cernych, E.N., E.E. Antipina, and E.Ju. Lebedeva. 1998. Produktionsformen der Urgesellschaft in den Steppen Osteuropas (Ackerbau, Viehzucht, Erzgewinnung undverhüttung. In B. Hänsel and J. Machnik (eds.), *Das Karpatenbecken und die Osteuropäische Steppe*, pp. 233–252.

Cernych, L. 2003. Spektralanalyse und Metallverarbeitung in den früh- und mittelbronzezeitlichen Kulturen der ukrainischen Steppe als Forschungsproblem. *EurAnt* 9: 27–62.

Chataigner, C. 1995. *La Transcaucasie au Néolithique et au Chalcolithique*. BAR International Series 624. Oxford.

Chernykh, E.N. 1992. *Ancient Metallurgy in the USSR*. Cambridge: Cambridge University Press.

Chernykh, E.N. 1997a. *Kargaly: Zabytyi Mir*. Moscow: "Nokh" Publisher.

Chernykh, E.N. 1997b. Kargaly – Krupneishii Gornometallurgicheskii Kompleks Severnoi Evrazii v Drevnosti. *RA* 1: 21–36.

Chernykh, E.N. (ed.). 2002a. *Kargaly Tom I*. Moscow: Languages of Slavonic Culture.

Chernykh, E.N. (ed.). 2002b. *Kargaly Tom II*. Moscow: Languages of Slavonic Culture.

Chernykh, E.N. 2002c. Vvedenie. In E.N. Chernykh (ed.), *Kargaly, Tom II* (supra), pp. 10–11.

Chernykh, E.N. 2002d. Drevneishie vyrabotki na kholme Gornogo. In E.N. Chernykh (ed.), *Kargaly Tom II* (supra), pp. 128–139.

Chernykh, E.N. (ed.). 2002e. *Kargaly International Field Symposium – 2002: Earliest Stages* of Mining and Metallurgy in Northern Part of Eurasia: Kargaly Complex. Proceedings of Symposium. Moscow.

Chernykh, E.N. 2002f. The Kargaly Phenomenon: Some Paradoxes and a Functional Interpretation. In Kargaly International Field Symposium(supra), pp. 87–88.

Chernykh, E.N. (ed.). 2004. *Kargaly Tom III*. Moscow: Languages of Slavonic Culture.

Chernykh, E.N. 2005. Puti i modeli razvitiya arkheometallurgii (staryi i novyi svet). *Rossiskaya Arkheologiya* 4: 49–60.

Chernykh, E.N., L.I. Avilova, and L.B. Orlovskaya 2000. *Metallurgicheskie provintsii i radiouglerodnaya khronologiya (Metallurgical Provinces and Radiocarbon Chronology* [in Russian and English]). Moscow.

Chernykh, E.N. and L.B. Orlovskaya. 2004a. Radiouglerodnaya khronologiya drevneyamnoi obshchnosti i istoki kurgannykh kul'tur. *RA* 1: 84–99.

Chernykh, E.N. and L.B. Orlovskaya 2004b. Radiouglerodnaya khronologiya katakombnoi kultur'no-istoricheskoi obshchnosti (srednii bronzovyi vek). *RA* 2: 15–29.

Childe, V. G. 1933. Is Prehistory Practical? *Antiquity* 7: 410–418.

Childe, V.G. 1964. *What Happened in History*, revised edition. Harmondsworth: Penguin Books Ltd.

Chippendale, C. 1993. Ambition, Deference, Discrepancy, Consumption: The Intellectual Background to a Post-Processual Archaeology. In N. Yoffee and A. Sherratt (eds.), *Archaeological Theory: Who Sets the Agenda?* Cambridge: Cambridge University Press, pp. 27–36.

Compagnoni, B. and M. Tosi. 1978. The camel: Its distribution and state of domestication in the Middle East during the third millennium B.C. in light of finds from Shahr-i Sokhta. In R.H. Meadow and M.A. Zeder (eds.), *Approaches to Faunal Analysis in the Middle East*. Peabody Museum Bulletin 2. Cambridge: Peabody Museum, pp. 91–103.

Connor, S.E., I. Thomas, E.V. Kvavadze, G.J. Arabuli, G.S. Avakov, and A. Sagona. 2004. A survey of modern pollen and vegetation along an altitudinal transect in southern Georgia, Caucasus region. *Review of Palaeobotany and Palynology* 129: 229–250.

Coudart, A. 1999. Is post-processualism bound to happen everywhere? The French case. *Antiquity* 73(279): 161–167.

Crawford, H.E.W. 1998. *Dilmun and Its Gulf Neighbours*. Cambridge: Cambridge University Press.

Dales, G. F. 1977. Shifting Trade Patterns between the Iranian Plateau and the Indus Valley in the Third Millennium B.C. In J. Deshayes (ed.), *Le plateau iranien et l'Asie Centrale des origins à la conquête islamique*. Paris: CNRS, pp. 67–78.

Dani, A.H. and V. M. Masson (eds.). 1992. *History of civilizations of Central Asia, vol. I. The dawn of civilization: Earliest times to 700 B.C.* Paris: UNESCO Publishing.

Debaine-Francfort, C. 2002. Xinjiang and Northwestern China around 1000 BC: Cultural Contacts and Transmissions. In R. Eichmann and H. Parzinger (eds.), *Migration und Kulturtransfer: Der Wandel vorder- und zentralasiatischer Kulturen im Umbruch vom 2. zum 1. vorchristlichen Jahrtausend*. Bonn: Dr. Rudolf Habelt GmbH, pp. 57–70.

De Cardi, B. 1970. *Excavations at Bampur, A Third Millennium Settlement in Persian, Baluchistan, 1966*. Anthropological Papers of the American Museum of Natural History, vol. 51 (3). New York.

Degen-Kovalevskii, B.E. 1939. Problema dati rovki "bol'shikh kubanskikh kurganov." *KSIIMK* 2.

Dergachev, V.A. 1998. *Kerbunskii Klad – Carbuna Deposit*. Kishinev: "Tipografia Academiei de Stiinte".

Dergachev, V.A. 2002. Two Studies in Defense of the Migration Concept. In K. Boyle, C. Renfrew, and M. Levine (eds.), *Ancient Interactions*, pp. 93–112.

Deshayes, J. 1973. La Date des tumuli de Sé Girdan. *Iran* 11: 176–178.

De Miroschedji, P. 2000. La céramique de Khirbet Kerak en Syro-Palestine: État de la question. In C. Marro and H. Hauptmann (eds.), *Chronologie des Pays du Caucase et de l'Euphrate aux IVe–IIIe Millenaires*, pp. 255–278.

Díaz-del-Río, P., P. López-García, J. A. López-Sáez, Mª I. Martinez-Navarrete, A.L. Rodríguez Alcade, S. Rovira Llorens, J.M. Vicent Garcí, and I. Zavala Morencos. 2006. Understanding the productive economy during the Bronze Age through archaeometallurgical and palaeoenvironmental research at Kargaly (Southern Urals, Orenburg, Russia). In D. L. Peterson, L. M. Popova, and A.T. Smith (eds.), *Beyond the Steppe and the Sown:*

Proceedings of the 2002 University of Chicago Conference on Eurasian Archaeology. Colloquia Pontica 13. Leiden: Brill, pp. 347–361.

Dietz, U.L. 1992. Zur Frage vorbronzezeitlicher Trensenbelege in Europa. *Germania* 70: 17–36.

Dietz, U.L. 2003. Horseback Riding: Man's Access to Speed? In M. Levine, C. Renfrew, and K. Boyle (eds.), *Prehistoric Steppe Adaptation and the Horse,* pp. 189–199.

Di Nocera, 2000. Radiocarbon Datings from Arslantepe and Norsuntepe: The fourth-third millennium absolute chronology in the Upper Euphrates and Transcaucasian Region. In C. Marro and H. Hauptmann (eds.), *Chronologie des Pays du Caucase et de l'Euphrate aux IVe–IIIe Millenaires,* pp. 73–93.

Dolukhanov, P.M. 1981. The Ecological Prerequisites for Early Farming in Southern Turkmenia. In P. L. Kohl (ed.), *The Bronze Age Civilization of Central Asia: Recent Soviet Discoveries,* pp. 359–385.

Drews, R. 1993. *The End of the Bronze Age: Changes in Warfare and the Catastrophe ca. 1200 B.C.* Princeton, NJ: Princeton University Press.

Dschaparidze, O. 2001. Zur frühen Metallurgie Georgiens vom 3. bis zum 1. Jahrtausend v. Chr. In I. Gambaschidze, A. Hauptmann, R. Slotta, and Ü. Yalcin (eds.), *Georgien: Schätze aus dem Land des Goldenen Vlies,* pp. 92–119.

Dshaparidse, O. 1995. Die kurgane von Martqopi. In A. Miron and W. Orthmann (eds.), *Unterwegs zum Goldenen Vlies: Archäologische Funde aus Georgien,* pp. 73–75.

Dubova, N.A. 2004. Mogil'nik i tsarskii nekropol' na beregakh bol'shogo basseina severnogo gonura. In M. F. Kosarev, P. M. Kozhin, and N.A. Dubova (eds.), *Yistokov tsivilizatsii,* pp. 254–281.

D'yachenko, A.I., A.S. Skripkin, and V.A. Demkin. 2004. Itogi arkheologicheskogo issledovaniya svyatilishcha y stanitsy Trekhostrovskoi v Volgogradskoi oblasti. *Istoriko-arkheologicheskie issledovaniya v Azove i na Nizhnem Dony v 2002 g.* 19: 178–183.

Dyson, R.H., Jr. 1973. The Archaeological Evidence of the Second Millennium B.C. on the Persian Plateau. In I.E.S. Edwards et al. (eds.), *The Cambridge Ancient History,* 3rd ed., vol. 2, pt. 1. Cambridge: Cambridge University Press, pp. 686–715.

Dyson, R.H., Jr. and S. M. Howard (eds.). 1989. *Tappeh Hesar: Reports of the Restudy Project, 1976.* Firenze: Casa Editrice le Lettere.

Dzhavakhishvili, A.I. and L. Glonti. 1962. *Arkheologicheskiye raskopi provedennye v 1954–1961gg. Na selishche Kvatskhelebi (Tvlepiakokhi).* Tbilisi.

Edens, C. 1992. The dynamics of trade in the ancient Mesopotamian "world system." *American Anthropologist* 94: 118–139.

Ellis, L. 1984. *The Cucuteni-Tripolye Culture. A Study in Technology and the Origins of Complex Society.* British Archaeological Reports – International Series 217. Oxford.

Epimakhov, A.V. 2002. Complex Societies and the Possibilities to Diagnose Them on the Basis of Archaeological Data: Sintashta Type Sites of the Middle Bronze Age of the Trans-Urals. In K. Jones-Bley. and D.G. Zdanovich (eds.), *Complex Societies of Central Eurasia from the 3rd to the 1st Millennium BC: Regional Specifics in Light of Global Models,* vol. I, pp. 139–147.

Epimakov, A.V., B. Hanks, and C. Renfrew. 2005. Radiouglerodnaya khronologiya pamyatnikov bronzovogo veka Zaural'ya. *Rossiskaya Arkheologiya* 4: 92–102.

Flannery, K.V. 1973. Archeology with a Capital S. In C. L. Redman (ed.), *Research and Theory in Current Archeology.* New York: John Wiley & Sons, pp. 47–53.

Fol, A. and J. Lichardus (eds.). 1988. *Macht, Herrschaft und Gold: Das Gräberfeld von Varna (Bulgarien) und Anfänge einer neuen europäischen Zivilisation.* Saarbrücken: Moderne Galerie des Saarland-Museums.

Fol, A. and J. Lichardus. 1988. Archäologie und Geschichte. In A. Fol and J. Lichardus (eds.), *Macht, Herrschaft und Gold,* pp. 19–26.

Francfort, H.-P. 1984a. The early periods of Shortughai (Harappan) and western Bactrian culture of Dashly. In B. Allchin (ed.), *South Asian Archaeology 1981.* Cambridge: Cambridge University Press, pp. 170–175.

Francfort, H.-P. 1984b. Commentaires. In P. L. Kohl, *Central Asia: Palaeolithic beginnings to the Iron Age (L'Asie Centrale des origines à l'Âge du Fer),* pp. 249–265.

Francfort, H.-P. 2003. La civilization de l'Asie Centrale à l'âge du Fer. In O. Bopearachchi, C. Landes, and C. Sachs (eds.), *Catalogue de L'Exposition: De l'Indus à l'Oxus Archéologie de l'Asie Centrale.* Lattes: Association IMAGO – musée de Lattes, pp. 29–59.

Francfort, H.-P. 2005. La civilization de l'Oxus et les Indo-Iraniens et Indo-Aryen en Asie Centrale. In G. Fussman, J. Kelllens, H.-P.

Francfort, and X. Tremblay (eds.), *Aryas, Aryens et Iraniens en Asie Centrale*. Paris: Collège de France, Publications de l'Institut de Civilisation Indienne, Diffusion de Bocard, fascicule 72.

Frangipane, M. 1998. Nel Segno del Leone. *Archeo* 14 (4): 28–41.

Frangipane, M. 2000. The Late Chalcolithic/EBI sequence at Arslantepe. Chronological and cultural remarks from a frontier site. In C. Marro and H. Hauptmann (eds.), *Chronologie des Pays du Caucase et de l'Euphrate aux IVe–IIIe Millenaires*, pp. 439–472.

Frangipane, M., C.M. Di Nocera, A. Hauptmann, P. Morbidelli, A. Palmieri, L. Sadori, M. Schultz, and T. Schmidt-Schultz. 2001. New Symbols of a New Power in a "Royal" tomb from 3000 BC Arslantepe, Malatya (Turkey). *Paléorient* 27 (2): 105–139.

Frank, A.G. 1993. Bronze Age World System Cycles. *Current Anthropology* 34 (4): 383–429.

Frankel, D. 2000. Migration and Ethnicity in Prehistoric Cyprus: Technology as *Habitus*. *European Journal of Archaeology* 3 (2): 167–187.

Frankel, D. and J. M. Webb. 2000: Marki *Alonia*: A prehistoric Bronze Age settlement in Cyprus. *Antiquity* 74: 763–764.

Frey, O.-H. 1991. Varna -Ein Umschlagplatz für den Seehandel in der Kupferzeit? In J. Lichardus (ed.), *Die Kupferzeit als historische Epoche*, pp. 195–201.

Gadzhiev, M. 1991. *Ranne-Zemedel'cheskaya Kul'tura Severo-Vostochnogo Kavkaza*. Moscow: Nauka.

Gadzhiev, M., P. L. Kohl, R. G. Magomedov, and D. Stronach. 1997. The 1995 Daghestan-American Velikent Expedition: Excavations in Daghestan, Russia (with an Appendix on the Velikent Fauna by A. Morales and an Appendix on the Velikent Flora by A. Arnanz). *Eur Ant* 3: 179–218.

Gadzhiev, M., P. L, Kohl, R. Magomedov, D. Stronach, and Sh. Gadzhiev. 2000. Daghestan-American Archaeological Investigations in Daghestan, Russia 1997–99. *Eur Ant* 6: 47–123.

Gaiduchenko, L.L. 1999. Osobennosti prirodopol'zovaniya drevnego Naseleniya 'strani gorodov' yuzhnogo Urala i Zaural'ya. In D.G. Zdanovich, N.O. Ivanova, and I.V. Predeina (eds.), *Kompleksnye obshchestva tsentral'noi Evrazii v III-I tys. do n.e.* (Chelyabinsk, in Russian and in English), pp. 309–312.

Gambaschidze, I., A. Hauptmann, R. Slotta, and Ü. Yalçin (eds.). 2001: *Georgien: Schätze aus dem Land des Goldenen Vlies*. Bochum: Deutsches Bergbau Museum.

Gamkrelidze, T.V. and Vyach.Vs. Ivanov. 1984. *Indoevropeiskii Yazyk i Indoevropeitsy: rekonstruktsiya i istoriko-tiplogicheskii analiz prayazyka i protokul'tury*, vols. I and II. Tbilisi: Publishing House of the Tbilisi State University.

Garazhian, O. 2004. Environment, archaeological remains and the formation process of complex societies in Northeastern Iranian Khorassan. In *Turkmenistan is a Native Land of Anau Culture and White Wheat (Ak Bugday)*. Abstracts of Reports of the International Scientific Conference (October 22–23, 2004). Ashgabat, pp. 197–199.

Gavrilyuk, N.A. 1999. *Istoriya Ekonomiki Stepnoi Skifii VI–III vv. do n.e.* Kiev: Institut arkheologii NAN Ukrainy.

Gayduchenko, L.L. 2002. Organic Remains from Fortified Settlements and Necropoli of the "Country of Towns." In K. Jones-Bley and D.G. Zdanovich (eds.), *Complex Societies of Central Eurasia from the 3rd to the 1st Millennium BC: Regional Specifics in Light of Global Models*, vol. II, pp. 400–416.

Geertz, C. 1963. *Agricultural Involution: The Processes of Ecological Change in Indonesia*. Berkeley: University of California Press.

Gei, A.N. 1991. Novotitorovskaya Kul'tura (predvaritel'naya kharakteristika). *Sovetskaya Arkheologiya* 1: 54–71.

Gei, A.N. 1999. O nekotorykh problemakh izucheniya bronzovogo veka na yuge evropeiskoi rossii. *RA* 1: 34–49.

Gei, A.N. 2000. *Novotitorovskaya Kul'tura*. Moscow: TOO "Staryi Sad".

Gening, V.F., G.B. Zdanovich, and V.V. Gening. 1992. *Sintashta*. Chelyabinsk: Yuzhno-Ural'skoe knizhnoe izdatel'stvo.

Gerskovic, J.P. 1999. *Studien zur spätbronzezeitlichen Sabatinovka-Kultur am unteren Dnepr und an der Westküste des Azov'schen Meeres*. Archäologie in Eurasien, Band 7. Rahden/Westf.: Verlag Marie Leidorf GmbH.

Gershkovich, J.P. 2003. Farmers and Pastoralists of the Pontic Lowlands during the Late Bronze Age. In M. Levine, C. Renfrew, and K. Boyle (eds.), *Prehistoric Steppe Adaptation and the Horse*, pp. 307–317.

Gevorkyan, A. Ts. 1980. *Iz istorii drevneishei metallurgii Armyanskogo Nagor'ya*. Erevan: Armenian Academy of Sciences.

Ghirshman, R. 1954. *Iran: From the Earliest Times to the Islamic Conquest.* Baltimore, MD: Penguin.

Gimbutas, M. 1977. The first wave of Eurasian steppe pastoralists into Copper Age Europe. *Journal of Indo-European Studies* 5: 277–338.

Gimbutas, M. 1979. The three waves of the Kurgan people into Old Europe, 4500–2500 BC. *Archives suisses d'anthropologie générale* 43: 113–137.

Gimbutas, M. 1989. *The Language of the Goddess.* New York: Harper Collins.

Gimbutas, M. 1994. Das Ende Alteuropas. Der Einfale von Steppennomaden aus Südrußland und die indogermanisierung Mitteleuropas. In E. Jerem and W. Meid (eds.), *Archaeolinqua Alapitvany.* Budapest: Akadémiai Kiadó, pp. 13–135.

Glonti, L.I. and A.I. Dzhavakhishvili. 1987. Novye dannye o mnogosloynom pamyatnike epokh eneolita-pozdney bronzy Shida Kartli. *KSIA* 192: 80–87.

Gogadze, E. 1972. *Periodizatsiya i Genezis Kurgannoy Kul'tury Trialeti.* Tbilisi: Metsniereba.

Govedarica, B. and E. Kaiser. 1996. Die äneolitischen abstrakten und zoomorphen Steinzepter Südost- und Osteuropas. *EurAnt* 2: 59–103.

Götzelt, T. 1996. *Ansichten der Archäologie Süd-Turkmenistans bei der Erforschung der 'mittleren Bronzezeit' ('Periode' 'Namazga V').* Archäologie in Eurasien, Band 2. Espelkamp: Verlag Marie Leidorf GmbH.

Gubaev, A., G. Kosholenko, and M. Tosi (eds.). 1998. *The Archaeological Map of the Murghab Delta Preliminary Reports 1990–95.* Roma: IsIAO.

Hakemi, A. 1997. *Shahdad: Archaeological Excavations of a Bronze Age Center in Iran.* Roma: Istituto Italiano per il Medio ed Estremo Oriente Centro Scavi e Richerche Archeologiche, Reports and Memoirs, vol. XXVII.

Hauptmann, A., E. Pernicka, T. Rehren, and Ü. Yalcin(eds.). 1999. *The Beginnings of Metallurgy: Proceedings of the International Conference "The Beginnings of Metallurgy", Bochum 1995.* Der Anschnitt, Beiheft 9.

Hänsel, B. and J. Machnik (eds.). 1998. *Das Karpatenbecken und die Osteuropäische Steppe: Nomadenbewegungen und Kulturaustausch in den vorchrhistlichen Metallzeiten (4000–500 v. Chr.).* München.

Häusler, A. 1981. Zur ältesten Geschichte von Rad und Wagen im nordpontischen Raum. *EAZ Ethnogr.-Archäol. Z.* 22: 581–647.

Häusler, A. 1985. Kulturbeziehungen zwischen Ost- und Mitteleuropa im Neolithikum? *Jahresschr. Mitteldt. Vorgesch.* 68: 21–74.

Häusler, A. 1994. Archäologische Zeugnisse für Pferd und Wagen in Ost- und Mitteleuropa. In B. Hänsel and S. Zimmer (eds.), *Die Indogermanen und das Pferd. Festschr. Bernfried Schlerath.* Budapest:, pp. 217–257.

Häusler, A. 1995. Die Entstehung des neolithikums und die nordpontischen Steppenkulturen: Bemerkungen zu einer neuen Hypothese. *Germania* 73: 41–68.

Häusler, A. 1998. Hat es Bestattungssitten "der Indogermanen" gegeben? *Mitteilungen der Anthropologischen Gesellschaft in Wien (MAGW)* 128: 147–156.

Hayen, H. 1989. Früheste Nachweise des Wagens und die Entwicklung der Transport-Hilfsmittel: Beiträge zur Transportgeschichte. *Mitteilungen der Berliner Gesellschaft für Anthropologie-Ethnologie und Urgeschichte* 10: 31–50.

Hayen, H. 1991. Ein Vierradwagen des dritten Jahrtausend v. Chr. – Rekonstruction und Nachbau (Oldenburg).

Henrickson, E.F. and I. Thuesen (eds.). 1989. *Upon This Foundation – The 'Ubaid Reconsidered.* Copenhagen. Museum Tusculanum Press.

Hernández Bermejo, J.E. and J. León (ed.). 1994. *Neglected crops 1492 from a different perspective.* FAO Plant Production and Protection Series, no. 26.

Hiebert, F.T. 1994a. *Origins of the Bronze Age Civilization in Central Asia.* American School of Prehistoric Research Bulletin 42. Cambridge, MA.

Hiebert, F.T. 1994b. Production evidence for the origins of the Oxus Civilization. *Antiquity* 68 (259): 372–387.

Hiebert, F.T. 2000. Bronze Age Central Eurasian Cultures in Their Steppe and Desert Environments. In G. Bawden and R.M. Reycraft (eds.), *Environmental Disaster and the Archaeology of Human Response.* Anthropological Papers No. 7. Albuquerque, NM: Maxwell Museum of Anthropology, pp. 51–62.

Hiebert, F.T. and R.H. Dyson, Jr. 2002. Prehistoric Nishapur and the frontier between Central Asia and Iran. *Iranica Antiqua* 37: 113–149.

Hiebert, F. T. and P. L. Kohl. 2000. Maps and commentaries of Merv–Bactra and Bactria. In R.J.A. Talbert (ed.), *Barrington Atlas of the Greek and Roman World*. Princeton, NJ: Princeton University Press.

Hiebert, F.T. and C.C. Lamberg-Karlovsky. 1992. Central Asia and the Indo-Iranian Borderlands. *Iran* 30: 1–15.

Hiebert, F.T. and K.M. Moore. 2004. A small steppe site near Gonur. In M.F. Kosarev, P.M. Kozhin, and N.A. Dubova (eds.), *U istokov tsivilizatsii*, pp. 294–302.

Hobsbawm, E.J. 1980. The Revival of Narrative: Some comments. *Past and Present* 86: 3–8.

Iessen, A.A. 1950. K khronologii "bol'shikh kubanskikh kurganov." *Sovetskaya Arkheologiya* 12.

Inanischwili, G. 2001. Metallurgische Verfahren und Kenntnisse im alten Georgien. In I. Gambaschidze, A. Hauptmann, R. Slotta, and Ü. Yalcin (eds.), *Georgien: Schätze aus dem Land des Goldenen Vlies*, pp. 142–149.

Isaac, B. and Z. Kikodze, P. L. Kohl, G. Mindiashvili, A. Ordzhonikidze, and G. White. 1994. Appendix A: Archaeological Investigations in Southern Georgia 1993. *Iran* 32: 22–29.

Isakov, A.I. 1994. Sarazm, an Agricultural Center of Ancient Sogdiana. *Bulletin of the Asia Institute* 8:1–12.

Ismailov, G.S. 1985. *Poselenie Garakapektepe.* Baku.

Itina, M.A. 1977. *Istoriya stepnykh plemen yuzhnogo Priaral'ya (II – nachalo I tycyacheletiya do n. e.).* Moscow: Nauka.

Ivanov, I.S. 1988. Die Ausgrabungen des Gräberfeldes von Varna. In A. Fol and J. Lichardus (eds.), *Macht, Herrschaft und Gold*, pp. 149–66.

Ivanov, I.S. 1991. Der Bestattungsritus in der chalkolithischen Nekropole von Varna (mit einem Katalog der wichtigsten Gräber). In J. Lichardus (ed.), *Die Kupferzeit als historische Epoche*, pp. 125–150.

Jarrige, J.-F. 1985. Continuity and change in the north Kachi plain (Baluchistan, Pakistan) at the beginning of the second millennium BC. In J. Schotsmans and M. Taddei (eds.), *South Asian Archaeology 1983*. Naples: Instituto Universitario Orientale, pp. 35–68.

Jones-Bley, K. and D.G. Zdanovich (eds.). 2002. *Complex Societies of Central Eurasia from the 3rd to the 1st Millennium BC: Regional Specifics in Light of Global Models.* Journal of Indo-European Studies Monograph Series 45, vols. I and II. Washington, DC: Institute for the Study of Man.

Jovanovic, B. 1971. *Metallurgija eneolitskog perioda Jugoslvavije.* Beograd.

Jovanovic, B. 1982. *Rudna Glava. Najstarije rudarstvo bakra na Centralnom Balkanu.* Bor-Beograd.

Kavtaradze, G. 1983. *K khronologii epokhi eneolita i bronzy gruzii.* Tbilisi.

Kavtaradze, G. 1999. The Importance of Metallurgical Data for the Formation of Central Transcaucasian Chronology. In A. Hauptmann, E. Pernicka, T. Rehren, and Ue. Yalçin (eds.), *The Beginnings of Metallurgy*, pp. 67–102.

Keall, E.J. and M. Roaf. 2000. Map and commentary of Hyrcania. In R.J.A. Talbert (ed.), *Barrington Atlas of the Greek and Roman World*. Princeton, NJ: Princeton University Press.

Kenoyer, J.M. 1998. *Ancient Cities of the Indus Valley Civilization.* Karachi: Oxford University Press.

Kes', A., V. P. Kostyuchenko, and G.N. Lisitsina. 1980. *Istoriya zaseleniya i drevnee oroshenie yugo-zapadnoi Turkmenii.* Moscow: Nauka.

Khachatryan, T.S. 1975. *Drevnyaya Kul'tura Shiraka III-I tys. do n.e.* Erevan.

Khalilov, Dzh. A., K.O. Koshkarly, and R.B. Arazova. 1991. *Arkheologicheskie Pamyatniki Severo-Vostochnogo Azerbaidzhana.* Baku.

Khazanov, A.M. 1994. *Nomads and the Outside World*, 2nd ed. Madison, WI: The University of Wisconsin Press.

Khlopin, I.N. 1997. *Eneolit Yugo-Zapadnogo Turkmenistana.* Sankt-Peterburg.

Kiani, M.Y. 1982. *Parthian Sites in Hyrcania. The Gurgan Plain.* Berlin: Dietrich Reimer Verlag.

Kiguradze, T. 1986. *Neolithische Siedlungen von Kvemo-Kartli, Georgien.* München: Verlag C.H. Beck.

Kiguradze, T. 2000. The Chalcolithic – Early Bronze Age transition in the Eastern Caucasus. In C. Marro and H. Hauptmann (eds.), *Chronologie des Pays du Caucase et de l'Euphrate aux IVe–IIIe Millenaires*, pp. 321–328.

Kiguradze, T. 2001. The Caucasian Chalcolithic. In P. N. Peregrine and M. Ember (eds.), *Encyclopedia of Prehistory, vol. 4, Europe.* New York: Kluwer Academic/Plenum Publishers, pp. 38–54.

Kiguradze, T. and A. Sagona. 2003. On the Origins of the Kura-Araxes Cultural Complex.

In A.T. Smith and K. Rubinson (eds.), *Archaeology in the Borderlands: Investigations in Caucasia and Beyond*, pp. 38–94.

Kircho, L.B. 2005. *Khronologiya Epokhi Pozdnego Eneolita – Srednem Bronzy Srednei Azii: Pogrebeniya* Altyn-depe. St. Petersburg: "Nestor Historiya" Press.

Kircho, L.B. and S.G. Popov. 2005. Prilozhenie 2: K voprosu o radiouglerodnoi khronologii arkheologicheskikh pamyatnikov Srednei Azii V–II tys. do n.e. In L.B. Kircho, *Khronologiya Epokhi Pozdnego Eneolita*, pp. 528–541.

Kislenko, A. and N. Tatarintseva. 1999. The Eastern Ural Steppe at the End of the Stone Age. In M. Levine, Yu. Rassamakin, A. Kislenko, and N. Tatarintseva (eds.), *Late prehistoric exploitation of the Eurasian steppe*. Cambridge: McDonald Institute Monographs, pp. 183–216.

Klengel, E. and H. Klengel. 1980. Zum fragment eines Steatitegefäßes mit einer Inschrift des Rimush von Akkad. *Rocznik Orientalistyczny* 41: 45–51.

Klochko, V.I. 1994. The Metallurgy of the Pastoral Societies in the Light of Copper and Bronze Processing in the Northern Pontic Steppe – Forest Steppe Zone: 4500–2350 BC. *Baltic-Pontic Studies* 2: 135–166.

Kohl, P. L. 1974. *Seeds of Upheaval: The production of chlorite at Tepe Yahya and an analysis of commodity production and trade in Southwest Asia in the mid-third millennium*, 2 vols., Ph.D. dissertation, Harvard University, Ann Arbor: University Microfilms.

Kohl, P. L. 1978. The Balance of Trade in Southwestern Asia in the Mid-Third Millennium B.C. *Current Anthropology* 19 (3): 463–492.

Kohl, P. L. (ed.). 1981. *The Bronze Age Civilization of Central Asia: Recent Soviet Discoveries*. Armonk, NY: M.E. Sharpe.

Kohl, P. L. 1984. *Central Asia: Palaeolithic beginnings to the Iron Age [L'Asie Centrale des origines à l'Âge du Fer]*. Synthèse no. 14. Paris: ERC.

Kohl, P. L. 1989. The use and abuse of world systems theory. In C.C. Lamberg-Karlovsky (ed.), *Archaeological Thought in America*. Cambridge: Cambridge University Press, pp. 218–240.

Kohl, P. L. 1992a. The Kura-Araxes 'Chiefdom/State': The Problems of Evolutionary Labels and Imperfect Analogies. In G.L.

Possehl (ed.), *South Asian Archaeology Studies*. New Delhi, pp. 223–232.

Kohl, P. L. 1992b. Central Asia (Western Turkestan). In R.W. Ehrich (ed.), *Chronologies in Old World Archaeology*, 3rd ed., vols. I and II. Chicago: University of Chicago Press, pp. 179–195 (vol. I) and 154–162 (vol. II).

Kohl, P. L. 1993. Limits to a post-processual archaeology (or, The dangers of a new scholasticism). In N. Yoffee and A. Sherratt (eds.), *Archaeological Theory: Who Sets the Agenda?* Cambridge: Cambridge University Press, pp. 13–19.

Kohl, P. L. 2002a. Bronze production and utilization in Southeastern, Daghestan, Russia: c. 3600–1900 BC (with an Appendix by L. Weeks, Summary of Velikent Compositional and Lead Isotope Analysis). In M. Bartelheim, E. Pernicka, and R. Krause (eds.), *Die Anfänge der Metallurgie in der Alten Welt*. Rahden/Westf.: Verlag Marie Leidorf GmbH, pp. 161–184.

Kohl, P. L. 2002b. Archaeological Transformations: Crossing the Pastoral/Agricultural Bridge. *Iranica Antiqua* 37: 151–190 (Festschrift for C.C. Lamberg-Karlovsky, ed. by D.T. Potts).

Kohl, P. L. 2005a. Invariant Homo Politicus and the Biological Constraints on Cultural Evolution. Review of T. Earle's *Bronze Age Economics: The beginnings of political economies* and B.G. Trigger's *Understanding Early Civilizations*. *Current Anthropology* 46 (4): 685–687.

Kohl, P. L. 2005b. Staryi i novyi svet: kontrasty evolyutsii. *Rossiskaya Arkheologiya* 4: 36–43.

Kohl, P. L., R. Biscione, and M.L. Ingraham. 1981. Implications of Recent Evidence for the Prehistory of Northeastern Iran and Southwestern Turkmenistan. *Iranica Antiqua* 16: 185–204.

Kohl, P. L. and E.A. Carson, C. Edens, and J. Pearce 1993. International Program for Research in the Caucasus: Field Seasons 1990 and 1991, pp. 143–150 in *Bulletin of the Asia Institute*, new series/vol. 6, 1992. 110.

Kohl, P. L. and E.N. Chernykh. 2003. Different Hemispheres, Different Worlds. In M.E. Smith and F.F. Berdan (eds.), *The Postclassic Mesoamerican World*. Salt Lake: University of Utah Press, pp. 307–312.

Kohl, P. L., M.G. Gadzhiev, and R.G. Magomedov. 2002. Between the Steppe and the

Sown: Cultural Developments on the Caspian Littoral Plain of Southern Daghestan, Russia, c. 3600–1900 BC. In K. Boyle, C. Renfrew, and M. Levine (eds.), *Ancient Interactions*, pp. 113–128.

Kohl, P. L. and D. L. Heskel. 1980. Archaeological Reconnaissances in the Darreh Gaz Plain: A short report. *Iran* 18: 160–172.

Kohlmeyer, K. and G. Saherwala. 1984. *Frühe Bergvölker in Armenien und im Kaukasus*. Berlin: Berliner Gesellschaft für Antropologie, Ethnologie und Urgeschichte.

Korenevskii, S. N. 1993. *Drevneishee Osedloe Naselenie na Srednem Tereke*. Moscow.

Korenevskii, S. N. 1995. *Galyugai – poselenie makopskoi kul'tury*. Moscow.

Korenevskii, S. N. 2001. *Drevneishie Zemledel'tsy i Skotovody Predkavkaz'ya*. Doctor of Historical Sciences Dissertation Abstract, Moscow.

Korenevskii, S. N. 2004. *Drevneishie zemledel'tsy i skotovody Predkavkaz'ya: Maikopsko-novosvobodnenskaya obshchnost' – problemy vnutrennei tipologii*. Moscow: Nauka.

Korobov, D. S. and S. Reinhold. n.d. Aerial photography and field survey – A new type of Late Bronze Age settlements in the North Caucasus discovered from the air.

Koryakova, L.N. 1996. Social Trends in Temperate Eurasia during the Second and First Millennia BC. *Journal of European Archaeology* 4: 243–280.

Koryakova, L.N. and A.V. Epimakhov. n.d. *The Urals and Western Siberia in the Bronze and Iron Ages*. Cambridge University World Archaeology Series. Cambridge: Cambridge University Press, in press.

Kosarev, M.F., P.M. Kozhin, and N.A. Dubova (eds.). 2004. *U istokov tsivilizatsii: Sbornik statei k 75-letiyu Viktora Ivanovicha Sarianidi*. Moscow: Staryi sad.

Kozhin, P. M. 2004. Kolecnyi ekipazh vpervye preodolevaet pustyni. In M. F. Kosarev, P. M. Kozhin, and N.A. Dubova (eds.), *U istokov tsivilizatsii*, pp. 282–289.

Kremenetski, K.V. 2003. Steppe and Forest-Steppe Belt of Eurasia: Holocene Environmental History. In M. Levine, C. Renfrew, and K. Boyle (eds.), *Prehistoric Steppe Adaptation and the Horse*, pp. 11–27.

Kruc, W.A. 1994. 'Osiedla-giganty' oraz niekótre problemy demograficizne kultury Trypolskiej. *Archeologia Polski* 39 (1–2): 7–30.

Krupnov, E.I. 1954. Prikaspiiskaya arkheologicheskaya ekspeditsiya. *KSIIMK*.

Kushnareva, K.Kh. 1997. *The Southern Caucasus in Prehistory: Stages of cultural and socioeconomic development from the eighth to the second millennium B.C.* Philadelphia: The University Museum.

Kushnareva, K.Kh. and T.N. Chubinishvili. 1970. *Drevniye kul'tury Yuzhnogo Kavkaza*. Leningrad.

Kushnareva, K.Kh. and V.I. Markovin (eds.). 1994. *Epokha Bronzy Kavkaza i Srednei Azii: Rannyaya i srednyaya bronza Kavkaza*. Moscow: Nauka.

Kutimov, Yu.G. 1999. Kul'turnaya atributsiya keramiki stepnogo oblika epokhi pozdnei bronzy yuzhnykh raionov Srednei Azii (Turkmenistana). *Stratum Plus* 2: 314–322.

Kuzmina, E.E. 1994. *Otkuda prishli Indoarii?* Moscow: Russian Academy of Sciences.

Kuzmina, E.E. 2003. Origins of Pastoralism in the Eurasian Steppes. In M. Levine, C. Renfrew, and K. Boyle (eds.), *Prehistoric Steppe Adaptation and the Horse*, pp. 203–232.

Kuz'minykh, S.V. 2005. 'Iz mednogo kronida pokolen'ya . . .': K yubeleyu E.N. Chernykh. *Rossiskaya Arkheologiya* 4.

Lamberg-Karlovsky, C.C. 1996. *Beyond the Tigris and Euphrates: Bronze Age Civilizations*. Jerusalem: Ben-Gurion University of the Negev Press.

Lamberg-Karlovsky, C.C. 2002. Archaeology and Language: The Indo-Iranians. *Current Anthropology* 43 (1): 63–88.

Larsen, M.T. 1976. *The Old Assyrian State and Its Colonies*. Copenhagen: Akademisk Forlag.

Lattimore, R. (trans.). 1967. *The Iliad of Homer*. Chicago: University of Chicago Press, Phoenix Editions.

Laufer, B. 1930. The Early History of Felt. *American Anthropologist* 32: 1–18.

Lazarovisi, Gh. and M. Lazarovisi. 2003. The Neo-Eneolithic Architecture in Banat, Transylvania Moldavia. In. V. Grammenos (ed.), *Recent Research in the Prehistory of the Balkans*. Publications of the Archaeological Institute of Northern Greece, no. 3. Thessaloniki: Archaeological Institute of Northern Greece, pp. 369–486.

Lebedeva, E.Yu. 2005. Arkheobotanika i Izuchenie Zemeledeliya Epokhi Bronzy v

Vostochnoi Evrope. *Opus: Mezhdistsiplinarnye Issledovaniya v Arkheologii* 4: 50–68.

Lechtman, H. 1980. The Central Andes: Metallurgy without Iron. In T.A. Wertime and J.D. Muhly (eds.), *The Coming of the Age of Iron*, pp. 267–334.

Lechtman, H. 1996. Arsenic bronze: Dirty copper or chosen alloy? A view from the Americas. *Journal of Field Archaeology* 23: 477–514.

Lecomte, O. 1999. Vehrkana and Dehistan: Late Farming Communities of South-West Turkmenistan from the Iron Age to the Islamic Period. *Parthica* 1: 135–170.

Levine, M., Yu. Rassamakin, A. Kislenko, and N. Tatarintseva (eds.). 1999. *Late prehistoric exploitation of the Eurasian steppe.* Cambridge: McDonald Institute Monographs.

Levine, M. 1999. Origins of horse husbandry. In M. Levine,Yu. Rassamakin, A. Kislenko, and N. Tatarintseva (eds.), *Late prehistoric exploitation of the Eurasian steppe*, pp. 5–58.

Levine, M., C. Renfrew, and K. Boyle (eds.). 2003. *Prehistoric Steppe Adaptation and the Horse.* Cambridge: McDonald Institute Monographs.

Lichardus, J. 1988. Der Westpontische Raum und die Anfänge der kupferzeitlichen Zivilisation. In A. Fol and J. Lichardus (eds.), *Macht, Herrschaft und Gold*, pp. 79–130.

Lichardus, J. (ed.). 1991. *Die Kupferzeit als historische Epoche. Saarbrücker Beitr. Altkde.* 55, Bonn.

Lichardus, J. and M. Lichardus-Itten. 1998. Nordpontische Gruppen und ihre westlichen Nachbarn. Ein Beitrag zur Entstehung der frühen Kupferzeit Alteuropas. In B. Hänsel and J. Machnik (eds.), *Das Karpatenbecken und die Osteuropäische Steppe*, pp. 99–122.

Lichardus. J. and J. Vladár. 1996. Karpatenbecken-Sintasta-Mykene: Ein Beitrag zur Definition der Bronzezeit als historischer Epoche. *Slovenská Archeológia* 46 (1): 25–93.

Ligabue, G. and S. Salvatori. 1990. *Bactria: An Ancient Oasis Civilization from the Sands of Afghanistan.* Venezia: Erizzo Editrice.

Linduff, K.M. 2002. At the Eastern Edge: Metallurgy and Adaptation in Gansu (PRC) in the 2nd Millennium BC. In K. Jones-Bley and D.G. Zdanovich (eds.), *Complex Societies of Central Eurasia from the 3rd to the 1st Millennium BC: Regional Specifics in Light of Global Models*, vol. II, pp. 595–611.

Linduff, K.M. 2005. Kak daleko na vostok rasprostranyalas' evrasziiskaya metallurgicheskaya traditsiya? *Rossiskaya Arkheologiya* 4: 25–35.

Lisitsina, G.N. 1978. *Stanovlenie i razvitie oroshaemogo zemledeliya v yuzhnoi Turkmenii.* Moscow: Nauka.

Lisitsina, G.N. 1981. Stanovlenie sel'skokhozyaistvennogo proizvodstva varidnykh raionakh SSSR. In B.A. Kolchin and E. Saiko (eds.), *Stanovlenie proizvodstva v epokhu eneolita i bronzy*, pp. 49–71.

Litscheli, W. 2001: Archäologie in Georgien. In I. Gambaschidze, A. Hauptmann, R. Slotta, and Ü. Yalcin (eds.), *Georgien: Schätze aus dem Land des Goldenen Vlies*, pp. 62–67.

Litvinskii, B.A. 2004. Viktor Ivanovich Sarianidi – Legenda Arkheologii Tsentral'noi Azii. In M. F. Kosarev, P. M. Kozhin, and N.A. Dubova (eds.), *U istokov tsivilizatsii*, pp. 5–22.

Litvinskii, B.A. and V.S. Solov'ev. 1972. Stoianka stpenoi bronzy v yuzhnom Tadzhikistane. *Uspekhi Sredneaziatskoi Arkheologii* 1: 41–47.

Liverani, M. 1997. Comment to J. McCorriston's "The Fiber Revolution." *Current Anthropology* 38 (4): 536–537.

Lombard, P. 2003. Fouilles à Aratashen, Automne 2003. In C. Chataigner (ed.), *Mission Caucase: Rapport Scientifique sur les operations effectuées en 2003*, Lyon:, pp. 3–14.

López Sáez, J.A., P. López García, and Mª.I. Martinez-Navarrete. 2002. Palinologicheskie issledovaniya na kholme Gornogo. In E.N. Chernykh (ed.), *Kargaly Tom II*, pp. 153–165.

Lordkipanidse, O. 1991. *Archäologie in Georgien; von der Altsteinzeit zum Mittelalter.* Heidelberg: VCH Acta humaniora.

Lordkipanidze, O. 2001. Georgien – Land und Raum. In I. Gambaschidze, A. Hauptmann, R. Slotta, and Ü. Yalcin (eds.), *Georgien: Schätze aus dem Land des Goldenen Vlies*, pp. 2–53.

Lyonnet, B. 1997. *Céramique et Peuplement du Chalcolithique à la Conquête Arabe*, vol. 2. Prospections Archéologiques en Bactriane Orientale (1974–1978). Paris: ERC.

Lyonnet, B. 2000. La Mésopotamie et le Caucase du Nord au IVe et au debut du IIIe millnaires av. n.è.: Leurs rapports et les problèmes chronologiques de la culture de Majkop. Etat de la question et nouvelles propositions. In C. Marro and H. Hauptmann (eds.), *Chronologies des Pays du Caucase et de l'Euphrate aux IVe–IIIe Millenaires*. Paris: De Boccard Edition-Diffusion, pp. 299–320.

Lyonnet, B. 2005. Another Possible Interpretation of the Bactro-Margiana Culture (BMAC) of Central Asia: The Tin Trade. In C. Jarrige and V. Lefèvre (eds.), *South Asia Archaeology 2001, vol. 1, Prehistory*. Paris: adpf – Éditions Recherche sur les Civilisations.

Lyonnet, B. n.d.a. *Mari et la Margiane ou 'la circulation des biens, des personnes et des idees' dans l'Orient ancien à la fin du 3ème et au début du 2ème millénaire avant notre ère*. Mémoire présenté dans le cadre d'une Thèse d'Habilitation, Avril 2001 (Paris).

Lyonnet, B. (ed.). n.d.b. *Les cultures du Caucase (VIème-IIIème mill. av. n. è.). Leurs relations avec le Proche-Orient*. Paris: CNRS editions (in press).

Lyonnet, B. n.d.c. La culture de Maikop, la Transcaucasia, l'Anatolie orientale et le Proche-Orient: Relations et chronologie. To appear in Madjidzadeh, Y. 2003. *Jiroft: The Earliest Oriental Civilization*. Teheran: Ministry of Culture and Islamic Guidance.

Magomedov, R.G. 1991. O kompleksakh maikopskoi kul'tury na territorii Dagestana'. In O.M. Davudov (ed.), *Gory i Ravniny Severo-vostochnogo Kavkaza v Drevnosti i Srednie Veka*. Makhachkala: DNTs RAN, pp. 13–38.

Magomedov, R.G. 1998. *Ginchinskaya Kul'tura*. Makhachkala: DNTs RAN.

Mair, V.H. (ed.). 1998. *The Bronze Age and Early Iron Age Peoples of Eastern Central Asia*. Vols. I and II. Washington, DC: Institute for the Study of Man Inc.

Maisuradze, B. and G. Gobedschischwili. 2001. Alter Bergbau in Ratscha. In I. Gambaschidze, A. Hauptmann, R. Slotta, and Ü. Yalcin (eds.), *Georgien: Schätze aus dem Land des Goldenen Vlies*, pp. 130–135.

Makarenko, M. 1933. *Mariupil'skii Mogil'nik*. Kiev.

Makharadze, Z. n.d. Nouvelles données sur le Chalcolithique en Géorgie orientale. To appear in B. Lyonnet (ed.), *Les cultures du Caucase*.

Mallory, J.P. 1989. *In Search of the Indo-Europeans: Language, Archaeology and Myth*. London: Thames and Hudson.

Mammaev, M.M. 2005. Ot sostavitelya. In *Drevnosti Kavkaza i Blizhnego Vostoka:*

sbornik statei, posvyashchennyi 70-letiyu so dnya rozhdeniya professora M.G. Gadzhieva. Makhachkala: Publishing House "Epokha", pp. 4–8.

Mandel'shtam, A.M. 1968. Pamyatniki epokhi bronzi v yuzhom Tadzhikistane. Materiali i Issledovaniya po Arkheologii SSSR 145. Moscow: Nauka.

Mantu, C.-M. 1998a. The Absolute Chronology of the Romanian Neolithic and Aeneolithic/Chalcolithic Periods. The State of the Research,. *Actes du colloque "C14 Archéologie"*, pp. 225–231.

Mantu, C.-M. 1998b. *Cultura Cucuteni: Evolutie, Chronologie, Legaturi*. Muzeul de Istorie Piatra Neamt: Biblioteca Memoriae Antiquitatis.

Mantu, C.-M., G. Dumitroaia, and A. Tsaravopoulos. 1997. *Cucuteni: The last great Chalcolithic civilization of Europe*. Bucharest: Athena Publishing and Printing House.

Markovin, V.I. and R.M. Munchaev. 2003. *Severnyi Kavkaz: Ocherki drevnei i sredneivekovoi istorii i kul'tury*. Moscow: RAN.

Marro, C. and H. Hauptmann 2000: *Chronologie des Pays du Caucase et de l'Euphrate aux IVe–IIIe Millenaires*. Paris: Institut Français D'Etudes Anatoliennes D'Istanbul De Boccard.

Martín Sánchez, M., P. López Garcia, and J.A. López Sáez. 2000. Palynological Estimate of the Evolution of the Vegetation of the Caucasus and the Level of the Caspian Sea during the Recent Holocene. *EurAnt* 6: 106–113.

Martinez-Navarrete, Mª.I., J.M. Vicent García, P. López-Garcia, J.A. López Sáez, I. de Zavala-Morencos, and P. Diaz del Rio. 2005. Metallurgicheskoe proizvodstvo na Kargalakh i rekonsruktsiya okrulzhayushchei sredy. *Rossiskaya Arkheologiya* 4: 84–91.

Mashkour, M. 2003. Equids in the Northern Part of the Iranian Central Plateau from the Neolithic to Iron Age: New Zoogeographic Evidence. In M. Levine, C. Renfrew, and K. Boyle (eds.), *Prehistoric Steppe Adaptation and the Horse*, pp. 129–138.

Masson, V.M. 1981. Altyn-depe during the Aeneolithic period. In P. L. Kohl (ed.), *The Bronze Age Civilization of Central Asia: Recent Soviet discoveries*, pp. 63–95.

Masson, V.M. 1988. *Altyn-Depe*. Philadelphia: The University Museum.

Masson, V.M. and N.Ya. Merpert (eds.). 1982. *Eneolit SSSR* (Moscow).

Masson, V.M. and V.I. Sarianidi. 1972. *Central Asia: Turkmenia before the Achaemenids*. London: Thames and Hudson, Ltd.

McConchie, M. 2004. *Archaeology at the Northeast Anatolian Frontier, V: Iron Technology and Iron-Making Communities of the First Millennium BC*. Louvain: Peeters.

McCorriston, J. 1997. The Fiber Revolution: Textile Extensification, Alienation, and Social Stratification in Ancient Mesopotamia. *Current Anthropology* 38 (4): 517–549.

Meadow, R. 1993. Continuity and Change in the Agriculture of the Greater Indus Valley. *Information Bulletin* 19: 63–77.

Mei Jianjun and C. Shell. 1999. The existence of Andronovo cultural influence in Xinjiang during the 2nd millennium BC. *Antiquity* 73 (281): 570–578.

Merpert, N.Ya. 1974. *Drevneishie skotovody volzhsko-ural'skogo mezhdurech'ya*. Moscow: Nauka.

Merpert, N.Ya. 1991. Die neolithisch-äneolithischen Denkmäler der pontisch-kaspischen Steppen und der Formierungsprozeß der frühen Grubengrabkultur. In J. Lichardus (ed.), *Die Kupferzeit als historische Epoche*, pp. 35–46.

Merpert, N.Ya. 2001. Rol' V.A. Gorodstova v sozdanii periodizatsii bronzovogo veka yuzhnoi poloviny vostochnoi evropy i voprocy istoriografii'. In Yu.I. Kolev (ed.), *Bronzovyi vek vostochnoi evropy: Kharakteristika kul'tur, khronologiya i periodizatsiya*, pp. 7–8.

Merpert, N.Ya. and R.M. Munchaev 1993. The Earliest Evidence for Metallurgy in Ancient Mesopotamia. In N. Yoffee and J.J. Clark (eds.), *Early Stages in the Evolution of Mesopotamian Civilization: Soviet Excavations in Northern Iraq*. Tucson, AZ: University of Arizona Press, pp. 241–248.

Michaud, R. and S. Michaud. 1978. *Caravans to Tartary*. London: Thames and Hudson Ltd.

Miron, A. and W. Orthmann. 1995. *Unterwegs zum Goldenen Vlies: Archäologische Funde aus Georgien*. Saarbrücken: Victor's Residenz-Hotel.

Molodin, V.I., H. Parzinger, J. Schneeweiß, J.N. Garkusa, A.E. Grisin, O.I. Novikova, N.S. Efremova, Z.V. Marcenko, M.A. Cemjakina, L.N. Myl'nikova, H. Becker, and J. Faßbinder. 2002. Cica – Eine befestigte Ansiedlung der Übergangsperiode von der Spätbronze- zur Früheisenzeit in der Barabinsker Waldsteppe.

Vorbericht der Kampagnen 1999–2001. *EurAnt* 8: 185–236.

Monah, D. and F. Monah. 1997. Cucuteni: The last great Chalcolithic civilization of old Europe. In C.-M. Mantu, G. Dumitroaia, and A. Tsaravopoulos (eds.), *Cucuteni: The last great Chalcolithic civilization of Europe*. Bucharest: Athena Publishing and Printing House, pp. 16–95.

Moore, K.M. 1993. Animal use at Bronze Age Gonur depe. *Information Bulletin* 19: 164–176.

Moorey, P.R.S. 1994. *Ancient Mesopotamian Materials and Industries: The Archaeological Evidence*. Oxford: Clarendon Press.

Morales-Muñiz, A. and E. Antipina. 2000. Late Bronze Age (2500–1000 B.C.) faunal exploitation on the East European steppe. In K. Boyle, M. Levine, and C. Renfrew (eds.), *Late Prehistoric Exploitation of the Eurasian Steppe: Papers presented for the symposium to be held 12 Jan. – 16 Jan. 2000, vol. 2*. Cambridge: McDonald Institute Monographs, pp. 267–294.

Morales-Muñiz, A. and E. Antipina. 2003. Srubnaya Faunas and Beyond: A Critical Assessment of the Archaeozoological Information from the East European Steppe. In M. Levine, C. Renfrew, and K. Boyle (eds.), *Prehistoric Steppe Adaptation and the Horse*, pp. 329–351.

Morgunova, N.L. 1995. *Neolit i Eneolit yuga lesostepi volgo-ural'skogo mezhdurech'ya*. Orenburg: RAN.

Motzenbäcker, I. 1996. *Sammlung Kossnierska. Der Digorische Formenkreis der Kaukasischen Bronzezeit*. Berlin: Museum für Vor- und Frühgeschichte SMPK.

Muhly, J. D. 1973. *Copper and Tin*. Transactions, The Connecticut Academy of Arts and Sciences 43: 155–535.

Muhly, J. D. 1980. The Bronze Age Setting. In T.A. Wertime and J. D. Muhly (eds.), *The Coming of the Age of Iron*. New Haven, CT: Yale University Press, pp. 25–67.

Munchaev, R. M. 1975. *Kavkaz na zare bronzovogo veka*. Moscow: Nauka.

Munchaev, R. M. 1994. Maikopskaya kul'tura. In K.Kh. Kushnareva and V.I. Markovin (eds.), *Epokha Bronzy Kavkaza i Srednei Azii: Rannyaya i srednyaya bronza Kavkaza*, pp. 158–225.

Munchaev, R. M. (ed.). 2002. *Problemy Arkheologii Evrazii: K 80-letiyu N.Ya. Merperta*. Moscow: Institut Arkheologii RAN.

Munchaev, R.M., N.Ya. Merpert, and Sh.N. Amirov. 2004. *Tell Khazna I: Kul'tovo-administrativnyi tsentr IV–III tys. do n.e. v Severo-vostochnoi Sirii*. Moscow: Paleograph.

Muscarella, O.W. 2003. The Chronology and Culture of Sé Girdan: Phase III. *Ancient Civilizations: From Scythia to Siberia* 9, 1–2: 117–131.

Muscarella, O. W. n.d. "Jiroft" and Aratta: a review of Yousef Madjidzadeh, *Jiroft The Earliest Oriental Civilization*, Teheran 2003.

Narimanov, I.G. 1985. Obeidskie plemena Mesopotamii v Azerbaidzhane. In *Vsesoyuznaya Arkheologicheskaya Konferentsiya 'Dostizheniya Sovestskoi Arkheologii v XI Pyatiletke' – Tezisy Dokladov*. Baku, pp. 271–272.

Narimanov, I.G. 1987. *Kul'tura Drevneishego Zemledel'chesko-Skotovodchesdogo Naseleniya Azerbaidzhana*. Baku: "Elm".

Nechitailo, A.L. 1991. *Svyazi Naseleniya Stepnoi Ukrainy i Severnogo Kavkaza v Ephoku Bronzy*. Kiev: Naukova Dumka.

Nekhaev, A.A. 1986. Pogrebenie maikopskoi kul'tury iz kurgana u sela Krasnogvardeiskoe. *Sovetskaya Arkheologiya* 1.

Nekhaev, A.A. 1990. Eneoliticheskie poseleniya Zakubanya, In A.M. Zhdanovsky and I.I. Marchenko (eds.), *Drevnie pamyatniki Kubani*. Krasnodar:, pp. 5–22.

Nekhaev, A.A. 1992. Domaikopskaya kul'tura Severnogo Kavkaza. *Arkheologicheskie vesti* 1: 76–94.

Neustupny, E. 2002. In P.F. Biehl, A. Gramsch, and A. Marciniak (eds.), *Archäologien Europas. Geschichte, Methoden und Theorien,*. Münster: Waxmann, pp. 283–288.

Oates, J. 2003. A Note on the Early Evidence for Horse in Western Asia. In M. Levine,C. Renfrew, and K. Boyle (eds.), *Prehistoric Steppe Adaptation and the Horse*, pp. 115–125.

Olsen, S.L. 2003. The Exploitation of Horses at Botai, Kazakhstan. In M. Levine, C. Renfrew, and K. Boyle (eds.), *Prehistoric Steppe Adaptation and the Horse*, pp. 83–103.

Oppenheim, A.L. 1954. The Sea-Faring Merchants of Ur. *Journal of the American Oriental Society* 74: 6–17.

Otchir-Goriaeva, M. 2002. Welchen Kultur- und Wirtschaftstyp repräsentieren die bronzezeitlichen Funde in den Wolga-Manyc-Steppen? *EurAnt* 8: 103–133.

Özdogan, A. 1999. Cayönü. In M. Özdogan and N. Basgelen (eds.), *Neolithic in Turkey: The Cradle of Civilization*. Istanbul: Arkeoloji ve Sanat Yayinlari, pp. 35–64.

Paléorient. 1999 (25 [1]). The Uruk Expansion: Northern Perspectives from Hacinebi, Hassek Höyük and Gawra. Paris.

Palumbi, G. 2003. Red-Black Pottery: Eastern Anatolian and Transcaucasian Relationships during the mid-fourth millennium BC. *Ancient Near Eastern Studies* 40: 80–134.

Palumbi, G. n.d. *Rosso e Nero: Ruolo e Significato ella Cultura Kuro-Araks nelle Trasformazioni delle Comunità dell'Anatolia Orientale tra IV e III Millennio a.C.* Unpublished doctoral dissertation, Università degli Studi di Roma "La Sapienza."

Parzinger, H. 1998a. Kulturverhältnisse in der eurasischen Steppe während der Bronzezeit. In B. Hänsel(ed.), *Mensch und Umwelt in der Bronzezeit Europas*. Kiel:, pp. 457–479.

Parzinger, H. 1998b. Der nordpontische Raum und das untere Donaugebiet in der späten Kupferzeit: Das Ende des Kodzadermen-Gumelnita-Karanovo VI-Verbandes und die Cernavoda I-Kultur. In B. Hänsel and J. Machnik (eds.), *Das Karpatenbecken und die Osteuropäische Steppe*, pp. 123–134.

Parzinger, H. 2003. Grundzüge der Vor- und Frügeschichte Sogdiens. In H. Parzinger and N. Boroffka, *Das Zinn der Bronzezeit*, pp. 260–286.

Parzinger, H. and N. Boroffka. 2003. *Das Zinn der Bronzezeit in Mittelasien I: Die siedlungsarchäologischen Forschungen im Umfeld der Zinnlagerstätten*. Archäologie in Iran und Turan, Band 5. Mainz am Rhein: Verlag Philipp von Zabern.

Pecorella, P.E. and M. Salvini. 1984. *Tra Lo Zagros e L'Urmia: Ricerche Storiche ed Archeologiche Nell'Azerbaigian Iraniano*. Roma.

Pernicka, E., F. Begemann, S. Schmitt-Strecker, H. Todorova, and I. Kuleff. 1997. Prehistoric Copper in Bulgaria. Its Composition and Provenance. *EurAnt* 3: 41–180.

Perrot, J. (ed.). 2003. *Jiroft: Fabuleuse Découverte en Iran. Dossiers d'Archeologie* 287.

Peterson, D. 2003. Ancient Metallurgy in the Mountain Kingdom: The Technology and Value of Early Bronze Age Metalwork from Velikent, Daghestan. In A.T. Smith and K.S. Rubinson (eds.), *Archaeology in the Borderlands*, pp. 22–37.

Philip, G. and A.R. Millard. 2000. Khirbet Kerak Ware in the Levant: the implications of radiocarbon chronology and spatial distribution. In C. Marro and H. Hauptmann (eds.), *Chronologie des Pays du Caucase et de l'Euphrate aux IVe–IIIe Millenaire,* pp. 279–296.

Pigott, V.C. 1999a. A Heartland of Metallurgy: Neolithic/Chalcolithic metallurgical origins on the Iranian Plateau. In A. Hauptmann, E. Pernicka, T. Rehren, and U. Yalçin (eds.), *The Beginnings of Metallurgy,* pp. 107–120.

Pigott, V.C. 1999b. The Archaeometallurgy of the Asian Old World: Introductory comments. In V.C. Pigott (ed.), *The Archaeometallurgy of the Asian Old World.* Philadelphia: The University Museum, pp. 1–13.

Pilipossian, A. 1996. Hachette de cérémonie en forme d'ancre. In J. Santrot (ed.), *Arménie: Trésors de l'Arménie ancienne.* Paris: Somogy Editions D'Art, p. 65.

Pizchelauri, K. 1984. *Jungbronzezeitliche bis ältereisenzeitliche Heiligtümer in Ost-Georgien.* München: Verlag. C.H. Beck.

Possehl, G.L. 2002. *The Indus Civilization: A Contemporary Perspective.* Walnut Creek, CA: AltaMira Press.

Potts, D.T. 1990. *The Arabian Gulf in Antiquity I.* Oxford: Clarendon Press.

Potts, D.T. 1997. *Mesopotamian Civilization: The Material Foundations.* Ithaca, NY: Cornell University Press.

Potts, D.T. 2004. Camel hybridization and the role of *Camelus bactrianus* in the ancient Near East. *Journal of the Economic and Social History of the Orient* 47: 143–165.

Potts, D.T. 2005. In the beginning: Marhashi and the origin's of Magan's ceramic industry in the third millennium BC. *Arabian Archaeology and Epigraphy* 16: 67–78.

Potts, D.T. n.d.. Exit Aratta: Southeastern Iran and the Land of Marhashi.

Potts, T.F. 1994. *Mesopotamia and the East. An Archaeological and Historical Study of Foreign Relations ca. 3400–2000 BC.* Oxford Committee for Archaeology, Monograph 47. Oxford.

Priakhin, A.D. and V.I. Besedin. 1999. The Horse Bridle of the Middle Bronze Age in the East European Forest-Steppe and the Steppe. *Anthropology & Archeology of Eurasia* 38 (1): 39–59.

Primas, M. 2002. Early Tin Bronze in Central and Southern Europe. In M. Bartelheim, E. Pernicka, and R. Krause (eds.), *Die Anfänge der Metallurgie in der Alten Welt.* Rahden/Westf.: Verlag Marie Leidorf GmbH, pp. 303–314.

Pumpelly, R. 1908. *Explorations in Turkestan, Expedition of 1904.* Vol. I. Washington, DC: Carnegie Institute of Washington.

Pustovalov, S.Z. 1994. Economy and Social Organization of Northern Pontic Stepp – Forest-Steppe Pastoral Populations: 2700–2000 BC (Catacomb Culture). *Baltic-Pontic Studies* 2: 86–134.

Pustovalov, S.Z. 1998. Nekotorye Problemy Izucheninya Kolesnogo Transporta Epokhi Bronzy. In *Problemy Izucheniya Katakombnoi Kul'turno-Istoricheskoi Obshchnosti (KKIO) i Kul'turno-Istoricheskoi Obshchnosti Mnogovalikovoi Keramiki (KIOMK),* Zaporozh'e, pp. 50–54.

Puturidze, M. 2003. Social and Economic Shifts in the South Caucasian Middle Bronze Age. In A.T. Smith and K.S. Rubinson (eds.), *Archaeology in the Borderlands,* pp. 111–127.

P'yankova, L.T. 1993. Pottery of Margiana and Bactria in the Bronze Age. *Information Bulletin (UNESCO International Association for the Study of the Cultures of Central Asia)* 19: 109–127.

P'yankova, L.T. 1994. Central Asia in the Bronze Age: Sedentary and Nomadic Cultures. *Antiquity* 68 (259): 355–372.

P'yankova, L.T. 1999. Stepnye komponenty v kompleksakh bronzogo veka yugo-zapadnogo Tadzhikistana. *Stratum Plus* 2: 286–297.

Rao, S.R. 1972. *Lothal and the Indus Civilization.* Bombay: Asia Publishing House.

Rassamakin, Yu. 1994. The main directions of the development of early pastoral societies of Northern Pontic Zone: 4500–2450. *Baltic-Pontic Studies* 2: 29–70.

Rassamakin, Yu. 1999. The Eneolithic of the Black Sea steppe: Dynamics of cultural and economic development 4500–2300 BC. In M. Levine, Yu. Rassamakin, A. Kislenko, and N. Tatarintseva (eds.), *Late Prehistoric Exploitation of the Eurasian Steppe,* pp. 59–182.

Rassamakin, Yu. 2002. Aspects of Pontic Steppe Development (4500–3000 BC) in the Light of the New Cultural-Chronological Model. In K. Boyle, C. Renfrew, and M. Levine (eds.), *Ancient Interactions,* pp. 49–73.

Ratnagar, S. 2000. *The End of the Great Harappan Tradition.* New Delhi: Manohar.

Ratnagar, S. 2001. The Bronze Age: Unique Instance of a Pre-Industrial World Sytem? *Current Anthropology* 42: 351–379.

Ratnagar, S. 2004. *Trading Encounters. From the Euphrates to the Indus in the Bronze Age*. New Delhi: Oxford University Press.

Renfrew, C. 1969. The Autonomy of the South-East European Copper Age. *Proceedings of the Prehistoric Society* 35: 12–47.

Renfrew, C. 1987. *Archaeology and Language: The Puzzle of Indo-European Origins*. Cambridge: Cambridge University Press.

Rezepkin, A.D. 1991. Kul'turno-khronologicheskie aspekty proiskhozhdeniya i razvitiya maikopskoi kul'turi. In *Maikopskii phenomenon v drevnei istorii Kavkaza i Vostochnoi Evropy*. Leningrad:, pp. 20–21.

Rezepkin, A.D. 1996. K probleme sootnosheniya khronologii kul'tur epokhi eneolita – rannei bronzy severnogo Kavkaza i Tripol'ye. In Yu.Yu. Piotrovskii (ed.), *Mezhdu Aziei i Evropoi: Kavkaz v IV–I tys. Do n.e.* Saint Petersburg: Gosudarstvennyi Ermitazh, pp. 50–54.

Rezepkin, A.D. 2000. *Das frühbronzezeitliche Gräberfeld von Klady und die Majkop-Kultur in Nordwestkaukasien*. Rahden/Westf.: Verlag Marie Leidorf GmbH.

Roaf, M. 1990. *Cultural Atlas of Mesopotamia and the Ancient Near East*. Oxford.

Rothman, M.S. (ed.). 2001. *Uruk Mesopotamia and Its Neighbors*. Santa Fe, NM: School of American Research.

Rothman, M.S. 2003. Ripples in the Stream: Transcaucasia-Anatolian Interaction in the Murat/Euphrates Basin at the Beginning of the Third Millennium BC. In A.T. Smith and K.S. Rubinson (eds.), *Archaeology in the Borderlands*, pp. 95–110.

Rovira, S. 2004. Tekhnologiya vyplavki metalla i ego obrabotki. In E.N. Chernykh (ed.), *Kargaly Tom III*, pp. 106–133.

Rovira, S. 2005. Tekhnologiya vyplavki medi v epokhu pozdnei bronzy na Kargalakh. *Rossiskaya Arkheologiya* 4: 79–83.

Rubinson, K.S. 1977. The Chronology of the Trialeti Culture. In L.D. Levine and T.C. Young, Jr. (eds.), *Mountains and Lowlands: Essays in the Archaeology of Greater Mesopotamia*. Bibliotheca Mesopotamica 7. Malibu: Undena Publications, pp. 235–249.

Safonov, I.E. 2001. Raskopki V.A. Gorodtsovym kurganov epokhi bronzy v izyumskom uezde letom 1901 g. (po arkhivnym materialam). In Yu.I. Kolev (ed.), *Bronzovyi vek vostochnoi evropy: Kharakteristika kul'tur, khronologiya i periodizatsiya*, pp. 11–18.

Sagona, A.G. 1984. *The Caucasian Region in the Early Bronze Age*. BAR International Series 214. London.

Sagona, A.G. 2000. Sos Höyük and the Erzurum region in late prehistory: A provisional chronology for Northeast Anatolia. In C. Marro and H. Hauptmann (eds.), *Chronologie des Pays du Caucase et de l'Euphrate aux IVe–IIIe Millenaires*, pp. 329–374.

Sagona, A. (ed.). 2004a. *A View from the Highlands: Archaeological Studies in Honour of Charles Burney*. Ancient Near Eastern Studies Supplement 12. Belgium: Peeters.

Sagona, A. 2004b. Social Boundaries and Ritual Landscapes in Late Prehistoric Trans-Caucasus and Highland Anatolia. In A. Sagona (ed.), *A View from the Highlands*, pp. 475–538.

Sahlins, M. and E. Service (eds.). 1960. *Evolution and Culture*. Ann Arbor: University of Michigan Press.

Salvatori, S. 1995. Protohistoric Margiana: On a Recent Contribution (Review of IASCCA [International Association for the Study of the Cultures of Central Asia] Information Bulletin 19, Moscow 1993). *Rivisita di Archeologia* 19: 38–55.

Salvatori, S. 1998. The Bronze Age in Margiana. In A. Gubaev, G. Kosholenko, and M. Tosi (eds.), *The Archaeological Map of the Murghab Delta Preliminary Reports 1990–95*. Roma: IsIAO, pp. 47–55.

Salvatori, S. 2000. Bactria and Margiana Seals: A New Assessment of Their Chronological Position and a Typological Survey. *East and West* 50 (nos. 1–4): 97–145.

Salvatori, S. 2003. Pots and Peoples: The 'Pandora's Jar' of Central Asia Archaeological Research. On Two Recent Books on Gonur Graveyard Excavations. *Rivista di Archeologia* 27: 5–20.

Sarianidi, V.I. 1977. *Drevnie Zemledel'tsi Afganistana*. Moscow: Nauka.

Sarianidi, V.I. 1986. *Die Kunst des Alten Afghanistan: Keramik, Siegel, Architektur, Kunstwerke aus Stein und Metall*. Leipzig: VEB E.A. Seemann Verlag.

Sarianidi, V.I. 1998a. *Margiana and Protozoroastrianism*. Athens: Kapon Editions.

Sarianidi, V.I. 1998b. *Myths of ancient Bactria and Margiana on its seals and amulets*. Moscow: Pentagraphic, Ltd.

Sarianidi, V.I. 2001. *Necropolis of Gonur and Iranian Paganism*. Moscow: World Media.

Sarianidi, V.I. 2002. *Margush: Ancient Oriental Kingdom in the Old Delta of the Murghab River.* Ashgabat: Türkmendöwlethabarlary.

Sarianidi, V.I. 2004. Strana Margush otkryvaet svoi tainy dvortsovo-kul'tovyi ansambl' severnogo Gonura. In M.F. Kosarev, P.M. Kozhin, and N.A. Dubova (eds.), *U istokov tsivilizatsii*, pp. 229–253.

Sarianidi, V.I. 2005. *Gonurdepe Türkmenistan: city of kings and gods.* Ashgabat: Türkmendöwlethabarlary.

Sarianidi, V.I., N.N. Terekhova, and E.N. Chernykh. 1977. O rannei metallurgii I metalloobrabotke drevnei Baktrii. *Sovetskaya Arkheologiya* 2: 35–42.

Schlanger, N. (ed.). 2002. Explorations in the History of Archaeology (Special section). *Antiquity* 76 (291): 127–238.

Schmidt, E.F. 1937. *Excavations at Tepe Hissar Damghan.* Philadelphia: The University Museum, University of Pennsylvania Press.

Shahmirzadi, S.M. 2004. Sialk und siene Kultur – Ein Überblick. In T. Stöllner, R. Slotta, and A. Vatandoust (eds.), *Persiens Antike Pracht: Bergbau – Handwerk – Archäologie.* Bochum: Deutsches Bergbau Museum, Band I, pp. 200–208.

Shchetenko, A.Ya. 1999. O kontaktakh kul'tur stepnoi bronzy c zemledel'tsami yuzhnogo Turkmenistana v epokhu pozdnei bronzy (po materialam poselenii Tekkem-depe i Namazga-depe). *Stratum Plus* 2: 323–335.

Sherratt, A.G. 1981. Plough and pastoralism: Aspects of the Secondary Products Revolution. In I. Hodder, G. Isaac, and N. Hammond (eds.), *Patterns of the Past: Studies in honour of David Clark.* Cambridge: Cambridge University Press, pp. 261–305.

Sherratt, A.G. 1983. The secondary exploitation of animals in the Old World. *World Archaeology* 15: 90–104.

Sherratt, A.G. 2003. The Horse and the Wheel: The Dialectics of Change in the Circum-Pontic Region and Adjacent Areas, 4500–1500 BC. In M. Levine, C. Renfrew, and K. Boyle (eds.), *Prehistoric Steppe Adaptation and the Horse,* pp. 233–252.

Shiomi, H. 1976. *Archaeological Map of the Gorgan Plain, Iran, no. 1.* Hiroshima.

Shiomi, H. 1978. *Archaeological Map of the Gorgan Plain, Iran, no. 2.* Hiroshima.

Shishlina, N.I. 1997. The Bow and Arrow of the Eurasian Steppe Bronze Age Nomads. *Journal of European Archaeology* 5 (2): 53–66.

Shishlina, N.I. 2003. Yamnaya culture pastoral exploitation: A local sequence. In M. Levine, C. Renfrew, and K. Boyle (eds.), *Prehistoric Steppe Adaptation and the Horse,* pp. 353–365.

Shishlina, N.I. and F.T. Hiebert. 1998. The steppe and the sown: Interaction between Bronze Age Eurasian nomads and agriculturalists. In V.H. Mair (ed.), *The Bronze Age and Early Iron Age Peoples of eastern Central Asia,* vol. I, pp. 222–237.

Shishlina, N.I., O.V. Orfinskaya, and V.P. Golikov. 2003. Bronze Age Textiles from the North Caucasus: New Evidence of Fourth Millennium BC Fibres and Fabrics. *Oxford Journal of Archaeology* 22 (4): 331–344.

Shnirelman, V.A. 1998. Archaeology and ethnic politics: The discovery of Arkaim. *Museum International* 50 (2): 33–39.

Shnirelman, V.A. 1999. Passions about Arkaim: Russian Nationalism, the Aryans, and the Politics of Archaeology. *Inner Asia* 1: 267–282.

Skripkin, A.S., A.N. D'yachenko, and V.A. Demkin. 2004. O naznachenii sooruzheniya y stanitsy Trekhostrovskoi. *Istoriko-arkheologicheskie issledovaniya v Azove i na Nizhnem Dony v 2002 g.* 19: 192–196.

Smith, A.T. 2003. *The Political Landscape: Constellations of Authority in Early Complex Polities.* Berkeley: University of California Press.

Smith, A.T. and K.S. Rubinson (eds.). 2003. *Archaeology in the Borderlands: Investigations in Caucasia and Beyond.* Monograph 47. Los Angeles: The Cotsen Institute of Archaeology, University of California.

Smith, M.E. 1996. *The Aztecs.* Malden, MA: Blackwell.

Snodgrass, A.M. 1971. *The Dark Age of Greece.* Edinburgh: Edinburgh University Press.

Stein, G. J. 1999. *Rethinking World Systems: Diasporas, Colonies and Interaction in Uruk Mesopotamia.* Tucson: University of Arizona Press.

Stein, G. J., R. Bernbeck, C. Coursey, A. McMahon, N.F. Miller, A. Misir, J. Nicola, H. Pittman, S. Pollock, and H. Wright. 1996. Uruk colonies and Anatolian communities: An interim report on the 1992–1993 excavations at Hacinebi, Turkey. *AJA* 100 (2): 205–260.

Stein, M.A. 1937. *Archaeological Reconnaissances in North-Western India and South-Eastern Iran.* London: Macmillan.

Steinkeller, P. 1982. The Question of Marhashi: A Contribution to the Historical Geography of Iran in the Third Millennium B.C. *Zeitschrift für Assyriologie* 72: 237–265.

Stone, L. 1979. The Revival of Narrative: Reflections on a New Old History. *Past and Present* 85: 3–24.

Tatarinov, S.I. 2003. *Drevnie gornyaki-metallurgi Donbassa.* Slavyansk: "Pechatnyi dvor."

Taylor, T. 1999. Envaluing Metal: Theorizing the Eneolithic 'Hiatus.' In S.M.M. Young, A.M. Pollard, P. Budd, and R.A. Ixer (eds.), *Metals in Antiquity.* BAR International Series 792. Oxford: Archaeopress, pp. 22–32.

Tekhov, B.V. 1977. *Tsentralny Kavkaz v XVI–X vv. do n.e.* Moscow: Nauka.

Tekhov, B.V. 1980. *Tliiskii Mogil'nik I.* Tbilisi: "Metsniereba."

Tekhov, B.V. 1981. *Tliiskii Mogil'nik II.* Tbilisi: "Metsniereba."

Tekhov, B.V. 1985. *Tliiskii Mogil'nik III.* Tbilisi: "Metsniereba."

Tekhov, B.V. 1988. *Bronzovye Topory Tliiskogo Mogil'nika.* Tbilisi: "Metsniereba."

Telegin, D.Ya. 1986. *Dereivka: A settlement and cemetery of Copper Age horse-keepers on the Middle Dnieper.* BAR International Series 287. Oxford: Archaeopress.

Telegin, D.Ya. 2002. A Discussion on Some of the Problems Arising from the Study of Neolithic and Eneolithic Cultures in Azov Black Sea Region. In K. Boyle, C. Renfrew, and M. Levine (eds.), *Ancient Interactions,* pp. 25–47.

Telegin, D.Ya., A.L. Nechitailo, I.D. Potekhina, and Yu.V. Panchenko. 2001. *Srednestogovskaya i Novodanilovskaya Kul'tury Eneolita Azovo-Chernomorskogo Regiona: arkheologo-antropologicheskii analiz materialov I katalog pamyatnikov.* Lugansk: "Shlyakh".

Teufer, M. 1999. Ein Scheibenknebel aus Dzarkutan (Süduzbekistan). *AMI* 31: 69–142.

Tiratsian, G. 1992. Découvertes récentes en Arménie. *Les Dossiers D'Archeologie* 177: 32–39.

Todorova, H. 1978. *The Eneolithic Period in Bulgaria. British Archaeological Reports* vol. S 49, Oxford: BAR

Todorova, H. (ed.). 1989 *Durankulak 1.* Sofia.

Todorova, H. 1990. Die Sozial-ökonomische Struktur der Varnakultur an der Westlichen Schwarzmeerküste. Sarajevo: *Godisnjak* Knjiga XXVIII Centar za Balkanoloska Ispitivanja Knjiga 26, pp. 233–238.

Todorova, H. 1991. Die Kupferzeit Bugariens. In J. Lichardus (ed.), *Die Kupferzeit als historische Epoche,* pp. 89–93.

Todorova, H. 1993. Die Protobronzezeit auf der Balkanhalbinsel. *Anatolica* 19: 307–318.

Todorova, H. 1995. The Neolithic, Eneolithic and Transitional Period in Bulgarian Prehistory. In D.W. Bailey and I. Panayatov (eds.), *Prehistoric Bulgaria.* Madison, WI: Prehistory Press, pp. 79–98.

Todorova, H. 1998. Der balkano-anatolische Kulturbereich vom Neolithikum bis zur Frühbronzezeit. In M. Stefanovich, H. Todorova, and H. Hauptmann (eds.), *James Harvey Gaul: In Memoriam.* Sofia: The James Harvey Gaul Foundation, pp. 27–53.

Todorova, H. 1999. Die Anfänge der Metallurgie an der westlichen Schwarzmeerküste. In A. Hauptmann, E. Pernicka, T. Rehren, and Ü. Yalcin.(eds.), *The Beginnings of Metallurgy,* pp. 237–246.

Todorova, H. (ed.). 2002a. *Die prähistorischen Gräberfelder* (Durankulak II; 2 vols.). Sofia: Deutsches Archäologisches Institut.

Todorova, H. 2002b. Die Sozialstruktur im Licht der Auswertungsergebnisse. In H. Todorova (ed.), *Die prähistorischen Gräberfelder,* pp. 267–280.

Todorova, H. 2002c. Einleitung. In H. Todorova (ed.), *Die prähistorischen Gräberfelder,* pp. 11–15.

Todorova, H. 2002d. Die geographische Lage der Gräberfelder (mit drei Karten). Paläoklima, Strandverschiebungen und Umwelt der Dobrudscha im 6.-4. Jahrtausend v.Chr. In H. Todorova (ed.), *Die prähistorischen Gräberfelder,* pp. 16–23.

Todorova, H. and K. Dimitrov. 2005. Sovremennye issledovaniya arkheometallurgii v Bolgarii. *Rossiskaya Arkheologiya* 4: 6–12.

Tolstov, S.P. 1962. *Po drevnim del'tam Oksa i Yaksarta.* Moscow: Vostochnoi Literaturi.

Tosi, M. 1977. The archaeological evidence for protostate structures in Eastern Iran and Central Asia at the end of the 3rd millennium BC. In J. Deshayes (ed.), *Le plateau iranien et l'Asie Centrale des origins à la conquête islamique,* Paris: CNRS, pp. 45–66.

Tosi, M. n.d. Reasoning about Magan, Marhashi, and the Shifting Frontiers of Meluhha.

Trifonov, V. A. 1987. Nekotorye voprosy peredneaziatskikh svyazei maikopskoi kul'tury. *KSIA* 192: 18–26.

Trifonov, V.A. 1991. Osobennosti lokal'no-khronologicheskogo razvitiya Maikopskoi kul'tury. In V.A. Trifonov (ed.), *Maikopskii fenomenon v drevnei istorii Kavkaza i Vostochnoi Evropy.* Leningrad:, pp. 25–29.

Trifonov, V.A. 1996. Popravki k absolyutnoi khronologii kul'tur epokhi eneolita – bronzy severnogo Kavkaza. In Yu.Yu. Piotrovskii (ed.), *Mezhdu Aziei I Evropoi,* pp. 43–49.

Trifonov, V.A. 2000. Maikop Type Tumuli in Northwestern Iran: Towards a More Precise Dating of the Tumuli at Sé Girdan. In *The Scholar's Destiny, to the Centenary of Boris A. Latynin.* St. Petersburg (in Russian, cited in Muscarella *op. cit.*), pp. 244–264.

Trifonov, V. 2001. Popravik absolyutnoi khronologii kul'tur epokhi eneolita-srednei bronzy Kavkaza, stepnoi i lesostepnoi zon vostochnoi Evropy (po dannym radiouglerodnogo datirovaniya). In Yu.I. Kolev (ed.), *Bronzovyi vek vostochnoi evropy: Kharakteristika kul'tur, khronologiya i periodizatsiya,* pp. 71–82.

Trifonov, V.A. 2004. "Tsarskie" Grobnitsy Arslantepe i Novosvobodnoi: Nekotorye aspekty sravnitel'nogo analiza. *Problemy Arkheologii Nizhnego Povol'zh'ya/ Mezhdunardnaya Nizhne volzhskaya arkheologicheskaya konferentsiya. Tezisi Dokladov.* Volgograd:, pp. 56–61.

Trigger, B.G. 1973. The Future of Archeology is the Past. In C. L. Redman (ed.), *Research and Theory in Current Archeology.* New York: John Wiley & Sons, pp. 95–111.

Trigger, B.G. 1989. *A History of Archaeological Thought.* Cambridge: Cambridge University Press.

Trigger, B.G. 2003. *Artifacts and Ideas: Essays in Archaeology.* New Brunswick, NJ: Transaction Publishers.

Trippett, F. 1974. *The First Horsemen.* New York: Time-Life Books.

Tschartolani, S. 2001. Alterbergbau in Swanetien. In I. Gambaschidze, A. Hauptmann, R. Slotta, and Ü. Yalcin (eds.), *Georgien: Schätze aus dem Land des Goldenen Vlies,* pp. 120–129.

Ucko, P.J. (ed.). 1995. *Theory in Archaeology: A World Perspective.* London: Routledge.

Videjko, M.Y. 1996. Grosssiedlungen der Tripol'e Kultur in der Ukraine. *EurAnt* 1: 45–80.

Vinogradov, A.V. 1979. Issledovaniya pamyatnikov kamennogo veka v severnom Afganistane. *Drevnyaya Baktriya* 2: 7–62.

Vinogradova, N.M. 1994. The farming settlement of Kangurttut (South Tadjikistan) in the Late Bronze Age. *AMI* 27: 29–47.

Vinogradova, N.M. 2004. *Yugo-Zapadnyi Tadzhikistan v epokhu pozdnei bronzy.* Moscow: Institut Vostokovedeniya RAN.

Voigt, M.M. and R.H. Dyson, Jr. 1992. The Chronology of Iran, ca. 8000–2000 B.C. In R.W. Ehrich (ed.), *Chronologies in Old World Archaeology,* vol. I (Chicago, 2nd ed.), pp. 122–178.

Waldbaum, J.C. 1978. *From Bronze to Iron: The Transition from the Bronze Age to the Iron Age in the Eastern Mediterranean.* Studies in Mediterranean Archaeology, vol. 54. Göteborg: Paul Aströms.

Wallerstein, I. 1974. *The Modern World System.* New York: Academic Press.

Watson, P.J., S.A. LeBlanc, and C.L. Redman. 1971. *Explanation in Archeology: An Explicitly Scientific Approach.* New York: Columbia University Press.

Webb, J.M. and D. Frankel. 1999. Characterizing the Philia Facies: Material Culture, Chronology, and the Origin of the Bronze Age in Cyprus. *AJA* 103: 3–43.

Weiss, H. and T.C. Young, Jr. 1975. The Merchants of Susa: Godin V and Plateau-Lowland Relations in the Late Fourth Millennium B.C. *Iran* 13: 1–18.

Weeks, L. R. 1999. Lead Isotope Analyses from Tell Abraq, United Arab Emirates: New data regarding the 'tin problem' in Western Asia. *Antiquity* 73: 49–64.

Weeks, L.R. 2003. *Early Metallurgy of the Persian Gulf: Technology, trade, and the Bronze Age world.* Leiden: Brill Academic Publishers, Inc.

Wolf, E.R. 1982. *Europe and the People Without History.* Berkeley: University of California Press.

Wolf, E. R. 1984. Culture: Panacea or Problem? *American Antiquity* 49 (2): 393–400.

Woolley, Sir C.L. 1953. *A Forgotten Kingdom.* London: Penguin.

Yazdi, L.P. 2004. Southern Turkmenistan and North Iranian Khorassan. In *Turkmenistan is a Native Land of Anau Culture and White Wheat (Ak Bugday).* Abstracts of Reports of the International Scientific Conference (October 22–23, 2004). Ashgabat, pp. 194–196.

Yoffee, N. 2005. *Myths of the Archaic State: Evolution of the Earliest Cities, States, and Civilizations.* Cambridge: Cambridge University Press.

Yoffee, N. and J. J. Clark (eds.). 1993. *Early Stages in the Evolution of Mesopotamian Civilization: Soviet Excavations in Northern Iraq.* Tucson: University of Arizona Press.

Young, T.C. 1967. Iranian Migration into the Zagros. *Iran* 5: 11–34.

Zdanovich, D.G. 1995. Mogil'nik Bol'shekaraganskii (Arkaim) i mir drevnikh indo-evropeitsev Uralo-Kazakhstanskikh stepei. In G.B. Zdanovich (ed.), *Arkaim: Issledovniya, poiski, otkrytiya.* Chelyabinsk: Trudy Zapovednika Arkaim Nauchno-Populyarnaya Seriya, pp. 43–53.

Zdanovich, D.G. 2002. Introduction. In K. Jones-Bley and D.G. Zdanovich (eds.), *Complex Societies of Central Eurasia from the 3rd to the 1st Millennium BC: Regional Specifics in Light of Global Models,* vol. I, pp. xix–xxxviii.

Zdanovich, G.B. (ed.). 1995. *Arkaim: Issledovniya, poiski, otkrytiya.* Chelyabinsk: Trudy Zapovednika Arkaim Nauchno-Populyarnaya Seriya.

Zdanovich, G.B. 1995. Arkaim: Arii na Urale ili nesostoyashayasya tsivilizatsiya. In G.B. Zdanovich (ed.), *Arkaim: Issledovniya, poiski, otkrytiya.* Chelyabinsk: Trudy Zapovednika Arkaim Nauchno-Populyarnaya Seriya, pp. 21–42.

Zdanovich, G.B. 1997. Arkaim – kul'turnyi kompleks epokhi srednei bronzy yuzhnogo zaural'ya. *RA* 2: 47–62.

Zdanovich, G.B. 1999. Yuzhnoe zaural'e v epokhu srednei bronzy. In *Kompleksnie Obshchestva Tsentral'noi Evrazii v III–I tis. do n.e.,* pp. 42–45.

Zdanovich, G.B. and I.M. Batanina. 2002. Planography of the Fortified Settlements of the Middle Bronze Age in the Southern Trans-Urals According to Aerial Photography Data. In K. Jones-Bley and D.G. Zdanovich (eds.), *Complex Societies of Central Eurasia from the 3rd to the 1st Millennium BC: Regional Specifics in Light of Global Models,* vol. I, pp. 121–138.

INDEX

Made in the USA
Lexington, KY
19 December 2013